797,885 Books

are available to read at

Forgotten Books

www.ForgottenBooks.com

Forgotten Books' App
Available for mobile, tablet & eReader

ISBN 978-1-330-17213-1
PIBN 10043996

This book is a reproduction of an important historical work. Forgotten Books uses state-of-the-art technology to digitally reconstruct the work, preserving the original format whilst repairing imperfections present in the aged copy. In rare cases, an imperfection in the original, such as a blemish or missing page, may be replicated in our edition. We do, however, repair the vast majority of imperfections successfully; any imperfections that remain are intentionally left to preserve the state of such historical works.

Forgotten Books is a registered trademark of FB &c Ltd.
Copyright © 2015 FB &c Ltd.
FB &c Ltd, Dalton House, 60 Windsor Avenue, London, SW19 2RR.
Company number 08720141. Registered in England and Wales.

For support please visit www.forgottenbooks.com

1 MONTH OF FREE READING

at

www.ForgottenBooks.com

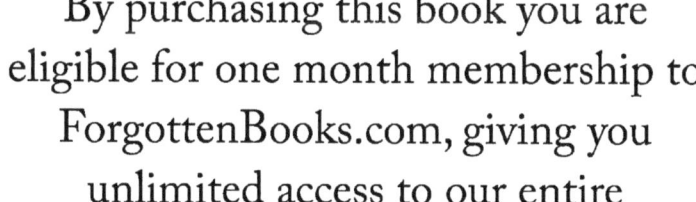

By purchasing this book you are eligible for one month membership to ForgottenBooks.com, giving you unlimited access to our entire collection of over 700,000 titles via our web site and mobile apps.

To claim your free month visit: www.forgottenbooks.com/free43996

* Offer is valid for 45 days from date of purchase. Terms and conditions apply.

Similar Books Are Available from
www.forgottenbooks.com

The Life of the Spirit and the Life of Today
by Evelyn Underhill

The Key to the Universe
by Harriette Augusta Curtiss

Optimism
The Lesson of Ages, by Benjamin Paul Blood

Spiritual Science
by Oliver Loraine Wroughton

In the Hours of Meditation
by A Disciple

The Inner Consciousness
How to Awaken and Direct It, by Swami Prakashananda

Spiritual Healing
by William Frederick Cobb

The Nature of Spirit, and of Man As a Spiritual Being
by Chauncey Giles

This Mystical Life of Ours
by Ralph Waldo Trine

Self-Knowledge and Self-Discipline
by B. W. Maturin

The Subconscious Mind and Its Illuminating Light
by Janet Young

The Pathway of Roses
by Christian D. Larson

The Hygiene of the Soul
Memoir of a Physician and Philosopher, by Gustav Pollak

The Smile
If You Can Do Nothing Else, You Can Smile, by S. S. Curry

Spiritual Reading for Every Day, Vol. 1 of 2
An Introduction to the Interior and Perfect Life, by Kenelm Digby Best

Vedanta Philosophy
Three Lectures on Spiritual Unfoldment, by Swâmi Abhedânanda

Angel Voices from the Spirit World
Glory to God Who Sends Them, by James Lawrence

Spiritual Director and Physician
The Spiritual Treatment of Sufferers from Nerves and Scruples, by Viktor Raymond

The Ten Commandments
An Interpretation, or the Constitution of the Spiritual Universe, by George Chainey

Cosmic Consciousness
The Man-God Whom We Await, by Ali Nomad

THE WORD

A MONTHLY MAGAZINE

DEVOTED TO

Philosophy, Science, Religion, Eastern
Thought, Occultism, Theosophy,
and
the Brotherhood of Humanity

H. W. PERCIVAL, *Editor*

VOLUME XI.

APRIL, 1910 — SEPTEMBER, 1910

1910
THE THEOSOPHICAL PUBLISHING COMPANY
OF NEW YORK
253 WEST 72d STREET

Copyrighted by
H. W. PERCIVAL
1910

INDEX.

A.—Adepts, Masters and Mahatmas, ...1, 65, 129, 193, 257, 321
    Atlantis, A Dream of..................49, 116, 178, 236, 288, 353
    Ancient Traveler, Tales of the
        Prologue 227
        The Romance of Svarat's King 229
        The River of Life 233
        The Twin Cities 284
        The Pearls of Khor 345
        The Bhahdishih 347

C.—Christ of the Soul. The Genesis and Growth of the.........25, 90
    Choice Extracts and Translations 96
    City of the Dead, The 167

D.—Dreams of Atlantis, A 49, 116, 178, 236, 288, 353

E.—Experience and its Results 302

F.—Florence, Savonarola of 31, 102, 137
    Friends, Moments with 60, 128, 191, 255, 316, 378

G.—Genesis and Growth of the Christ of the Soul, The............25, 90

H.—Hand, The Marvels of 330

I.—Inner Life and the Tao-Teh-King, The 11, 75, 152, 218, 278
    Immortality and Modern Scientists 265

M.—Master and Mahatmas, Adepts 1, 65, 129, 193, 257, 321
    Moments with Friends 60, 128, 191, 255, 316, 378
    Modern Scientists, Immortality and......................... 265
    Marvels of the Hand, The 330
    Magazine Shelf, Our
        The Way of Initiation 62
        The Life and Doctrines of Paracelsus 382
        From Passion to Peace 383

S.—Savonarola of Florence 31, 102, 137
    Sepher Ha-Zohar, The Book of Light, The....123, 187, 247, 307, 368
    Shelf, Our Magazine,
        The Way of Initiation 62
        The Life and Doctrines of Paracelsus 382
        From Passion to Peace 383

T.—Tao-Teh-King, The Inner Life and the 11, 75, 152, 213, 278
    Translations, Choice Extracts and 96
    Tales of the Ancient Traveler
        Prologue 227
        The Romance of Svarat's King 229
        The River of Life 233
        The Twin Cities 284
        The Pearls of Khor 345
        The Bhahdishih 347
Z.—Zohar, The Book of Light, The Sepher Ha....123, 187, 247, 307, 368

THE WORD

A MONTHLY MAGAZINE

Published and Edited by
H. W. PERCIVAL, 253 West 72d Street, New York City

London—Kegan Paul, Trench, Trubner & Co., 43 Gerrard Street

CONTENTS FOR APRIL, 1910

ADEPTS, MASTERS AND MAHATMAS, . . .	Editorial	
THE INNER LIFE AND THE TAO-TEH-KING,	C. H. A. Bjerregaard	11
THE GENESIS AND GROWTH OF THE CHRIST OF THE SOUL AND SOME OF ITS MODES OF LIFE	James L. Macbeth Bain	25
"SAVONAROLA" OF FLORENCE, .	Dr. W. Williams	31
UNDINE, A POETIC DRAMA IN THREE ACTS, . .	Justin Sterns	42
A DREAM OF ATLANTIS—THE LAND OF MU,	Alice Dixon Le Plongeon	49
MOMENTS WITH FRIENDS, ...	A Friend	60
OUR MAGAZINE SHELF, ...	B. B G.	62

Yearly Subscription - - - - - -	$4.00 or 16s.
Single Copies - - - - - - -	.35 or 1s. 6d.
Six Months' Subscription - - - - -	2.00 or 8s.
Three Months' Subscription - - - -	1.00 or 4s.

Bound Volumes of The Word
Vols. I-X in Cloth and Half Morocco

The ten completed volumes of The Word are a valuable addition to any Library

They are a library in themselves

[Entered as Second-class Mail Matter, May 2, 1906, at the Post Office at New York, New York, under the Act of Congress of March 3, 1879.]

NEW

THE MAGICAL MESSAGE
according to
IÔANNÊS
commonly called
The Gospel according to [St] John

A verbatim translation from the Greek done in modern English, with introductory essays and notes

BY

JAMES M. PRYSE

Price, Cloth, $2.00

The root of Mr. Pryse's claim is that the Gospel by John is altogether mystical in intention and that the mystical meanings of the words should never be distorted. According to Mr. Pryse the fourth gospel is much more than an account of the physical career of Jesus. He sees in it the history of the purification of the soul and so well does he buttress his claim that the best exponents of biblical criticism and Greek scholarship will be hard put to it to find anything to say in disproof.

The Theosophical Publishing Company of New York, 253 W. 72d Street

---

NEW

"OSRU"

The History of a Soul

A Tale of Many Incarnations

BY

JUSTIN STERNS

Cloth, $1.25

"You never read a stranger story"

The Theosophical Publishing Company of New York, 253 W. 72d Street

When ma has passed through mahat, ma will still be ma; but ma will be united with mahat, and be a mahat-ma. —The Zodiac.

THE WORD

ADEPTS, MASTERS AND MAHATMAS

(Continued from Vol. X., page 331.)

WHAT the disciple had before learned while in contact with the men of the world he now verifies to be true or false by bringing the faculties of his mind to bear on whatever subject is considered. The disciple finds that that thought into which all other thoughts had blended and by which he had found himself as disciple, and had known himself to be an accepted disciple in the school of the masters, was in fact the opening up of and ability to use his focus faculty consciously; that he had, after his long and continued efforts, been able to bring together his wandering thoughts which had been attracted by and were operating through his senses, was due to the use of his focus faculty; that by the focus faculty he had collected and centered those thoughts and so quieted the activities of the mind as to allow the light faculty to inform him where he was and of his entrance into the mental world. He sees that he could not then use his focus faculty and light faculty continuously, and that to be a master he must be able to use the five lower faculties, the time, image, focus, dark and motive faculties consciously, intelligently and at will as continuously as he may decide.

When the disciple begins to use his focus faculty intelligently it seems to him as though he is coming into great knowledge and that he will enter all realms in the different worlds by the use of his focus faculty. It seems to him that he is able to know everything and answer any question by using his focus faculty, and all the faculties seem to be at his disposal and ready for his use, when operated from his focus faculty, so that when he would know by any subject the meaning or nature of any object or thing, he centralizes the aforenamed faculties on that subject, which he holds steadily in mind by his focus faculty. As by the focus faculty he holds the subject and draws the other faculties to bear on it, the I-am faculty brings the light, the motive faculty directs matter by the time faculty into the image faculty, and all these together overcome the dark faculty, and out of the darkness which had obscured the mind the object or thing appears and is known in its subjective state, in all that it is or may be. This is done by the disciple at any time and anywhere while in his physical body.

The disciple is able to go through this process in the course of one inhalation and exhalation of his natural breathing without stoppage. As he gazes at any thing or hears any sound or tastes of any food or senses any odor or contacts any thing or thinks of any thought, he is able to find out the meaning and nature of that which has been suggested to him through his senses or by the faculties of the mind, according to the nature and kind of motive which directs the inquiry. The focus faculty acts in the physical body from the region of sex, libra ($\triangle$). Its corresponding sense is the sense of smell. The body and all the elements of the body are changed during one inbreathing and outbreathing. One inbreathing and outbreathing are only half of one complete round of the circle of breath. This half of the circle of breath is taken in through the nose and lungs and heart and goes in the blood to the organs of sex. This is the physical half of the breath. The other half of the breath enters the blood through the organ of sex and returns by the blood to the heart through the lungs and is exhaled through the tongue or the nose. Between these swings of the physical and magnetic breath there is a moment of balance; at this moment of balance all objects or things become known to the disciple by the use of his focus faculty.

The experience which made of the disciple a disciple put him in possession and gave him the use of the focus faculty, and with that first use of this faculty the disciple began its conscious and intelligent use. Before its first use the disciple was like an infant which, though having the organs of sense, is not yet possessed of its senses. When an infant is born, and for some time after its birth, it cannot see objects though its eyes are open. It senses a buzzing sound though it knows not whence comes the sound. It takes its mother's milk, but has no sense of taste. Odors enter through the nose, but it cannot smell. It touches and feels, but cannot localize the feeling; and altogether the infant is an uncertain and unhappy waif of the senses. Objects are held before it to attract its notice, and at some time the little thing is able to bring its eyes to a focus on some object. There is a moment of joy when the object is seen. The little thing sees into the world of its birth. It is no longer a waif in the world, but a citizen of it. It becomes a member of society when it knows its mother and is able to relate its organs to the objects of sense. That by which it was able to bring the organs of sight, hearing and of the other senses in line with the object seen, heard or otherwise sensed, was the power of focus. Every human who comes into the physical world must go through the processes of relating his organs of sense and his senses to the things of sense. Nearly all men forget the first object seen, forget the first sound heard, do not remember the things first tasted, what odor it was that was first smelled, how they got into touch with the world; and most men have forgotten how the focus faculty was used and how they still use the focus faculty by which they sense the world and the things of the world. But the disciple does not forget the one thought into which all his thoughts had been centered and by which he seemed to know all things and by which he knew himself as an accepted disciple.

He knows that it was by the focus faculty that he knew himself to be in another world than the world of the senses, though he was in the senses, even as the infant discovered itself in the physical world when it was able to focus its organs of sense in the world of the senses. And so having intelligent use of this faculty the disciple is as a child in relation to the mental world, which he is learning to enter through his faculties, by means of his focus faculty. All his faculties are adjusted to each other by means of his focus faculty. This focus faculty is the power of the mind to bring in line and relate any thing to its origin and source. By holding a thing in the mind and by use of the focus faculty, on and in that thing, it is made known as it is, and the process through which it became as it is, and also what it may become. When a thing is directly in line with its origin and source it is known as it is. By the focus faculty he can trace the path and events by which a thing has become as it is through the past, and by that faculty he can also trace the path of that thing to the time when it will have to decide for itself what it chooses to be. The focus faculty is the range finder between objects and subjects and between subjects and ideas; that is to say, the focus faculty brings into line any object of the senses in the physical world with its subject in the mental world and brings into line through the subject in the mental world the idea in the spiritual world, which is the origin and source of the object or thing and of all its kind. The focus faculty is like a sun-glass which gathers rays of light and centers them at a point, or like a searchlight which shows the way through the surrounding fog or darkness. The focus faculty is of a vortex-like power which centers movements into sound, or causes sound to be known by shapes or figures. The focus faculty is like an electric spark which centers two elements into water or by which water is changed into gases. The focus faculty is like an invisible magnet which attracts and draws in and holds in itself to itself fine particles which it shows in a body or form.

The disciple uses the focus faculty as one would use a field glass to bring objects into view. When one places a field glass to his eyes, nothing is at first seen, but as he regulates the lenses between the objects and his eyes the field of vision becomes less foggy. Gradually the objects take on outline and when they are focussed they are plainly seen. In like manner, the disciple turns his focus faculty on the thing which he would know and that thing becomes more and more clear until the moment of focus, when the thing is adjusted to its subject and is made plain and clear to and is understood by the mind. The balance wheel by which an object is made known to the mind by means of the focus faculty is the wheel or circle of the breath. The focus faculty is in focus at the moment of balance between the normal inbreath and outbreath.

The disciple is happy in this period of his life. He is asking and knows of objects and things in the physical world and their causes in the mental world; this affords happiness. He is in the childhood of his discipleship and enjoys all experiences in his retirement from the world, as a child enjoys itself in the life of the world and before the hardships of life have begun. The sky shows him the plan of creation. The wind sings to him its history as the song of life in the constantly flowing time. The rains and the waters open to him and inform him how the formless seeds of life are carried into form, how all things are replenished and nourished by water and how by the taste which water gives, all plants select their food and grow. By her perfumes and odors, earth discloses to the disciple how she attracts and repels, how one and one become blended into one, how and by what means and for what purpose all things come or pass through the body of man and how heaven and earth unite to temper and test and balance the mind of man. And so in the childhood of his discipleship the disciple sees the colors of nature in their true light, hears the music of her voice, drinks in the beauty of her forms and finds himself encircled by her fragrance.

The childhood of discipleship ends. Through his senses he has read the book of nature in the terms of the mind. He has been mentally happy in his companionship with nature. He tries to use his faculties without using his senses, and he tries to know himself as distinct from all his senses. From his body of sex, he trains the range of his focus faculty to find the mental world. This puts him out of range of the senses in the physical body, though he is still possessed of his senses. As he continues to so use his focus faculty, one after another the senses are stilled. The disciple cannot touch or feel, he cannot smell, he has no sense of taste, all sounds have ceased, vision is gone, he cannot see and darkness surrounds him; yet he is conscious. This moment, when the disciple is conscious without seeing or hearing or tasting or smelling and without touching or feeling anything, is of vital importance. What will follow this moment of being conscious without the senses? Some keen minds in the world have tried to find this state of being conscious without the senses. Some have shrunk back with horror when they had almost found it. Others have gone mad. Only one who has been long trained in and who has been tempered by the senses can remain steadily conscious during that crucial moment.

What follows the experience of the disciple has already been decided by his motives in attempting it. The disciple comes out of the experience a changed man. The experience may only have been for a second by the time of his senses, but it may have seemed an eternity to that which was conscious in the experience. During that moment the disciple has learned the secret of death, but he has not mastered death. That which was steadily conscious for a moment independently of the senses is to the disciple like coming to life in the mental world. The disciple has stood in the entrance to the heaven world, but he has not entered it. The heaven world of the mind cannot be joined to or made one with the world of the senses, though they are related to each other as opposites. The world of the mind is dreadful to a thing of the senses. The world of the senses is as hell to the purified mind.

When the disciple is able he will again repeat the experiment which he has learned. Whether the experiment is dreaded or is eagerly sought by him, it will lead the disciple into a period of negation and darkness. The physical body of the disciple has become a thing distinct from himself though he is still in it. By the use of his focus faculty in attempting to enter the mental or heaven world he called into action the dark faculty of the mind.

The experience of being conscious without seeing, hearing, tasting, smelling, touching and feeling is a mental demonstration to the disciple of all he has previously thought and heard concerning the reality of the mental world and of its being different and distinct from the physical and astral worlds. This experience is thus far the reality of his life, and is unlike any previous experience. It has shown him how little and transitory is his physical body and it has given him a taste or prescience of immortality. It has given him distinctness of being from his physical body and from sensuous perceptions, and yet he does not really know who or what he is, though he knows he is not the physical or astral form. The disciple realizes that he cannot die, though his physical body is to him a thing of change. The experience of being conscious without the senses gives the disciple great strength and power, but it also ushers him into a period of unutterable gloom. This gloom is caused by the awakening into action of the dark faculty as it had never before acted.

Through all periods and existences of the mind the dark faculty of the mind had been sluggish and slow, like a gorged boa or a serpent in the cold. The dark faculty, blind itself, had caused blindness to the mind; itself deaf, it had caused a confusion of sounds to the senses and dulled the understanding; without form and color, it had prevented or interfered with the mind and senses from perceiving beauty and from giving shape to unformed matter; without balance and having no judgment it has dulled the instincts of the senses and prevented the mind from being one-pointed. It had been unable to touch or feel anything, and had bewildered the mind and produced doubt and uncertainty in the sense. Having neither thought nor judgment it prevented reflection, blunted the mind and obscured the causes of action. Unreasoning and without identity it opposed reason, was an obstacle to knowledge and prevented the mind from knowing its identity.

Although having no senses and opposed to the other faculties of the mind, the presence of the dark faculty had kept the senses in activity, and allowed them or aided them to cloud or obscure the faculties of the mind. It had fed in the senses the activities which have paid it constant tribute, and that tribute had kept it in a torpid state. But the disciple trying to overcome the senses and to enter the mental world has in great degree withheld tribute from this thing of ignorance, the dark faculty of the mind. By his many efforts toward overcoming and control of his desires, the disciple had seemingly stilled the dark faculty and had seemingly enjoyed the use of his other faculties in interpreting his senses. But he finds that his desires were not really conquered and the dark faculty of the mind was not really overcome. When the disciple was able to be conscious without the use and independently of his senses, he called at that time and by that experience the dark faculty of his mind into activity as never before.

This, the dark faculty of his mind, is the adversary of the disciple. The dark faculty has now the strength of the world serpent. It has in it the ignorance of the ages, but also the cunning and wiles and glamour and deception of all bygone times. Before this awakening, the dark faculty was senseless, sluggish and without reason, and it still is. It sees without eyes, hears without ears, and is possessed of senses keener than any known to physical man, and it makes use of all the wiles of thought without thinking. It acts directly and in a way most likely to overcome and prevent the disciple from crossing through its realm of death into the mental world of immortal life.

The disciple has known of the dark faculty and been informed of its wiles and of having to meet and overcome them. But that old evil, the dark faculty, seldom attacks the disciple in the way he expects to be met, if he does expect. It has innumerable wiles and subtle ways of attacking and opposing the disciple. There are only two means which it can employ, and it invariably uses the second only if the first has failed.

After being conscious without the senses, the disciple is more sensitive to the world than ever before. But he is so in a different manner than before. He is aware of the inside of things. Rocks and trees are so many living things not seen, but apprehended as such. All the elements speak to him, and it seems to him that he may command them. The world seems a living, throbbing, being. The earth seems to move with the movement of his body. The trees seem to bend to his nod. The seas seem to moan and the tides to rise and fall with the beating of his heart and the waters to circulate with the circulation of his blood. The winds seem to come and go in rythmic movement with his breath and all seems to be kept in movement by his energy.

This the disciple experiences by being aware of it rather than sensing it. But at some time while he is aware of all this, his inner senses spring into life and he sees and senses the inner world of which he had been aware mentally. This world seems to open out to him or to grow out of and include and beautify and enliven the old physical world. Colors and tones and figures and forms are more harmoniously beautiful and exquisite and immeasurably more delightful than any the physical world did offer. All this is his and all things seem to be for him alone to direct and use. He seems the king and ruler of nature which had been waiting for him through the ages until he should, as now, at last have come to rule in her kingdoms. All the senses of the disciple in the school of the masters are now keyed to their highest pitch. In the midst of the delights of sense, there comes to the disciple one thought. It is the thought by which he sees through things and knows them as they are. By it, the disciple in the school of the masters knows that the new world in which he stands is not the world of the masters, the mental world, beautiful though it is. As he is about to pass judgment on this glorified world, the world of the inner senses, figures and forms and all elements cry out to him. First to enjoy with them and, as he refuses, then to remain with them and be their ruler, their savior, and lead them onward to a higher world. They plead; they tell him they have waited long for him; that he should not leave them; that he alone can save them. They cry out and appeal to him not to forsake them. This is the strongest appeal they can make. The disciple in the school of the masters holds the thought of his discipleship. By this thought he makes his decision. He knows that this world is not his world; that the forms which he sees are impermanent and decay; that the tones and voices which appeal to him are the crystallized echoes of the world's desires, which can never be satisfied. The disciple pronounces his thought to the world which has claimed him. He shows it that he knows it and will not give his word to the inner world of the senses. Immediately there is within him a sense of power with the knowledge that he has wisely judged of the sense world and refused its allurements.

His thoughts now seem to penetrate all things and to be able to change the forms of things by the very power of his thought. Matter is easily moulded by his thought. Forms give way and change into other forms by his thought. His thought enters the world of men. He sees their weaknesses and their ideals, their follies and ambitions. He sees that he can wield the minds of men by his thought; that he may stop bickerings, quarrels, contentions and strife, by his thought. He sees that he might compel warring factions to enjoy peace. He sees that he can stimulate the minds of men and open them to keener vision and to ideals higher than any they have. He sees that he may suppress or remove disease by speaking the word of health. He sees that he may take away sorrows and assume burdens of men. He sees that with his knowledge he may be a god-man among men. He sees that he may be as great or as lowly among men as he wills. The mental world seems to open and disclose its powers to him. The world of men calls him but he gives no response. Then the men struggling call in mute appeal to him. He refuses to be the ruler of men, and they ask him to be their savior. He may comfort the sorrowing, raise the lowly, enrich the poor in spirit, quiet the troubled, strengthen the weary, remove despair and enlighten the minds of men. Mankind needs him. The voices of men tell him they cannot do without him. He is necessary to their progress. He can give them the spiritual vigor which they lack and may begin a new reign of spiritual law if he will go out to men and help them. The disciple in the school of the masters dismisses the call of ambition and position. He dismisses the call to be a great teacher or a saint, though he listens well to the cry for help. The thought of his discipleship is again with him. He focusses on the calls and judges them by his one thought. Almost had he gone out to the world to help.

To be continued.

The Best of Value of Books.

There is no luck in literary reputation. They who make up the final verdict upon every book are not the partial and noisy readers of the hour when it appears, but a court as of angels, a public not to be bribed, not to be entreated and not to be overawed, decides upon every man's title to fame. Only those books come down which deserve to last. Gilt edges, vellum and morocco, and presentation-copies to all the libraries will not preserve a book in circulation beyond its intrinsic date. It must go with all Walpole's Noble and Royal Authors to its fate. Blackmore, Kotzebue, or Pollock may endure for a night, but Moses and Homer stand for ever. There are not in the world at any one time more than a dozen persons who read and understand Plato,—never enough to pay for an edition of his works; yet to every generation these come duly down, for the sake of those few persons, as if God brought them in his hand. "No book," said Bentley, "was ever written down by any but itself." The permanence of all books is fixed by no effort, friendly or hostile, but by their own specific gravity, or the intrinsic importance of their contents to the constant mind of man. "Do not trouble yourself too much about the light on your statue," said Michael Angelo to the young sculptor; "the light of the public square will test its value."

—*Emerson*, "Spiritual Laws."

THE INNER LIFE AND THE TAO-TEH-KING.

By C. H. A. Bjerregaard.

XI.

IN the last chapter I described how to live the life which is of Teh by using a phrase of Goethe's: "Im Ganzen, Guten, Schönen resolut zu leben." I will now show how this fourfold life connects with corresponding powers within our own constitution, and, that this corresponding fourfoldness makes it not only possible, but easy to live with determination in the Whole, the Good and the Beautiful.

On Diagram II.[1] I designate the four inherent powers as Life, Love, Light and determined Will. The terms are entirely my own, and not used by anybody else, as far as I know. I have used them for many years in my studies of the subject, but I would not lay any special weight upon them. Other terms may be as suitable and perhaps convey the same ideas. What I do mean by them I shall explain, and, I shall hope that you for yourself will substitute other terms if you have such and if they convey to you the ideas I intend to express. The main point is the idea or the psychological fact, not the name we give the fact.

These four terms inscribed in the respective four corners of Diagram II. represent ideas connected with the ancient classification of temperaments into four groups, usually attributed to Hippocrates: the sanguine, choleric, melancholic and phlegmatic. I say ideas distinctly connected with this classification, because I do not bind myself to it nor do I think that classification exhaustive. However, defective as it is, it serves admirably for a broad classification of our congenital constitution, and it has the advantage of being biological. We get the best psychology where we begin biologically, on sure foundations in nature. Moreover, back of these four temperaments lie the elements, fire, air, earth, water, such as the ancients named them,

---

[1] Diagram II. appeared in the issue of February, 1910.

and, also the four forms of the spiritual world: supreme goodness, nous, psyché, hylé, and, also the influences from the four corners of the universe.

Our bodily constitution gives a bias to our disposition, and that bias is usually called temperament and distinguished in a four fold way as sanguinic, choleric, melancholic and phlegmatic. Temperament is nothing else than a predominant characteristic of our natural inclinations and tendencies, and the four names I have put on the diagram are simply my transcriptions of the four terms: sanguinic, choleric, melancholic and phlegmatic, which I have not put down on the diagram, because I wanted to avoid the confusion that was apt to arise if I wrote too much on it. I only mention this about the temperaments to give you a clue to my terms: life, love, light and will, and to indicate that I begin in biology, the true psychological basis. Besides the four terms I have used, there are others which I might have written on the diagram, but which I also have left out in order to avoid confusion. You can readily add them yourself if you wish.

Among such terms are those of a four-foldness described in Paul's letter to the Ephesians (Eph. 4.11-15). Paul speaks of the appointment of apostles, prophets, evangelists and pastoral teachers, who were set in the church in order to perfect the saints, to build up the church, that all might attain to the unity of faith and grow to be full grown men and no more be children driven by any and every wind of doctrine. That which Paul here describes as the order of the ministry of the early church is admirable psychology. If we understand what apostles, prophets, evangelists and pastoral teachers mean, the whole psychological system of the Path and of Teh, as understood by Paul, is marvellous in its simplicity. I will try to elucidate.

The apostolic power is the spirit in rational preëminence. It is the power that has the eye upon the Whole, both in its outer features and in its inner. It is the embodiment of Logos-Reason or the fundamental human power which is the spring of all mental, moral and spiritual manifestations. In the apostolic power there is something dominant like that silent but weighty force which the earth exhibits everywhere. In the catacombs, the apostle's symbol is a lion and his robe is yellow, like the earth under the burning sun in the Orient. The apostolic character lies in the first Kabbalistic world of Aziah, the world of activity or earth.

The prophetic power spoken of is the Wisdom-power or, as the classical people called it, the Hermes. Hermes was messenger from the Highest and his nature was represented as being that of the Wind, a term which to the ancients was synonymous with Spirit. The prophet was not a soothsayer but a divine messenger or witness. In the ancient church he was the preacher or which was the same the witness, the witness or proclaimer of the divine truth. The prophet was a sort of executive officer of the Spirit. The ancient symbol used as an expression for his office was an eagle and usually shown on blue felt, clearly indicative of his soaring spirit. The prophetic character lies in the second Kabbalistic world of Yetzirah, the world of formation.

The evangelist is also a messenger, but one sent by an authority, not directly from heaven like the prophet. The evangelist is the man with the large warm heart who goes out into the world with the "glad tidings" and who brings milk and honey to the hungry. His symbol is double. He is represented by the "human face divine" back of him, and with the figure of an ass at his side. The idea being that he has human feeling as motive power and also the steadiness, ye, obstinacy of the ass, that will not be driven away by stripes, and, which morever is satisfied to eat that on the fields which the ox or other animals will not eat. The evangelistic character lies in the third Kabbalistic world, the world of Briah, the world of creation.

The pastoral teacher is symbolically represented as the patient ox on the threshing floor in the East, which treads out the corn by steady and patient walking round and round. This symbol explains him as the more or less phlegmatic or patient teacher who by persistent labor brings out the fruit in the pupil, who is being trained in spiritual life. He is not original like the prophet, nor authoritative like the apostle, nor fiery like the evangelist, but he is really the cornerstone in the spiritual edifice, for what does all the work of the other offices amount to, if the teaching pastor did not teach the initiate how to masticate and assimilate? The pastor and teachers' character lies in the fourth Kabbalistic world, the world of Atziloth, the archetypal world.

Reviewing the four offices as now described, you can readily see the truth of Paul's statement, that they are necessary for full growth, for unity and perfection, not only in an outer organization made up of people of the four temperaments, but also in each one of us. Though we have only one temperament predominant, we have the other three in less degree and they need training and guidance as much as the one which is dominant. I shall come back to this fourfoldness at the end of this chapter and make a personal application of it.

The square represents man as a temple. The square is ethically an emblem of sincerity; it means wholeness, health and harmony on a plane of life different from that of nature. The circle, the line that runs into itself, stands for similar perfections in nature. The square in the sense I use it was discovered, or at any rate is credited, to operative Masonry and Free-Masonry. The circle could not be used as a symbol for temple, and has not been used, because a temple is not a nature-product; a temple is a human symbol for a human creative act. The word square has gone into human language as a term for integrity and beauty. We are square physically when we form an equilateral quadrature by standing upright, feet joined and arms outstretched. We are square spiritually when the events of our lives follow the principle of fourfoldness expressed by the law of "the limbs." The metaphysical and physical supplement one another. We are square cosmologically and theologically by other figures and measurements unnecessary to detail at present.

The idea of the square I have derived from the Apocalypse of St. John. I use it because of its psychological character. I will explain what that means. St. John saw the New Jerusalem descend in the form of a man and that form was described as being a square. That mystery only becomes intelligible when you place the human figure with outstretched arms inscribed in a square, making the length of the body from head to sole equal to the length of the arms and hands from finger tip to finger tip. A square drawn around such a figure may well represent the human temple and the psychological fourfoldness of man in his temperamental actions. Such a figure in a square is to be recommended to all who study man's constitution and their own. For microcosmic man it answers to the macrocosmic man's figure in that temple I gave in a former chapter, and located geographically from China to the Mediterranean sea and a few degrees north of the tropic of Cancer.

Laotze knew the fourfoldness. The cosmogony of the Tao-Teh-King is this:

Tao gave birth to 1 (Tao-sen-yit).

1 gave birth to 2 (Yit-sen-ri).
2 gave birth to 3 (Ri-sen-sam).
3 gave birth to 4 (Sam-sen-wan-wut or the 10,000 things), and the 10,000 things carry (1) Yin on the back and hold, (2) Yang in the arms, and these two produce, (3) Harmony, or the living principle, and, these three together constitute (4) the world; in other words Yin, Yang, Harmony and the world also constitute a fourfoldness. Rather interesting; is it not? Yin and Yang mean Mother and Father.

So much for Diagram II. and its construction. The word Teh, stands in the centre of the Diagram and I shall now try to make you see these four as emanations from Teh.

Those who have given serious attention to the life that seems to rush by them; anybody who has observed phenomena and thought about their causes, must have become aware that existence, either in cosmic or human form, is something dynamic, something living, is much like a stream. To be sure, none of us know either the stream's spring nor its outlet to an ocean, if there be any ocean. We see only that something under space and time conditions. It is even possible that there is no stream and that we read our own changeable nature into that which we call the universe.

However, we see change. Even fire, if it be not stirred, will go to sleep and die. Like ships swinging around on the anchor chain, we do not really get away, but nevertheless we are always in motion, because life itself moves by ebb and flood. Water without circulation becomes stagnant and pollutes itself. Moral bugles are always calling us; we are never allowed rest except we wed ourselves to death. Streams, physical, mental and moral; winds, spiritual or otherwise, keep up a circulation everywhere. Some of us in pessimistic moods see these currents only as destructive and point to all the flotsam and jetsam they carry along. Others more optimistic see only how great majestic ships of human dignity and worth sail down in the deep waters and safely pass all dangers.

Wherever mankind has had an eye for such a movement it has usually also seen that movement under a twofold aspect and named these aspects variously. In China the twofold aspect was seen long ago, and by Laotzse the two were named Tao and Teh; and he, like the other ancient sages, by these two terms described what he perceived, and he did it in the Tao-Teh-King. I have already set forth what Laotzse meant by Tao and there is but little more to say. I began to speak about Teh in the last chapter and shall now give some more information. I will claim that the word Teh represents such movements, changes, emanations, streams and dynamic forces, as those I have hinted at as descriptions of That which takes place around us.

I have frequently used the word Teh and given suggestions about it; yet much is still left to be said. Something of that still unsaid I shall try to bring out by placing the Teh in relationship to the conceptions evolution and karma, and thereby gain some means by which to explain it.

I shall not define evolution nor karma. By evolution I shall in general understand the movement in the universe so aptly defined by Herbert Spencer and Science in general, and I shall take the word largely in a physical sense. By Karma I shall understand practically the same as I understand by evolution, but I shall take the word mainly in a moral and spiritual sense. At any rate I shall give the word a very wide and universal meaning.

These two words, evolution and karma, have many equivalents, varying according to views taken, and it will have its interest that I give you some of these equivalents and explain them to some extent, because the equivalents will help to explain Tao and Teh, the two old Chinese terms for thoughts similar to some aspects of evolution, karma and the other terms, as I shall now mention them in the following and elucidate them.

The classical people, Greeks and Romans, used the term destiny or fate, and the fullest explanation of this word is that given by Seneca in his epistles. I will therefore reproduce this Stoic's words. I will quote Seneca in full because his definition is probably least known.

"They (our ancestors) did not by any means believe this, that Jupiter, as we worship him at the Capitol and in other shrines, sent down thunderbolts from his hand; but they recognized the same Jupiter as we do, the same director and guardian of the universe, the mind and soul of the world, the lord and maker of this work, to whom each name belongs. You wish to say that he is Providence, you will speak correctly; for he is the one by whose wisdom the world is cared for, so that it may proceed safely and perform its tasks. You wish to call him Nature; you will not sin. He is the One from whom all come; by whose spirit we live. You wish to call him the World, you will not be deceived, for he is all this which is visible, set in his own members, sustainng himself and his." (1)

"If you speak of Nature, Fate, Fortune, all are names of the same God, who is manifesting himself in these various ways." (2)

I need not say much in explanation of Seneca. As you noticed, he advises not to care for names but to get at the fact behind names. And speaking in the language of the Tao-Teh-King, the fact he cares for is named Teh. And Teh as a fact is presented by Laotzse as a "power that makes for righteousness," a power that has its being in all our modes of existence. A power and purpose, a will and a way, name it as we may, exists as a fact and cannot be denied. Look upon it as evolution, as karma or under any of the aspects mentioned by Seneca —there it is, and, as Seneca (Ep, 107.11) also says, "it leads the willing and drags the unwilling."

An ancient Greek poet describing the mother of the gods, said she was "One shape of many names." That description fits Teh admirably. Not only is Teh of motherly nature (though the Tao-Teh-King knows no gods) but Teh is multiform and many named, as I have said, and that because Teh enters into all human actions as the organizing reason, the forming and plastic principle, and gets its many names from these incarnations.

Such a principle as Teh is peculiar to humanity. Throughout the organic world, action is regulated mainly by hereditary structure; and secondarily by reflex action or instinct derived from hereditary structure. But action with man is modified by intelligent use of experience, by the reflex action of the accumulated results of mankind's past experiences. That action and those accumulated results of mankind's past experiences is in Chinese called Teh; with us, scientifically, Morals, principles of morals or principles for the conduct of our spiritual life.

The Calvinist among christian theologians chose the term election and understood one small action of that which other christians call Providence, a term so personal that they are constantly in trouble when asked to explain it.

Among scientists you meet with the biologist who has a term of his own, by which he accounts for both cause and effect and motion, too. "Selection" is his magic word. I need not spend

¹Seneca Naturallum Quest. Lib. 11. Cap. 45.1, 2, 3.
²Seneca. De Beneficiis Lib. iv.8.

any time on it; you are familiar with it if you have followed the literature of the last thirty years. The same is the case with the phrase "cosmic process," so handy to the evolutionist as an explanation of facts he does not understand and which his narrow science has no room for.

Pantheistic poets of modern days speak of "cosmic emotion" and quote Sidgwick and Romanes as their authorities; other poets of the same color have varied the phrase and speak of "tides of eternal emotions." The mystics of all ages have called the same phenomena and their causes "love." The future will probably see other terms and hear other expressions. And it is well that new terms and expressions should come forth. They prove that some parts of mankind are neither dead nor asleep. Whatever terms be applied, they all signify that the power they name is one that works for uplift, for evolution, for progress, for spiritual life, for the Inner Life. The terms employed always signify quality in contradistinction to quantity, and they all have a tendency to be personal in character and all stand somewhat in opposition to something impersonal. It seems that no teacher can avoid personification. Whatever terms be employed and whether they be considered personally or impersonally they can all be translated by Teh, as the Tao-Teh-King uses that word.

I, myself, shall not offer new terms. I am engaged in restoring Teh to its right place and I mean to use with perfectly liberty and whenever I want any of the terms I have just now enumerated, because they express various aspects of the Chinese conception of Teh. But this I will say right here, that with the exception of Seneca's explication of all that which lies in the word fate, all the other terms apply principally to Tao and only secondarily to Teh. With the exception of Stoicism, the West knows next to nothing of such a conception as that of Teh as the mother of the universe; or as we can say, since Goethe, the "eternally feminine." Western thought is so exclusively masculine in cast and formal in its philosophy, that it has become terribly one-sided and barren. If it were not for the mystic leven of love, that, here and there, now and then, has softened its rudeness and added a little affection and color to its mentality, the Western mind would be a dreary desert and look like barren rocks. And the pity is, the West believes itself superior.

The names given to Deity by the ancients were always

descriptions of the character of their deity, such as they perceived it. In conformity to that practice, I shall give Teh the sense of "the eternally femine," the sense of "a power that makes for righteousness," the sense of "providence," the sense of "cosmic process," the sense of "moral force," the sense of "mother," besides all the other senses already given the word.

The reason for these many names of Teh or senses given to Teh is this, that Teh is as an old saw says a soul and a light that reveals all things, but hides itself from sight. All the world sees by Teh, but never saw Teh.

I find thee, O Most High, where'er my glance I send,
At the beginning Thee; Thee also at the end.
If towards the source I fly, in Thee 't is lost to me.
The outlet would I spy,—that, too, breaks forth from Thee.
Thou the beginning art, that doth its end enclose.
Thou art the end that back to the beginning flows.
And in the midst art Thou, and all things are in Thee,
And I am I, because Thou art the midst in me.   (3)

According to the Tao-Teh-King, the relationship of Tao and Teh is something like this: "If Tao perishes," it is said, "then Teh will also perish." Teh is called the manifestation of Tao, and, Tao cannot be reached except by means of Teh. Teh is multiform, but Tao is a unit. These two ideas, that Teh is the manifestation of Tao and is multiform, explain the synchretism of the Teh. All virtue is necessarily manifold and ever varying. In one moment it is heavenward and a worthship; in the next it is earthward or love to the neighbor. These two ideas of "manifestation" and "multiformity" explain the great variety of names and descriptions of Teh already given. In one place it is said that Tao is the Lord of Teh, but nowhere does any commentary explain in what that lordship consists. Whatever it does mean, it does not mean that Tao is superior to Teh, because Tao does not and cannot exist without Teh.

It will not do to call Tao the masculine and Teh the feminine principle of existence, because the Tao-Teh-King not only does not do it, but knows both Yang and Yin and calls them the masculine and feminine principles. If Tao and Teh are related to Yang and Yin, then it must be as superior spiritual principles behind them and it is in this sense that I take Teh, when I call it "the eternally feminine."

---

[3]Friedrich Rückert: The Wisdom of the Brahmin, iv.50. Translated by C. T. Brooks, Boston, 1882.

It is exceedingly difficult to define Tao and Teh fully and satisfactory to a Western critical and intellectual mind. Both terms are too elastic for logic and both represent something universal, that cannot be put into a philosophical form. Truly the Tao-Teh-King declares that their nature "baffles investigation"; but the same book also declares that if we "use" Tao and Teh, we shall know them.

Thus an examination of the nature of Tao and Teh ends like all examinations of mystic principles; they are beyond comprehension, but ready for our use at any time and anywhere. The mystic principles desire incorporation; they wish to be placed in the human heart and to be allowed to lead man to his eternal good. They never mislead, however exacting they may be. They never teach us, as we understand teaching, but they are ready to lead us, and, they are always near us, yea, they dwell in our hearts.

I have just said that I should give Teh the sense of "the eternally feminine" and the sense of "mother." These two senses have been given Teh by explicit language. All the other senses are implied in various teachings. But before I draw out the colors and the life that lies in the terms of the sixth chapter of the Tao-Teh-King on the mother-power Teh, I will give you a translation of it. And I will say a few words about the direct meaning before I apply this conception mother-power to Teh, for Teh is the mother-power, considered morally, out of which springs our whole mental, moral and spiritual life. Teh as the mother of all things is described in the sixth chapter as follows:

"The Valley-God never dies. I call it the Mother of the Abyss and she is the Root of Heaven-Earth (or the All-things.) She endures forever, and forever she produces."

I might have disposed of this short chapter by saying that this Valley-God is the same as sakti, as deva matri, but I should then have been reading Brahminical ideas and modern methods into Chinese Theosophy and that would have been a false commentary. It has been done by others, I am sorry to say.

I will admit, that the root idea of the Tao-Teh-King's description is probably physical and sexual. So much in the East begins that way. So much in the East is cast mainly in prehistoric forms, and only too many of modern students of Eastern lore stick in these forms.

While the signs and forms of the Tao-Teh-King are often physical and sexual, simply because the writer had no other means at hand for his use, these signs and forms of the Tao-Teh-King always bear a high and noble, a spiritual and transcendental signification, and are so understood by genuine Taoists. In this case, "the Valley-God" cannot mean anything else than Teh or Virtue. The sign for Valley-Spirit is a double one. It is composed of ku and sen.

The sign for ku is a mouth out of which flows water, hence it is a sign for valley, but simply for a valley without a stream. To indicate that the valley gives out water, the sign sen is added, which indicates that the valley is living. That is the way the Chinese commentator understands it. For short, the signs is a name for the activity of Teh in all the realms of its operation. But the realistic conception connected with the term must not be ignored. There is such an one in it, which is evident from the fact that Laotzse also calls it "nourishing mother" (ssï-mu).

A prominent Taoist and philosopher, Liet-tsi (400 B. C.), declares Laotzse's teaching and words to be cited from the books of the fabled King Hoang-ti (about 27 Cent. B. C.). If so, then the meaning of the sign and term would be physical and sexual. Be this declaration of Liet-tsi so or not, we cannot prove or deny the allegation. The word ku-sen means now the "emanating spirit" or "the out flowing spirit," indicating the invisible power behind all objective appearances, or, in other words, the spiritual or invisible mother of all things already mentioned in the opening chapter of the book.

The chapter on the valley-god already given in translation divides itself naturally into three thoughts. The first relates to the valley-god as the original power through which as the mysterious mother all things come forth; the second thought relates to the valley-god as the root of heaven and earth specially; and the third thought is this that these two already mentioned do not exist separately but are really one, and, it has been suggested by the German commentator, Strausz, that these two in union correspond to Chokma of the Old Testament, to the Idea of Plato, to Sophia of the Gnostics and the Magic of Jacob Böhme. I think the suggestion an admirable one. I would add that the two in union also correspond to Sephira, mother of the Sephiroth, of the Kabbalah.

It would be very interesting to work out the details of these correspondences, but space and time forbid it, at present. I wish to bring Teh down to the level of our own daily life and individual existence. That will be more practical and useful, at present.

Let me now apply this fourfoldness of Teh to you and myself and try to find out our exact place in the temple, and thereby necessarily the work we can and must do in that universal ministry of Teh to which we all without exception are called.

If we find ourselves individually of a warm and pure red blood condition; if our blood is not leaded with foreign substances, but readily heals a wound; if our nerves are in a corresponding healthy condition and neither "cracked" nor weak; if we enjoy to live and to be active in great and good work and do a work for the benefit of mankind, not merely because we are paid for it or profit by it in some way, but do such a work because we find our call in it and an innermost satisfaction in doing it; then, I say, we are Life people, people of the apostolic temper, workers in the universal ministry. Our genius is activity and it will be a sin for us to be unfaithful. Our place on the Diagram and in the temple is readily seen. We know what Teh wants of us.

If we are introspective of disposition; if we always are inclined to look behind a phenomenon to see its spirit, if possible; if the blue sky draws us out of ourselves and robs us of the solid ground under our feet; if things and persons do not appear to our souls like the seeming solid things our senses declare them to be; if we are disinclined for all kinds of "small talk," "gossip," or the like, but from time to time are moved by a mighty impulse to "speak out," to "witness," to give testimony in the name of the Highest; then, we are of the prophetic temper, or at least poets or philosophers. Our genius is clearly spirit and our work in the universal ministry so clearly marked off for us that we never can mistake it. We know our place on the Diagram and in the temple. We know what Teh wants of us.

If our hearts bleed at the sight of human misery, both physical and spiritual; if we burn to go out into the world to preach the glad tidings that there is hope for all, even the deepest fallen; if we proclaim that hope in love to mankind and without any condemnation, not even with reproach; if we cheerfully stand abuse, even stripes and never lose courage in our work; if we persist in working for others as if they were our own relatives, though separated from us by race or color or enmity; then, I say, we are of the evangelistic temper. Our genius is clearly Love and nobody can do the work laid out for us in our ministry as well as we can. We know our place in the temple and what Teh wants of us.

If we are disposed to teach and take care, to lead and to

guide, and be a daily and hourly sacrifice of which others take freely and eat, never even realizing that they torture us; if we have a patience that never wearies over repetitions and monotony; if compensation is never thought of; if we run after the lost sheep, comfort the obstinate ones, and bear over with the unreasonable; then, our work in the temple of humanity is pastoral teaching and we are indeed pillars in the sanctuary of Teh.

It is evident that this last group of sanctified tempers and human beings are those who live with determnation (see Diagram II.). That the first group described (the apostolic) is living in the Whole is self-evident. I hardly need to say that the prophetic temper as described is the light bearer of beauty, and that the evangelistic temper is a real incarnation of goodness.

Let none try to stifle their own conscience and say that they have not felt any motion in the direction of the four forms mentioned. They do not speak the truth, ignorantly or wilfully. All feel the motions of Teh! The Tao-Teh-King (Ll) declares "To produce and not possess—to act and not expect—to enlarge and not control—that is Teh." If such people have not felt the drawings of Teh under such forms as those I have described, they have felt them under other forms. Perhaps the four to them should be named, God, Reason, Nature, Highest Life; perhaps they should be named Right, Justice, Love, Reciprocity of life; perhaps they should be named as on Diagram I. No matter how they are named. Each age has named them differently, but each age has known the fact that Teh manifests itself in a temple square or human individuality. Not only each age knows the fact, but the fact presents itself to each individual, even to those who cannot express the fact or translate the moving power into words.

No man is sufficient for himself. Life is so constituted that we need reservoirs of every kind of excellence, of intelligence, of knowledge, of power. The four forms are such reservoirs in which Teh is present and they are for us to draw from, both to live by and to work by.

Now in which ever of these four groups our work may lie, it is the spirit of Teh, the Great Mother, that works that temper in us. And to be in Truth, we must obey, yea we wish to obey and we do obey as surely as the water runs out of the valley. You remember the sign of ku-sen, the great symbol of Teh!

I say it is Teh that both works in us and wishes to work in us, and, if we amount to anything at all in the universal ministry to which we all are called by Teh, even while we still struggle on the Path, then we show eagerness to do that work as we say "with a will"; we do it determinedly and that eagerness proves what we amount to.

This is Teh and teaching about Teh. And Teh now witnesses within each one of us for or against us, according to the truth in which we stand in this matter.

There is a spurious Biblical phrase which reads, "It is a terrible thing to fall into the hands of the living God." It may be spurious as regards the Bible, but this I say, "It is a terrible thing to fall into the hands of Teh" for those who are unfaithful. It can only mean destruction.

I said in the beginning of this chapter that the fourfold life of Teh corresponded to similar powers within our constitution and that this corresponding fourfoldness made it not only possible but easy to live with determination in the Whole, the Good, the True and the Beautiful.

I have shown you the corresponding forms, both the inner in yourself and the outer in Teh's universal life, and, I have said that Teh works spontaneously in us all, because Teh is a river of active goodness or virtue that flows into the world from out a valley, which is called the Abyss of Abysses. It is now for you and me to live up to this light and make ourselves living realizations of that stupendous fact.

Terstegen was a Dutch mystic. As a mystic, he is especially remarkable on account of his intuitive perceptions of the motions of the Spirit, of Teh such as I have defined Teh. Here are a few lines from his poetry describing these motions of Teh:

"Hath not each heart a passion and a dream—
Each, some companionship forever sweet—
And each, in saddest skies some silver gleam—
And each, some passing joy too faint and fleet—
And each, a staff and stay, though frail it prove—
And each, a face he fain would ever see?"

These are some of the beckonings of Teh, that come to all. He finally asks:

"And what have I?—a glory and a calm,
A life that is an everlasting psalm,
A heaven of endless joy in Thee," that is Teh.

Terstegen thus declares that Teh is an "everlasting presence" and an endless joy.

May that be your lot! You shall then know that all this about Teh is of the Inner Life.

(*To be continued.*)

THE GENESIS AND GROWTH OF THE CHRIST OF THE SOUL AND, SOME OF ITS MODES OF LIFE.

By James L. Macbeth Bain.

(*Continued from Vol. X., page* 338.)

WHILE all the richness of the whole Christ are hid in every human soul, yet not through any one soul may all the fulness of it be manifested. For it needs all souls to show forth the fulness of the richness of the Beauty infinite and manifold.

Yet is the Christ ever revealing this Beauty to those who can see. And just as we can see, so is the revealing. And Love is the opener of the eyes. But when Love is not yet awakened in us it often happens that the Holy One is even with us, sitting by us, and we know it not. For our familiarity with the soul in whom It dwells hides the Beauty of the presence from us. But It is there, ever willing to bless us by the vision of the Great Beauty. And if we only give It our love and reverence, ay, and our adoration, It will give us of the power of Its Beauty to become like unto It. For, sure as we give to the Holy One our whole heart, so surely is It henceforth unto us the power of the undying Life, the strength of the Beauty eternal.

And this leads us to a very great theme on which a word must be given for the completing of what has already been said and it is the potency of the Christ in us.

Now the Holy One of the soul may be thought of as the human, microcosmic counterpart of the universal or cosmic Christ. We cannot rightly use the language of sex here, and yet we men can hardly speak in other terms even of our Holy One of Blessing than as the individualised, corresponding affinity of the Christ of the Great Cosmos, the Holy One of Universal Blessing.

Thus the new-born or little Christ in us, is as a sunflower, open, ever open to receive the radiance of the Sun of the Cosmos of the innermost heaven of the Great Love. It is as a sun shining within the soul, a little sun, yet living and strong in all the potency of the One Sun of our human universe. For it hath been kissed of the Holy One into life. And being a center of living energy it now generates in the soul the divine radium or Christ power of blessing in modes fit for the use of the human need.

Or, the Christ of the soul may be likened to the female principle in life, ready and waiting for the enrichening of the male. And yet the age-long blessing of the Holy One may well be spoken of as the gentle brooding of the Mother of the ages over the unborn, and the actual inflow of the Great Love as the coming of the heavenly Bride to her own.

Thus the language of sex, though necessary, is not adequate, and may even lead the feebler ones into mistaking the sensuous for the spiritual. And this subtle snare of the old enemy of the pure whiteness of the Dove has caught not a few of the finest mystics of our day in the meshes of Psyche.

For in the innermost of pure spirit, even the holy place of the Christhood, there is no more sex. All who have even once come unto the Center know that, in the Great Deep of spaceless and timeless Being, all sex-differentiation is transcended, ay, lost in the Great Love whose essence is neither male nor female but the two in one.

And so it is that this holy correspondence is best uttered in the words of the impersonal. May we say then that in the little Christ of the soul as related to the great Christ of the cosmos there is the passive or receptive principle of the Cosmic Body, while in the Christos universal there is the positive principle of the energizer.

And yet the Christ of the soul, being a microcosmic counterpart of the Cosmic Christ, possesses and manifests the power of these dual principles. This we speak of as the potency of the whole Christ, the indwelling Unity.

And the way of its coming is somewhat after this manner. Soon as the house is ready, the dweller is there—*i.e.*, as soon as your psyche is worthy of the indwelling Christ, so soon is the Universal Christ in her as the home-Christ.

True, the Cosmic Christ-potency has been working in her heretofore, but in the way of preparing Its dwelling-place. It has been shedding Its life-power in and through her, thereby washing her from all unworthiness, bringing by the sweet power of Its vibrations, harmony out of her discord, and thus healing her into the wholeness or unification of her powers. But It has not yet been able to dwell in her, for It cannot dwell where there is any uncleanness. The Christ visits our disordered soul as the Healer. The Christ in us visits even now the souls that are in the prison-house of despair as the Comforter or Light-bearer. And as the healer comes to heal and not to dwell in the house of the patient, so the Holy One comes often to visit the diseased soul, though It cannot yet find in that soul an abiding.

But when the soul has been cleansed of the impurities of its olden selfhood, when the house is of a pure and sweet air, whereon may grow the fragrant plants of the Beauty of the Spirit of Life in whose aroma is the very power of healing, then will it be a fit dwelling-place for the Universal Christ; and the Holy One will be drawn as by the beauty of Love to Its home. And so It becomes our Emmanuel.

Now in receiving the energising kiss of the Mother-Christ our psyche is blessed of the holy power, and even as the sunflower awakes to full life by the shining into it of the power of earth's sun, so our Christ-soul awakes to the fulness of her life by the power in her of the Sun of the Great Love.

And she is henceforth the bearer of the fruit of blessing unto many. And never again throughout the ages will she be unfruitful. For she hath been blessed of the potency of the Holy One. And this blessing once given, its power never passes away. And in her will dwell the silent joy of the deep peace.

And the power who hath thus blessed her into new life, she, as the ageless Christ of the soul, knows, speaks to, prays to and sings of as her radiant Christ of the Great Love, the Sun of the human Universe.

And so in a very real sense all the hymns or prayers of faith and love, yearning and gladness, ay, of anguish and despair that have been offered of the spiritual soul of man to the Spirit of Life are cries of the little Christ of the Soul unto the Cosmic Christ, the Mother of the Ages of our race, the Soul of the Great Love.

Now it is possible to communicate of the potency of the Great Love principle thus generated in the soul, to other souls. And it will work the great work of love in these souls in modes corresponding to their degree of unfoldment. Thus if you communicate this divine potency to one yet bound in the degree of personal limitation, who, receiving the divine gift, would appropriate it for the pleasure of self, and transmute it into the baseness of self, and whose affectional stuff is therefore in the light of the Spirit, unclean, it will work therein as a cleansing power, bringing unto the state of burning all her elements that must be consumed of the Fire of Love. And this process of burning or consuming will be to her great suffering, that corresponds in degree to the power these psychic elements contain and give as a fuel unto the burning. Yet is it the good work of Love all through, and the anguish is purgatorial. For the soul is being refined, and the flame is of the Great Love and in the power of the Holy One.

To another soul who yearns only for the light of truth this divine potency will be as a gentle flame shining within her deeps, and giving the yearned-for illumination.

To another who is hungry and faint for want of the living bread, the love principle communicated will be the very food of the angel; and that soul will be nourished well. And so, throughout all the needs of the soul of man, in the Great Love or Christ principle communicated there is all that meet our need.

Now this body of Love is a heavenly or spiritual body. It is indeed the body we shall use when we enter our full heaven; and in and by it alone do we now enter our heaven even while we are dwelling in the flesh. Through its mediation alone we have as constant communion with the many and blessed potencies in the unseen as we can well receive and enjoy. Through it we pass to and from the heavenly state as often as we will, perceiving in it and bearing through it back to the needy soul of this earth the sweet fruits and life-giving essences of the homeland of the soul. Ay, we thus cross and recross the Jordan as we will; and we are the carriers of the grapes of the Promised Land unto the needy ones who still must abide by the borders of the wilderness of mortality.

And even in this mediatorial service is the work both of feeding the new body and of its continuous refining. For in giving of our present good, we, as the living vessels of communion, are ever receiving of a higher and purer good to refill our emptiness. And, as every body is formed out of its food, so our body of Love, in being nourished of the higher, is refined and ever refined unto a degree of potency that is always becoming higher and finer.

For, like any other live body, this body can be nourished or starved; it can be kept in health and increased in effective activity by the free and full exercise of all its faculties, or it can be so denied the right to function that its faculties will dwindle away into the atrophy of inefficiency. Also it may be overwrought, even unto its hurt, and may need a period of rest and even healing.

But what is more serious is that it may be poisoned by the death-thoughts of the olden selfhood, the denier of the new Life. And there is here so serious a peril that I shall speak of it now. This denying is the work of the old will of death in us; for it still imagines itself to be our true reality. So it claims to have its rights, ay, its own sweet home in us, and will be heard of us for very clamouring, if we only allow it a hearing.

But, like every soul who claims its rights, it is a liar to the truth of the Spirit of Life, and its baneful word is always pessimistic. It is the old enemy of our life, the adversary of our joy, the foe of the newborn who would indeed gladden our days; and it seeks by all means to kill this child, the bearer of our good cheer, who even in our deepest gloom must remain optimistic. Now, we can judge of the truth of its word, and we know that it is lying even as it has lied to us before. Its word has not been true to the facts of our experience and inasmuch as we have listened to it we have been held in the bondage of fear or despair. Therefore, knowing this, it is out wisdom to deny it utterly, to banish it from our soul as an ally of death by affirming the will of the new Life. And thus will our body of Love be preserved from hurt.

Again, it can be retarded in its growth by the unwholesome influence of our past mental attitudes arising from crudities in our spiritual education or errors of our unenlightened judgment. Now these mental attitudes, though false to the new mind and no more real to us, are still potent with the power of our olden psyche. And inasmuch as we have lived in them, in so much is their potency. And inasmuch as they are thus potent, in so much will the adversary of our Life use them for the service of death. And they, too, claim you, the free born child of the new Life, for they too are blind to the fact that you no longer belong to them.

And as you cannot but deny them, refusing them sustenance, they cry as abandoned children after you, clinging to you in virtue of their yet active potency. And the pain of their crying and clinging will be according to the degree and intensity of soul-force you gave them in the past.

And they will continue so to cry, to cling to and distress you as long as they can draw any sustenance from you through sympathy. For they, too, live on the good of psyche, and they would eat up the food of the unborn Christ, and so retard its growth in the soul.

And the only way of deliverance from them is to deny them this food. For they must die, and the deathless One, though unborn, must live. And this is the word of the Christ of the Ages: He who would come to me must deny the dear ones of the old selfhood, saying in the power of the Truth: Ye are no more me, and I am no more ye; nay, for I am Thou and Thou art I.

Now this Love body must be fed on the food of its own heaven. And there is a spiritual food for this new Christ-body. For it can no longer be nourished on the stuffs which are the foods convenient and good for the soul or mind of the past degrees. Indeed, these foods are now hurtful unto it; and it desires them not. This spiritual or heavenly food is the livng bread, who is the holy substance, the cosmic Christ-Spirit, in essence diffuse and universal, so far as our human need is concerned, whether we be in the flesh or out of the flesh.

This food is not only administered to the spiritual soul at all times in a common way, but also at special times and in special conditions. Thus, during sleep it may be, and is, administered, and it is well to realize before falling asleep that He giveth it to his beloved during sleep.

It is also specially given during the periods of the utter quiet of the soul and of the external or mundane consciousness whether it be in the modes of contemplation and prayer, or of simple and pure passivity. And it is important to know, to find and to enter if possible the conditions physical and psychical which conduce to this state of passivity.

To be concluded.

"SAVONAROLA" OF FLORENCE.

THEOSOPHIST, REFORMER AND MARTYR. A PORTRAITURE OF
SPIRITUAL GROWTH AND DEVELOPMENT.

BY DR. W. WILLIAMS.

(*Continued from Vol. X., page 368.*)

"THE ORDEAL OF FIRE."

THE surest and most certain method to ruin an enemy is to destroy his prestige and discredit him in the public estimation. Popularity is an unstable thing, changeable, indiscriminate, unreliable and subject to sudden alterations. No dependence can be placed on it; no confidence reposed in it. Its admiration is liable to be changed into unreasonable hatred and cruelty, and in a sudden ebullition of unbridled rage it knows no bounds of restraint. Of this characteristic, Florence herself was about to afford a lamentable instance which will ever remain a dark blot on the annals of her history.

After the prohibition of Savonarola from preaching, by the signory, the popular mind became excited and unsettled giving rise to heated discussions and disputes between the various political parties again existent in the city. All recognized the gravity of the act, doubting and dreading the issue of it to the detriment of the state. Speculation ran riot and opinions the most discordant were expressed, and a feeling of uncertainty and apprehension as to the future universally prevailed. It was the prelude to the tragedy about to be enacted, the exordium was soon to begin and the curtain rung up. The first act was commenced by a Franciscan friar, who at this time was delivering a series of sermons in the church of San Croce. Acting under orders he began to attack and stigmatize Savonarola, denouncing him as a heretic, a schismatic and a false prophet and concluded his diatribes by challenging him to the proof of his teachings and doctrines by the ordeal of fire. Similar challenges had at times been thrown out, but had been ignored and unnoticed by Savonarola as beneath and inconsonant with the dignity of a christian minister and regarded as needless and unnecessary for the detection and apprehension of truth. This same friar when preaching in the preceding year in Prato, had reviled Savonarola and challenged him to prove his teaching by submitting to pass through the fire, but on being confronted with Fra Domenico, Savonarola's most valiant and intimate friend and intrepid defender, and after agreeing to a public discussion, suddenly decamped and fled out of the town under the pretext of having received a summons to Florence from his superiors. On repeating his challenge in Florence Fra Domenico who was then preaching in place of Savonarola at San Marco promptly accepted it, declaring himself prepared to go through the ordeal by fire, as now being the chief exponent of his master's teachings and who, he said, was reserved for greater things. The Franciscan finding Domenico so intrepid and ready to accept the challenge refused to carry out his proposition, on the ground that the quarrel was with Savonarola alone and that though he expected to be consumed, he was willing to enter the fire with him in order to procure the death of such a disseminator of scandal and false doctrine, but with Domenico he would have nothing whatever to do. On hearing and becoming acquainted with what had occurred, Savonarola reproved his friend's imprudent zeal. And here the miserable affair might have terminated, had it not become widely circulated and discussed throughout the city. It was something strange and extraordinary. The idea caught like wildfire on the popular mind, it being regarded as the best and most effectual means of confounding and triumphing over his foes and enemies and reinstating him in his former position of eminence and dignity. Both the Arrabbiati and Compagnacci saw their chance and reasoned thus: If Savonarola enters the fire, he will undoubtedly be burnt alive. If, however, he refuses, he will lose all credit with his followers and the citizens in general and then will come our opportunity of raising a tumult during which it will be easy to seize his person and kill him. They therefore applied to the signory, a majority of whose members they found ready and willing to fall in with their ideas and undertake the direction and execution of the shameful and inhuman scheme. Taking a note of the principal doctrines of Savonarola that Fra Domenico had declared himself ready to defend even with his life, the signory arranged they should be transcribed by the public notary and then invited the signatures of those who were willing to maintain them by passing through the fiery ordeal. It was an artful and insidious ruse and proved successful. Several of Savonarola's friends at once volunteered to submit themselves to it, but Domenico claimed precedence and prayed earnestly to be allowed to undertake it, so great was his affection for his master and concern for his safety. Again the Franciscan cowardly declined to affix his signature for the same reasons he had previously given. At the same time he proposed as his substitute a certain Rondinelli who would pass through the fire along with Fra Domenico, but when the time for signing the challenge arrived, Rondinelli failed to appear. He was an artisan of weak intellect whom the Compagnacci had induced to act as their tool, Dolfo Spino assuring him that no harm should befall him; that he only needed to declare himself willing to endure the ordeal, but would not be required to do so. Acting on this assurance though reluctantly, Rondinelli affixed his signature, stating, "He would enter the fire, although certain he would be consumed and that he did it for his soul's salvation." Thus the details of the wretched farce were arranged by the members of the signory who, oblivious of the dignity of their position and station now set themselves to carry them out, trusting they would succeed and bring about not only the death of Savonarola, but also lead to the subversion and abolition of the republic.

The Ordeal by Fire.

Whilst the preliminaries were being arranged in Florence respecting the ordeal by fire, Alexander from his eyrie in Rome watched keenly the plot elaborated for the downfall and ruin of Savonarola. It was his duty as head of the Christian Church to condemn and forbid such an outrageous exhibition and relic of pagan and barbarous times. He, the secret mover, the *Deus ex machina* of the dark transaction, was aware that to save appearances he must take some steps to shield himself from suspicion of complicity in an affair that was revolting to the public conscience and general opinion of the age. This he accomplished by writing and sending a brief wherein he condemned and forbade the ordeal, but so contrived that it did not reach Florence until two days after it had taken place, the result of which as we shall presently see filled him with feelings of joy and delight as he inwardly gloated over the approaching ruin of Savonarola, thinking thereby to escape the danger of a general council and thus preventing the revelation of the wickedness of his infamous pontificate.

Owing to various reasons, a common agreement was come to between the signory and Arrabbiati to call a public meeting of the citizens to discuss the matter of the ordeal by fire; whether it should or should not take place. It was an artful device to rid themselves of the responsibility of their action. It was attended by a minority of Savonarola's friends, who on perceiving the real object of it and disgusted with the sham proceedings of it, retired after giving expression to their indignation at a subterfuge so base and shameless. A resolution in favor of it was formally proposed and carried after a great deal of deceitful discussion so evident that one of Savonarola's opponents regaining his sense of honesty and fair dealing rose up and in agitated tones exclaimed, "When I hear such things as have been said I scarcely know whether life or death is most to be preferred. I truly believe that if our forefathers, the founders of this city could have divined that a like question would be discussed here and that we were to become the jest and opprobrium of the whole world, they would have refused to have anything to do with us. And now that our city is come to a worse pass than has occurred for many long years and one sees it is now all in confusion, I would therefore implore your excellencies to deliver our people from all this wretchedness at any cost and put an end to these things in order that no misery or hurt may befall our city." Such honest advice however proved of no avail in the most cultured and civilized city of Europe, to save it from the degradation of witnessing in its midst such a barbarous and inhuman proof of truth as was the ordeal by fire. Savonarola knowing full well that his Franciscan opponents would never have the courage to face the burning pyre and that they were mere puppets in the hands of the pope and the Arrabbiati,—did his utmost to prevent the miserable exhibition, not because he had any doubt or mistrust whatever of the ability of himself or Fra Domenico to come out of the ordeal unscathed and uninjured, but as he said:

"God would certainly make a miracle if necessary, but it is not for us to command one. Besides, had not the citizens of Florence had enough miracles and proofs of his sincerity and truthfulness in predictions already and actually fulfilled and in the work he had accomplished in the moral elevation and political renovation of Florence itself. Miracles are useless where reason and common sense suffice. Yet we neither compel nor exhort any man to believe in them more than he feels able. We only exhort to lead righteous lives and for this the fire of charity and the miracle of faith are required; all the rest is of no avail."

Notwithstanding the deprecatory words respecting having recourse to such methods of proof as the proposed ordeal by fire for the ratification and confirmation of any article of faith or doctrinal teaching, the signory regardless of consequences and urged on by the Arrabbiati who were resolved that their intended victim should not escape out of their hands, finally fixed on the 7th of April as the day of trial, which was accepted by Savonarola who clearly perceived and was fully acquainted with their insidious designs and intentions. He knew well that the whole affair was an artful pretext to bring about his assassination and discredit, and that their blatant champion would fail to appear and submit himself to the fiery proof. He was also aware that in case he refused to allow Fra Domenico to do so, it would afford his enemies a specious excuse for banishing him out of Florence as a cowardly impostor or of arresting him and sending him a prisoner to Rome and moreover discerned that even Domenico's success in passing through the burning faggots would be attributed to the use of enchantments and Satanic or black magic. For his own personal safety he cared not so much as for the honor and establishment of the great principles of the divine life, for the reality and vindication of which he was prepared and willing to lay down his life and endure everything as a gage and proof of its existence. Thus he proved himself a true student of occultism and a veritable and trusty initiate of the great mystic brotherhood whose chief maxim of conduct is, "Not for thyself, nor for thy own advantage, but for the good of humanity must thy knowledge be subordinated and used. Act well thy part in life, discharging its duties and placing all thy trust and confidence in the good law that never errs or fails them who rely upon it."

On the day preceding the ordeal a huge platform was laid down by order of the signory, eighty feet in length and ten feet wide and two and a half feet high, in the Piazza or public square. It was covered with earth and bricks on which was placed a large quantity of conbustibles including wood, gunpowder, oil, pitch and rosin, and leaving a pathway or avenue two feet wide to be traversed by the rival champions through the burning flames.

News of the appproaching trial had circulated throughout the whole of Tuscany and Florence was thronged and filled with crowds from all quarters, anxious to be eye witnesses of such an extraordinary and uncommon spectacle. At the dawn of day the piazza was lined with soldiers and its opening strongly guarded. Every available space was occupied, every window and house-top and railing commanding a view of the huge pyre was packed and crowded by the excited partisans of both sides whose hearts and minds were stirred and agitated with feelings and emotions they could not conceal or restrain, the Arrabbiati and Compagnacci being elated with the opportunity of creating a riot and killing Savonarola, the Franciscan friars trusting some mode of escape for their champpion would be found, whilst the Piagnonior adherents of Savonarola inwardly prayed that the event would result in a convincing and triumphant proof of their beloved teacher's doctrines. The signory secretly uneasy concerning the result of the trial and fearful lest a revolt against their deceitful scheme if discovered would sweep them out of existence in case that Fra Domenico proved the victor, filled the Palace of Justice with armed men belonging to their own party and at the same time ordered the city gates to be closed and troops to be stationed in different parts and threatened instant death to anyone who dared to disobey orders issued by themselves.

    Savonarola on learning this and distrustful of their good faith, sent to the Council of Ten, composed of members favorable towards him, to take steps to prevent either of the champions shirking the ordeal and leaving his competitor in the flames. He suggested at the same time that the pyre should be fired at one end and lighted at the other after the two friars had entered it so that all retreat might be cut off. He further requested that the trial should take place before the dinner hour that the minds of spectators might be clear and unobscured. During the consideration of these arrangements, he celebrated high mass in San Marco and delivered a short address in which he recommended all his hearers to continue instant in prayer and supplication for the overthrow of the enemies' wicked and inhuman designs. Scarcely had he formed the frati to march in procession to the Piazza when the mace-bearers of the signory appeared and stated that all things were ready prepared for the ordeal. There were two hundred of frati of the convent who marched out of the convent gates in double file with a large crucifix borne aloft in front. Fra Domenico followed after wearing a fiery red colored cope and holding a great cross in hand was accompanied by a deacon and subdeacon. Savonarola marched in the rear carrying the Host and was followed by a great multitude with lighted torches. Emerging from out of the convent, they chanted the psalm, *"Exurgat Deus et Dissipentur enemici ejus"* (let God arise and his enemies be scattered) in deep and sonorous tones which on being heard, was taken up by vast multitudes thronging the thoroughfares. *Exurgat Deus* pealed forth from ten thousand throats so that the city vibrated with the mighty sound and every soul thrilled with the resonance of the sublime words of the majestic psalm.

All eyes were turned in the direction of San Marco. For a few moments as the procession came in sight, every voice was hushed. Not a sound was heard save the deeply resounding chant *Exurgat Deus et dissipentur enemici ejus,* instilling fear into the hearts of the Arrabbiati and terror into the minds of the signory as they beheld Savonarola and Fra Domenico marching along with the solemn procession, guarded and accompanied with a strong band of armed friends into the piazza and taking up their appointed places. *Exurgat Deus* like the blast of a mighty trumpet resounded again throughout the square and the vast multitude of spectators overwhelmed and carried away with a force and power that moved and pulsated through them, took up the ringing refrain *et dissipentur enemici ejus,* that like the bruit and low rumbling of distant thunder reverberated throughout and shook the city. As it died away and silence again prevailed the gaze of everyone was turned upon Savonarola and Domenico standing calm and erect at the further end of the pyre and waiting for the appearance of the Francescan champion, whilst the frati on bended knees were engaged in silent prayer. Amidst the vast assembly they alone remained tranquil and unmoved. Savonarola cowled as was his custom, and Domenico clasping the Host to his breast. Thus they stood and waited and in those few moments of hushed suspense and expectancy, their forms stood forth serene and majestic in mien and appearance as though natives of a superior world invested with a radiant something, an aura of brightness strange and unaccountable to the comprehension of the on-gazers who could only ask themselves the question, what is it?

But where is Rondinelli the Franciscan champion, why comes he not forth? Everything is prepared and the torch is ready to be applied to the sombre pile of faggots and combustibles, why delays he to present himself and pass through the fiery ordeal? What are the signory doing? Why do they not come forth and take their appointed places as arbiters and judges? To these questions no answer was given for some time and a feeling of general disgust and disappointment began to arise and prevail amongst the excited spectators. Terrified and frightened, the Franciscans were now holding secret consultations with members of the signory because of the intrepidity of Fra Domenico and his eagerness to enter the flames. The Arrabbiati were planning how best to accomplish their purposes of turning the ordeal into a miserable fiasco and in the tumult that would inevitably ensue, assassinate both Savonarola and Domenico.

Scarcely knowing what to do, the signory sent and asked why they did not commence proceedings, to which Savonarola replied that they themselves should come forth and no longer keep the people in suspense. Driven to bay, they had recourse to several annoying pretexts and petty demands by the rejection of which by Domenico, they had hoped to cast the oppprobrium of failure upon Savonarola and his party and to this end caused it to be noised about, that he had enchanted his champion and his red cope. They demanded that he should not stand near him when Domenico entered the flaming pyre. In these excuses they were foiled as Domenico readily consented to strip and array himself in the robes of any other Domenican brother they might choose. These concessions proved of no avail but gave rise to further requests on the part of the Franciscans and the signory to whom Savonarola sent a note of remonstrance against such dilatory and vexatious proceedings and urged them to put an end to the suspense by producing Fra Rondinelli according to the terms of the written contract drawn up by themselves.

It was now past midday and the impatience of the vast crowd at these delays began to manifest itself in hoarse murmurs and shouts of anger and resentment, especially when the Franciscans and their champion asked for and obtained another private interview with the judges appointed to preside over the ordeal. The majority of the onlookers now began to think that the whole affair was a farce, a cunning device to entrap Savonarola, as they noticed the suspicious tactics and expedients resorted to by his opponents. The Arrabbiati in order to counteract this rising surmise, and seeing the danger to themselves, unless they could allay and quash it, succeeded in creating a disturbance that resulted in a fight and caused great uproar and commotion. Shouts of recrimination passed between the various parties, and groans filled the spacious piazza. A tumultuous rush was made towards the palace of the signory. Judging that now had come the opportunity for the accomplishment of their deep laid plot, the Arrabbiati and Compagnacci together made a furious onset against Savonarola whom, however, they found surrounded and guarded by a strong cordon of friends who fully aware of their intentions had come fully armed for his protection and defense. One of these named Salviati observing their approach rushed in advance and tracing a line on the ground with his sword, shouted in stentorian and resolute voice: "Whoever dares to cross this line shall taste the steel of Salviati." As the uplifted blade gleaned threateningly in the rays of the sun, it daunted the intending assassins and caused them to shrink back dismayed and frustrated in their dastardly attempt. Still the angry crowd surged towards the council chamber, but were kept back by the soldiery on guard. It had come buoyed up with the expectation and desire of witnessing a miracle and now after hours of weary waiting, hungered, disappointed and ignorant of the true reason of the procrastinating tactics and insidious schemes of the signory, it became maddened, enraged and disgusted with the unaccountable delay that had occurred.

It was now well on in the afternoon and so excited were all minds that yells, hootings and shouts to begin the ordeal became general. They had gathered and come to witness a miracle, and with nothing less than a miracle would they be satisfied. This state of discontent and unrealized expectation became intense, notwithstanding a great storm of wind and rain that swept over and deluged the city. Though the peals of thunder and the flashes of lighting were terrific and awful, yet the crowd stirred not, so great were their desire and determination to witness a miracle. The tempest suddenly ceased and as the sun appeared again, expectation ran high that the wished for exhibition would now begin. Still the Franciscans and their champion came not forth but kept themselves within the council building raising fresh objections and excuses for delay to secure which, they resorted to every imaginable pretext, demanding now that Fra Domenico should relinquish the cross he held in his hand and on expressing his willingness to do this and would enter the fire bearing the Host instead, they stoutly demurred again, declaring it would be sacrilege to burn the consecrated wafer. A heated theological discussion on the question led to further delay and ended in Domenico refusing to give way to further demands.

The sun was now going down and daylight disappearing and the signory now issued a proclamation stating it was impossible to carry out the details in connection with the ordeal. By this artifice they hoped to escape the public indignation at the ignominious failure, which their emissaries and myrmidons moving amongst the greatly exasperated crowd attributed wholly to Savonarola, saying that he by refusing to pass through the fire himself, had proved himself a fraud and an imposter. The Franciscans loudly claimed the victory, though their champion through fear of his personal safety had not dared to come forth, but had kept himself concealed within the precincts of the council buildings. The angry surging multitude whose trust and confidence in Savonarola had up to the commencement of the trial remained firm and unshaken, ignorant and unaware of the shameful plot against his life and deceived by the infamous lies and falsehoods now assiduously circulated by the confederates of the Arrabbiati and Compagnacci in a moment of capricious fickleness and maddened disappointment, rushed towards Savonarola and his friends whom they regarded as the cause of the fiasco and failure. Amidst the greatest uproar and confusion, Salviati with his guards had great difficulty in preserving Savonarola and Fra Domenico from attack and checking the onrush of the now infuriated mob of assailants. With sword in hand they struggled and fought courageously and finally succeeded in reaching the convent of San Marco and closing the gates, were safe for a while from harm and the insults of enraged opponents and foes.

Entering the church where a vast congregation of females had remained engaged in prayer, Savonarola gave a brief outline of what had occurred and then retired to his dormitory overwhelmed with sorrow and anguish both of mind and heart at the ingratitude of Florence, whom he had so greatly loved and for whose welfare and happiness he had willingly sacrificed the best years of his life, watching over and guarding her from danger with anxious affection greater than that of a mother over her sickened and suffering child. Sitting in his lonely cell, in that moment of desolate solitude, his soul tasted of a bitterness and endured pangs of anguish keener than those of death, and never felt and experienced in all their awful intensity and fulness save by those divinely sent teachers and messengers of truth and light whose strange destiny and unhappy doom is, at the finish of their life career of incessant toil and thankless labors in the world, to be cast off like a sucked orange, to be crucified or endure the pain and agony of a cruel martyrdom.

To be continued.

Causes and Effects.

Every act rewards itself, or in other words integrates itself, in a two-fold manner; first in the thing, or in real nature; and secondly in the circumstance, or in apparent nature. Men call the circumstance the retribution. The causal retribution is in the thing and is seen by the soul. The retribution in the circumstance is seen by the understanding! it is inseparable from the thing, but is often spread over a long time and so does not become distinct until after many years. The specific stripes may follow late after the offense, but they follow because they accompany it. Crime and punishment grow out of one stem. Punishment is a fruit that, unsuspected, ripens within the flower of the pleasure which concealed it. Cause and effect, means and ends, seed and fruit, cannot be severed; for the effect already blooms in the cause, the end pre-exists in the means, the fruit in the seed.

—*Emerson*, "Compensation."

UNDINE.

A Poetic Drama in Three Acts.

By Justin Sterns.

Act III.

(Concluded from Vol. X., page 360.)

A ROOM in the palace. The furnishings are dark tapestries and ancient oak. At the back, seen between a row of dark stone columns, is the sea. The Prince is lying on a divan in the center of the stage. Undine stands back of the divan, leaning slightly over him. His eyes are on her face.

Undine:
Lo! I am more than glory and more than honor!
More than fair fame! ah! reckon not the cost!
Oh, what are all the treasures of earth beside me?
Take me! and count the world well lost!
(She bends over him slowly and kisses him.)
Ah, my beloved! why do you strive to withstand me?
Why do you hold aloof and reckon the cost?
(She throws her head back and her hands out, still looking at him.)
Behold! I am more to be desired than Heaven!
Take me! and count your soul well lost!
Prince: Undine! (He gropes for her hand but she evades him. Seeking to touch her he raises himself to a sitting position.) Undine! let us fly together!
Undine: It is your wedding day!
Prince: Oh! fly with me!
Undine: The guests are even now within the palace!
Prince: I know! I know! But let us sail away and seek an unknown land!
(Undine moves slowly away and he rises and follows her imploringly.)

Undine: Have you forgotten
Your princess and your kingdom?
Prince: I have forgotten!
Oh, Undine, Undine! let us fly together!
Take all I have! Scatter it to the wind!
Ah! would I had the wealth and power of Ind
To squander for the treasure of your love!
I am all wonder that I ever strove
To keep what once I vainly thought had worth!
At last I know—that all I want of earth
   Is you—is you!

Take all I am! Do with me as you will!
I am no longer judge of good and ill.
I am no longer aware of right and wrong.
Ah, God! You bind me with a spell so strong!
But I will strive no more as I have striven
For now I know that all I want of Heaven
   Is you—is you!

 Undine turns and faces him.)
 Undine: Is it I you love—or the maiden of your dreams?
 Prince: Come! I will follow you to the edge of the world.
 Undine: You love me?
 Prince: Whithersoever you lead I will go.
 Undine: You do not love me!
 Prince: Let us fly together.
 (Undine walks slowly back to the divan, the Prince following hesitatingly. Undine seats herself on the divan.
 Undine: (Sadly, to herself.)
Yea! even so as the Enchantress said!
He is mine—if I will rob him of his soul!
 (The Princess in her bridal veil enters in time to see the Prince lean and kiss Undine's hand, which lies along the back of the divan. She comes to them quietly, looking from one to the other. Undine rises slowly and faces her. The Prince drops on the divan and buries his face in his hands.)
 Princess:
Alas! My maidens decked me with a veil
I have no right to wear. For you have taken
His love. And since you could, it never was mine!
Ah! never mine! and this was never mine!
 (She slowly lifts the veil from her hair and drops it quietly

in a heap at Undine's feet. The Prince raises his head and looks at Undine, but his right hand reaches out blindly towards the Princess, and when he has found her hand he clings to it with both of his. Undine looks at the discarded veil. Then she looks at the Prince and from the Prince to the Princess.)

    Undine: (To the Princess.)
He loves you! I have bound him with a spell
And yet he loves you! He would follow me
To the ends of the earth and down to the pit of Hell
And yet he loves you! He would lose his soul
To gain me, yea! Yet it is you he loves!
Behold! though the spell is even now upon him
How he clings to you blindly! Nevertheless if I will
I may take him. For the charm is old as Eve
That I have laid upon him. As old as Eve
And subtle as the serpent that beguiled her. (Wearily.)
And such as I have ever had the power
To use it. If I will, he shall forget you.
He shall even believe he loves me, for I must take
Away his soul if I would make him mine,—
His soul, that steadily, stubbornly refuses
To be turned from you.
(Very wearily.) Are you not content?
(She picks up the veil.)
And this is yours. By all the laws of Heaven.
(She puts it herself upon the Princess's head. Then walks slowly away. The Prince follows her.)
    Prince: Fly with me, Undine!
(Undine turns and holds out her hand. He drops on one knee and takes it. She lays the other for a moment over his eyes.)
    Prince: Undine! little sister!
(He rises and draws his arm and the back of his hand dazedly across his eyes.)
What were you saying? Have I slept, perchance?
(He sees the Princess and comes to her swiftly. Takes both her hands and kisses them. He leads her to the divan and sitting down would draw her down beside him. Instead she stands beside him and draws his head for a moment tenderly against her breast. Then she releases him, leaving both her hands in his. Undine, meanwhile, has gone to the back of the stage and is leaning wearily against a column, one arm stretched up and wound around it, looking at the sea.)

Princess: (Very tenderly.)
They tell this tale of a woman's love,
How she was fain that love to prove.
She sought a secret shrine and pressed
The knife that lay there to her breast.
    (Ah! bitter-sweet are the pangs of love.)

While the blood flowed, she besought for her lover—
Whispering the same rune over and over—
The greatest good, O wondrous prize!
That the god's wisdom could devise.
    (Ah! bitter-sweet are the pangs of love.)

The red knife on the alter stirred,
And then she knew her prayer was heard.
Like a homing bird to her lover she went.
He was not in the bower, he was not in the tent.
    (Ah! bitter-sweet are the pangs of love.)

He was not on the lea, he was not on the strand.
A boat was bearing him from the land!
He gave no glance to the vanishing shore,
And she knew she would never see him more.
    (Ah! bitter-sweet are the pangs of love.)

(She draws his head down on her breast again for a moment.
Then she releases him and steps back.)

Thus, even thus, do I love you! Would you be free?
    Would you be happier so?
    Behold! I bid you go!
Behold! I bid you think no more of me!

    (The Prince comes to her.)
    Prince:
I love you! If some god, most cruel-kind,
Should deign to look upon me, and should dare
Carry me from you for my greater good—
Ah! I should curse him while he let me live!
    I want no joy you may not share,—
      You may not share.

I want no joy you may not share.   But oh!
If the god, cruel-kind, unsealed my eyes
And bade me know that you must go from me,
Or fail forever of some wondrous good,
   Then love itself would still love's cries,
      Would still love's cries.

(He raises her hands to his lips. The church bells peal out. They start hurriedly apart. Two of the Princess's ladies in waiting appear at one entrance, right. She goes to them and accompanies them off, with a single backward glance. The Prince also goes off right, but by another exit. The two sisters of Undine appear, walking to her on the other side of the yard-high wall which forms the base of the row of columns at the rear of the stage. They cling there, delicately poised, as though at the first sound of an approaching footstep they would plunge into the sea and hide themselves.)

   Younger Sister: Alas! today he weds another, Undine!
You have lost!
   Undine: All.   Today, within the hour,
He weds the maiden of his dreams.
   Younger Sister: Ah! no!
This must not, must not be.   There is a way,
O sister! There is even yet a way.
Lo! We have braved the Enchantress for your sake!
This knife—ah, do not shrink! Have we not paid
What price the Enchantress demanded that we might save you!
(She leans over and hides the knife in the bosom of Undine's robe.)
So! Let it lie there till your heart gains courage!
This hour a life is forfeit—yours—or his!
And why not his? Nay, do not shrink from me!
For is not immortality his dower?
I do not bid you take his soul away
But his life only.   Thus shall you win again
Your thrice a hundred years of careless joy—
Nor harm him overmuch.   Ah! do not spurn me!

   Elder Sister: Hasten, Undine! seek him at the altar.
And ere the priest has uttered the last words
Plunge the knife to his heart—ah! do not falter!
Then leap from the open casement to the sea,

And you shall be once more a daughter of Neptune,
Care free and soulless, all the past forgotten.
 Younger Sister: The hour draws near. Ah, hasten, Undine,
  hasten!
Or ere the moment be forever past.
Beneath the casement we will wait for you.
 Undine: And wherefore not? yea! I will do as you bid me!
Yea, I will do it! I have suffered much
And striven much, in vain. Now all is finished.
Lo! it shall be as a dream that is past and forgotten,
And I shall sport again amid the breakers,
Soulless and well content. Yea! I will do it!
Wait me beneath the casement.
 (They drop abruptly out of sight. Undine comes slowly forward, drawing out the knife.)
 Undine:
Oh, heart of my heart! how shall I do you this wrong?
How shall I bear your unbelieving eyes
What time the knife sinks home! And how endure
To see the agony of death engulf you!
Lo! any wound to you from any hand
Would pierce my heart! How shall I wound you, then,
With mine own hand?
 (She presses the dagger against her breast.)
  Come! let me see if I
Have strength to bear the answering pang that hurt
To you must bring me! O most dear! most dear!
 (She tries a little to press the knife into her flesh.)
Ah ,God! there is no prize in earth or Heaven
That I could hurt you so to make my own!
 (She goes swiftly and flings the knife into the sea.)
I am content. I am content to die. (A pause.)
Lo, now! my prayer was heard! was heard and answered!
That I might serve him in his hour of need!
Oh! bitter is the mockery of the gods!
For I have this day saved him—from myself!
 (The stage is momentarily in darkness, and the Enchantress, bathed in rosy light, is there.)
 Enchantress: Undine, daughter of Neptune, this hour you
  die.
They stand before the altar even now!
 Undine: Yea, most dread Enchantress! Ere the sun redden

Undine shall be but a fleck of foam on the ocean
Tossing forever beneath the untroubled stars.
    Enchantress: Not so! not so! for you have won your querdon.
When the knife sank beneath the waves,—wherewith
By one swift stroke you might have rent forever
The web that you have woven patiently
Through the long days and sleepless, tortured nights,—
The soul that you have travailed for was born.
    Undine: And somewhere—sometime—?
    Enchantress: Yea! some time, somewhere,
Eternity shall yield you your desire!
    (There is darkness and the Enchantress is gone.
    Undine: (looking like one in a trance of bliss)
        Oh! all is well!
For I have won to the open gate of Heaven
That lieth beyond the thorn-strewn paths of earth
By the road that windeth through the heart of Hell!

    Ah! now I behold
What no one hath told, or can tell!
What no one hath known, or can know!
Till he tread the path I trod,
Till he face the fires of Hell,
Till he win to the gate of Heaven!

    Yea!
By the road that windeth through Hell
Beyond the thorn-strewn places of earth I have come,
And I know—what the angels know!
(But God hath forbidden that we tell!)

    Oh! I have done, I have done,
With sorrow and striving and pain,
With anguish and weeping. For lo!
    I, even I, have won
    To the open gate of Heaven!

    (In the distance, so far away that only the melody and not the words can be distinguished, is heard the bridal chorus. Before it is finished the bells begin to peal joyously. At their first stroke Undine puts her hand to her heart, and a moment later drops to the floor, dead. The bridal chorus finishes.)
                    CURTAIN.
                  THE END.

A DREAM OF ATLANTIS—THE LAND OF MU.

By Alice Dixon Le Plongeon.

(Continued from Vol. X., page 375.)

To Kera, lady of his court, he came
Impatient to address the dame
Who had to him a promise made—
Compliance now from her he bade.
"Yea, Majesty, the hour draws near,
E'en while at thy command I'm here
Perchance we lose important light—
Dismiss thy servant from thy sight
Without delay to soon return,
That she the truth may quickly learn.
If word I cannot have with thee
O King, regard with scrutiny
A jeweled butterfly I'll wear
Reposing high upon my hair—
Its wings shall speak—if lifted these,
This very night our princess flees."
The stars are peeping from the clouds;
Night with her shadowy veil enshrouds
A drowsy world; soft murmurs creep
Along the grass while nodding flowers
Their petals close in tranquil sleep
Until the sun its radiance showers.

The palace heights with radiance gleam
Where rosy lights bestow their beam
On objects beautiful and grand
Upon this most enchanting land,
Where every joy that sense may crave
Is granted by a royal knave,
And orgies well deserving scorn
Will meet the blushing face of Morn.

But while the foolish joy in sin
The princess must her freedom win
From tyrant's thrall, by Can's command
For he the way hath wisely planned.

In darkness now young Nalah, clad
In vestal's garb, forth ventures, sad,
Tho' well content to leave the home
So loved, in distant lands to roam—
Her greatest loss and deep lament
That Manab dear will not consent
To save herself with those who flee,
Escaping dire calamity.

Beneath the house of vestal maids,
In times of which the memories fades,
A path was cut and chambers wrought;—
Here virgins penitent were brought
To dwell in solitude awhile
If passion threatened to beguile
Their hearts from duties freely vowed
When they with office were endowed.
This pathway bent to where the land
Was circled by an azure band
Of ocean wave. Here Manab led
The fugitives, and here they said
Those tender words, a last farewell
To her whom duty would impel
To bide her fate, that awful hour
When great and small alike must cower.

But Can now urged, "No more delay;
For night is swiftly chased by day"—
And while alone the priestess took
That narrow path again, Can's look
Was searching eagerly the dark
Where forth they ventured to embark—
Itzat by Nalah's side,
While Can the fair Pelopa led—
Her mind unparted from the dead,
Great Atlas deified.

A DREAM OF ATLANTIS

Kadimo too and little Cho,
The only child with these to go,
Awaited where the small boat lay
In shadow, safe from every ray,
In trusty rowers' care,
Whose vigorous strokes would quickly gain
The vessel riding on the main
And wooed by breezes fair.

A fleecy veil each star enshrouds;
The moon is wading thro' the clouds—
But stealthily upon them creep
Stout villains who in silence leap
To seize the princess. Swift as light
The rowers hasten to the fight.
Now clashing steel rings deadly blow
As fierce they grapple, foe to foe.
Can's dagger thrusts the hardy breast
Of him who would the princess wrest
From Itzat; plucks it forth again
All reeking with its crimson stain
And drives it thro' a cursing knave,
The heart of his dear son to save,—
While Itzat, striking right and left,
Fells others, soon of life bereft

The victory won was swift and sure,
For love aids courage to endure,
And, save one lusty sailor dead,
The fugitives, tho' wounded, fled—
Lest other minions should appear
Ere from the shore the boat could clear.
Unseen the dead and wounded lay
No more to greet the light of day;
While bleeding men the oars applied
To reach the waiting vessel's side.

The first on deck was nimble Cho
Who cried, "Good Can is there below
With those who sail this night;
Scarce one but has a wound that bleeds

And urgently your succor needs
So sorry is their plight."

Strong arms their prompt assistance gave
The valiant and the fair to save,
And soon each fainting hero found
Repose. Then tenderly were bound
The stabs, by Can and Kadimo;
And generous wine restored life's glow.
By leaves, whose surface smooth could yield
A tender magic, wounds were sealed;
And drowsing balms from nature culled
To sleep each sufferer gently lulled.

But Can and Kadimo were strong
Tho' not unscathed, and all night long,
While favoring winds filled every sail,
Both watched and tended Itzat pale,
Whose fluttering breath was near to fail;
While for him grieving Nalah wept
As slow the hours of danger crept.
But life obeys a potent force
When love would hold it on its course;
And as the sun rose o'er the deep
Death fled before life's balmy sleep.

The great ship sped before the wind—
Its port the land where Can would find
A thousand stalwart arms to toil—
Good men who, fleeing dangerous soil,
Abroad had gone with sisters, wives,
And youths whose force in active lives
Would seek expression, and renew
Their powers as each maturer grew.

But parting looks must lingering dwell
On shores that fade—Farewell, farewell!
Dear land our fathers loved, most blest!
Fair valleys, mounts with snowy crest;
Sweet waters, clear and purling streams
Whose ripples float to us in dreams.

A DREAM OF ATLANTIS

Upon the ocean's fickle way
Becalmed ere long the good ship lay;
And when the welcome gale at last
Arose, it swelled to tempest blast;
Till, as the sunless daylight waned,
The sails were rent and timbers strained.
From dark to dawn the seamen bold
Strove lustily against the cold
And moaning winds that would assail
Their ears, like agonizing wail
Of giants tortured unto death,
For mercy pleading with each breath.
How bitter is the icy blast
That pierces to the soul at last—
Relentless cold! thy hateful touch
Is close allied to Death's grim clutch;
Detested thou amid the woes
That fate on suffering life bestows.

Loud shriek the winds, and howl despair
While crashing thunders roar—Beware!
And fiery bolts from lightning shaft
Are hurled upon the quivering craft.

Now Heppel, never self-forgiven,
Cries out, to madness nearly driven,
"Ye thunders, rend the skies! Flash, flash,
Ye lightnings! Roar ye winds, and lash
The billows into fiercer strife—
Let raging storm engulf my life!"
Despair his vitals tear again
Since out upon this seething main
The beings loved by Atlas great
Are menaced with disastrous fate.
Thus on the heaving deck he stood
Petitioning the death he wooed.
Him Can restored to saner thought—
For tho' the storm much havoc wrought,
It passed like other storms before,
And onward sailed the ship once more;
While smiling Nature won the mind

THE WORD

From thrilling dangers left behind.
While Itzat on the deck reposed,
His eyelids dreamily half closed,
'Twas Nalah who beside him stayed
Quite still, to weary him afraid.

Upon the sad Pelopa's brow
The light of hope spread not its glow;
For constantly she mourned her dead;
And Can unto his student said—
"If grieving saps from day to day
Her strength, life too must ebb away."

Kadimo tender care bestowed
On them whose blood had freely flowed;
And little Cho his aid would lend
Obedient to his guide and friend.

Fair winds now filled the sails and sped
The ship, while ancient tales were read
By Can, from out a treasured tome,
Of Mu, the lost but well-loved home.
These records told how long ago
Had been submerged by ocean's flow
A goodly portion of that land,
Waves rolling high above the strand
Where hills of mud and mounts of fire
Had spouted forth disaster dire;
And from that time beneath the main
Grand cities lost to view had lain.

Kadimo, hearing, sadly mused,
With melancholy oft infused—
"How wretched is the fate of man!
Existence galls, tho' brief its span;
For every smile that joy bestows
On us, we suffer untold woes."

No sooner was the thought expressed
Than, smiling, Can himself addressed
To banish from the youthful mind
Its gloom, and better reason find

A DREAM OF ATLANTIS

In Nature's moods, if bad or good,
By mortals little understood:
"For tho' life bringeth grief and pain,
If some the cup of anguish drain,
While sorrow broods upon the earth
Compassion ever comes to birth.
The skies are blue above our head
Far oftener than with storm-clouds spread.
We view creation, but it keeps
Unfathomed truths within its deeps.
This dazzling gem, called life, betrays
A flaw, we think, amid its rays.
Perchance beneath the flaw we see
A glorious light may hidden be."
Existence many joys will give
When mortals learn the way to live;
To love, to work, to earn repose;
To feel how warmly friendship glows;
To see on all sides passing by
What loveliness invites the eye.
When man is noble, good and just,
He tempers Nature's hardy thrust;
A kindness done to aught that moves
The universal love approves.
Look upward, not in sadness down;
On sunlight, not the shadow's frown."

While each his thoughts expression gave
The vessel safely plowed the wave,
Till Zinaan's lovely isles were neared,
Upon whose verdant shores appeared
Men, women, children, everywhere
On land, amid the meadows fair;
While vessels gaily came and went
For profit, or on pleasure bent.
Here water sweet the voyagers found,
And wholesome products of the ground,
Then journeyed on apace
To reach the very ancient strand
Called Mayach, the fatherland
Of Atlas' noble race.

THE WORD

At last from heavy seas and gales
Escaped, the brave men furled their sails,
While every eager foot the sand
Soon pressed upon the promised land.
The land of beauty far behind
Awaits its doom. No ties now bind
These venturers unto what they've left—
For here, of luxury bereft—
They'll fashion from their brain and brawn
A kingdom where new hopes shall dawn.

The forests soon with voices ring,
And sturdy arms keen axes swing
Where sons of industry stand forth
To prove their courage and their worth
In building homes and halls of state
Where Wisdom should on Justice wait.
From Nature's crude supplies alone
Mind fashions all that mortals own:
To man the earth its bounty yields
In metals, wood, and stone; he wields
His forces; fire and water lend
Their welcome aid to serve his end.
All objects, little, great, or fine,
That human genius may design,
Must ever be a protean birth
That springs from water, fire, and earth.

No mountain hath this ancient land
To send its fire upon the strand
The virgin forests and the plain
Are level as the surging main.
No rivers on the surface speed
To where the ocean currents lead;
But far below the soil there stream
Deep waters where blind fishes gleam
In caverns vast whose walls are formed
Of shells long turned to stone,
Tho' once in watery vast they swarmed
Beneath the tempest moan.
Here too fantastic shapes appear

A DREAM OF ATLANTIS

And garlands marble white
That droop where pinnacles uprear
Within that home of Night
Where orgies dwell and evil sprites,
Defending their abode
From mortals who would find delights
Where healing streamlets flowed
To lakes whose placid waters spread
Where valor never yet hath led.
Tho' rivers none above the ground
Appear, vast circling wells are found
Below whose deep and sloping brink
Clear sunlit waters stay;
Here panting leopards crouch to drink
When night enshroudeth day.
To such a spot, where water pure
Is found to fill all needs
And each infirmity to cure,
The wise Can onward leads.

Anon foundations broad are reared
Of solid earth and rock
That may resist the trembling feared
From Homen's awful shock.
Of marble, ready to the hand,
The builders fashioned temples grand
And palaces that might defy
The centuries as they flitted by.

Nor gold, nor orichalcum red
Within that soil had made their bed,
Nathless, the mazy sculptures wrought
In sacred emblems, precepts taught
By learned men,—and bold designs,
Appear as from Mu's richest mines
Brought here to gladden every eye—
For ardent red and golden dye
Abound beneath the sunny sky
Of Mayach the old:—
Ix-Chel her glories forth had sent

THE WORD

Throughout the years untold,
To trees, that of their bounty lent
In lustrous hues, that feigned the gleam
Of orichalcum's ruddy beam
Or ray of burnished gold.

While art and industry kept pace
To build and beautify the place,
Some men of wisdom council held,
Consulting how the state to weld
In bonds of lasting brotherhood,
For universal strength and good.
The people with acclaim desired
That he who had the state inspired
As monarch there should reign;
For none his goodness could assail,
And none appeal without avail
Who justice would obtain.

"Propitious is thy name, O Can!"
Exclaimed a venerated man
Tho' brief in sound 'tis fraught
With meanings that are gifts of power,
Our learned ones have taught—
These gifts thou wilt upon us shower."

No gorgeous rite nor pageant gay,
No feasting, marked the happy day
When Can was hailed, by hearts sincere
And words of truth, as sovereign dear.
"Simplicity," he said,
"Must guide within this new domain
Where Fate our steps hath led.
Forget the luxury and the vain
Conceits that breed a million wrongs
In vicious ways where misery throngs."

To tranquil days and joyous thought
The princess once again is brought,—
For youthful hearts must glow
With hope revived when love conspires

His rosy flame to throw
Upon the one that he inspires
With ardor to bestow
The self on Nature's altar vast,
Where myriad creatures, snared, must cast
Them down to satisfy her greed
Insatiate;—unending need
Of countless shapes that live their day
And back to Mystery find their way.

Lord Itzat on his conquest bent
Pleads well, and not in vain,
With Nalah who erstwhile had lent
A hearing to that strain
In days of blissful promise; now
The winsome maid renewed her vow,
Disdaining other suits to heed—
Of noble chieftains come to plead.

To be continued.

Effect of Belief in One's Statement.

I have heard an experienced counsellor say that he never feared the effect upon a jury of a lawyer who does not believe in his heart that his client ought to have a verdict. If he does not believe it his unbelief will appear to the jury, despite all his protestations, and will become their unbelief. This is that law whereby a work of art, of whatever kind, sets us in the same state of mind wherein the artist was when he made it. That which we do not believe we cannot adequately say, though we may repeat the words ever so often. It was this conviction which Swedenborg expressed when he described a group of persons in the spiritual world, endeavoring in vain to articulate a proposition which they did not believe; but they could not, though they twisted and folded their lips even to indignation.
—*Emerson*, "Spiritual Laws."

MOMENTS WITH FRIENDS.

"Is darkness the absence of light, or is it something separate in itself and which takes the place of light. If they are distinct and separate, what is darkness and what is light?"

Darkness is not "the absence of light." Light is not darkness. Darkness is something in itself, not light. Darkness may for a while take the place of light and obscure light, but light will dispel darkness. Light will eventually overcome darkness by the raising of and causing darkness to become light. The light and darkness which we perceive through the senses are not light and darkness in themselves, though that which we perceive as light and dark have their origin in the true light and in darkness. As a thing, darkness is homogeneous substance, which is the root, basis or background of all manifestation as matter. In its original state, it is quiet and is the same throughout itself. It is unconscious, unintelligent and undisturbed. Light is the power which comes from the intelligences who have passed through the evolutions and are above or beyond manifestation. When intelligences direct their light power on unconditioned and homogeneous substance, which is darkness, that portion of substance or darkness, and on which light is directed, springs into activity. With the beginning of activity, the substance which was one becomes dual. In action darkness or substance is no longer substance, but is dual. This duality of substance or darkness is known as spirit-matter. Spirit and matter are the two opposites of the one thing, which is substance in origin, but spirit-matter in action. The units into which substance is thus divided as spirit-matter, as well as the manifesting spirit-matter as a whole, have impressed upon them and it the origin of their root parent, and also the cause of their action or manifestation. Substance is the root and parent of every indivisible unit particle of the manifesting mass as well as of the mass as a whole. Light is the cause of the manifestation and of the action in each unit as well as of the manifesting mass as a whole. So that in each indivisible unit, as well as throughout the manifesting mass as a whole is represented: the root parent as substance and the acting power as light. In each unit called spirit-matter there is potentially the parent, substance, and the power, light. Substance is represented by that portion of the indivisible unit which is called matter, and light is represented by the other side or portion of the same indivisible unit called spirit. All universes or manifestations are called out of the unfathomed substance or darkness into manifestation by the light power of intelligences, and this light keeps the spirit-matter thus called into action continuously in action throughout its period of manifestation. During the period of the manifestation the light which is present in manifestation with darkness is the cause of that which we call light. The matter which is manifesting is the cause of what we call darkness. Light and darkness seem ever in conflict and seem to give place to each other throughout manifestation. Day and night, waking and sleeping, life and death, are the opposites or reverse sides of the same thing. These opposites act alternately in short or long periods, until darkness is turned into light. Each seems to the other as the undesirable though each is to the other a necessity. Man has in him darkness and the light power. To man the senses are his darkness and his mind is his light. But this is not usually so considered. To the senses the mind seems as darkness. To the mind the senses are darkness. That which to the senses seems to come from the sun, we call sunlight. To the mind the senses and that which they call light is as darkness when it, the mind, is illuminated by the light power of its parent intelligence. The sunlight and the intelligent perception of it may come to us even while the mind is immersed in and in conflict with the darkness; then we shall see the sunlight as a reflection or symbol of the real light. Darkness gives place to and is changed into permanent light as it is overcome by perceptions and by actions of the mind. When our minds have won in the conflict with darkness we shall perceive the true light which shines in the darkness even though darkness now knows it not.

What is radium and how is it possible for it to throw off continuously a great energy without any apparent waste and loss of its own power and body, and what is the source of its great radio-activity?

It is supposed that the writer of the question is familiar with the scientific statements concerning the recent discovery of radium, such as its being extracted from pitchblende, its discovery by Madame Curie, its light power, the effect of its action on other bodies, its scarcity and the difficulties attending its production.

Radium is a physical state of matter through which force and matter finer than physical are manifested to the senses. Radium is physical matter in contact with other matter and forces usually speculated about as being hypothetical. Ether and these forces are states of matter finer than the physical and they act on or through what is called physical matter, whether the physical matter is a diamond or a molecule of hydrogen. Were it not for ethereal or hypothetical matter acting through the physical matter there would be no change or decomposition of physical matter. The action of finer through gross matter causes the "chemical" combinations and changes of the matter in ordinary use and as dealt with by chemists.

Radium is physical matter which is acted directly upon or through by astral matter without a third factor and without being perceptibly changed by the action of astral matter. Other physical matter is acted on by astral matter, but in lesser degree than radium. Generally, the results of the action of the astral on other physical matter are not perceptible because physical matter cannot offer the contact and resistance to astral matter which is offered by radium, and most other matter is not so directly in contact with astral matter as is radium. Infinitesimal and imperceptible particles of radium are present in all matter. But thus far pitchblende seems to be the source from which they may be collected in the greatest amount, little though it is. When the particles called radium are compacted into one mass, astral matter acts directly on and through it in a quality and power apparent to the senses.

The radio-activity of radium is not, as is now supposed, due to its generating or throwing off from itself particles of its own body. The physical matter of which radium is composed does not furnish the radio-activity or other power which manifests through it. Radium is not a force, but a medium of force. (Matter is twofold and exists on different planes. On each plane, it is matter when it is passive and force when it is active. So physical matter is passive matter and force is active matter. Astral matter is passive astral matter and force on the astral plane is active astral matter.) Radium is the body through which astral matter manifests. Radium is matter of the physical world; radio-activity is astral matter from the astral world which becomes visible by means of physical radium. The astral world is around and through the physical world, and, as its matter is finer, it is in and through gross physical matter, as science says that ether is in and through a crowbar, or as it is known that electricity acts in and through water. Like a candle which gives light, radium emits light or energy. But unlike the candle, it is not burnt out in giving the light. Like a generator or an electric wire which seems to generate heat or light or power, radium seems to generate or throw off energy; and so it does, perhaps. But the light or other power which seems to be generated is not furnished by the wire. It is known that the power of electricity does not originate in a dynamo or in an electric wire. It is also known that the electricity which manifests as heat or light or power is directed along the wire. In a similar manner, that quality or force known as radio-activity manifests through radium from a source which is at present unknown to science. But the source is not radium any more than the source of electricity is a dynamo or a wire. The particles of its body are thrown off and burnt out or used up in a less degree than the particles of a dynamo or electric wire by the action of electrical energy. The source of that which is manifested through radium is the same as the source of the manifestations of electricity. Both come from the same source. The difference between the manifestation of electricity as heat, light or power and that which is manifested through physical radium is in the medium of manifestation and not in electricity or radio-activity. The particles of which are composed the dynamo, generator or wire, are not of the same quality as the particles of which radium is made up. Astral matter and the forces which act in astral matter act directly on radium without any other factor or mediation. The current which plays through an electric wire is made manifest by other factors, such as batteries, magnets, generators, dynamos, steam and fuel. None of these factors are required by radium because it is directly in contact with and itself allows astral matter to manifest through or about it, the radium.

It is known that the electric current does not go through the wire, but around the wire. It will also be found that in a similar manner the radio-activity is not in the radium, but around or about the radium. Electricians have tried and are still trying to devise some means by which electric energy can be made to manifest and directed without the use of steam or fuel or galvanic action. Radium suggests and illustrates how this may be done. A FRIEND.

OUR MAGAZINE SHELF.

NOTICE.—Books coming under the subjects to which this magazine is devoted, will be received, and as space permits, impartially reviewed, irrespective of author or publisher.

The duty of the reviewer is to present to our readers a true and unbiased account of his charge. There will be no deviation from this principle.—Ed.

THE WAY OF INITIATION or How to Attain Knowledge of the Higher Worlds. By Rudolf Steiner. From the German by Max Gysi; 163 pages; octavo; $1.00. Macoy Publishing and Masonic Supply Co., New York.

This book is prefaced by biographical notes of Rudolf Steiner by the eminent French student of the inner life, Edouard Schuré. There is also a picture of Mr. Steiner. Mr. Schuré says of Mr. Steiner: "Standing before those deep and clear-seeing eyes, before that countenance, hollowed by inward struggles, moulded by a lofty spirit which has proved its balance on the heights and its calm in the depths, my friend exclaimed: 'Behold a master of himself and of life.'" Is this truth? Is it fulsome praise?

The best part of the book are general remarks on The Higher Education of the Soul (p. 135), by which term is meant "mind," and on the Conditions of Discipleship (p. 149). The following quotations show the author at his best: "The qualities which have to be combated, in addition to anger and vexation, are such as ambition, timidity, curiosity, superstition, conceit, the disease of prejudice, idle love of gossip, and the making of distinctions in regard to human beings according to the merely outward marks, of rank, sex, race, and so forth. In our time it is difficult for people to comprehend that the combating of such qualities can have any connection with an increase of capacity for knowledge. But every devotee of occultism is aware that much more depends upon such matters than upon the expansion of the intellect, or the employment of artificial practices." (p. 142.)

Speaking of Conditions of Discipleship (pp. 149-163), the author is clear and generally conservative and at times lofty, as in the following demand (p. 158): "A sixth condition is the development of a sense of gratitude with regard to everything which relates to Man. One must realize that one's existence is, as it were, a gift from the entire universe. Only consider all that is needed in order that each of us may receive and maintain his existence! Consider what we owe to Nature and to others than ourselves! Those who desire an occult training must be inclined toward thoughts like these, for he who cannot enter into such thoughts will be incapable of developing within himself that all-inclusive love which it is necessary to possess before one can attain to higher knowledge."

Throughout the book the ethical teachings are sound and reasonable. If they could be separated from the rest, the book would have to be praised. The language is not magisterial, but inviting and kindly. The underlying thought is friendly, quiet, tactful and seems to be guided by the maxim which the author professes (p. 143), that it matters little whether the reader differs in his views from the author, but the vital point is whether he will discover the right view for himself if Mr. Steiner is able to contribute something towards it.

Yet the book is not satisfactory. It is misleading in many respects. It is not what was to be expected of one heralded as a master of life. It suffers from a lack of precision in the use of essential terms—that may be partially the fault of the translator. It carries the inaccuracy and generalities of mysticism into proposed teaching concerning steps in occultism; that is, the more scientific, unemotional, tranquil, judicious traveling on The Path with an open and discerning mind. No distinction is made between occultism and mysticism.

He speaks of the necessity of controlling "one's feelings and ideas" (p. 61). Feelings can be controlled, so can thoughts. But ideas are generally considered to be in the highest of the manifested worlds (the manasic)—how can *they* be controlled? Here thoughts are presumably meant. There are many instances of misconceptions in the book.

What was the use of Madame Blavatsky's presenting a sevenfold classification of human principles and of her pointing to four distinct planes in the manifested cosmos, if the terminology she enabled the west to use and further perfect is cast away and "soul" and "spirit" are used for astral and desire principles, "spiritual" eye for clairvoyance? Such methods lead the ignorant into astralism, always dangerous and pernicious.

The book first speaks of The superphysical world and its gnosis. That is the astral world. He treats it as "spiritual." He says that the life of the spirit can be understood only when we do not presume to criticize it with the lower mind, but rather when we develop it reverently within ourselves (p. 48). The author does not seem to favor too much reliance upon one's own judgment. In the chapter, "How to Attain Knowledge," he says the student of occultism must have as a fundamental attitude of the soul—meaning mind—(p. 53), devotion, veneration, no thought of criticism or opposition. He advises that a would-be disciple abstain, whenever his duties or circumstances permit, entirely from judgment. Then why has man a mind; why the power to observe, to reason? Clearly, the path here advocated is not a path into and in the schools of the mental world, in the school of the Masters, but a road into the astral world, where the use of the mind is superfluous and obnoxious. Hence, the author's recurrence to colors which the disciple is promised to see with the "spiritual" eye at certain stages. He says, in the case of a soul which is devotional, the yellowish-red or brown red tints will vanish, and tints of bluish-red will replace them; that a clairvoyant will perceive soul and spirit which formerly had a dull glimmer of "reddish or reddish brown color, or perhaps of reddish-yellow," as assuming after growth "a brilliant yellowish-green or yellow-blue hue" (p. 135); that the disciple will see around a man who has had some wish fulfilled a flame-like appearance which is yellow at the center and greenish at the edges (p. 111).

He generally uses the word soul for astral body and also for mind, and thus the book looses the clearness which ought to be a mark of a book dealing with steps on the path of discipleship. So he says of the devotional disciple, "now he can listen with his soul" (p. 75); and that occult science gives the means of developing the spiritual ears and eyes.

He uses spiritual for astral. So he speaks of the spiritual body having instruments of perception (p. 81) and that the organs of clairvoyance evolve themselves out of spiritual feelings; that the "Spiritual" world, the so-called astral plane, begins to dawn upon the disciple (p. 84). He speaks of "culture of soul and spirit" (p. 136), and that the student learns "to see with the soul and to speak and hear with the spirit" (p. 148).

The teachers of occultism he mentions are clearly teachers in the astral world and of astral things. The teaching, in so far as it tends to develop astral organs and enables an entrance into the astral world before the faculties of the mind have been developed, is opposed to the old theosophical scheme, and this, Mr. Steiner claims to represent. Instead, it falls in line with movements which ignore the dangers of the astral world and ignore the importance of training mental powers. The theosophical method was and still is to let the would-be disciple not only ignore but shun the astral powers and schools and beings and guides, and instead conquer the mental plane and then from there descend with safety into the deceptive worlds of astral reflections, reflections from the physical and reflections from the mental world.

The kindly mood in which the book is evidently conceived and the calm presentation do not lack persuasiveness. Many truths are interspersed with the errors, inaccuracies and dangerous precepts. The lack of a definite terminology tends to hide dangers. Therefore, the book should be read with great care and caution. Much may be retained as of value. The fundamental scheme here advocated is not to be followed except by one who wants to go in for astralism and challenge its dangers—with the usual result.

B. B. G.

To honor Science means to respect its limitations. Science is not and cannot be, and ought never to try to be, an expression of ultimate reality. When Science seeks to be a philosophy, it not only oversteps its rights, but weakens at the same time, its own position.

—*Hugo Munsterberg.*

THE
WORD

A MONTHLY MAGAZINE

PUBLISHED AND EDITED BY
H. W. PERCIVAL, 253 West 72d Street, New York City

LONDON—KEGAN PAUL, TRENCH, TRUBNER & Co., 43 Gerrard Street

CONTENTS FOR MAY, 1910

ADEPTS, MASTERS AND MAHATMAS, ... EDITORIAL		65
THE INNER LIFE AND THE TAO-TEH-KING,	C. H. A. BJERREGAARD	75
THE GENESIS AND GROWTH OF THE CHRIST OF THE SOUL AND SOME OF ITS MODES OF LIFE,	JAMES L. MACBETH BAIN	90
CHOICE EXTRACTS AND TRANSLATIONS,	A FELLOW OF THE ROSICRUCIAN SOCIETY	96
"SAVONAROLA" OF FLORENCE, ...	DR. W. WILLIAMS	102
A DREAM OF ATLANTIS—THE LAND OF MU,	ALICE DIXON LE PLONGEON	116
THE SEPHER HA-ZOHAR—THE BOOK OF LIFE, .	NURHO DE MANHAR	123
MOMENTS WITH FRIENDS, ...	A FRIEND	128

Yearly Subscription   -   -   -   -   -   - $4.00 or 16s.
Single Copies   -   -   -   -   -   -   -   .35 or 1s. 6d.
Six Months' Subscription   -   -   -   -   -   2.00 or 8s.
Three Months' Subscription   -   -   -   -   -   1.00 or 4s.

BOUND VOLUMES OF THE WORD
Vols. I-X in Cloth and Half Morocco

The ten completed volumes of The Word are a valuable addition
to any Library
They are a library in themselves

[Entered as Second-class Mail Matter, May 2, 1906, at the Post Office at New York, New York, under the Act of Congress of March 3, 1879.]

NEW
THE MAGICAL MESSAGE
according to
IÔANNÊS
commonly called
The Gospel according to [St.] John

A verbatim translation from the Greek done in modern English, with introductory essays and notes

BY

JAMES M. PRYSE
Price, Cloth, $2.00

The root of Mr. Pryse's claim is that the Gospel by John is together mystical in intention and that the mystical meanings of the words should never be distorted. According to Mr. Pryse the fourth gospel is much more than an account of the physical career of Jesus. He sees in it the history of the purification of the soul and so well does he buttress his claim that the best exponents of biblical criticism and Greek scholarship will be hard put to it to find anything to say in disproof.

The Theosophical Publishing Company of New York, 253 W 72d Street

---

A Book of practical Development
is
WILLIAM J. FLAGG'S
Yoga
Or Transformation.

It gives the Facts.

It shows the true Magic which underlies the Akkadian, Hindu, Taoist, Egyptian, Hebrew, Greek and Christian Religions.

It gives a comparative statement of the various Religious Dogmas concerning the Soul and its Destiny.

It is a religious Education to read this Book carefully.

Price, cloth, $3.00.

Send for Descriptive Catalogue.

Charles G. Leland,

The well-known writer, has written a fascinating volume, called,

HAVE YOU A
Strong Will?

Or How to develop and strengthen the Will-Power, Memory, or any other Faculty or Attribute of Mind.

It is written, so all will grasp it.
Brilliant, so you will enjoy it.
Powerful, so you will not forget it.

It will help you to do what you want.

Price, cloth, $1.50.

Send for a booklet, "Books for the Higher Life." It will tell you all about this Book.

The Theosophical Publishing Company of New York, 253 W. 72d Street

When ma has passed through mahat, ma will still be ma; but ma will be united with mahat, and be a mahat-ma.
—The Zodiac.

THE WORD

Vol. 11   MAY, 1910.   No. 2.

Copyright, 1910, by H. W. PERCIVAL.

ADEPTS, MASTERS AND MAHATMAS.

(Continued from page 10.)

THE adamantine rocks of the ages crumble. Color leaves form and forms vanish. Music goes out of sound and sounds end in wails of sadness and reproach. The fires are dead. Sap dries up. Everything is cold. The life and the light of the world are gone. All is still. Darkness prevails. The disciple in the school of the masters now enters his death period.

The inner world is dead to him; it vanishes. The outer physical world is also dead. He treads the earth, but it has the unsubstantiality of a shadow. The immovable hills are as shifting to him as the clouds and like so many veils; he sees through them into the beyond, which is emptiness. The light has gone out of the sun though it still shines. The songs of birds are as screams. All the world is seen to be in a constant state of flux and reflux; nothing is permanent, all is change. Life is a pain, though the disciple is dead to pain as to pleasure. Everything is unreal; all is a mockery. Love is a spasm. Those who seem to enjoy life are seen to be only in a delirium. The saint is self deluded, the sinner is mad. The wise are as the foolish, there is neither bad nor good. The heart of the disciple loses feeling. Time is seen to be a delusion, yet it seems to be the most real. There is no up nor down in the universe. The solid earth seems to be a dark bubble floating in darker and empty space. Though the disciple in the school of the masters walks about and physically sees things as before, the mental darkness thickens about him. Waking or sleeping, the darkness is with him. The darkness becomes a thing of horror and continually encroaches. Silence is upon him and his words seem to have no sound. The silence seems to crystallize into a formless thing which cannot be seen, and its presence is the presence of death. Go where he will, do what he will, the disciple cannot escape this dark thing. It is in everything and around everything. It is within him and around him. Annihilation were bliss as compared to the nearness of this dark thing. But for the presence of this dark thing the disciple is alone. He feels as though he is the living dead in a dead world. Though without a voice, the shapeless darkness recalls the delights of the inner world of the senses to the disciple, and when he refuses to listen he is shown that he may escape or pass out from this utter gloom if he will answer the call of men. Even while in the midst of darkness the disciple of the masters is aware that he should not heed the darkness, though he is crushed down by it. For the disciple all things have lost attraction. Ideals have disappeared. Effort is useless and there is no purpose in things. But although he is as dead the disciple is still conscious. He may struggle with the darkness, but his struggles seem useless. For the darkness eludes him while it crushes. Believing himself strong he throws himself at first against the darkness in his efforts to overcome it, only to find that it becomes heavier as he opposes it. The disciple is in the coils of the ancient serpent of the world against which human strength is as weakness. It seems to the disciple that he is in eternal death, though the life and the light have gone out of things and hold nothing for him and although his body is as his grave, yet he is still conscious. It dawns upon him that if he cannot overcome the darkness, yet the darkness has not quite overcome him, for he is conscious.

This thought of being conscious in the dark is the first glimmering of life for the disciple since he entered his death period. The disciple lies softly in the coils of death and does not fight, but remains conscious; the darkness carries on the fight. The dark neighbor urges the fight, but seeing that struggle was useless, the disciple no longer struggles. When the disciple is willing to remain perpetually in utter darkness if need be, and when he feels conscious in eternity, even though in darkness and will not yield, that thought by which things are known comes to him. He now knows that the utter gloom in which he is surrounded is his own dark faculty, a very part of his own being which is his own adversary. This thought gives him new strength, but he cannot fight, for the dark faculty is of himself though it eludes him. The disciple now trains his focus faculty to find his dark faculty. As the disciple continues to exercise his focus faculty and bring the dark faculty into range there seems to be a sundering of mind and body.

The dark faculty spreads if possible a deeper gloom. The focus faculty brings into range the disciple's thoughts of the ages. Great strength is needed by the disciple to continue the use of his focus faculty. As some old thought is thrown up from the past by the dark faculty, the disciple's attention is momentarily diverted by the thing of the past, the child of desire. Each time the disciple turns his focus faculty to bring into light the dark brother faculty, the thing of the olden time uses a new device. When seemingly within range and about to be discovered, the thing of darkness, like a devil fish, emits an impenetrable blackness which surrounds it and darkens everything. While the darkness prevails the thing again eludes the focus faculty of the disciple. As the disciple brings the focus to bear steadily into the blackness, it begins to take on form, and out of the dark gloom there come most loathsome forms. Huge worm-like creatures ooze themselves out of the blackness and around him. Giant crab-like shapes crawl out of the blackness and over him. Out of the blackness lizards waddle up and project slimy and fork-like tongues at him. Hideous creatures which were nature's failures in her early attempts to produce living things, swarm around the disciple from out of the blackness which his focus faculty makes known. They cling to him and seem to enter him and would possess his being. But the disciple continues to use his focus faculty. Out of the seemingly impenetrable darkness and in the range of the focus faculty there crawl and squirm and hover and brood things with and without form. Bats of incarnate blackness, wickedness and malice, with human or mishapen head flutter about and flap their noxious wings around him, and with the horror of their dread presence there come male and female human figures expressive of every human vice and crime. Creatures of loathsome and sickening loveliness insinuate themselves around and fasten to the disciple. Composite male and female reptilean, vermin-like human creatures beset him. But he is fearless until he discovers that they are his own creations. Then fear comes. He sickens in despair. As he looks at or feels the awful things, he sees himself reflected in each. Each looks into his heart and brain, and looks to the place it had there filled. Each cries out to him and accuses him of a past thought and action which gave it form and called it into being. All of his secret crimes through the ages rise up in the black terror before him.

Each time he ceases using his focus faculty he finds relief, but not forgetfulness. Ever he must renew his efforts and must uncover the dark faculty. Again and again he seeks out the dark faculty and as many times does it elude him. At some time, it may be in one of the darkest moments or one of relief, the one thought of the disciple comes again; and again he knows things as they are. They are the children of his past thoughts and deeds conceived in ignorance and born in darkness. He knows that they are the ghosts of his dead past, which his dark faculty has summoned and which he must transform or be borne down by. He is fearless and wills to transform them, by the one thought which he knows. He begins this, his work. Then he becomes aware of and awakens and uses his image faculty.

As soon as the disciple comes into possession of his image faculty he discovers that the dark faculty is unable to produce forms. He learns that the dark faculty had been able to throw up before him the past in forms by means of the image faculty, but as he has now taken possession of it and learns its use, the dark faculty though it still remains elusive, cannot create form. Gradually the disciple gains confidence in himself and learns to look fearlessly on his past. He marshals the events of that past in order before him. Through his image faculty he gives them the forms in which they were, and by the one thought which he knows he judges them for what they are. By the image faculty he holds the matter of his past as represented by the forms, and he returns it to the matter of the world or to the dark faculty, from either of which it came. That which is returned to the world is given direction and order and a high tone. That which is returned to the dark faculty is subdued, controlled, refined. By his image faculty the disciple is able to give form to the darkness and to image the dark faculty, but he is still unable to know the dark faculty in itself. As the disciple judges, transforms and refines his matter of the past he is able by his image faculty to inquire into the earliest forms of nature and to trace matter through its various forms from the earliest periods of involution into form, through its consecutive stages, link by link, through the entire chain of its evolutionary period to the present time. By use of his image faculty the disciple is able to trace by analogy of the past and the present the forms which will be evolved from nature and by the use of the faculties of the mind. By his image faculty and with his focus faculty he may make forms large or small. By the use of the image faculty the disciple can trace all forms to that of the mental world, but not within or beyond it. By use of the image faculty the disciple knows of the processes of the formation of present man, of his metempsychoses, transmigration and reincarnations and is able to image the processes by which he as disciple will become master of his faculties in the mental world.

The disciple may try to image to himself who he is and what is his form. But by his one thought which he knows he will know that he is as yet unborn and that though he knows of his "I" he is unable to image himself. The disciple finds that from the very first of his attempts to center the focus faculty on the dark faculty, even though it were possible, he could not have discovered the dark faculty because his attention had been diverted from it by the creatures which it made present to him. As he learns this he knows that he has stilled the dark faculty. He knows himself to be unborn, like a foetus.

Up to the present time and at the present time the disciple in the school of the masters has met with masters and knows of their presence, but only through their physical bodies. The disciple is not able to perceive a master body independently of a master's physical body and though the disciple is able to know when a master is present yet he cannot perceive distinctly of a master body; because a master body is not a sense body and cannot be perceived through the senses. And the disciple has not yet learned the use of the motive faculty independently of the senses and by its use only can a master body be known. While the disciple struggled with the dark faculty a master could not help him because the disciple was then testing his own strength, proving his steadfastness of purpose, transmuting his own matter, and to have given assistance at such time would have caused the disciple to remain mortal. But when the disciple by his own steadfastness and courage has proven himself true to his purpose and by the use of his focus and image faculties and by the one thought which he knows, has stilled the dark faculty, then the disciple is shown by a master the difficulties through which he has passed and the purpose which it has served. He finds or has shown to him that that with which he has struggled is the uncontrolled and blind desire of his human kind and that by subduing desires he aids and stimulates mankind to so act with theirs.

As yet the disciple has not overcome sleep; he has not overcome death. He knows that he cannot die, though he is in a womb of death. He no longer struggles. He awaits the maturing of time which will bring him to birth. He cannot see nor sense the processes which are passing within his physical body, though he may follow these processes in thought. But soon there comes a new movement within him. There seems to be a new influx of intelligent life. He takes mental life within his physical body, as when a foetus takes life in the womb. The disciple feels as though he might rise out of his physical body and soar where he pleases and at will. But he does not. There is a new lightness and buoyancy throughout his body and he is mentally sensitive to all things within his sphere. His thoughts will take form before him, but he knows that he should not yet give matter the form of his thought. As his time of birth approaches, the one thought which he knows is ever present with him. His focus faculty is fixed in this one thought. All things seem to blend into this thought and this one thought which he knows is through all things. He becomes more conscious of this one thought; lives in it, and while his physical body will perform its functions naturally his whole concern is in his one thought which he knows. A calm joy and peace are within him. Harmony is about him and he quickens according to his thought. Power of motion enters him. He wills to speak, but does not at once find mental voice. His effort sounds a note in the song of time. The song of time enters his being and bears him up and up. His one thought is stronger. He tries again to speak and again time responds, but he has no voice. Time seems to flood him. Power comes and his speech is born within him. As he speaks, he ascends out of the dark faculty as out of a womb. He, a master, has risen.

His speech, his voice, is his birth. It is his ascension. Never again will he pass through death. He is immortal. His speech is a word. The Word is his name. His name, his word is as the keynote of a song which is sounded throughout the time world, surrounding and permeating the physical world. His name is the theme of the song of life which is taken up and sung by every particle of time. As the harmony of time is understood, the disciple perceives himself to be a mental body. His mental body is a body of faculties, not of senses. His focus faculty he uses readily. By it he finds that he, his mental body, is the one thought by which he became a disciple in the school of the masters, the same thought which guided him through all difficulties and by which he knows things as they are; it is his motive faculty.

The master seems to have always existed. His immortality seems not to have just commenced, but to extend indefinitely into the past. He is not a physical body, he is not a psychic or astral body. He is a master body, the matter of which is thought. He thinks and time adjusts itself by his thoughts. He is in the heaven world of humanity, and finds that all humanity are there represented. He finds that though all humanity are represented in his world, the heaven world, the mental world, the world of the masters, that humanity are constantly appearing and reappearing in some new aspect. That the heaven of one is changed by that one and enjoyed differently with each reappearance and that the heaven world of anyone is changed with the changing of the ideal of that one. The master perceives that this heaven world is dimly perceived by mankind, even while they are on earth, though they fail to realize their heaven while on earth. He perceives that the heaven of mankind is made of their thoughts and that the thoughts of each build his own heaven which each realizes when the power of his mind leaves the physical body at death and is united with the ideals which are his heaven world and which he experiences between lives. The master perceives the individuals of humanity coming and going from the heaven world, each extending or limiting the period of his experience according to his ideal and according to the motive by which he learns from his experience and the causes of his experiencing. The master perceives that the mind of the personality of a life thinks of itself in connection with the highest thoughts, as its personality, but does not realize the different periods of incarnation while in the heaven world. But the master does not yet follow the minds in their coming and going from the heaven world.

The master sees in the heaven world that those who come

and enter it after death and were by their ideals represented in it during physical life, do not know of the heaven world as he knows it. The unborn men yet resting in the heaven world, enjoy heaven as they had known of it in their physical lives. Though there are beings who live consciously and throughout time in the heaven world, yet mortal men resting in this heaven world do not know these beings, and during their stay they are unaware of the presence of masters, unless the thought of masters had been part of their ideals in physical life. The master sees that in the heaven world man is a thought body, stripped of his physical body; that man's heaven is a transitory state though a state more real to him than was his physical life; that as a thought body without his physical body, man uses his image faculty and thereby constructs his heaven-world; that the kind of a man's heaven world is decided by the motive of the mind who made it.

Of all this the master had known while he was a disciple; now it is known by him. The heaven world which is to the mind of a mortal an immense expanse of years, is, to a master, a brief dream only. Time in the mental world when conceived by the mind of a mortal is endless eternity as compared with the time of the physical world. The mortal in his heaven state cannot use his time faculty; the master does. The time faculty of the master is brought into use, by his motive faculty, as he thinks. As he thinks, the atoms of time group themselves and are related to each other as his thought, and that is determined and caused by his motive. The master thinks of time, its comings and goings. He follows time and sees the circulations from the beginnings of time, its constant flow from the spiritual world, its fludding and turning back into the spiritual world. The motive causes its comings and decides its goings, in periods necessary for the realization and working out of its ideals.

The master thinks of his motive and his motive faculty makes known to him the motive which prompted his becoming a master. While he seems to have always been a master, he knows that his becoming one is the fullness of his time. The beginnings of this, though far removed in the lower time worlds are present in the mental world, his world. He knows that the completion of his beginning is his becoming, and its uniting with the beginning. But he knows that the processes of the becoming are not here; they are in the lower time worlds.

Other motives than the motive which caused him to become

what he is, are made known to him as he thinks and uses his motive faculty. He has followed time in its beginnings and in its completions, but he does not see all the processes of his becoming a master. He thinks of the processes and uses his image and focus faculties. The flowing of time continues. He follows it in its groupings and formation of the worlds. The worlds take on form as form-time, which is form-matter, and forms appear upon them. The atoms of time fill in the forms, which are the time molecules. The atoms of time pass through the form molecules; they pass through the form world, and while they are flowing on the forms become physical. The physical world, as the form world made visible and concrete, is seen to be a constant flowing on of time and not to be concrete and solid: Forms appear and disappear like bubbles, and time which flows on continues through the forms which are thrown up on it and borne away on it. These throwings up and drawings in are the lives and deaths of things which come into the physical world. The human forms are among them. He sees a continuous line of forms, graduated in perspective, stretching over the bounds of the physical world and ending in himself. These forms or bubbles lead into himself. By his focus faculty he lines them up and sees that they are the forms or the shadows of himself. He focusses them, and all end now and blend into and disappear in the physical body, his present physical body, from which he has but just risen, ascended as a master.

He is immortal; his immortality is the whole of time. Though the whole becoming has extended throughout time, it has been lived through while he has taken voice and given name to himself, and during his ascension. His physical body is in the same position and, according to physical time, not many moments seem to have lapsed.

The master now is in full possession of his physical organs; he is aware of the physical world; he is in full possession of five of his mental faculties and uses them independently of his senses. His physical body rests; peace is upon it; he is transfigured. He, the master, as a master body, is not of the form of the physical body. He is in the physical, but he extends beyond it. The master is aware of and sees other masters about him. They speak to him as one of them.

The disciple who was and who has now become a master, lives and acts consciously in the physical and mental worlds. His physical body is within the master body, as the physical world is within and permeated by the mental world. Through or by use of the physical body the physical world is alive to him. Everything in the physical world is more pronounced. The sun shines, birds sing, the waters pour forth their melody of joy, and manifested nature greets the master as her creator and preserver. The world of the inner senses which beckoned him as disciple now gladly offers obedience and submissive service to the master. That to which he did not yield as disciple he now will guide and direct as master. He sees that to the world of men, which had offered him glory and had asked his aid, he may now render service and he will give it aid. He regards his physical body with sympathy and compassion. He looks on it as the thing through which he has come into his own.

To be continued.

The great distinction between teachers sacred or literary—between poets like Herbert, and poets like Pope—between philosophers like Spinoza, Kant and Coleridge, and philosophers like Locke, Paley, Mackintosh and Stewart—between men of the world who are reckoned accomplished talkers, and here and there a fervent mystic, prophesying half insane under the infinitude of his thought,—is that one class speak *from within,* or from experience, as parties and possessors of the fact; and the other class *from without,* as spectators merely, or perhaps as acquainted with the fact on the evidence of third persons. It is of no use to preach to me from without. I can do that too easily myself. Jesus speaks always from within, and in a degree that transcends all others. In that is the miracle. I believe beforehand that it ought so to be. All men stand continually in the expectation of the appearance of such a teacher. But if a man do not speak from within the veil, where the word is one with that it tells of, let him lowly confess it.

* * * * * * * * * * *

It makes no difference whether the appeal is to numbers or to one. The faith that stands on authority is not faith. The reliance on authority measures the decline of religion, the withdrawal of the soul. The position men have given to Jesus now for many centuries of history is a position of authority. It characterizes themselves. It cannot alter the eternal facts.

EMERSON, *"The Over-Soul."*

THE INNER LIFE AND THE TAO-TEH-KING.

XII.

By C. H. A. Bjerregaard.

IN the last chapter, I introduced and discussed several new subjects, necessarily leaving a great deal for this and the following chapters. The subjects were Teh, the human temple, our temperaments, and the work we are called to do both on the Path and in the Universal Ministry for the benefit of our fellowmen.

I shall now continue the same subjects and endeavor to explain certain important aspects of them by means of a folklore tale from our American plains. Strange as it may appear, the story I shall read contains the most valuable material for a study of Teh and a life on the Path, the life of regeneration.

The story I shall read is a Shawnee tale, and I give it as told in Schoolcraft's "Algic researches" under the title of "The Celestial Sisters." The book is now scarce. Inner evidences and the undisputed veracity of Schoolcraft is sufficient evidence against any charge or suspicion of a manipulation of the story, in the interest of romance or continuity or spiritual symbolism. This is the story.

The Celestial Sisters.

Waupee, or the White Hawk, lived in a remote part of the forest, where animals abounded. Every day he returned from the chase with a large spoil, for he was one of the most skillful and lucky of hunters of his tribe. His form was like the cedar; the fire of youth beamed from his eye; there was no forest too gloomy for him to penetrate, and no track made by bird or beast of any kind which he could not readily follow.

One day he had gone beyond any point which he had ever before visited. He traveled through an open wood, which enabled him to see a great distance. At length he beheld a light breaking through the foliage of the distant trees, which made him sure that he was on the borders of a prairie. It was a wide plain, covered with long blue grass, and enameled with flowers of a thousand lovely tints.

After walking for some time without a path, musing upon the open country, and enjoying the fragrant breeze, he suddenly came to a ring worn among the grass and the flowers, as if it had been made by footsteps moving lightly round and round. But it was strange, so strange as to cause the White Hawk to pause and gaze long and fixedly upon the ground, there was no path which led to this flowery circle. There was not even a crushed leaf nor a broken twig, nor the least trace of a footstep, approaching or retiring, to be found. He thought he would hide himself and lie in wait to discover, if he could, what this strange circle meant.

Presently he heard the faint sounds of music in the air. He looked up in the direction they came from, and as the magic notes died away he saw a small object, like a little summer cloud that approaches the earth, floating down from above. At first it was very small, and seemed as if it could have been blown away by the first breeze that came along; but it rapidly grew as he gazed upon it, and the music every moment came clearer and more sweetly to his ear. As it neared the earth it appeared as a basket, and it was filled with twelve sisters, of the most lovely forms and enchanting beauty.

As soon as the basket touched the ground they leaped out, and began straightway to dance, in the most joyous manner, around the magic ring, striking, as they did so, a shining ball, which uttered the most ravishing melodies, and kept time as they danced.

The White Hawk, from his concealment, entranced, gazed upon their graceful forms and movements. He admired them all, but he was most pleased with the youngest. He longed to be at her side, to embrace her, to call her his own; and unable to remain longer a silent admirer, he rushed out and endeavored to seize this twelfth beauty who so enchanted him. But the sisters, with the quickness of birds, the moment they descried the form of a man, leaped back into the basket, and were drawn up into the sky.

Lamenting his ill-luck, Waupee gazed longingly upon the fairy basket as it ascended and bore the lovely sisters from his view. "They are gone," he said, "and I shall see them no more."

He returned to his solitary lodge, but he found no relief to his mind. He walked abroad, but to look at the sky, which had withdrawn from his sight the only being he had ever loved, was painful to him now.

The next day, selecting the same hour, the White Hawk went back to the prairie, and took his station near the ring; in order to deceive the sisters, he assumed the form of an opossum, and sat among the grass as if he were there engaged in chewing the cud. He had not waited long when he saw the cloudy basket descend, and heard the same sweet music falling as before. He crept slowly toward the ring; but the instant the sisters caught sight of him they were startled, and sprang into their car. It rose a short distance when one of the older sisters spoke:

"Perhaps," she said, "it is come to show us how the game is played by mortals."

"Oh no," the youngest replied; "quick, let us ascend."

And all joining in a chant, they rose out of sight.

Waupee, casting off his disguise, walked sorrowfully back to his lodge, but ah, the night seemed very long to lonely White Hawk! His whole soul was filled with the thought of the beautiful sister.

Betimes, the next day, he returned to the haunted spot, hoping and fearing, and sighing as though his very soul would leave his body in its anguish. He reflected upon the plan he should follow to secure success. He had already failed twice; to fail a third time would be fatal. Near by he found an old stump, much covered with moss, and just then in use as the residence of a number of mice, who had stopped there on a pilgrimage to some relatives on the other side of the prairie. The White Hawk was so pleased with their tidy little forms that he thought he, too, would be a mouse, especially as they were by no means formidable to look at, and would not be at all likely to create alarm.

He accordingly, having first brought the stump and set it near the ring, without further notice became a mouse, and peeped and sported about, and kept his sharp little eyes busy with the others; but he did not forget to keep one eye up toward the sky, and one ear wide open in the same direction.

It was not long before the sisters, at their customary hour, came down and resumed their sport.

"But see," cried the young sister, "that stump was not there before."

She ran off, frightened, toward the basket. Her sisters only smiled, and gathering round the old tree-stump, they struck it, in jest, when out ran the mice, and among them Waupee. They killed them all but one, which was pursued by the young sister. Just as she had raised a silver stick which she held in her hand to put an end to it, too, the form of the White Hawk arose, and he clasped his prize in his arms. The other eleven sprang to their basket, and were drawn up to the skies.

Waupee exerted all his skill to please his bride and win her affections. He wiped the tears from her eyes; he related his adventures in the chase; he dwelt upon the charms of life on the earth. He was constant in his attentions, keeping fondly by her side, and picking out the way, for her to walk as he led her gently toward his lodge. He felt his heart glow with joy as he entered it, and from that moment he was one of the happiest of men.

Winter and summer passed rapidly away, and as the spring drew near with its balmy gales and its many-colored flowers, their happiness was increased by the presence of a beautiful boy in their lodge. What more of earthly blessing was there for them to enjoy?

Waupee's wife was a daughter of one of the stars; and as the scenes of earth began to pall upon her sight, she sighed to revisit her father. But she was obliged to hide these feelings from her husband. She remembered the charm that would carry her up, and while White Hawk was engaged in the chase, she took occasion to construct a wicker basket, which she kept concealed. In the meantime, she collected such rarities from the earth as she thought would please her father, as well as the most dainty kinds of food.

One day when Waupee was absent and all was in readiness, she went out to the charmed ring, taking with her her little son. As they entered the car she commenced her magical song, and the basket rose. The song was sad, and lowly and mournful, and as it was wafted far away by the wind, it caught her husband's ear. It was a voice which he well knew and he instantly ran to the prairie. Though he made breathless speed, he could not reach the ring before his wife and child had ascended beyond his reach. He lifted up his voice in loud appeals, but they were unavailing. The basket still went up. He watched it till it became a small speck, and finally it vanished in the sky. He then bent his head down to the ground, and was miserable.

Through a long winter and a long summer Waupee bewailed his loss, but he found no relief. The beautiful spirit had come and gone, and he should see it no more!

He mourned his wife's loss sorely, but his son's still more; for the boy had both the mother's beauty and the father's strength.

His wife had reached her home in the stars, and in the blissful employments of her father's house she had almost forgotten that she had left a husband upon the earth. But her son, as he grew up, resembled more and more his father, and every day he was restless and anxious to visit the scene of his birth. His grandfather said to his daughter, one day:

"Go, my child, and take your son down to his father, and ask him to come up and live with us. But tell him to bring along a specimen of each kind of bird and animal he kills in the chase."

She accordingly took the boy and descended. The White Hawk, who was ever near the enchanted spot, heard her voice as she came down from the sky. His heart beat with impatience as he saw her form and that of his son, and they were soon clasped in his arms.

He heard the message of the Star, and he began to hunt with the greatest activity, that he might collect the present with all dispatch. He spent whole nights, as well as days, in searching for every curious and beautiful animal and bird. He only preserved a foot, a wing, or a tail of each.

When all was ready, Waupee visited once more each favorite spot—the hill-top when he had been used to see the rising sun; the stream where he had sported as a boy; the old lodge, now looking sad and solemn, which he was to sit in no more; and last of all, coming to the magic circle, he gazed widely around him with tearful eyes, and, taking his wife and child by the hand, they entered the car and were drawn up—into a country far beyond the flight of birds, or the power of mortal eye to pierce.

This is the story.

I would indeed like to dwell minutely upon all the details of the rich symbolism of the story, but that would lead beyond the limits of my present discourses on the Inner Life and the Tao-Teh-King. I must therefore take only the salient features of the story and they happen to be just the very details, that I need to explain how Teh comes to us; what Wu-Wei is and how our temperaments are to be ruled and turned into use for the spiritual life.

Now then, to the application.

First about Waupee. He is plainly what we ordinarily call "the natural man"; a fine specimen of human possibilities, but he is not on the Path as yet. He is truly a man of temperaments, both as these are potentially in themselves and also as hindrances to spiritual life. The natural man is seen in the hunter and his skill. The un-free man is also seen in this same skillful man, who at first is only killing such passions and dispositions as he meets with in the forest of his own spiritual wilderness. It is not till he, as the story has it, on the third day comes upon the Open that he enters upon the larger life. He passes through three degrees of development before he is ready to concentrate upon the one object in his life. On the first day he discovers that there is an "opening" and on the next he, like the natural man, who knows nothing about "Wu Wei" or "non-action," fails because his very temperamental strength and natural excellence is in his way. His faults are these, he hides and lies in wait; he rushes out to seize the youngest sister; he plays possum; these are temperamental faults, but perfectly natural on his part. He, an Indian, could not be expected to act otherwise. His whole character is determined by his natural will and by his training. His actions are simply forms of his habits. The only hope we can see for him in the story, and, before we learn of the trick of the mice, is his boldness, his frankness and courage. He is not a weakling, either in soul or body. He is full of determination, and in those traits appear the first rudiments of the future spiritual man. Though the conflicts that arise within him at the sight of the sister threaten to destroy him, the very conflict is the sign of coming freedom.

And how does he finally succeed? After having tried several kinds of direct methods for the attainment of his object and failed, he becomes a mouse and is about to be destroyed, and then he succeeds, that is, he becomes humble so humble that he is no more than a mouse. Could an Indian well conceive of an animal more insignificant, even more contemptible than a mouse? And when he is about to be destroyed he has reached the very point of "non-action," or Wu Wei, which he, and all of us must reach before we embrace the heavenly maiden, Teh. Teh comes out of Wu Wei, "non-action"; Teh is taken possession of in Wu

Wei "non-action"; and Teh really is Wu Wei, "non-action," and thus the very soul of the story, the motive force of all that takes place.

And here for the present, I must drop Waupee as a subject and talk about Wu Wei. Waupee and his history is not my main subject. He is only an illustration. The main subject is Wu Wei and the ideas connected with that conception.

In my last chapter, I have treated Teh from the universal point of view. Now I came to Teh as the sum total of practical virtue or Wu Wei, as it is called in the Tao-Teh-King. It is of greatest importance that we should get a clear understanding of that term, not only because an understanding of the moral tendency of the whole book depends upon it, but also because Wu Wei represents the wisdom of all ages on how to begin to travel on the Path, and how to continue on the Path, and on how to be identified with the Path.

The word in literal translation is this: "Wu" means "not having"; "to be destitute of"; "Wei" means "small," "fading away," "bodiless," "secret," or, put together in Wu Wei we get the conception, "not doing," "non-action," "non-assertion." That is the literal signification of the two words.

Based upon this literal translation of the two Chinese signs, we may establish the doctrine which we in the West call Quietism, and which also exists under the name of Wu Wei in China, though not elaborated so definitely as it was in Southern Europe by John of the Cross, Molinos, Teresa, Madam Guyon, Fenelon, and among the Germans by Angelus Silecious, and many others.

Quietism means first of all, resignation and absolute subjection under the Universal Will; but this is not its main characteristics; in resignation and absolute subjection it resembles all other mysticism. It is also a passive and receptive mode of receiving a divine influx and making little or nothing of activity in religious matters, whether ceremonial or moral. In this respect it is known to the Tao-Teh-King and implied in the word Wu Wei! Next, Quietism has been practiced as a disinterested love for a personal god. In this last form it is not known in China, simply because the Tao-Teh-King knows no personal God. It is the form especially practiced by Madam Guyon, Molinos and Fenelon. Practical forms of Quietism, such as the form among the Quakers, is also implied in Wu Wei. Forms of Quietism which have run into extremes of Pietism are unknown to Wu Wei and Tao-Teh-King. This is enough about Quietism and Wu Wei in general.

If you wish a literary and poetic interpretation, but no translation of Wu Wei, I can recommend no better than that little charming book by Henri Borel called "Wu Wei, a phantasy based on the philosophy of Laotzse." It is indeed the cream of the Tao-Teh-King, and if you read that you can get no better practical insight into the mind of the Tao-Teh-King and Laotzse. If you can absorb the sense of Borel's book, you may forget all these twelve chapters of mine and you shall find that you have lost nothing but the husks that covered the nut.

As I said, this is enough about Wu Wei in general. I will now go into details. Wu Wei defined as a principle for the "conduct of life" means "non-interference," "non-exertion," "not-doing," "masterly inactivity"; that is, we must discard all thoughts of helping nature in her work. It is laid down as a *sine qua non* (LXIII.) "Act non-action. Be occupied with non-occupation. Taste the tasteless. Find your great in what is little, and your many in the few."

This is metaphysical. But the same chapter says also, "Recompense injury with kindness." That savors of the New Testament and is intensely practical and useful in real life. It is said in Chapter 79, "to let matters rest will be found to be the best way. Therefore, the wise man takes care of his own part of the compact and exacts nothing of others"; and "he who undertakes to do the work for the Great Architect rarely fails to cut his own hands." It is so hard for people to learn that to be passionless and motionless does not mean stupidity and mental or spiritual ruin, but the contrary. Rigid inactivity frees a man from entanglements and bad karma. All efforts defeat themselves, because they are efforts and not spontaneous actions. Wu Wei means "non-interference" in politics as well as in people's personal affairs. The Taoist demands that the people be left to develop their own resources. Conformity to nature will bring best results. In my next chapter I shall speak of Wu Wei in Chinese politics and ancient history.

The metaphysics of Wu Wei or "non-action" is this, that "emptiness" or "vacancy" or "space," words which also correctly translate Wu Wei, is not a negative force, but a most positive one; one, of which it is said (V) that "though empty, it never collapses, and the more it is exercised the more it brings forth." Emptiness is even called "the abyss-mother," which is "the root of heaven and earth"; because the sage, the holy man, the mystic, employs "emptiness" as a working principle (VII.), and as he "puts himself last, he is first; abandoning himself, he is preserved."

To get at the full meanings of "emptiness" or "vacancy" or "space" as a translation of Wu Wei I must come back to the term Ku-sen as I explained it in the last chapter. Ku means literally a valley, that is, the space or empty room enclosed by hills; not the valley as it appears to the eye or as civilization uses it for railroads or cities. It is the cosmic emptiness symbolized, but not marked off by mountain ridges. It is taught (XI.): "thirty spokes unite in one nave, and by that part which is non-existent (that is, the hole in the center of the nave) it is useful for a carriage wheel. Clay is moulded into vessels and by their hollowness they are useful as vessels. Roofs and floors, doors and windows, are arranged in such a way that they make a house by the hollowness they produce."

You understand then that it is the hole in the nave that represents but does not constitute the essential of the wheel, that the space inside of the clay walls represents but does not constitute the essential of the vessels, and that the hollow space of the room stands for the real part of the house. Of course it is so, because the number of spokes, or their length, is certainly immaterial to the main office which the wheel is to serve as a wheel; and it is immaterial whether the vessel is made of clay or silver; whether it is round or square or oblong. The main thing is that it can contain something, and the same is the case as regards the house. In the Tao-Teh-King much is made of this vacuum, this emptiness, this hollow space and that tendency is thoroughly oriental and mystic.

That which Laotzse here illustrates by realistic terms, Buddha also illustrated and in his own characteristic way. In the Milinda Panha there is reported a conversation between the Buddhist sage Nagasena and King Milinda, which runs as follows. The sage tells the king: "My fellow-priests address me as Nagasena, but that is merely a name, for I am no independent ego-entity, no atman." The king replies: "If you are no ego-entity, pray tell me who it is that acts, that eats, that drinks, that thinks ———?" And the king continues to ask if Nagasena is hair, nails, lungs, sensation, perception or consciousness, and receives a denial to all his questions. Finally the king comes to the natural conclusion that he fails to discover any Nagasena; that Nagasena is an empty sound and at last declares: "Venerable Sir, you speak a falsehood, a lie. There is no Nagasena."

Then comes the turning of the tables. The sage asks the king if he came in a chariot or on foot, and the king answers: "I came in a chariot." Nagasena then asks: "What is a chariot." Is it the axle, the wheels, the box, the yoke or the reins? The king answers no! to all the questions and Nagasena then declares: "I fail to see any chariot. The word chariot is an empty sound. Your majesty speaks a falsehood, a lie. There is no chariot." The king defends himself and says: "Venerable Sir; I speak no lie; the word 'chariot' is only a way of speaking, a term, a name for that which is made up of pole, axle, box, wheels." Nagasena now draws the conclusion he has been waiting to make, which is, that in an absolute sense there is really no more person or chariot than the unity that is made by the combination of the various phenomenal parts that go to make a person or a chariot. In other words a person, a chariot, is no reality, but only a name for a combination.

In Plato the same problem was discussed under the form of "the One and the Many." In the Middle Ages, it was again discussed in Scholasticism and the problem was called "Nominalism and Realism." Both with Plato and in Scholasticism the result was the same as in Buddhism, that is, the thing is not real, and the name we give it is a name merely and not an equivalent expression for reality. All mystics and Inner Life people hold that the Real is not known and that which we call real is only a name for a mystery. The mystery cannot be known, but may be communed with in the Inner Life.

When Laotzse uses the illustration of the valley, the hole in the nave, he means to lead the thoughts from the phenomenal to the real; from the name of the thing to that which in earlier chapters I defined as Simplicity and Stillness.

In our own conception we approach this idea of emptiness, vacuity, when we say for instance "beauty unadorned is most adorned." A human body can never be truly represented in its native beauty except by its nakedness.

The older mystics preferred nakedness to dress while meditating, because nakedness gave them a freedom, that never can be attained with garments on. This, of course, may not appear intelligent to those who do not know what meditation and contemplation are. We have the same idea symbolized in the hermit, the yogi, who sacrifices everything in withdrawing to the desert. He wishes to liberate himself, that freedom from cares may help him to escape all trammels; he literally "empties" himself. But perhaps the idea of emptiness may be clear when I tell you that innermost in all Egyptian temples there was an adytum, a most holy chamber, and that that chamber was dark and empty—why? It was the residence of the god! the god resided in space and space was symbolized by emptiness! Can you see the mystery?

Here is another illustration taken from a totally different sphere of life. The Japanese have tea-rooms, which they call the "Abodes of Vacancy." The tea-room is an empty room. It is absolutely empty, except for what may be placed there for the time being to satisfy some aesthetic mood. In its emptiness the tea-room answers to the adytum or the innermost of the Egyptian temples, which was dark and empty. The tea-room gets its significance from its temporary use by visitors and their presence. It is nothing but emptiness in itself. The visitors give it its character; they are the main thing; the room itself is nothing.

A room or its name means nothing to the Japanese mystic, it is its use he inquires about; its consecration. Its name means nothing; its character is the all to him. Yet a room is of course a room and of architectural signification whether consecrated or not. In the tea-room the wall decorations are landscapes, birds, flowers, rather than the human figure, the latter being present in the person of the beholder himself. How subtle that, too! How ingenious is not the teaching that the tea-room is for silence or solitude, for Man; for Presence; for the Real!

In short the idea of emptiness, nakedness, is expressed. Nakedness, that individual truth may be revealed. Again the idea of isolation is expressed by the very emptiness of the room. Man is to learn emptiness, which in China and Japan means vastness or the Great Mother, Teh, the universal womb in which and out of which the actual comes forth. Space is the divinity thought of as female. In India it is Aditi, the "boundless one" and sometimes Sakti. In China it is Ku-sen, the "valley spirit."

You see how different the Oriental and mystic sanctuaries are from the Western and the church peoples! Look into a real blue sky and you shall see how full and rich it is in its emptiness! You will see how much more rational and sublime the Orientals are! How overwhelmingly so. No cathedral can rival them in their simplicity and forceful teachings. Truly said Jesus, that the lilies in their simplicity or nakedness or emptiness surpassed Solomon in all his glory; lilies and the lotus are sanctuaries on account of their very simplicity, emptiness in their purity, which is a sublime Nakedness. We do not obtain the Real by simply "having our will." Obtaining the thing is not obtaining it at all. The object of our desire does not fascinate; it is the life which passes through it that fascinates. The flower I put in my buttonhole is a victim of my greed and cannot be expected to give me any real pleasure. It is the moonlight that bewitches, not the moon. It is beauty that elevates, not the art object. It is the dignity in a man that a woman submits to, not to the mere man. And vice versa it is the "eternally feminine" a real man worships, not flesh and blood.

We are such "spaces," or "emptiness," or we ought to empty ourselves that we may be such a room filled with the mysterious presence, symbolized by the Japanese Tea-room and the adytum of Egyptian temples. Any and all endeavor to realize such a condition is called Wu Wei, "non-action," and you must have understood that it is not a negativity, that on the contrary it is Reality.

Now apply these later teachings to the definitions of Wu Wei, given before, and you observe how the terms already used have expanded enormously. Literally translated they were merely negative terms on our ordinary plan of life, but they have now grown to positive statements of occult truths. Wu Wei is now no more "not having" nor merely Quietism and resignation; it is now an eternal quality, a Presence. And that presence is Teh. Follow the word further and see how it keeps on growing as we get nearer and nearer to it, by what I now shall state. You shall now hear why non-action, Wu Wei, is so highly praised in the Tao-Teh-King.

It is because "The non-existent enters into all things without any crevice" (XLIII), and by non-action there is nothing that may not be done" (XLVIII), and "there is no sin greater than giving rein to desire." There is no misery greater than discontent" (XLVI). It is, therefore, also advised, "Shut the lips and close the portals of eyes and ears and as long as you live you will have no trouble; but open your lips and meddle with things and as long as you live you will not get out of trouble." (LII).

All these statements would have no meaning if Wu Wei, or "non-action," had not become something positive. The West is active in its excellence: It strives for the first place by doing. The East is passive in its excellence; it does not strive, it yields, and it attains the first place spiritually, by yielding. It is this latter method which the Tao-Teh-King recommends on every page, and calls Wu Wei, and understands to be the essence of Teh.

It is difficult for the West to understand this method. The method of "not-doing" is unfortunately always understood as doing nothing, and that is not at all the sense of "not doing." And it can be truly asserted that "not doing" is the under-current of all spiritual life in the world. Buddhism and Christian Mysticism meet Taoism in teaching the same method. They have their own way with it, but they aim exactly at the same point.

Buddhism in world-weariness tells disciples to leave the world and have nothing to do with it. Taoism does that, too; but at the same time exhorts its followers to rule the world by non-resistance, by subjection, by not desiring it, and, not even acknowledge to self that they rule it by that method. You shall now hear some singular teachings on that subject. Such as that the real world comes from something not real (that "existence comes from non-existence") and that "the sage manages affairs without doing anything, and conveys his instructions without the use of speech."

The Buddha looks upon the world through the large glass end of the telescope and rejects all its things as insignificant, because he sees everything diminutively as you do when you look in at the large end of a telescope. Taoism looks in from the small glass end of the telescope and sees the "infinitely great," and identifies itself with it, calls it Tao and Teh and means thereby the Primal Force, the Absolute, Brahm (neuter), Buddhism comes in from one end of the bridge and Taoism from the other. They meet in the Middle, in the recognition that the bridge is not "it," but that the Middle is the Path, the way of "not doing."

As it is, Buddhism produces intermediaries between God and man, real saints. Taoism by Wu Wei or non action is suitable for a practical world and makes wise men, who can be in the world and rule it and yet not be of it, nor lost in it. A Taoist knows as much as a Buddhist about sin and sorrow and the illusoriness of the phenomenal world, but he does not run away from any of these. A Taoist knows no "Sorrows of Werther" and "Weltschmertz." He practices Wu Wei because he has no use for fraudulent phenomena; he does not shun them because of any pathological condition. The Taoist by Wu Wei becomes the sage among the unwise; the physician among the sick and a teacher to those who are blind. A Buddhist cannot fight, a Taoist can!

And, about "not doing" it should here be stated, that the Christian Mystics of the Middle Ages, had a sensible understanding of it in spite of all their insane ascetic practices. They were intensely practical people, which they proved by their actions during the Black Death horrors, and the papal interdict, details of which I must pass over for the present. This terribly active world of ours places a man's value on what a man does, not on what he is. And in overlooking quality and preferring quantity, we of the West have lost the best parts of life. Go into public institutions and, in many cases, you there find moral outcasts in important positions, because they can labor much. If you ask why the institution keeps such people, you will be told that the institution is soulless and therefore does not care about morals, but only about the amount of labor they can perform. Not so in the Greater Life as lived by mystics and true people. To them the eternal personal value of the worker is the most important. They place a man's value not in what he does, but in what he is; upon quality, not upon quantity. It is that which a man is, which makes his acts good; the deeds do not make the man. There is nothing to hinder a mystic from being active in the world. No; nothing! He will, however, not follow the world's methods. He may sell his services to the world, but he never sells his person or his soul or his convictions.

Again, there is nothing the modern man will object to more vigorously than to be told to be quiet, to lie low, to become reconciled to things, even if they are bad. We cannot blame him. He has seen how church and state have frightfully misused the principle of quietness, and that is his reason for fears and noncompliance.

Rebellion against restraint is the keynote to all that is going on in modern progressive society, politics, social affairs, yet I must maintain against all contradiction that the principle of Wu Wei is fundamentally right and that we shall never come to a true reorganization of society unless we re-adopt it; not as it is preached by the hirelings of the various crafts, but as Nature enforces it and as the Tao-Teh-King teaches it. Nature everywhere calls for submission. On this subject of submitting we must persuade our fellowmen and ourselves that Wu

Wei does not mean the ruin of ourselves and our eternal purposes and aims. It means that we must still the noise of the senses and the clamorous desires, which constantly are in our way for the attainment of truth, and we must also eliminate all intellectual notions. All sages, and none of them have been hypocrites or time-servants, have realized for themselves and have taught their disciples that life is only found by losing it; that "a man is rich in proportion to the number of things he can afford to let alone" (Thoreau); that desires are limitless and cause all our troubles; that they only create more thirst, as does salt water when we drink it; that our senses, our tempers, are to be used but are not to rule us, and that death follows if they rule; that our desires sing like the Sirens of old and prevent our hearing "the voice of the silence," and, that they color the images that arise in our minds and consequently blurr them and their truth; that silence, solitude and lowliness are the soil, the sun, the air, in which spiritual life grows. All these facts of the spiritual life we must persuade ourselves and our fellowmen to learn and to submit to. They are wisdom! They are power! They are Wu Wei. On none of these points are we expected to destroy ourselves, whether by submitting to the will of another or to an abstract principle. We are simply to bow down to wisdom, to place the individual under the universal and no more. It ought to be easy, for as one master said: "the yoke is easy and the burden light."

But let it at once be understood that Wu Wei, Quietism, is not merely submission, not merely a negative virtue. It is in itself very positive. A Quietist radiates happiness, and good cheer flows from him. A Quietist is never discouraged, and is therefore able to be a rallying point for others. A Quietist is resolute and never turns back from his purpose, and his purpose is always sublime. A Quietist is brave, and others have confidence in him. His presence inspires confidence. And all this because we feel his presence permeated with a deep power, and his nearness gives us the impression of something sublime. Ask anybody who has met a great soul, and they will tell you about the influence that comes from him. In the third chapter, I gave an illustration of a Quietist, in the beggar at the church door, who converted Tauler.

To be continued.

THE GENESIS AND GROWTH OF THE CHRIST OF THE SOUL AND SOME OF ITS MODES OF LIFE.

By James L. Macbeth Bain.

(Concluded from page 30.)

NOW every body draws its food from its own sphere of being. I need the pure air of God's open sky for the health of my whole psyche. And the fragrance of the Holy Breath in the grass and plants of mother earth is the sweet incense of my temple of adoration.

And it is so with every true lover of nature. For pure air is the food of the fine magnetic body, and to do without it is to withhold from the whole psyche as from the body of flesh the gift of God, thus robbing her of her divine right and hurting her life.

Since my boyhood I have had to betake me to the lonely places where the trees and the hills and the running waters are my companions; and there merged and at peace in their fellowship I am fed of this sweet substance.

Very beautiful and wonderful are the modes of this soul-feeding, and of one mode I have sung in "Breaths of the Great Love's Song," p. 109. And what I give as my experience I know to be the experience of many; and so I think it will serve a use to say more of it now.

Sometimes it is felt as if passing by the brain to the spine and through the whole nerve body, sometimes as if by the solar plexus. And there is at the time a reason for this in the state of either the nerve or magnetic body. In either case the consciousness of it is equally pure.

The sweetness of this food is such as no word can utter. For in it is the sweetness of the Body of the Christ-mother, and the Christ-child is always fed on the finest of the substance of the Holy One. And one is very conscious of the inflow and assimilation. And this conscious state of receptivity is in duration according to the need and capacity of our psyche at the time. Thus it may last five minutes, or an hour, or more.

And while one's consciousness of external life is intensified one is unconscious of the passing of time and superior to ordinary physical conditions. Thus the body, even though in the normal state very sensitive to cold, feels it not then nor is hurt thereby. All lassitude vanishes, and the heart, whose power may be depleted by much service, beats steady and strong during and after the period of feeding. And there is no more weariness nor feebleness in the whole body; and sweet sleep comes in good time. And this state of joyous health passes not with the influx. But, so far as it has become effective in the soul, so far is the body of flesh quickened in its forces of blessing and renewed in all its powers of service. And were it not that there are karmic debts to be paid in this flesh I do believe that the power of this living food might even redeem this body from the power of the elements of death. For it is the essence of the One who is the resurrection and the life of our whole being.

To every soul this food is of the substance of its own heaven. Thus, to the poet or artist it is the very beauty of the Holy One of Life; to the mystic it is the essence of the Love of God; to the prophet it is the fine fire of the pure Spirit; to the saintly mind it is the sweet light of interior illumination. And to the human soul it is the power of the Healing of the Holy One of Blessing. And so to us all it is just what we can receive.

To illustrate the need for this feeling we cannot do better than study the records of the life-work of Jesus Christ, for what was needful to the stronger is surely needful to the feebler.

Nothing, we may be sure, did the brother of the blessed life desire more than to serve and ever to serve the feeble bodies and souls who crowded about him and followed him in their more or less blind hunger for what they felt he had to give them. But even he had out of very necessity to withdraw his body from them at certain times and after certain periods of service. And why so? This Christ-body in Jesus demanded its own food. And this need constrained him to go where alone it could both receive and assimilate the heavenly food. And to receive it he had to go apart. He had to leave the multitude, ay, and his most near disciples, in order to go in the deep silence of God's peace unto the hill of high devotion and pure, rarefied spiritual perception, and there the angels of God communed with him and thus ministered to the need of his spiritual soul. For there was no one in the flesh who could thus minister to him the strong one.

I would not imply by this that all spiritual ministration is necessarily mediated through the angelic host, for I feel that the spiritual soul does receive of the divine or Christ-substance immediately from the Cosmic Christ soul. But sure, sure we are that in times of need these good spirits of the Christhood do fulfil this sweet service of mediation.

But in fine modes this feeding is continuous and is being effected even when we may not be at all conscious of it. And so we must not imagine that because we do not feel the joy of the influx nor taste the sweetness of the food as we have in times past we are therefore not in communion. For, I repeat, this communion never ceases. And were it not so the spiritual soul would not continue to live.

But there are soul states wherein there is generated a psychic stuff which we may compare to a fine oil. For it gives unto the holy inbreathing a body of manifestation when it is being consumed of the Breath. And in the soul a fire of unutterable sweetness is kindled; and this fire pervades the whole body from the innermost ions unto the outermost tissues and nerves. But when once this oil is consumed, the holy Breath, even while still inflowing, may not be so intensely felt, or may not be felt at all. And this privation may last for days or weeks or months or years, according to the richness or poverty of our psyche in generating this body for the manifesting of the Presence. And this is the opportunity for the trial, the triumph and the strengthening of our faith. For inasmuch as our faith in the ever-abiding Presence is strong to endure throughout this period of privation in so much do we gain real or abiding strength as a spiritual soul. And this is the power to bless. Thus the power to bless depends not on our feelings. These are of the realm of psyche, and must be apprehended to be the manifestors of the psychic senses, but not the holy Essence who manifests. Therefore let those unselfish souls, who, through some poverty of their psyche, cannot give unto the holy Power this oil for burning, be of good cheer. For, inasmuch as they serve in the self-transcending Love, insomuch are they verily in communion with the Holy One, receiving the sweet food of the Christ substance, even though they may not have the joy of feeling its inflow.

But, while it is true that the whole psyche can be fed in the loneliness of the high mountain air in a way that cannot be in the heavier air of the low-lying plain or the devitalised air of the city of men, and that our body may become too fine even to exist in these conditions, and must have the purer if it would live, we are not to understand that we must go into lonely places of this earth's surface or ascend high hills in order to find God and to be fed of the substance of the Christ. To recognize this as an utter necessity would be to acknowledge our complete subjection to material conditions. And this no spiritual soul, whose great victory is to triumph over such conditions, can admit.

But to those, and they are the many dwellers in cities, to whom this retreat into the quiet of God's holy nature is denied, it is only needful to enter into the silence of God through the silence, either spontaneous or induced, of the olden selfhood, even the lull of the fearful or querulous or despairing worldly mind, and then by a conscious turning of the quiet soul towards the Great Love, even as we would turn the silent face towards the sun when we would be more abundantly blessed of his radiance, thus to ascend unto the purer air of the Hill of God, and here, as in a great calm, to yield our waiting soul to the ministration of the heavenly host, or to the quiet and, it may be, imperceptible permeation of the holy Substance, her only, her very food.

For, now that it has risen beyond the discordant vibrations of the earthly mind, the fine body of Love can receive and respond to the fine vibrations of the spiritual cosmos.

And, sure as in that moment of perfect receptivity you ask for the heavenly food, so surely will it be given unto you and that abundantly. Indeed the very asking is in itself an earnest or sure forerunner of the gift of the substance of the Great Love. I have never once known this to fail, and I have proved it true unnumbered times during my earthly life.

But we must see the other side of the whole truth and realize that soul must blend with soul in mutual service if the living Christ, the sweetness of God, is to be given as a food unto the body of Love-service.

For, even in the physical and psychic degrees, it is necessary that bodies and souls come together in order that love be generated. The power of life cannot be born in the state of complete separateness. Unless there be contact of body with body or communion of soul with soul there can be no birth of love. And this holds good through all we have just said.

Thus the Great Love or essence of the Christ-spirit is generated through the fellowship of souls who, being in the Will of the Life-Giver, must fulfil the great law of their nature, and give, ever give of their good unto those who can receive it. For it is not possible for them to keep any good for the service of self, and, when they receive, it is only to give. And wheresoever it is generated there is the Christ brought forth into manifestation as the service of Love.

For there is only one way of life possible to the new-born, so far as it is related to the goods of this passing world. It is a non-possessor, and it can be none other. Sure as it lives it has given them all away. For it belongs not to their realm. And its greatest labor is to be yet constrained for the service of others to administer any of these goods. And its greatest luxury would be to have no more the handling of any of them. And while fulfilling this service which it can do well if duty so calls (for its wisdom is finer than the wisdom of the earthly mind), it looks forward with patience to the laying aside of these bonds of hard labor. Is it not so with thee, Christ-soul a-weary of the toil? Indeed, it is so. For thou art Love, and Love hath nothing, nothing of her own. And the Commune is thine only ideal state; and thy Christ will surely bring thee unto they haven of rest, even thine own home, O Love-soul, where service is always joy.

Now this body of Love-service is well. tried and proved to the uttermost, so that any weakness in it may be made known and that it may not fail in the hour of the most trying service.

And the more potent it is to be for service the more searching will be the process of trial. And the keener or more tense the strain of proving, ay, even unto the limit of enduring and the point of breaking, the stronger and more efficient does it become for service. And that it can suffer much is a sure sign that it can serve well.

But it cannot break, though we often foolishly feel it must; for it is not our personal soul but the deathless Christ who now lives and serves in us. And the Christ can never fail, and there is nothing It cannot endure. For It is the very Power of the Great Love, who beareth all things and who faileth never.

A high ideal have we set before you, dear human soul, for the priceless gift of the Christ service. And who of us can yet say that he has come unto this ideal? Not I, not I, is the unfeigned word of the soul who is nearest unto it. But let us be of good cheer, for there is a sure way of attainment. And it is the way of the Cross.

And ere we can enter the way of the Cross of Christ what toll must we pay? Only the value of the old, weary selfhood with all the prides and insanities thereof, the highest price in the eyes of the payer, but in the light of the Truth a valueless one.

For, having indeed kissed the utmost lowliness of the Christ in giving your sweetest love and its best service unto that one of his human body who has most cruelly wronged or most subtly and persistently tormented and debased you in the eyes of men either wilfully or unknowingly, and just because it has done so, thus denying the natural hate of the heart, or, having given your highest service of Life to what appears to you as the basest or more repulsive member of His Body, loving it most strongly, not wilfully but in the pure spontaneity of the free Spirit, even because to your eyes it is so repulsive, thus denying the natural likings and dislikings of the soul, having thus laid your old self lower than the soil on which men tread, you are now, in virtue of this utter sacrifice of your dearest self-pride unto the Great Love, clean in fact from the taint of the virus of the olden selfhood, and so fit to be a vessel of the service of Life in this our temple of the Holy One, a bearer of the wine of joy unto man, a channel for the inflow of the divine essence unto every soul who comes to you thirsting for the living God.

Soul, dear unto the Christ, when you know what the joy is so to fulfil the service of the holy Grail unto others, you will bless, bless, and ever bless the Spirit of Life for all the distresses, ay, for all the pains of the hells through which the Great Love has led you in order that you might come unto this cleanness needful for the sweet service of our Holy Christos. Here is the key to the mystery of suffering. And this is only the teaching of all the strongest spiritual seers of the ages. And they bear us witness.

The End.

CHOICE EXTRACTS AND TRANSLATIONS.

BY A FELLOW OF THE ROSICRUCIAN SOCIETY.

"HUMAN PRE-EXISTENCE."

(An extract from the writings of an author whose name has sunk into oblivion and who lived in the beginning of the 19th century about sixty or seventy years before the advent of modern Theosophy).

THAT mankind had existed in some state previous to the present was the opinion of the wisest sages of the most remote antiquity. It was held by the Gymnosophists and Brahmins of India, the Magi of Persia, and the greatest philosophers of Greece and Rome; it was likewise adopted by the fathers of the Christian church, and frequently enforced by her primitive writers; why it has been so little noticed, so much overlooked, rather than rejected by the divines and metaphysicians of later ages is almost unaccountable, seeing that it is undoubtedly confirmed by reason, by all the appearances of nature, and the doctrines of revelation.

In the first place, then, it is confirmed by reason, which teaches us that it is impossible that the conjunction of a male and female can create or bring into being an immortal soul; they may prepare a material habitation for it, but there must be an immaterial pre-existent inhabitant ready to take possession. Reason assures us that an immortal soul, which will exist eternally after the dissolution of the body, must have eternally existed before the formation of it, for whatever has no end, can never have had any beginning, but must exist in some manner which bears no relation to time, to us totally incomprehensible; if therefore the soul will continue to exist in a future life, it must have existed in a former.

Reason likewise tells us that an omnipotent and benevolent Creator would never have formed such a world as this, and filled it with inhabitants, if the present was the only, or even the first state of existence, a state which, if unconnected with the past and the future, seems calculated for no one purpose intelligible to our understandings; neither of good or evil, of happiness or misery, of virtue or vice, of reward or punishment, but a confused jumble of them altogether, proceeding from no visible cause and tending to no end. But as we are certain that infinite power cannot be employed without effect, nor infinite wisdom without design, we may rationally conclude that this world could be designed for nothing more than a prison or house of correction in which we are awhile confined to receive punishment for the offenses committed in a former, and an opportunity of preparing ourselves for the enjoyment of happiness in a future life. Secondly. These conclusions of reason are sufficiently confirmed by the face of nature; this world is evidently formed for a place of punishment, as well as probation; a house of correction, to which we are committed, some for a longer, and some for a shorter period, some to the severest labor, others to more indulgent tasks; and if we consider it under this character, we shall perceive it admirably fitted for the end for which it was intended. It is a spacious, beautiful and durable structure. It contains many various apartments, a few very comfortable, many tolerable, and some extremely wretched: it is enclosed with a fence so impassable, that none can surmount it but with the loss of life. Its inhabitants likewise exactly resemble those of other prisons: They come in with malignant dispositions and unruly passions, from whence, like other confined criminals, they receive great part of punishment by abusing and injuring each other.

As we may suppose, that they all have not been equally guilty, so they are not equally miserable; the majority are permitted to procure a tolerable subsistence by their labor, and pass through their confinement without any extraordinary penalties, except from paying their fees at their discharge by death. Others, who perhaps stand in need of more severe chastisement, receive it by a variety of methods; some by the most acute, and by the most tedious pains and diseases; some by disappointments, and many by success in their favorite pursuits; some by being condemned to situations peculiarly unfortunate, as to those of extreme poverty, or superabundant riches; of despicable meanness, or painful pre-eminence, of galley slaves in a despotic, or ministers in a free country. If we survey the various regions of the globe, what scenes of wretchedness everywhere present themselves to our eyes! In some, thousands chained to the oar, and perpetually suffering from the inclemency of all weathers and their more inclement masters: In some, not fewer condemned to wear out their miserable lives in dreary mines, deprived of air and daylight; and in others, much greater numbers torn from their native country, their families and friends, and sold to the most inhuman of all tyrants, under whose lash they are worn out with fatigue or expire in torments.

The history of mankind is indeed little more than a detail of their miseries, some inflicted by the hand of Providence and many more by their own wickedness and natural ill usage. As nations, we see them sometimes chastised by plagues, famines, inundations, and earthquakes; and continually destroying each other with fire and sword, we see fleets and armies combating with savage fury and employing against each other every instrument of torture and death, which malevolence can invent or ferocity make use of. We see the dying and the dead huddled together in heaps and weltering in each other's blood; and can we be spectators of this horrible tragedy, without considering the performers as condemned criminals, compelled, like the gladiators of the ancients, to receive their punishment from each other's hands? The orator, the poet and the historian may celebrate them, as heroes fighting for the rights and liberties of their respective countries, but the theosophical student and philosopher can look upon them in no other light than as self-condemned spirits exiled into human forms and come to chastise each other for past offences.

As individuals, we see men afflicted with innumerable diseases, which proceed not from accident, but are congenial with their original formations, designed for the most important ends; the stone grows in the human bladder, under the law and direction as in the quarry, and the seeds and germs of scurvy, rheumatism and gout are sown in the blood by the similar law that has scattered those of vegetables over the face of the earth. From these various instruments of torture, numberless are the miseries which mankind endure; nor are those perhaps less numerous, though less visible, which they suffer from that treachery, injustice, ingratitude, ill-humor and perverseness, with which they every hour torment one another, interrupt the peace of society, and embitter the comforts of domestic life; to all which we may add, that wonderful ingenuity which they possess of creating imaginary, in the absence of real misfortunes and that corrosive quality in the human mind which, for want of the proper food of business or contemplation, preys upon itself, and makes solitude intolerable, and thinking a most painful task. Who, that surveys this melancholy picture of the present life, can entertain a doubt but that it is intended for a state of correction and learning and must therefore be subsequent to some former life to which this correction was necessary.

Again, the opinion of pre-existence is no less confirmed by Scripture, than by reason, and the appearances of things; for although perhaps it is nowhere in the New Testament explicitly enforced, yet throughout the whole tenor of those writings it is everywhere implied; in them mankind are constantly represented as coming into the world under a load of guilt, as condemned criminals, the children of wrath, and objects of divine indignation; placed in it for a time to give them an opportunity of expiating this guilt by sufferings and regaining, by virtuous conduct, their lost state of happiness and innocence: this is styled working out their salvation, not preventing their condemnation, for that is already past, and their only hope now is redemption, that is, being rescued from a state of captivity and sin in which they are universally involved. This is the very essence of the Christian dispensation and the grand principle in which it differs from the religion of nature, in every other respect they are nearly similar: they both enjoin the same moral duties and prohibit the same vices; both inculcate the belief of a future state of rewards and punishments, but here they essentially disagree; natural religion informs us, that a just and benevolent Creator could have no other design in placing us in this world, but to make us happy, and that if we commit no extraordinary crimes, we may hope to be so in another; but Christianity teaches a severe and more alarming lesson and acquaints us, that we are admitted into this life oppressed with depravity and wrongdoing, which we must atone for by suffering its usual calamities and consequences and work them off by acts of positive virtue, before we can hope for happiness in another.

Now, if by all this a pre-existent state is not constantly supposed, that is, that mankind have existed in some state previous to the present, in which this guilt was incurred, and this depravity contracted, there can be no meaning at all, or such a meaning as contradicts every principle of common sense—that guilt can be contracted without acting, or that we can act without existing

—so undeniable is this inference, that it renders any positive assertion of a pre-existent state totally useless; as if a man at the moment of his entrance into a new country was declared a criminal, it would surely be unnecessary to assert that he had lived in some other before he came there.

In all our researches into abstruse subjects, there is a certain clue, without which, the further we proceed the more we get bewildered, but which being fortunately discovered, leads us at once through the whole labyrinth, puts an end to our difficulties, and opens a system perfectly clear, consistent and intelligible. The doctrine of pre-existence, of human re-incarnation, or the acknowledgment of some past or former state of guilt and disobedience is this very clue; which if we constantly carry along with us, we shall proceed unembarrassed through all the intricate mysteries both of nature and revelation, and at last arrive at so clear a prospect of the wise and just dispensation of our Creator, as cannot fail to afford complete satisfaction to the most inquisitive skeptic. For instance: are we unable to answer that important question, Whence came evil? that is, why a Creator of infinite power, wisdom and goodness, should have formed a world replete with so many imperfections, and those so productive of calamities to its inhabitants? This clue will direct us to this satisfactory reply, so far as the question relates to the evils of the present life—because he designed it for a place of corrective punishment and probationary discipline; for which it is perfectly adapted; and we can be no more surprised to see such a world as this make a part of the universal system, than to see a magnificent prison, with all its appendages of punishment, make a part of a large, populous and well governed city. Do we find it difficult to comprehend why the same omnipotent and benevolent Creator should fill this world with inhabitants so wicked and so miserable? This clue will immediately lead us to a solution of them, and point out the true reason—because they are sent hither to be corrected, disciplined and reformed. Do we reject all those passages in the New Testament, as derogatory to the divine wisdom and goodness, which declares that mankind come into this world under a load of guilt and depravity and under the displeasure of their Creator?

No sooner are we brought by this clue within sight of a preexistent state, in which this guilt and depravity may have been contracted, but our incredulity vanishes, and we perceive plainly that their admission into this world under those circumstances is not only consistent with the justice of God; but the strongest instance of his mercy and benevolence, as by it they are enabled to *purge* off this depravity, to *expiate* their offences and thus to *attain* to a higher and diviner life.

Thus is a pre-existent state clearly demonstrated, by the principles of reason, the appearances of things and the sense of revelation; all which agree, that this world is intended for a place of corrective punishment and discipline, as well as of probation, and must therefore refer to some former period, for as probation implies a future life, for which it is preparatory, so corrective punishment must imply a former state or existence, in which offences were committed, for which it is due; and indeed there is not a single argument drawn from the justice of God and the seemingly undeserved sufferings of many in this present state which can be urged in proof of a future life, which does not prove with superior force the existence of another which is already past.

ACTORS IN ETERNITY.

By John B. Opdycke.

Eternity of Space—the cosmic stage
  On which the soul's great drama is portrayed;
Eternity of Time—the Brahmic age
  In which the lines are variously essayed;
Eternity of Subject—sacred theme
  The Playwright has so subtly dramatized;
Eternity of Action—the supreme
  Interpretation to be realized.
All men in turn play seven parts, indeed,—
  A versatility of high design,—
Thru seven acts unfold the plots they read,
  Each role, each scene, demanding art divine.
Such opportunity denotes the plane
  To which discerning actors may attain.

"SAVONAROLA" OF FLORENCE.

Theosophist, Reformer and Martyr. A Portraiture of Spiritual Growth and Development.

By Dr. W. Williams.

(*Continued from page* 41.)

"Savonarola's Arrest and Imprisonment."

ALL Florence rang with menacing cries and threats against Savonarola and his friends, several of whom were foully murdered. The Franciscan friars were exultant at the turn of events and the sudden change of popular opinion in their favor. As a reward for their services on the day of ordeal the signory debased itself by assigning to them for a period of twenty years a pension of sixty lire payable on the 7th of April of each year. Events quickly followed each other. "Now or never" was the cry of the Arrabbiati who resolved to strike a final blow, and for this end, took counsel with several members of the signory and the canons of the cathedral how best to effect the ruin and downfall of Savonarola and his party and thus obtain power and control of public affairs in Florence. They fully recognized the necessity of acting promptly and vigorously in order that the friends of Savonarola might not be able to organize any defensive measures on his behalf.

The following morning, it being Palm Sunday, passed without any commotion, yet the ordeal by fire and its egregious failure formed the subject of general discussion. Savonarola in the evening preached for the last time in the church of San Marco with sadness and gloom both of heart and mind. In tones of deepest emotion he declared his willingness to become a sacrifice for the truths he had inculcated, and face death for the welfare of his flock, and ended his discourse by giving them his final benediction and urging them to take heed and doubt not, for the good work began would go on increasing and my death will hasten it on. "Take comfort," he cried, "take up the cross and by it shall you find the way of salvation."

As the shades of evening came on and deepened into darkness, a mob composed of the lowest orders of the citizens, in defiance and disregard of all law, and unrestrained by the signory, assembled again in the piazza and under the leadership of the Arrabbiati began insulting and ill-using the followers of Savonarola in the public streets, shouting, "Our turn has come at last." Urged on by Dolfo Spino and others and becoming more and more emboldened, they commenced assailing the houses of the Piagnoni and hurling stones at the windows. Their numbers increasing and further inflamed by passion and a mad feeling of mischief, which invariably manifests itself in street mobs and ends in riot and tumult, they now unsheathed their swords, and brandishing all kinds of weapons, marched, shouting and yelling, "To San Marco! to San Marco, fire in hand!" During these unlawful proceedings the signory remained quiet, taking no steps to quell the disturbance. The train they had laid was being fired by others and they waited the results, which they trusted would bring about and eventuate in the death of Savonarola. Like a prairie fire, gathering force and impetus on its destructive course, so the mob on its way to San Marco cast away all self-restraint and feelings of humanity and cruelly slaughtered and ruthlessly butchered several individuals, one of whom returning home and singing to himself a psalm as he went, they slew on the spot. Another, a poor spectacle maker who, hearing the noise and tumult, had come forth and was standing in his doorway with slippers in hand, they killed by a sword thrust through his head. And now, like wild, savage animals having tasted blood, they rushed with mad and headlong speed towards the church of San Marco, which they found filled and thronged with worshippers engaged in the vesper services. Notwithstanding this, showers of stones were hurled through the door and windows of the church, which now resounded with the cries of the wounded and shrieks of the frightened congregation. In a few moments it became emptied, and the door and gates of the convent were locked and strongly barred against further ingress of the foremost of the infuriated assailants. About thirty of Savonarola's friends and devoted adherents, along with the frati, were now the only defenders of the convent. Unknown to their master, they had secretly conveyed a store of arms and ammunition and deposited them in a cell beneath the cloisters in oredr to be ready prepared against all emergencies. One of these, Francesco Davanzati, a man of indomitable courage and energy of character, took command and placed the frati at the weakest points as guards, who, with breastplates over their Dominican robes and helmets on their heads and huge halbards in hand, stood prepared to defend San Marco to the death, their watchword being, "Viva Christo!" On observing this, both Savonarola and Fra Domenico were greatly grieved and implored them to cast away their weapons, saying: "You must not stain your hands with blood. You must not disobey the precepts of the gospel." These injunctions proved in vain, for now deafening and furious yells of the mob outside were head, endeavoring to batter in and smash down the doors and gates of the convent. Seeing that all resistance would be futile and unwilling to prolong a struggle so unequal and involving the shedding of blood, Savonarola, true to himself and faithful to the principles of self-sacrifice, of which he had been so great an exponent, resolved to put an end to the fruitless contest against such fearful odds.

Arraying himself in his priestly robes, he addressed his companions and friends, " Suffer me," he said " to go forth, since through me *'orta est haec tempestas'* (this storm has arisen.)" On hearing these words, consternation was depicted on every face. Every heart was rent with feelings of pain and anguish, as friends and frati alike crowded around him, and with tears and supplications fervently besought him not to leave them. " No," they said, " do not leave us, you will be torn in pieces, and what then will become of us without you? " Overwhelmed and deeply affected with this exhibition and expression of their love and affection towards him, he bade them follow him into the church. Carrying the host on his breast through the cloisters and entering the choir, he turned and reminded them that prayer was the only weapon that should be used by ministers of religion and the higher life. The little band at once fell on their knees, and there amidst the sound of shot and the clashing of arms, whilst doors were being battered and windows smashed in on all sides and through which sounded the yells and imprecations of enemies thirsting for their blood, they turned their hearts and eyes heavenward and prayed as only a human soul in its *extremis* can pray, "*salvum fac tuum populum Domine*" (Save thy people, Oh Lord).

And now the besiegers had fired the gates and scaled the outside walls of the convent and forced their way into the choir of the church. Rising from their knees, Savonarola's friends finding themselves attacked, turned in self-defence, and seizing the burning torches and using their crucifixes of wood and metal, faced their opponents, and fighting stoutly for their lives belabored the assailants with such energy that they fled in great fear and terror, declaring that a band of angels was defending the convent. Though the invaders were driven back out of the church, they shortly returned with redoubled force and fury, and setting fire to the doors and seats, the edifice soon became enveloped in flames and filled with smoke, so that it was impossible to breathe and discern friend from foe. Everywhere resounded the cries of the wounded mingled with the wails of the dying.

During their riotous and illegal proceeding, the signory were sitting in council, and though fully aware of them, yet took no steps to stop them and sent no troops in aid and succor of the besieged at San Marco. On learning of the stubborn and determined resistance of Savonarola's adherents, and apprehensive lest his friends in the city and suburbs hearing of what was taking place would rush to deliver him out of danger, they issued a decree commanding him and his two most intimate friends, Fra Domenico and Fra Sylvester, to present themselves forthwith at the Palace of Justice, promising at the same time that no harm or injury should befall them. Their official mace-bearers proceeded to San Marco, but on Domenico asking to read the order, it was found they had in their haste forgotten to bring it and at once returned to fetch it. In the meanwhile the assailants, becoming masters of the convent, and their leader threatened to knock down the walls with his guns in case the order of the signory was not obeyed. Though having no authority for so doing, he acted on the suggestion of Fra Sacramoro, a professed friend of Savonarola, who now in the hour of his master's extremity and danger like another Judas, turned traitor, exclaiming in scornful mockery: "Should not the shepherd lay down his life for his lambs." These words touched Savonarola to the heart, but he made no reply to them. Turning, he kissed the few friends now gathered around him, beseeching him to seek safety in flight, for they knew that death was foredoomed. The macebearers, returning at this moment, Savonarola and Domenico, his ever faithful and inseparable friend surrendered themselves into their custody and keeping. As they emerged out of the church into the cloisters, they were at once surrounded by the raging and ferocious mob, who gave vent to their feeling of elation in hoarse and horrid shouts of exultation, so that outsiders thought that the prisoners were slain or crushed to death, which, however, was not the case.

It was now past midnight and through the surging rabble the officials found it exceedingly difficult to force their way through the crowds of ruffians, who, holding aloft their burning torches and lighted lanterns and with faces black with smoke and dust and eyes gleaming with fury, gazed on Savonarola with threatening mien and shouted, "Behold the true light!" as they singed his cowl and garments with their blazing torches. Waxing bolder, they savagely seized hold of his hands and cruelly twisted his fingers. "Prophesy," they cried, "who is it that has buffeted thee?" The details of the barbarous insults and outrages heaped upon Savonarola are most revolting and shocking to relate. No language can express, no words or terms describe, the cruel suffering and horrifying indignities he had to endure from the vilest of mobs on his way to the signory. Of such an exhibition of callous inhumanity, history preserves no record save that which was witnessed nineteen centuries ago, when Savonarola's master, the great and despised Prophet of Nazareth, amidst rude Roman soldiery, followed by jeering priests and hooting crowds, wended his weary way, bleeding and fainting under the burden of a heavy cross up the steep hill of Calvary, outside the city walls of Jerusalem, to endure the pangs of crucifixion. Like him, Savonarola, with hands bound behind him, was led surrounded and jeered at by pitiless Arrabbiati and scoffing Compagnacci in the early hours of that April morn into the presence of the signory, whose magisterial representative, the chief Gonfalonier, after addressing questions to the prisoner relative to predictions uttered in the past, ordered him, along with Domenico, to be consigned to separate cells, and there immured for the time being, until a plan had been elaborated and a juridical process drawn up to bring about their death.

On the day following, Fra Sylvester, who had succeeded in concealing himself within the precincts of the convent, was discovered in his hiding place and made prisoner also, and there in the narrow cells of the public jail the three friends whose inner lives were so intimately bound together, were incarcerated. Yet though dissevered and separated and denied that fraternal intercourse and mutual exchange of thought that had constituted the great joy and delight of their lives, stone walls nor iron cage could not obstruct or debar them from holding spiritual intercommunion and holding fellowship upon another and higher plane of devachanic existence, where it is the grand privilege of the children of light to meet at times and assemble together during their earth pilgrimage in the body, even though the tale of reincarnations necessary for the attainment of human prefection be not exhausted and completed.

Great was the joy and delight of Pope Alexander on learning of the success of his deep laid plan and the result of the ordeal by fire, as also of the arrest and imprisonment of Savonarola. He gloated over the prospect of his deportation to Rome, and reducing him to silence in the dank and darksome dungeons of the Papal Castle St. Angelo, by methods in which he was most expert. On receiving an official letter from the signory, giving a minute account of all that had happened, and praying his Holiness to grant them absolution for their past disobedience of his orders to arrest Savonarola and also for having seized hold of ecclesiastics and deprived them of their liberty and freedom, they begged permission to institute judicial proceedings against the prisoners. At the same time, as a *quid pro quo* for what they had done to gratify him, they took the opportunity of asking him to allow them to tax church property in order the better to provide for State necessities, against which Alexander had strongly objected. In his reply he extolled and praised them in glowing and fervent terms as most worthy sons of the church and sent them his blessing and a plenary absolution for the illegalities they had committed and readily granted them authority to institute proceedings and bring to trial the delinquents under arrest, to try, examine and torture them in case they refused to make a full confession of their errors and misdeeds. He also praised them for their zeal and devotion to their Holy Mother, the Church, and sent a plenary indulgence during the Easter octave, but as a condition insisted that at the conclusion of the trial the prisoners should be delivered over to him to suffer and undergo the punishment they merited. With reference to the authority to tax church property, though lavish in promise, he cautiously refrained from committing himself and indulged in vague expressions and ambiguous phrases.

The Intrigues and Illegalities of the Signory.

Leaving now Savonarola and his two faithful followers, Fra Domenico and Fra Sylvestro, confined within their narrow and dismal cells, calm and unaffected by the terrible doom awaiting them, that has cowed and broken down the fortitude of many brave hearted and tortured martyrs of the truth they gave forth to an ungrateful and unappreciative world, we come in the immediate presence and contact with an assembly of most wicked and infamous individuals whose only object and aim was the death and degradation of one by whose labors and toil in the cause of political freedom and spiritual enlightenment, most of them enjoyed the privilege of returning from exile in other lands and territories, the hateful tyranny and injustice of whose rulers had caused them to sigh after and long to enjoy the peace and liberty Savonarola had inaugurated and made possible in Florence. Of all degrading and foulsome passions incident to human nature, that of political rancor and hatred and enmity are the most baneful in their effects upon individuals, changing and transforming them into demons of atrocious cruelty and ferocious brutality. Such were the Arrabbiati who, though it was the season known as the Holy Week, now assembled to consult on the readiest and most effective means to accomplish their designs for the ruin and death of Savonarola and his two friends. They were fully aware of the illegality of their arrest and imprisonment, yet so intent were they upon the consummation of their infamous purpose, that they were determined nothing should thwart and prevent the execution of it. To this end they caused search to be made throughout the city to find out and arrest the most notable and principal followers of Savonarola on the pretense of having taken part in the defense of San Marco from the attacks of a riotous mob of which they themselves had been the instigators and leaders. Still more to influence the minds of the citizens and excite feelings of prejudice and doubt of the purity and integrity of the fallen teacher, they collected all the weapons found in the convent church and stacked them, all bloodstained, in a cart that was drawn by a few of their most audacious myrmidons through the streets and alleys and thoroughfares of the city and shouting in hoarse stentorian voices, "Behold the miracles of San Marco. Come and behold for yourselves the miracles of the friar, and judge of his love for the people of Florence." This cunning and wily device was in a great measure successful, so much so, that the signory were emboldened to call a practica or public meeting of the electors to discuss the course to be taken with prisoners who, instead of releasing and protecting from injury as they had sworn to do, were detained in close custody in defiance of all public law and justice. In order the better to conceal their ulterior design, they submitted for discussion the question, whether the three friars whom they had been obliged to seize and keep in custody for the honor and safety of the republic, should be examined in Florence or sent to Rome in accordance with the pope's request.

Another question was, what should be done with the Council of Ten and Ottanta in whose jurisdiction was vested the sole right to judge and determine legal proceedings in state trials and prosecutions? It was most important that these state judicial officials, the majority of whom were friendly disposed towards Savonarola, should be got rid of and superseded, in order to carry out successfully their preconceived and secret designs. Again it was most imperative that what was done, should be done quickly, as the end of their term of office was fast approaching and a new signory would most probably be elected who would quash and nullify their proceedings and thus their intended victims would escape out of their hands. In such a partisan meeting, it was easy to pass resolutions abolishing the Councils of Ten and Ottanta and electing in their places members of the Arrabbiati and Compagnacci who at once appointed seventeen of their party as examiners to conduct the trial and were entrusted with full power to use any kind of torture in order to extort confessions of guilt from Savonarola and the two other prisoners. One of these appointed judges was Dolfo Spino, the most bitter and inveterate enemy of Savonarola, whose assassination he had on several occasions attempted. So evident was the intention of this unprincipled man and his coadjutors to set at naught all rules of equity and principles of law and justice, that one of them, a certain Bartolo Zoti, indignantly refused to act on the commission, declaring he would be no party in a murder so atrocious and heinous.

The Examination and Torture of Savonarola.

Knowing that time was against them, the examiners commenced at once their flagitious work by proceeding to the Bargello tower, and by threats and insults and acts of indignity endeavored to extort from Savonarola a confession of his imposture and deceit as a lying prophet and a deceiver of the people. Failing in this, they resorted to modes of torture most barbarous in their cruelty, that caused the unhappy sufferer to endure most horrible and excruciating pain and agony. Hoisting him with his hands tied behind, on a pulley they jerked him several times, so that the muscles were lacerated and torn and his limbs quivered and writhed with pain. Yet no such confession as they wanted could they extort from Savonarola. In vain were all efforts to induce him to give the lie to his whole life and career that had been spent in the advocacy of uprightness and the proclaiming of the reality and existence of the higher and diviner life in the soul of man that, in proportion as it becomes assimilated to its higher self, becomes also imbued with those attributes of power and strength that enable it to endure affliction and the torments of persecution with a calmness and inflexibility of mind most heroic and sublime. Again and again they subjected his frail and sensitive frame weakened as it had been by frequent austerities and nightly vigils and years of unceasing ministration to the spiritual happiness and political welfare of Florence, inflicting further tortures and plying him with subtle and ambiguous questions, in the hope, that in moments of bodily agony and delirium verging on madness, some word of self incrimination would escape his lips and warrant his condemnation. Thus they crowded round him and waited with the official notary who, pen in hand stood ready to write down Savonarola's confession. Only once was the sufferer heard to speak in tones of anguish that would have softened their hearts had they not been of stones. *"Tolle Domine, tolle animam meam,"* (Receive Oh, Lord, receive my soul). Finding again further efforts futile to force from him any incriminatory avowals without which they could not legally condemn him, Savonarola was unbound and led back to his cell whilst the signory and the examiners deliberated on still more cruel and fiendish methods to induce him to confess. On entering it he knelt down and prayed: "Forgive them, Oh thou Divine

One, for they know not what they do." A feeling of fear and dread of exposure seized hold of the minds of the conspirators as they consulted together on their failure.

By the spread of lies and slanders, they had succeeded in exciting a prejudice against their victim and raised doubts in the public mind as to his integrity of character and purpose which, if they could not substantiate by facts or prove by his own avowals, however obtained, would recoil upon themselves and reveal their deep laid and treasonable designs for the overthrow of the state. In their extremity and bewilderment, it was suggested by one of their number, a notary named Ser Ceccone, to fabricate a fictitious confession. "Where no real case exists," said he, "it is necessary to invent one" and further added, he was not afraid of finding a way of doing it. It was the only feasible escape out of their terrible dilemma and therefore they bargained to give him the sum of six hundred ducats on the successful accomplishment of his infamous and villainous proposal. They found him a fit and clever tool and skilled in drawing up depositions expressing, by alteration of words and phrases, what was altogether opposite to their original and intended meaning. He was a most unscrupulous and unprincipled character and had been implicated in Piero's conspiracy against the state. To avoid arrest and escape conviction, he had fled and found refuge amongst the frati of San Marco and professing to be converted, had become a follower of Savonarola to whom he owed life and safety. His hypocrisy however became manifest after the imprisonment of his superior whom he reviled now in most rancorous and embittered terms. A few days after this nefarious compact, a second examination of their prisoner was held when similar methods of torture were resorted to, as at first, in order to force Savonarola to avow his duplicity in posing as a prophet and a lying propagator of predictions and visions that were pure inventions of his imagination.

All the questions put to him, with their answers, were duly noted down by Ser Ceccone and drawn up in depositions so flagrantly falsified and jumbled in their statements, as to render it impossible to separate and distinguish truth from falsehood, sometimes a "yes" being turned into a "no" and whole paragraphs being omitted and words interpolated such as "this was my hypocrisy," "this was my pride," "I did it for the sake of worldly glory," statements Savonarola would have scorned to avow and were altogether foreign to his nature and from which we may justly infer that these iniquitous examiners failed a second time to extort any such like admissions, and so they forged reports to hide and cloak their own perfidy and damage his reputation in the minds of his remaining followers whose faith and implicit confidence in Savonarola as an exponent and exemplar of the higher life was as yet firm and unshaken. This trust and credence blighted and shattered by his own admissions that his teachings had been bolstered up by pretended and fictitious prophecies and visions, they knew full well, would overwhelm his name and prestige with lasting shame and obloquy. Great and universal was the consternation and dismay when the forged and falsified depositions were published and circulated in Florence.

The loyalty of Savonarola's friends and their belief in his integrity and uprightness were rudely shaken, if not destroyed; so much so that like the disciples of the great prophet of Nazareth on the night of his arrest, they forsook him and fled. They had learned to regard and revere him with feelings of the deepest respect and admiration as a teacher of the truths of the higher life and venerated him as a divinely sent messenger or prophet and placed implicit confidence in his predictions, visions and ratiocinations of coming events. Throughout his whole public career, as a preacher, a statesman and reformer of the church, they had remained his firm and faithful adherents and never faltered in the love and affectionate esteem they extended to him, so that his very name was a watchword, a synonym of integrity, and of the highest type of christian virtue and character. In all his actions, his indefatigable labors and efforts for their spiritual interests and political welfare, they had detected not a single trait of selfishness, of personal ambition or desire for popularity for the furtherance of his own benefit, or the attainment of anything that would subserve to advance his power and authority in the state; and now to read these, unknown to them, forged and false depositions wherein Savonarola their beloved master had formally confessed that his life had been an imposture and all his visions and predictions, deceitful lies and fabrications, was a blow both to their hearts and minds so overwhelming in its pain and anguish, that one of them whose children had marched in the holy bands at carnival time, writes: "He confessed he was not a prophet and had not from God the things he preached. When

I heard this confession read, I stood in stupor and amazement, my heart became filled with grief and anguish. I was waiting to see Florence a New Jerusalem from whence should go forth the laws and example of a good life. I felt it was all the contrary and could only heal and assuage my woe by the cry, "Oh thou Divine One, in thy hands are all things." Another follower, Fra Benedetto, who had always proved himself a faithful and loving disciple and an unwearied defender of Savonarola, overcome with feelings of doubt and mental anguish, left Florence and retired to Viterbo as he expresses himself, like a thrush struck by a falling bough. This much however may be pleaded on their behalf; they knew not and had not the least idea or suspicion of the shameless deceit and perfidy of the signory in the proclamation of the forged confession. From their own questions and Savonarola's answers to them were drawn up two forms of depositions, one of which incriminatory in its avowals of self-confessed guilt Ser Ceccone had fabricated and by an artful stratagem and trick, succeeded in getting Savonarola to affix his signature to the forged and false copy, in presence of eight witnesses and a few monks who were totally unaware of the deceit that had been practiced.

Thus ended the examination of Savonarola after eleven days of continuous torture. In writing to the pope, who had complained of the slowness with which it had been conducted, the signory endeavored to excuse themselves by informing him, "We have had to do with a man of most enduring body and sagacious wit, who, hardening himself against torture, had involved the truth in a thousand obscurities and appeared determined by his feigned sanctity to win lasting fame in future ages, to suffer incarceration and death. Even after long and assiduous examination continued for several days and with the aid of torture, we could barely extort from him anything and we preferred not to reveal what he said, hoping to succeed in discovering the numerous windings of his mind." From the contents of this letter we may gather what nefarious and execrable means they adopted to accomplish their object of discrediting Savonarola in public estimation and, against all legality and justice, condemning him as a malefactor and impostor worthy of death. Several accounts of the circumstances attending the conclusion of the examination have been preserved and handed down; many of which are of an apochryphal character, but there is a general agreement, that when the depositions were placed before Savonarola for signature he turned to his judges and spoke the following words: "My teachings are known to all of you. In my present tribulation I ask only two things, to have care of the novices and preserve them in the christian doctrine in which we have hitherto kept them steadfast"; whereupon Fra Maletesto Sacramorr, the Judas who had so cruelly deserted and betrayed him, asked: "But are the things which thou hast subscribed true or false?" To this question Savonarola vouchsafed no answer but regarding him with a look that struck terror and dismay into his blackened soul, turned away and was led back to his cell a condemned criminal; and there we leave him for a time, alone and yet not alone, for the light that is the life of man glows within him and out of the gloom and darkness of his dungeon raises him into a world of tranquility and peace where the wicked cease from troubling and torturing and earth's wearied and suffering children find peace and rest at last.

Fra Domenico's Noble Defense of Savonarola.

The examination of Savonarola's two faithful friends began and was carried on in like manner to his, both being subjected to the torture of the pulley, rack and iron boot, in order to extort admissions and confessions convicting them of complicity in their beloved leader's guilt and imposture. As with Savonarola, all efforts proved in vain, especially with the brave lion-hearted Domenico whom no infliction of bodily torture and laceration of his limbs could prevail to deny the master, the one being in the world whom he truly loved and revered with an affection stronger than death; for notwithstanding the excruciating agonies of the rack and boot, he remained firm and unshaken in his faith in Savonarola even after being informed that his master had confessed and acknowledged his imposture and deceit. Foiled in this attempt to undermine and shatter his faith, the examiners requested Domenico to write out a confession which they altered and interpolated with concocted and false statements, as they had done with that of Savonarola. Finding, however, that there was nothing in it to convict him, they further urged him to write his opinion of his master and his pretended prophecies. Complying with their request he wrote, "From an inward conviction, I have ever believed and still firmly believe in all the prophetic predictions of Savonarola.

This I affirm though I am all shakened and my arms are useless, especially the left which by torture is now dislocated for the second time." This declaration being by no means satisfactory to his judges, they tortured him further, whereon he again wrote, "I know no more, for my sole concern has been to live a virtuous life with Jesus Christ as King of Florence. This if not believing, ye put me to the torture again, you will discover no more, for there is nought to be said." Still intent and determined upon making him deny his master, they racked him anew with greater cruelty and bade him write again. Unshaken and fearless of all consequences he wrote, "God's will be done! I have never perceived nor had the least occasion to suspect that my father Fra Savonarola was a deceiver or that he acted falsely in anywise; on the contrary, I have ever esteemed him to be a truly upright and most extraordinary man. And having a great reverence for him, I hoped by this means to receive grace from God and be enabled thereby to be a man of God, and I obeyed him as my superior with all single mindedness and zeal. To my brethren and a few laymen, I have sometimes declared from the pulpit that were I to detect the least error or deceit in Savonarola, I would openly reveal and proclaim it and I would do it now, if I knew of any duplicity in him, but none has ever come to my knowledge." Noble and brave, true hearted Domenico! greater in faith and trust in thy master than the cowardly Peter who seasoned denial of his, with oaths and curses.

To be concluded.

But Nature, it might seem, strives, like a kind mother, to hide from us even this, that she is a mystery: she will have us rest on her beautiful and awful bosom as if it were our secure home; on the bottomless boundless Deep, whereon all human things fearfully and wonderfully swim, she will have us walk and build, as if the film which supported us there (which any scratch of a bare bodkin will rend asunder, any sputter of a pistol-shot instantaneously burn up) were no film, but a solid rock-foundation.

—Carlyle, *"Characteristics."*

A DREAM OF ATLANTIS—THE LAND OF MU.

By Alice Dixon Le Plongeon.

BOOK IV—PART II.

(Continued from page 59.)

Among the men that willing dared
   The deep to cross, was one
Who what he owned had freely shared
   And every danger run,
Partaking in this enterprise
   To found an empire new
Where valiant sons might soon arise
   And virtues stern imbue:
A priest was he, and well inspired
   With learning of his creed—
Much wisdom patiently acquired
   Thro' years of thought and deed.
On him good Can, the king bestowed
The rank of pontiff; thus endowed
He will the lovely Nalah mate
With Itzat, heir to royal estate—
"As he for wisdom long hath striven,
Unto his years be honor given."
The king ordained, and every voice
Hailed Tohil as the monarch's choice.

The dear betrothed of Atlas dead
Learned not to smile again; grief fed
Upon her heart, and dimmed the face,
Once rosy, with a tender grace.
Beholding this, Can ever strove
To gratify her faithful love,
   And now the dame besought—
"Would'st thou, dear lady, see arise
   Ere other works be wrought,
A monument to glad thine eyes,—

In memory of our Atlas great,
Erected in this new-born state?"
Pelopa answered, "Yea, good Can"—
At once the laborers began
To build foundations where would arise
A temple to the mighty Kin,
And there an altar, shrined within,
King Atlas would immortalize.

Within this temple, scarce begun,
The princess and the monarch's son
Ahe wedded by Tohil, the Just,
Rejoicing in his sacred trust.

Within the woods trooped lads and maids
To gather from the forest shades
The brightest flowers and clinging vine
That slender fingers might entwine,
To deck with garlands hall and fane,
While joy in every heart must reign;
Sweet copal too its fragrance there
Is wafting on the balmy air.

Upon that most auspicious day,
While all the populace were gay,
Itzat his bride unto him drew
To hear the vows he would renew.
And now within her hand he placed
A gem. Once only had it graced
Her slender form. All smiling she
Exclaimed, "How came this unto thee?"

"When I by Gadeirus was sent
As envoy of his government,
This gem found me in Lobil's name,
With lying words that sought to blame
   A maiden pure and true—
Declaring she the gift bestowed
On him for whom her heart now glowed.
   His villainy I knew,
And not a sign the knave received

Anent the bauble he had thieved—"
"Nay, nay," the bride at this breaks in,
"Lobil committed not this sin;—
The jewel, from my raiment lost,
Upon the marble floor was tost
That very night when joyously
This token I received from thee.
But thou, my Itzat, well hast proved
Thy perfect faith in her who loved
Thee well, Distrust cannot assail
That heart where faith prevail."

Her gaze upon the bauble set,
The princess sighs, "Could I forget
That eve so filled with sunny joy?
Alas! that fate could so destroy
Those happy days, forever fled
When I beheld my father dead.
O Itzat! let my sorrow find
A refuge in thy heart so kind—
This land unbeautiful and drear
But keeps alive the memories dear
Of that grand realm where every bliss
Was found, that here we constant miss.
How sad the change! Our palace there
Was stored with objects fine and rare:
While here naught lovely greets the eye—
Ah, would that hence we two could fly;
Chastise that evil man, and reign
In our dear palace once again!"

While she laments the king draws near
And smiling says, "The words we hear
Proclaim that ere a day goes by
Our bride is eager to comply
With mandates by Tohil expressed—
Since now she hath herself confessed.
Ah! daughter, turn thee from the past—
Rejoice that here thy lot is cast;
Glad years and happiness on thee
Await, from enemies quite free.
　Not so in yonder land

Where desolation soon will be
  From mountain-peak to strand.
What knew the princess in her bower
Of wretches, who forsaken cower,
  Despairing, ill, unfed;
Of morals crushed by evil power
  And into bondage led.
In that far land of luxury
  A million creatures daily plead,
Amid the opulence they see,
  For succor in their urgent need,
These hapless ones will cease to groan
When rich and poor alike shall moan
And Mu herself be overthrown."

While hopeful life stirred everywhere
More pale and wan Pelopa fair
Became. The king beholding grieved
With Kadimo—"Be not deceived
I pray," said he, "Once wholly round
The sun we've rolled since Atlas found
A place among the hosts who bide
Where evil chance may not betide.
Her sorrow yet no respite knows;
More languid day by day she grows,
And life is drawing to its close."

E'en while he spake a maiden pale
  Came running to his side—
"Ah! Majesty, Pelopa frail
  Is dead!" she weeping cried.
"Alas!" the king exclaimed, and sped
Where faithful Yanyan, sobbing, led.

Upon her couch the bride of Death
A marble statue seems; the breath
Scarce flutters in the heart whose love,
To find its mate, must soar above.
Kadimo eager was to aid
The lovely one; but Can forbade
  The breaking of that peace
That o'er each sense so calmly glides

As nearer draws the power that guides
  The soul to its release—
When lo! the watchers see those eyes,
Within whose deeps shine glad surprise,
  Unfold their drooping lids—
As lotus-bud that sleping lies
  Awakes if sunlight bids—
And O, the glory of those orbs!
Whose ecstacy each gaze absorbs.

"Heart of my heart!" the lady sighed,
"Ah! well knew I thou had'st not died:—
Thy face beloved I see again.
O Can, for thee a happy reign
Begins. Mourn not, dear Nalah, Fate
Hath frowned; her smiles on thee await;
Thou'lt long survive thy place of birth,
Doomed soon to disappear from earth.
Pelopa lingers not; her joy
The head of Death cannot destroy.
My body place upon the pyre
When sunrays meet the leaping fire"—

With sobs each swelling bosom heaved,
And Nalah swooned, thus sore bereaved;
While Heppel, driven to despair,
Again would self-destruction dare—
  Kadimo barred his way:—
"Withhold!" said he, "thy hands restrain;
Recall thy promise to refrain
  From casting off this clay."

Then Heppel, "Verily I gave
My word; and grieving here must dwell;
Altho' my heart and soul rebel;
But from no danger will I save
Myself, since death my sorrow crave."

Before that temple late begun
In homage to the mighty sun,
The couch of liberation high
Was raised, of fragrant cedar dry.

Thereon, in virgin white arrayed,
Pelopa, beautiful, was laid;
Her lily hands, smooth brow and cheeks,
Like snow upon Atlantean peaks.
The holy, purifying breath
Of fire will banish icy death;
While priests their requiems chant aloud
'Mid lamentations of the crowd;
The hungry flames forbid the way
To earth-assoiling, slow decay:—
When sinks the sun below the west,
Pelopa's but a memory blest.

A piteous sight is Nalah's grief;
But tender sympathy relief
Bestows upon her buoyant heart—
Life's sunshine bidding woe depart.
Fond dreams their pinions wave o'erhead
When Joy and Innocence are wed.

From dawn to dark industrious hands
Obey the architects' commands,
As round a vast and central place
White marble structures rise apace—
Upon the east that temple high,
The mighty orb to glorify.
Broad avenues are formed close by,
Of columns cunningly inwrought—
That generations might be taught
Of virtuous kings who long had reigned
Ere Gadeirus, daring all, had gained
The Sacred Height, by murderous deed,
To sate his own ambitious greed.
These pillars side by side uprose
To mark the years thus made to close
  By crime that none could trace;
And to the nation bringing woes
  Unnumbered, and disgrace.
But these true records, stone on stone,
Three lustrums thence were overthrown
By earthquake, when great Mu went down;—

And in the ages yet unborn
The rambler in those halls forlorn,
Admiring would demand, amazed,
What force those piles of blocks had razed.

As Cho had loved to watch the throng
Of city streets the whole day long,
So now, such times as he can play
For him too swiftly pass away,
Beholding *alux*, while these slave,
All skillfully, the stones to grave;
For eager are these pigmy bands
To see designs grow 'neath their hands.
So close the lad observed one day,
  A dwarf named Haleb spoke:—
"Thou art as big as I—Why stay
  So idle? Give a stroke
Upon that stone and learn the way
  Its voices to evoke.
Our ears are pleased the whole day long
In listening to its cheery song."
Now gives he implements to Cho
  Who earnestly essays
To cut a line, for he would show
  How gladly he obeys.
Thenceforth each day a little while
In graving stone he will beguile.
His Butterfly Cho dreams of still,
Exclaiming oft, "Return I will
And bring my Pepen to this land
  Where she a home will find;
Its stones well carved by this my hand
  All prettily designed."

To be continued.

THE SEPHER HA-ZOHAR—THE BOOK OF LIGHT.

By Nurho de Manhar.

Containing the doctrines of Kabbalah, together with the discourses and teachings of its author, the great Kabbalist, Rabbi Simeon ben Jochai, and now for the first time wholly translated into English, with notes, references and expository remarks.

(Continued from Vol. X., page 380.)

RABBI SIMEON was walking one day in the country accompanied by Rabbi Eleazar, his son and his students, Rabbi Jose and Hiya. As they wended on their way, Eleazar said to his father: "That this our walk may be profitable, instruct us further, we pray thee, in the secret doctrine."

Then spake Rabbi Simeon and said: "It is written, 'When he that is a fool goeth on his way, his heart faileth him and he saith to everyone that he is a fool' (Eccles. X. 39). When a man desires that his ways may be agreeable to the Holy One and before going on a journey he ought first of all to seek counsel from his Lord (higher self) and repeat the traveler's prayer, as saith the scripture, 'The upright shall walk before him and follow him on his way' (ps. LXXXV. 13). That is, the Divine Shekina will never forsake us on our pilgrimage through life. But he who lives without faith in his Lord is as the fool whose heart or courage when on his way faileth him. The occult meaning of the word heart (leb) is the Holy One, who never accompanies a fool on his way nor grants him the aid and assistance he needs, because by his infidelity and indifference to the teachings of the good law, his heart faileth him, or in other words, the Divine Presence goeth not with him and he becomes known to others as a fool, for whenever he hears others speaking and discussing together on divine things, he derides and despises them. It is related of such an one, after pondering over the mark of the covenant, that every son of Israel bears on him, he affirmed it was a mere rite and no sure sign either of true religion or of faith in the Divine Being. When the venerable Rabbi Yebba heard these words he directed his looks and gaze upon the heretic, who gradually shrivelled up into a lifeless mass

of skin and bone.   As however it is our desire to be blessed
with divine help and guidance whilst on our way, we will endeavor to give expression to a few teachings out of the secret
doctrine.   It is written, 'Teach me thy way oh Lord, I will walk
in thy truth, unite my heart to fear thy name' (ps. LXXXVI.
11).   The interior signification of these words is difficult to
understand, yet they inculcate that all things are in the hand or
power of God except the purity or impurity of our lives and
deeds.   What David meant by them was, open my eyes that I
may understand thy secret mysteries, then shall I be assured I
am walking in the true path of light, swerving therefrom neither
to the right or left; 'Unite my heart to thee,' then shalt thou
become my strength and portion forever and it shall be filled with
the fear of thee and thy Holy name.   Observe that everyone who
reveres the Holy One, in the proportion of his reverence, makes
himself recipient of the higher life and daily approximating to
it becomes eventually united with the Divine.   On the other
hand, he who is lacking in reverence and faith in the divine,
makes himself unworthy and unfitted for entering into the joys
of the world to come.   We read that the path of the upright is
as a shining light that shineth more and more unto the perfect
day (Prov. IV. 18).   Blessed are the upright both in this world
and the world to come for the Holy One, blessed be he! takes
delight and joys in their progress and ascension towards the
higher life. The light here spoken of, is the light that the Holy
One created at the beginning of the world and reserved for those
who by their obedience to the good law, become united to their
higher self and so are qualified to enter into its enjoyments in
the world to come.   But of the worldly minded and selfish it is
written, 'The way of the wicked and unjust, is as darkness—
they know not at what they stumble' (Prov. IV. 19).   If the
question arise, know they not why they stumble and fall? scripture informs us, it is because their paths are tortuous and serpentine, their irrational lives are spent in the indulgence of sensual desires and unredeemed with few if any generous deeds of
self-sacrifice or consideration for the welfare and happiness of
others, and thus they live on never realizing that for all these
things they shall be brought into judgment and stand self-convicted and self-condemned at the bar of their own conscience,
filled with unavailing regrets and crying, 'Woe unto us that we
never gave heed nor opened our hearts whilst in the world for
the entrance and reception of truth, woe unto us!' Note, that for

their good deeds, the Holy One will grant unto the upright and unselfish, abundance of light and enjoyment in the region on high which eye hath not seen, nor hath it entered into the heart to conceive of (Is. LXIV. 3), the celestial sphere of the Beatific Vision. Happy the lot of the just and pure in both worlds, for of them scripture affirms, the righteous, the unselfish shall inherit the earth forever; (Is. LX. 21), they shall praise thy name, and the upright shall dwell in thy presence (Ps. CXL. 12). Blessed be the Divine Being forevermore, Amen and Amen."

It is written, "These are the generations of Noah" (Gen. vi. 9). The students of Rabbi Simeon were assembled together and meditating upon the secret doctrine. Then spoke Rabbi Hiya and said: "Thy people also shall be all righteous, they shall inherit the land forever, the branch of my planting, the work of my hands, that I may be glorified" (Is. lx. 21). Blessed is Israel who delights in the study of the secret doctrine, the knowledge of the mysteries of which qualifies them to live the higher life of the world to come. Observe that every Israelite or initiate in the mysteries never fails to attain unto it, inasmuch as he obeys the good law of the universe, and therefore it is written of him, "Had I not made my covenant with day and night, I should not have prescribed the laws that govern the heavens and the earth" (Jer. xxxiii. 25). True Israelites are moreover called zaddikim (righteous) on account of the purity of their lives, symbolized and distinguished by the mark or sign of the covenant (circumcision). Whence do we infer this fact? From the example of Joseph who was termed a Zaddik or just one, because of his purity of life and observance of the covenant.

Said Rabbi Eleazer: "Wherever in scripture the word 'Aleh' (these) occurs there is an antithesis of some kind between what precedes and what follows it. For instance, in (Gen. ii. 10) it is said, 'and a river went out of Eden to water the garden and from thence it was parted and became into four heads.' This said river that went out of Eden and entered into paradise, brought into it waters of celestial origin which gave life to the plants and flowers which grew therein and which only ceased on the completion of creation when, as it is written, 'God rested from all his work that he created and made.' Herein consists the mystery of the word aleh, occurring in the verse, 'These are the generations of Noah,' marking an antithesis between the generation of Noah and those preceding him, namely, the generations of Adam, or in other words, comes between the manifestation and development of life on the celestial and earthly planes of existence. Noah symbolized humanity beginning its earth career and for this reason is said to be 'aish ha-adamah,' the earthly man (Gen. ix., 20). The biblical account of Noah and the deluge contains a deep mystery that explains why it was necessary that Noah should enter the ark. It was in order to keep seed (human race) alive upon the face of all the earth (Gen. vii., 3). If so, of what then was the ark a symbol? The ark of the covenant (the good law) by which celestial or Adamic humanity was kept and preserved and without which it could not have entered upon its mundane career of existence and progression; that is, without the continuance of the good law in the world, the higher self could not have operated in the progressive development of the lower self, which therefore would have perished and reverted back to its pre-evolutionary or elemental state. Ere present humanity began evoluting on the earth, the Holy One entered into a covenant with the Higher Self, as it is written, 'But with thee I will establish my covenant and thou shalt come into the ark' (Gen. vii., 8). Scripture states that Noah was a just man (Gen. vi., 9) because a type of the ideal man Adam Kadmon, who is described as 'the righteous or just,' and also the foundation of the world (Prov. x. ,25). Both alike have the same appellation of *'just,'* the one in the celestial world, the other in the terrestrial world. This occult mystery is contained in the words 'Noah walked with Alhim' (Gen. vi., 8); that is to say, that Noah and Alhim were never disjoined or separated, one being the reflection of the other on the earth plane, and therefore it is written, 'Noah found grace in the eyes of the Lord' (Gen. vi., 8). Noah, moreover, is said to have been 'a just man and perfect in his generations' (bedorothav). The word 'perfect' (thamin) here denotes that he was born circumcised, and was also the source of perfection not only to his generation but also to his future posterity. This being so, it appears that Noah from the time of creation was predestined to enter and be incorporated within the ark, and also that previous to this event, humanity was not in a perfect state or condition, and only after his abode in the ark is it written, 'and of them was the earth overspread' (Gen. ix., 19). The word 'overspread' (naphzali) here has the same meaning 'ipared' (divided itself), as in Gen. ii., 10 'and a river went out of Eden to water the garden and from thence it was parted, that is, became divided into four heads.' In the work of creation it was at the moment of this dividing that the fertilizing and fructifying principle from on high entered into the world and made the earth fruitful as it does on the celestial plane, and therefore scripture states that 'aleh,' this principle of life, descended into Noah in order that through him the human race might appear and be perpetuated on the earth plane."

After Rabbi Eleazar had ceased speaking, Rabbi Abba went and embraced him, saying: "Oh lion! that breaketh rocks and dasheth them to pieces. Truly hast thou exposited the occult signification of the ark."

Rabbi Eleazar, continuing his discourse, said furthermore: "It is written, 'And he called his name Noah, saying this shalt comfort us concerning the work and toil of our hands' (Gen. v., 29). Here the word 'ath' is found before 'shemo' (his name). That is not so in the words 'And he called him Jacob.' What is the reason of this commission? Noah and Jacob symbolize two different divine principles of operation. Thus in vision Isaiah says, 'I saw the (ath) Lord' (Is. vi., 1), the prophet using 'ath' to intimate that he beheld both the Schekina and the Lord together. So is it also found with the name of Noah, teaching us that he was named by the Holy One and Schekina together, whilst Jacob, another patriarch symbolizing a lower state of existence, received his name from the Holy One only."

"These are the generations of Noah," said Rabbi Jehuda, 'A good man is gracious and lendeth (to the poor); he will guide his affairs with prudence' (Ps. cxii., 5). The term 'good man' designates the Holy One, and therefore is it written, 'The Lord is good to all (Ps. cxlv., 9). 'The Lord is a man of war,' for he alone giveth light and nourishment to this lower world and guideth it with judgment, as it is said, 'Righteousness and equity are the foundation of thy throne' (Ps. lxxxix., 14). Furthermore, the Just One or the ideal man is also designated as 'a good man,' and so it is written, 'Say unto the Just One that he is good, for he shall gather the fruit of his labors' (Is. iii., 10)."

Said Rabbi Jose: "This verse refers to Noah, as it is expressly said of him 'Noah was a just man.'"

Said Rabbi Isaac: "I think the words are an eulogy of the Sabbath, in the honor of which the Psalmist begins his praise of it by the word 'good.' It is good to praise the Lord (Ps. xciii., 2)."

To be continued.

MOMENTS WITH FRIENDS.

"Is it possible to develop a new species of vegetable, fruit or plant, totally different and distinct from any other known species? If so, how is it done?"

It is possible. One who has achieved in that line a most remarkable and widely known success is Luther Burbank of Santa Rosa, in California. Mr. Burbank has not yet, as far as we know, developed a wholly different and new species, but there is nothing to prevent him from so doing if he continues with his work. Up to the present time, so far as we are aware, his efforts have been directed to the crossing of certain varieties of fruits and plants, producing not a totally different species, but one having the characteristics of both or of one of the two or more varieties used in developing the new growth. Many accounts have been published of Mr. Burbank's work, though it is quite likely that he has not told all he knows and all he does, to achieve the success which is his. He has rendered inestimable service to man: he has taken some hitherto useless and objectionable growths and developed them into useful shrubs, wholesome foods or beautiful flowers.

It is possible to develop any vegetable, plant, fruit, or flower, of which the mind can conceive. The first thing necessary to develop a new species is: to conceive it. If a mind cannot conceive a new species, that mind cannot develop one, though he may by observation and application produce new varieties of old species. One who desires to invent a new species must ponder well on the genus of the species which he would have and then must brood intently and confidently over it. If he has confidence and will use his mind industriously and will not let his thought wander on other types nor indulge in idle fancies, but will think and brood on the species which he would have, then, in the course of time, he will conceive the thought which will show him the type he has so desired. This is the first proof of his success, but it is not enough. He must continue to brood over the thought which he has conceived and think patiently of that particular thought without wandering to others. As he continues to think, the thought will become clearer and the means by which the new species may be brought into the world will be made plain. In the meantime, he should set himself to work with those species which are nearest the one which he has in mind; to feel in them; to know the different movements and to be in sympathy with and impress the sap of the plant running through its arteries and veins, to feel its likes and to supply them, to cross the plants which he has selected and then to think his species into the crossing, to feel it develop from the two varieties he has chosen, and to give it physical form. He should not, and he will not, if he has gone thus far, be discouraged if he does not see at once his new species as the product. He should try and try again and as he continues to try he will in time rejoice to see the new species coming into being, as it will surely do if he does his part.

One who would bring a new species into being need know little of botany when he first begins, but he should acquaint himself with all he can learn of this work. All growing things have feeling and man must feel with them and love them, if he would know their ways. If he would have the best there is in them, he must give the best that he has to them. This rule holds good through all kingdoms.

A FRIEND.

THE
WORD

A MONTHLY MAGAZINE

Published and Edited by

H. W. PERCIVAL, 253 West 72d Street, New York City

London—Kegan Paul, Trench, Trubner & Co., 43 Gerrard Street

CONTENTS FOR JUNE, 1910

ADEPTS, MASTERS AND MAHATMAS, ...	Editorial	129
"SAVONAROLA" OF FLORENCE, . .	Dr. W. Williams	137
THE INNER LIFE AND THE TAO-TEH-KING,	C. H. A. Bjerregaard	152
THE CITY OF THE DEAD, ...	Samuel Neu	167
A DREAM OF ATLANTIS—THE LAND OF MU,	Alice Dixon Le Plongeon	178
THE SEPHER HA-ZOHAR—THE BOOK OF LIGHT,	Nurho de Manhar	187
MOMENTS WITH FRIENDS, ...	A Friend	191

Yearly Subscription - - - - - -	$4.00 or 16s.
Single Copies - - - - - - -	.35 or 1s. 6d.
Six Months' Subscription - - - - -	2.00 or 8s.
Three Months' Subscription - - - - -	1.00 or 4s.

Bound Volumes of The Word
Vols. I-X in Cloth and Half Morocco
Cloth, $21.00; Half Morocco, $26.00

The ten completed volumes of The Word are a valuable addition to any Library

They are a library in themselves

[Entered as Second-class Mail Matter, May 2, 1906, at the Post Office at New York, New York, under the Act of Congress of March 3, 1879.]

NEW

THE MAGICAL MESSAGE
according to
IÔANNÊS
commonly called
The Gospel according to [St] John

A verbatim translation from the Greek done in modern
English, with introductory essays and notes

BY

JAMES M. PRYSE

Price, Cloth, $2.00

The root of Mr. Pryse's claim is that the Gospel by John is altogether mystical in intention and that the mystical meanings of the words should never be distorted. According to Mr. Pryse the fourth gospel is much more than an account of the physical career of Jesus. He sees in it the history of the purification of the soul and so well does he buttress his claim that the best exponents of biblical criticism and Greek scholarship will be hard put to it to find anything to say in disproof.

The Theosophical Publishing Company of New York, 253 W 72d Street

---

A Book of practical Development
is
WILLIAM J. FLAGG'S

Yoga

Or Transformation.

It gives the Facts.

It shows the true Magic which underlies the Akkadian, Hindu, Taoist, Egyptian, Hebrew Greek and Christian Religions.

It gives a comparative statement of the various Religious Dogmas concerning the Soul and its Destiny.

It is a religious Education to read this Book carefully.

Price, cloth, $3.00.

Send for Descriptive Catalogue.

Charles G. Leland,

The well-known writer, has written a fascinating volume, called,

HAVE YOU A
Strong Will?

Or How to develop and strengthen the Will-Power, Memory, or any other Faculty or Attribute of Mind.

It is written, so all will grasp it.
Brilliant, so you will enjoy it.
Powerful, so you will not forget it.

It will help you to do what you want.

Price, cloth, $1.50.

Send for a booklet, "Books for the Higher Life."
It will tell you all about this Book.

The Theosophical Publishing Company of New York, 253 W. 72d Street

When ma has passed through mahat, ma will still be ma; but ma will be united with mahat, and be a mahat-ma. —The Zodiac.

THE WORD

Vol. 11   JUNE, 1910.   No. 3

Copyright, 1910, by H. W. PERCIVAL.

ADEPTS, MASTERS AND MAHATMAS.

(Continued from page 74.)

THE master enquires concerning the processes by which he has become what he is, and reviews the terrors which had beset him in the darkness in which he was immersed while a disciple. There is no pang of suffering now. Fear is gone. The darkness has no terrors for him, for darkness is subdued though not completely changed.

As the master reviews the transformations of his becoming, he perceives the thing which was the cause of all past hardships and heart stifling gloom, and above which he has risen, but from which he is not quite separated. That thing is the old elusive, formless darkness of desire, from which and out of which came myriad forms and formless dread. That formless thing is at last formed.

Here it lies now, a sphinx-like form asleep. It waits to be called to life by him if he will speak the word of life for it. It is the sphinx of the ages. It is like a half human beast which can fly; but now it rests. It is asleep. This is the thing which guards the Path and allows no one to pass who does not conquer it.

The sphinx calmly gazes on, while man dwells in the coolness of groves, while he throngs the market place, or makes his abode in pleasing pastures. However, to the explorer of life, to him to whom the world is a desert and who boldly tries to pass over its wastes into the beyond, to him the sphinx propounds her riddle, nature's riddle, which is the problem of time. Man answers it when he becomes immortal—an immortal man. He who cannot give answer, he who does not master desire, to him the sphinx is a monster, and it devours him. He who solves the problem, masters death, conquers time, subdues nature and he goes over her subdued body along his path.

This the master has done. He has outgrown physical life, though he remains still in it; he has conquered death, though he may still have to take on bodies which will die. He is a master of time, though in time, and he is a worker with its laws. The master sees that at the birth from his physical body, which was his ascension, he had in passing freed the sphinx body from his physical body, and to that which was formless he has given form; that in this form are represented the energies and capacities of all animal bodies in physical life. The sphinx is not physical. It has the strength and courage of the lion, and is animal; it has the freedom of the bird, and the intelligence of the human. It is the form in which all the senses are and in which they may be used in their fullness.

The master is in the physical and mental worlds, but not in the astral-desire world; he has silenced it by subduing the sphinx body. To live and act in the astral world also, he must call into action his sphinx body, his desire body, which now sleeps. He calls; he speaks the word of power. It arises from its rest and stands beside his physical body. It is in form and feature the same as his physical body. It is human in form, and of exceeding strength and beauty. It rises to the call of its master and answers. It is the adept body, an adept.

With the coming to life and into action of the adept body, the inner sense world, the astral world, is sensed and seen and known, as when returning to his physical body the master again knows the physical world. The adept body sees his physical body and may enter it. The master is through them both, but is not the form of either. The physical body is aware of the adept within, though it cannot see him. The adept is aware of the master who has called him into action and whom he obeys, but whom he cannot see. He knows his master as an ordinary man knows but cannot see his conscience. The master is with them both. He is the master in the three worlds. The physical body acts as a physical man in the physical, but it is ordered and directed by the adept who is now its ruler. The adept acts in the astral world, the inner world of the senses; but though having free action, he acts in accord with the master's will, because he feels the master's presence, is aware of his knowledge and power, and knows it is best to be guided by the mind of the master rather than by influence of his senses. The master acts in his own world, the mental world, which includes the astral and physical worlds.

To man acting in the physical world, it seems strange, if not impossible, that he should have three bodies or be developed into three bodies, which may act separately from and independent of each other. To man in his present state it is impossible; yet, as man, he has these three as principles or potential bodies which are now blended and undeveloped, and without either of which he would not be man. His physical body gives man a place in the physical world. His desire principle gives him force and action in the physical world, as man. His mind gives him the power of thought and reason. Each of these is distinct. When one leaves, the others are incapacitated. When all act together man is a power in the world. In his unborn state man can have neither his physical body, nor his desire, nor his mind, act intelligently and independently of the other two, and, because he does not know himself apart from his body and his desire, it seems strange that he, as a mind, could act independently and intelligently apart from his desire and his physical body.

As has been stated in the preceding articles, man may develop either his desire or his mind, so that either will act intelligently and act independently of his physical body. What is now the animal in man may be trained and developed by the mind who acts with and in it, so that it will become an entity independent of the physical body. The development or birth of the desires into a body in which the mind acts and serves, similarly as the mind of man now serves his physical body, is that of an adept. An adept does not usually destroy or leave his physical body; he uses it to act in the physical world, and though he may act independently of his physical body and move freely even when away from it, yet, it is his own form. But the desire body of man is merely a principle and is without form during his life.

It may seem strange that man's desire may be developed into form and given birth, and that that desire form may act separately from his physical body, and that similarly his mind may act as a distinct body independently of either. Yet it is no more strange than that a woman should give birth to a boy who is in appearance and tendencies different from her own nature and that of the father.

Flesh is born of flesh; desire is born of desire; thought is born of the mind; each body is born from its own nature. Birth comes after conception and maturity of body. That which the mind is able to conceive it is possible for it to become.

The physical body of man is like a man asleep. Desire does not act through it; mind does not act through it; it cannot act of itself. If a building is on fire and the fire scorches, the flesh does not feel it, but when the burning reaches the nerves it awakens the desire and calls it into action. Desire acting through the senses causes the physical body to beat down women and children, if they stand in its way of escape to a place of safety. But if, while on the way, the cry of a wife or child should reach into the heart and the man rushes to their rescue and risks his life to save them, this is the mental man, who overcomes the maddened desire and guides its power, so that through the physical body it lends its efforts at rescue. Each of the men is distinct from the other, yet all act together.

That an adept, being of the same form as his physical body should enter and act through his physical body is no more strange than that the white blood cells of the body should pass through other cells or the connective tissues of the body, yet they do. It is no more strange than that some semi-intelligence which is the control of a medium should act in the medium's body or emerge from it as a distinct and separate form; yet the truth of such occurrence has been attested by some able men of science.

Things which are strange should not be therefore ignored. Statements which are strange should be taken for what they are worth; it is not wise to speak of what one does not understand, as being ridiculous or impossible. It may be called ridiculous by one who has looked at it from all sides and without prejudice. He who discards as ridiculous an important statement without having used his reason is not making use of his prerogative as a man.

One who becomes a master does not bend the efforts of his mind to become an adept by developing his desire body. He turns all effort to the overcoming and subduing of his desire and developing as distinct the entity of his mind. It has been

ADEPTS, MASTERS AND MAHATMAS

explained that one who becomes a master does not first become an adept. The reason is that by becoming an adept the mind is bound more securely to the desires than while in the physical body; for the desire body, as an adept, acting in the inner and astral world of the senses has there more power over the mind than has the unformed desire body, while the mind of man acts in his body in the physical world. But when man has bent all efforts toward entering the mental world consciously and intelligently, and after he has so entered, he does by the power of mind that which is done by the aspirant to adeptship, by the power of desire. One who becomes a master becomes first aware of and lives consciously in the mental world, and then descends to the inner sense world of the adepts, which then has no power over him. The unborn mind of the adept has an unequal struggle with the fully developed desire body which is the adept, and so a man who becomes first an adept is not likely to become a master in that period of evolution.

This applies to the races of men as they now are. In earlier times and before desire had gained such ascendency over the minds of men, the natural way of development after incarnation into physical bodies was, that the desire body was developed and born through and from the physical body. Then the mind could, through its efforts at management of its desire body be born through its adept desire body, as that was born through its physical body. As the races of men developed further and the minds were more dominated by desire those who became adepts remained adepts and did not or could not become masters. With the birth of the Aryan race, the difficulties were increased. The Aryan race has desire as its dominant principle and force. This desire controls the mind which is developing through it.

Mind is the matter, the thing, the power, the principle, the entity, which is developing through all other races, from the earliest periods of the manifested worlds. Mind in its development, passes through the races, and is developed through the races.

The physical body is the fourth race, represented in the zodiac by libra ♎, sex, and the only race which is visible to man, though all the other preceeding races are present inside and about the physical. Desire is the fifth race, represented in the zodiac by the sign scorpio ♏, desire, which is striving to take on form through the physical. This fifth, desire race, should have been controlled by the mind in earlier periods and especially while operating those physical bodies usually called the Aryan race. But as the mind has not dominated and controlled desire and as it has and is becoming stronger, desire overcomes and attaches the mind to itself, so that it now has the ascendency. Therefore, the mind of a man who works for adeptship is held captive in the adept body, even as man's mind is now held captive in the prison house of his physical body. The fifth race, if developed naturally to its fulness, would be a race of adepts. The incarnate mind of man acting freely, and being fully developed, is or will be the sixth race, and is shown in the zodiac by the sign sagittary ♐, thought. The sixth race began in the middle of the fifth race as the fifth race began in the middle of the fourth race, and as the fourth race began in the middle of the third race.[1]

The fifth race is not fully developed, because desire acting through man is not developed. The only representatives of the fifth race are adepts, and they are not physical but are fully developed desire bodies. The sixth race will be thought bodies, not physical bodies nor desire (adept) bodies. The sixth race when fully developed will be a race of masters and that race is now represented by the masters. The master's work is to aid the incarnate minds of men to reach up by effort to their attainment in the mental world, which is their native world. The Ayran race, which is a physical race, has more than half run its course.

There is no exact line of demarcation where one race ends or another race begins, yet there are distinct markings according to the lives of men. Such markings are made by events in the lives of men and are at or about the time of such changes recorded in the writings as history or marked by records in stone.

The discovery of America and the landing of the Pilgrims marked the beginning of the formation of the sixth great race. Each great race develops on its own continent and spreads out into branches over all the world. The landing of the Pilgrims was a physical landing, but it marked the beginnings of a new era in the development of the mind. The characteristic and dominant feature of the sixth race, which began in America and is now developing in and through the United States, is thought. Thought characterizes the race which is forming in the United

---
[1]This figure will be shown in the July issue of THE WORD.

ADEPTS, MASTERS AND MAHATMAS 135

States, as desire is the dominant feature of the fifth race which was born in Asia, spread over the world and is wearing out in Europe.

The types of thought of the thought race will give different features and physical types to the fourth race bodies of the sixth or thought race, which will be as distinct in their way as a Mongolian body is from a Caucasian. The races have their seasons and run their courses as naturally and according to law, as one season is followed by another. But those among a race who so will, need not die with their race. A race decays, a race dies, because it does not attain its possibilities. Those of a race who will, by individual effort, may attain what would be possible to the race. Hence one may develop to be an adept because he has the force of the race behind him. One may become a master because he has the power of thought. Without desire, one could not be an adept; with it, he can. Without the power to think one cannot become a master; by thought, he can.

Because the mind is working in the desire world and with desires; because desire has dominance over mind; because the time has passed for man to try by natural development to become an adept, he should not try for adeptship first. Because man cannot likely grow out of adeptship and become a master; because the new race is one of thought; because he may with safety to himself and others develop by thought and because he can be of more service to himself and his race by attaining the possibilities of his race, it is better for him who seeks progress or attainment to place himself in thought with and seek entrance in the school of the masters, and not in the school of the adepts. To try for adeptship now, is like planting grain in late summer. It will take root and it will grow· but will not come to perfection and may be killed or stunted by the frosts. When planted at the proper season in the spring it develops naturally and will come to full growth. Desire acts on the mind as do the frosts on unripe grain, which they wither in its husk.

When man becomes a master he has passed through all that the adept passes through but not in the way in which the adept develops. The adept develops through his senses. The mind develops as master through his mind faculties. The senses are comprehended in the faculties. That which a man goes through in becoming an adept, and what he experiences in the sense world through his desires, the disciple of the masters passes through mentally, overcoming the desires by the mind. In the overcoming of the desires by the mind, desire is given form, because thought gives form to desire; desire must take form according to thought if the thought will not take form in desire. So that when the master by his faculties reviews the processes of his becoming from discipleship, he finds desire has taken form and that the form awaits his call to action.

To be continued.

THE PROPHETS OF INTELLECT.

But I cannot recite, even thus rudely, laws of the intellect, without remembering that lofty and sequestered class who have been its prophets and oracles, the high-priesthood of the pure reason, the *Trismegisti,* the expounders of the principles of thought from age to age. When at long intervals we turn over their abstruse pages, wonderful seems the calm and grand air of these few, these great spiritual lords who have walked in the world,—these of the old religion,—dwelling in a worshop which makes the sanctities of Christianity look *parvenues* and popular; for "persuasion is in soul, but necessity is in intellect." This band of grandees, Hermes, Heraclitus, Empedocles, Plato, Plotinus, Olympiodorus, Proclus, Synesius and the rest, have somewhat so vast in their logic, so primary in their thinking, that it seems antecedent to all the ordinary distinctions of rhetoric and literature, and to be at once poetry and music and dancing and astronomy and mathematics. I am present at the sowing of the seed of the world. With a geometry of sunbeams the soul lays the foundations of nature. The truth and grandeur of their thought is proved by its scope and applicability, for it commands the entire schedule and inventory of things for its illustration. But what marks its elevation and has even a cosmic look to us, is the innocent serenity with which these babe-like Jupiters sit in their clouds, and from age to age prattle to each other and to no contemporary. Well assured that their speech is intelligible and the most natural thing in the world, they add thesis to thesis, without a moment's heed of the universal astonishment of the human race below, who do not comprehend their plainest argument; nor do they ever relent so much as to insert a popular or explaining sentence, nor testify the least displeasure or petulance at the dullness of their amazed auditory. The angels are so enamored of the language that is spoken in heaven that they will not distort their lips with the hissing and unmusical dialects of men, but speak their own, whether there be any who understand it or not.—EMERSON, *"Intellect."*

"SAVONAROLA" OF FLORENCE.

THEOSOPHIST, REFORMER AND MARTYR. A PORTRAITURE OF SPIRITUAL GROWTH AND DEVELOPMENT.

BY DR. W. WILLIAMS.

(*Concluded from* page 115.)

FRA SYLVESTRO, THE MYSTIC; HIS CHARACTER, AND REMARKS ON MYSTICISM.

WE come now to the examination of Fra Sylvestro, of whom there exists a general consensus of opinion amongst historians and biographers that, after being subjected to torture and severe racking of his limbs, he succumbed at last and made a confession incriminating and most damaging to the credit and reputation of Savonarola. For this reason his name and memory have been handed down and referred to in terms of reproach and animadversion because of his perfidious betrayal of one for whom he had always professed respect and regarded as his master and teacher in the science of the higher and diviner life. Thus hostile criticism and severe judgments that have been passed upon Fra Sylvestro for conduct so treacherous and disloyal to Savonarola are chiefly, if not altogether, based upon the forged and therefore worthless depositions drawn up by his examiners and their servile tool and instrument, the miscreant Ser Ceccone. Assuming as real and genuine Sylvestro's avowals and admissions of the guilt and impostures of Savonarola his censors have regarded and alluded to him as a sickly, nervous and visionary creature and gaged him as a mystic weakling subject to strange attacks of epilepsy and ecstacy which he mistook for divine inspiration and spiritual illumination.

These misconceptions and detractions of Fra Sylvestro's true nature and character are due to the prevailing ignorance of the principles of Mysticism and also of the philosophy of the facts and laws relative to the divine life and its operations within the human soul, that need the application for their comprehension of a higher system of logic than what is taught in the schools and colleges of modern learning and science. The fact was that he was a mystic pure and simple. His was more a subjective than objective life and wholly given up and devoted to the contemplation and meditation upon those spirtual verities that exist outside and beyond the range and cognizance of ordinary human vision and consciousness. Though in the world he was not of the world and thus by the instincts of his nature and the law of his being was unqualified to descend into and play an active part in the arena of earth life and experience, or wage a successful struggle against its many and diverse antagonisms of ambition and strife for the acquisition of ephemeral objects as fame, wealth and position, the ordinary and great incentives to human action and endeavor. He was essentially a recluse delighting in the solitude of his cell in which, far from madding crowds and remote from the hurly-burly, the janglings and discords of human intercourse that would have jarred the chords of his sensitive nature and blunted its spiritual intuitions and receptivities, he acquired a knowledge of those invisible and noumenal forces that manifest themselves in daily life and experience under forms attractive or repellent. He had attained to that state of inner silence in which the mystic feels that a new life is being developed within him and a higher consciousness awakened that becomes as it were a torch that lights and a compass that directs him on his way; but owing to the blinding distractions of worldly objects as also to the passions and the insatiable pursuit after shadows, we fail to see the one and consult the other. He, however, who attains unto this exalted state of spiritual development and progress finds himself the recipient of lofty thoughts and sentiments and ennobling ideas and is able to observe the working and operation of the karmic law in the universe. To mystics, this earth life is an interlude during which it behooves them to gather all that is essential to progress in the life beyond. To them, charity and brotherhood are paramount virtues. So penetrated with these become they, as to forget self for others, considering no sacrifices too great in the attempt to do good. At times the stupendous differences they note prevailing between their former and present states of existence, the new light that now irradiates and lightens the path of their earthly pilgrimage and spiritual ascension, the new faculties with which they find themselves endowed, the immensity of the horizon opening before them, revealing a wide domain of exhaustless transcendental knowledge waiting for exploration, all these to them are indubitable evidences and sure tokens of the dawning of the beatific vision within them, so that what they speak and teach seems to be dictated by a voice from within; what they see is pointed out to them and, whilst regarding themselves as instruments of a superior intelligence, it is without any feeling of vanity arising therefrom. They love to reflect in silence, and when they address hearers and listeners it is only to give utterance to what will conduce and prove beneficial to their moral guidance and spiritual progress and happiness. Happy and blest are they who have attained unto the inner life, to the union of the higher and lower natures; for, as the Great Master has described and stated, they bear the kingdom of God, the true kingdom of heaven, within them.

Such an one was the greatly defamed and traduced Fra Sylvestro. Had he been as some have represented, surely he would not have enjoyed the confidence, the respect and affection both of Savonarola and Domenico and many other distinguished and influential citizens of Florence, noted for their learning and high social position, who chose him as their confessor and depositor of their secret thoughts, and found in him a true friend, a sympathetic counsellor and guide, who by his words and admonitions of light and wisdom led them safely and without stumbling along their life's intricate and mazy path. After the examination and torture of Fra Sylvestro had finished, falsified depositions as in the case of Savonarola and Domenico were drawn up and submitted to the signory, the examiners being asked no questions, and no inquiries raised as to their authenticity and the truthfulness of the statements they contained. There were other prisoners, all adherents of Savonarola, or members of San Marco, who, at first, persistently and courageously maintained their belief and confidence in his integrity, even after enduring the pain and torture of the pulley, to which they were subjected, but afterwards wavered and became filled with indignation when informed that their superior had denied the truth of his prophecies and visions and confessed himself an impostor. One of these, Roberto di Gagliano, wrote to the signory, "Having some learning as a theologian, I knew his doctrine to be sound and in no wise heretical. I could discern no fault in Fra Savonarola, but always beheld in him manifest signs of holiness, devotion, humility, goodly words, an excellent life and example, admirable conversation, sound, firm and solid doctrine, so that I would have testified to these things at the risk of my life. But since he has so subtly feigned and deceived, I return thanks to God and your excellencies for having opened our eyes." In thus writing also to the pope and endeavoring to excuse themselves for their implicit faith in their fallen and imprisoned superior, they unwittingly became the best witnesses in his defence. Not these friars but also men of far greater talents and position were imposed upon and deceived by the forged depositions of Savonarola. One of these wrote, "The fineness of his doctrine, the rectitude of his life and actions, the holiness of his manners, his devotion and the good results he achieved by purging Florence of immorality, usury and every species of vice, together with the different events that confirmed his predictions in a manner beyond all human power and imagination, that had he not made confession declaring himself, that his words were not inspired by God, we would never have been able to renounce our faith in him, for our belief in him was so firm that we were all most ready to go through the fire in support of his doctrine." In concluding their letter to the pope and entreating his holiness to absolve them from the ban of excommunication they had incurred as followers of Savonarola and for having used arms in his defence at the attack on the convent, they wrote, "May it be enough for your holiness to have seized the source and chief of all error. Let him suffer condign punishment if there be any meet for wicked men such as he, and let us strayed sheep return to the true shepherd."

The Pope Sends Commissioners to Florence.

It has been observed that the tender mercies of the wicked are cruel, and so both the signory and Alexander VI. proved themselves. As the latter read the letter of these simple-minded friars, unsuspicious and ignorant of the foul scheme and plot that were in operation, he gloated over the prospect of getting Savonarola at last into his hands and wreaking vengeance upon one whom he both hated and dreaded, and therefore continued insisting that Savonarola should be sent to Rome. To this request the signory were unwilling to accede, fearing lest their deceit and the illegality of their proceedings and ulterior project for the overthrow of the Republic would become too patent and glaring and cause a revulsion of public feeling that would result in their downfall and destruction and the escape of Savonarola out of their clutches. After a great amount of correspondence, a compact was made and an arrangement come to, that in consideration of granting Florence permission to tax church property for three years, the prisoners should be handed over to a commission appointed by his holiness to examine into the infamous crimes and iniquities of these three children of perdition. This agreement, whilst it effectually concealed their secret intentions to bring about the ruin and death of Savonarola, shifted the onus of condemning him and his two friends to death on to an ecclesiastical tribunal against whose decision, owing to the high status in the church its members occupied, there could not be raised the slightest objection or demur, neither the least suspicion entertained of their honesty and integrity.

The papal commissioners Torreano, general of the Dominican order and a Spaniard, Francesco Romolino Bishop of Ilerda, were immediately despatched to Florence and arrived there on May 19th, 1498. On their entry they were greeted by a crowd composed of the Arrabbiati and Compagnacci whose cry was "Death to the friar!" to which Romolino replied "that he should die without fail though he were another John the Baptist."

Savonarola and His Two Companions Sentenced to Death.

The pope's commissioners commenced their examination on the following day, attended by Ser Ceccone and others to help him in the falsification of the depositions. For the third time Savonarola was most cruelly and barbarously tortured and racked in order to force admissions of guilt from him. Again and again they jerked his frail form on the pulley, but to no effect. No incriminating words escaped his lips. Romolino becoming furious and enraged and despairing of extorting anything to warrant and justify their intended condemnation to death, began to threaten and menace his victim with further and greater tortures and ordered him to be placed again on the rack. The sufferer whilst being stripped and strapped again on the engine of torment, turned his gaze upon Romolino standing near, exclaimed: "If I must perforce suffer, I will suffer for the truth. All that I have taught and declared hath come to me from the Divine." Seeing all further attempts would prove vain and ineffectual in drawing out of Savonarola any confession of guilt and greatly exasperated at the failure to elicit any admission to justify his condemnation, the commissioners ordered him to appear before them on the following morning to receive their decision. "I am a prisoner of state," he exclaimed, "I will come if my jailers bring me." The pope's emissaries then consulted together. Their verdict needed no lengthy consideration as it had already been determined upon ere they entered Florence. To avoid any appearance of harshness and inclemency, Romolino whilst decreeing the death of Savonarola and Sylvestro, was inclined to spare the life of Domenico, but on some one remarking, that all Savonarola's teachings would be kept alive by this friar, he heartlessly exclaimed: "A vile friar more or less matters not, let him also die."

Thus ended the final trial and examination of Savonarola and his two companions. They had lived together in loving friendship and harmony of spirit each of them endowed with his peculiar gifts and attainments in the divine life; each of them working in his own sphere of labor having but one object, the revealing and making known the existence and reality of the higher and diviner life within the soul of man. Toilers together in this great work they had lived, and by the good law it was decreed they should not be separated and sundered in death but, bound by the threefold cord of faith, hope and charity, should pass the dark portal of death which to those who have found the Christ within them, become the *"Ianua Vitae,"* the gate of life, through which wends the Via Sacra leading into the domain of eternal light of which it is written, "There shall be no more pain nor suffering, for the former things are passed away." It is in apocalyptic language, "the Holy City, the New Jerusalem, that shall not pass away."

Savonarola's Last Interview With His Companions.

As soon as the ecclesiastical commission had given their sentence condemning the prisoners to be hanged and their bodies burned, the signory, to save appearances, summoned a public meeting of their partisans for the purpose of discussing the advisability and manner of executing it. Amongst the assembly packed with Arrabbiati was found only one individual who had the honesty and courage to raise his voice on behalf of Savonarola and plead for a mitigation of the iniquitous sentence passed upon him. "It is a grave crime," he said, "to put to death a man of such excellent qualities whose like was scarcely to be found in a hundred years. This man," he continued, "would not only succeed in restoring faith to the world, if it were extinct, but in diffusing the learning with which he is so rarely endowed. Hence I would advise you to keep him in prison if you choose, but preserve his life and grant him the use of writing materials, so that the world may not lose the fruits of his learning." This wise and humane suggestion was not entertained, as another pertinently said: "No one can count on future signories subject to be changed every two months. It is quite probable, Savonarola may be restored to liberty and again cause disturbance in the city. A dead enemy fights no more." These words deeply impressed the minds of the aiders and abettors in this wretched farce with a sense of their danger of incurring the punishment they had meted out to their innocent and guiltless prisoners. They had implicated themselves too deeply in intrigues with the pope to draw back from the execution of their premeditated design and from staining their hands with innocent blood by the commission of a most heinous and revolting crime. They therefore ratified the sentence of the papal commissioners and voted the death of Savonarola and his two faithful companions.

No time was lost in communicating the dread decree to the doomed ones, who listened to and received it with unexampled calmness, especially Domenico who, on learning the kind of death they were to suffer, begged to be burned alive that he might the more testify his attachment and fidelity to Savonarola and his teachings, and then wrote a farewell letter to the frati of San Domenico of Fresole, of which he was the prior, enjoining upon them to remain humble, united in charity and diligently occupied in religious exercises. "Let my body," he wrote, "be buried in some lonely spot without the church, in some corner near the door. Pray for me and I, being where I hope to be, will do as much for you. Have all the pamphlets of Savonarola in one cell collected and binding them together, place a copy in the library. Let another copy be kept to be read at the second table of the refectory. Let it be fastened thereto with a chain so that the lay brothers also may sometimes read it." Thus his chief thought as the sands of life were fast running out was for the honor and credit of his cherished master and the perpetuation of his teachings. The lives and actions of men like Domenico are tonic to the soul and refreshing to the heart and mind, giving rise to the assurance that the fellowship of kindred souls is no figment of fiction, but one of those basic facts in human nature that declare its divine origin and the rationale of its ulterior destiny paraphrased in the apostle's creed as "the communion of saints."

"Blest be the tie that binds all hearts
In bonds of friendly love!
The fellowship of kindred souls
Is like to that above."

When the death messengers deputed to inform Savonarola of his doom, entered his cell, they found him engaged in silent prayer and rapt meditation. He listened to his sentence unmoved and then continued his devotions. He had foreboded it and was ready to face his doom with that calmness and intrepidity of soul exhibited by the early martyrs of a church that by a strange reversal of fate had itself, from being persecuted become a merciless and barbarous and cruel persecutor and whose pope or spiritual head at the time was an incarnation of diabolical wickedness and crime unparalleled, and distinguished by the cunning and odious hypocrisy under the cloak of which he perpetrated them and accomplished his dreadful purpose. Shortly after Savonarola had been informed of his sentence, food was offered him but he declined it because, as he said, he wished to meet death with mind and soul ready and prepared to face it calmly. A member of a society, the Battuti, formed for visiting prisoners condemned to die and administer to them the consolations of religion in their last hours, now entered the cell and kindly inquired of Savonarola if he had any request to make, and tendered his good offices in obtaining it for him. On learning that he greatly wished to have a short interview with his two faithful friends, Domenico and Sylvestro, the Battuti promptly betook himself to the signory who, after some discussion, granted the request on being assured it was always an invariable custom to accede to the last wishes of the dying so that they need not be afraid of any extraordinary and unexpected event on the part of Savonarola. And thus the three friends met together for the last time in the hall of the great council and stood with clasped hands gazing upon the face of the master they loved so deeply and well, with faith unshaken and their love unabated. One thought only, one feeling of

"SAVONAROLA" OF FLORENCE

joy filled their souls, arising from the consciousness that after the endurance of the torturing pulley, the boot and rack, they could truly say, "We know in whom we have believed and are persuaded that he is able to keep that which we have committed unto him. We have fought the good fight and kept the faith."

SAVONAROLA'S LAST WORDS TO HIS COMPANIONS. HIS VISION ON THE NIGHT BEFORE EXECUTION.

The moments sped fast away and, addressing Domenico, Savonarola said: "I know you have asked to be cast alone into the fire, but I know also it is not well, since it is unmeet for us to choose what death we would die. How can we know whether we shall find strength to bear that to which we are condemned. This dependeth not upon ourselves but on the grace that shall be granted unto us of God." Then taking and clasping warmly the hand of Fra Sylvestro: "I know," he said, "you would like to protest your innocence in sight of the people. Abandon the idea and thus follow the example of the sufferer on Calvary's hill who refrained from declaring his innocence even on the cross." As he ceased speaking they both knelt before him and after receiving his blessing were led back to their separate cells to prepare themselves for death on the following morning. Wearied and overcome with bodily weakness, Savonarola sank on the floor, his head resting on the lap of his kindly disposed and sympathetic personal attendant. A few moments and his soul was in another world. A placid smile, an air of peaceful serenity crept over and suffused his wan and pallid countenance, as in vision he beheld himself ascending out of a huge dark valley that, like a Gehenna lighted with lurid flames, resounded with cries of hate and shouts of furious rage confused and mingled and confounded together like a wild chorus of maddened and infuriated wolves disappointed of their prey. But he heeded them not. His gaze was fixed and his course directed towards the opening of a vale in the distance, lighted and radiant with a sheen and splendor exceeding that of the rays of the rising sun. Reaching its entrance and whilst standing entranced with feelings and emotions of joy and delight that thrilled and pulsated through his whole soul, his ear caught the tones of a sylphlike voice, low yet sweet and gentle as those of an Eolian harp vibrating with the summer breeze. Turning, he beheld coming towards him a bright and glittering angel-like form of surpassing loveliness and beauty. It was the beloved of youthful and byegone days. A moment and he knelt before her and as he gazed into the limpid depths of eyes beaming with the light of an ineffable and inextinguishable love, again as she had once done in years long ago, she bent and kissed his throbbing brow and softly whispered: "To-morrow, oh Savonarola, claim thou my love! to-morrow! we meet never to be parted nor sundered again throughout time's countless ages." As the vision slowly dissolving faded away, the dreamer was awakened by the noises and hoarse voices of men engaged in erecting platforms and rearing the scaffold on which the three condemned ones were to take their exit out of earth life.

SAVONAROLA'S LAST MOMENTS AND MARTYRDOM AND LAST WORDS.

As the morning dawned and the rays of the rising sun beamed and shot above the horizon, they were allowed to meet again in order to receive the sacrament ere being led forth for execution. Savonalora officiated and as he raised on high the sacred host, his face and head again and for the last time, became irradiated with that strange and mystic light or luminosity, the cause and rationale of which are unknown and incomprehensible save and except to students of occult and spiritual science. "Oh thou Divine Being," he prayed, "I acknowledge thee to be the perfect, invisible Trinity, the Father, Son and Holy Spirit. I acknowledge thee, the Eternal Word, by whom all things were made and didst become incarnate in the virgin's womb and suffered the death of the cross. I pray thee for remission of my sins and implore thee to forgive them, likewise pardon for every offense or hurt brought on this city, and for every error of word, thought and deed I may have unwittingly committed." Having himself partaken of the communion and whilst administering it to his fellow suppliants kneeling before him, a holy peace entered into their souls. It was the peace of God that passeth all human understanding, that the world cannot give nor impart, nor can it take away from the enlightened and purified soul of man.

Scarcely had ended this last solemn ceremony when the civic guards appeared at the doorway to lead them to the place of execution. In the great piazza or public square, three platforms had been erected during the night and draped in black.

The one nearest the Hall of Justice was to be occupied by bishops, the central one by the pope's commissioners and attendants, whilst the other was allotted to the civil magistrates appointed by the signory for the carrying out of the sentence on the condemned. Again as at the ordeal by fire a few weeks before, an immense concourse of people had assembled in the vast open market place, in the middle of which was seen a scaffold, and at its further end a gibbet in form of a cross. Thousands of citizens and inhabitants of the suburbs and adjacent towns and villages had flocked in at early dawn, expecting that in some marvellous manner a miracle would be wrought of some kind, but what they could not tell. Every available inch of ground favorable for witnessing the dread scene was taken up; windows, house tops, palisades, parapets and towers and stories of buildings, all were packed and crowded by men and women, young and old, anxious to witness the ending of Savonarola's career, and all alike forgetting and unthinking of the benefits of liberty and freedom they were now enjoying and owed to his unselfish devotion to the welfare and happiness of Florence and who had rescued and raised her out of the depths of moral pollution and delivered her from the tyranny of the hypocritical Medici whose great ambition and policy were personal rule and self-aggrandizement. From slaves and parasites, he had converted her citizens into freemen and, breaking the power of faction, had given them a constitution that invested them with the right of self-government and of choosing and electing their own rulers and magistrates and also forgetting that many of them, now his foes and enemies but for his sense of humanity and clemency in securing the repeal of their sentence of banishment, would never have been allowed to return from exile, but have languished out their lives in foreign lands. Of all sins that of political ingratitude "hardens all within and petrifies the feeling."

A deathly silence pervaded the vast crowd, and in a moment all eyes were turned towards a narrow door of the Hall of Justice as the civic magistrates, the pope's commissioners and bishops were observed issuing forth and proceeding to their allotted platforms. Not a sound was heard nor a tongue moved as Savonarola, followed by Domenico and Sylvestro, appeared in view accompanied by a Dominican friar who commanded them to be stripped of their dark robes. On undergoing this indignity, Savonarola was greatly moved and exclaimed: "Holy gown! how dearly have I loved to wear thee. Thou wast granted me by God's grace, and I have ever kept thee unstained. Now I forsake thee not, but am bereft of thee." Reclothed, the condemned were led before the first platform occupied by bishops, the spokesman of whom was the Bishop of Vasona, who had formerly been a professed follower and friend of Savonarola. His duty was to read the sentence of priestly degradation. So overwhelmed with shame and confusion he became that he dared not look on the face of Savonarola, but with downcast looks ordered him and his fellow sufferers to be stripped of their robes. On taking the hand of his former friend and master, his form was seen to shake and tremble. His tongue faltered and for a moment he became as one struck dumb and unable to utter the formula of degradation he was appointed to pronounce. At last, recovering somewhat from his perturbation and bewilderment and forgetting the usual form of scission from the church militant and scarcely knowing what he said, he stammered forth: *"Separo te ab Ecclesia militante et triumphante."* (I cut thee off from the church militant and the church triumphant), which latter words were added without rule or authority. "Yes," Savonarola promptly replied, "from the church visible and militant, but from the church invisible and triumphant, No! that is not in your power to do."

They were the last words of Savonarola, uttered by him in public, and form no inappropriate finale of his life, career and mission, being the expression of a great truth: that no human soul can be precluded from the enjoyment of the divine life, either by pope or priest who imagine that in their hands are the keys to open or close the gates of heaven. That is beyond their fancied prerogative. Nothing can bar entry therein save and except a man's own self. It is the common heritage of every human soul that makes itself recipient of it by self-control and discipline of its natural and selfish instincts, by education of mind and heart to observe the good law and obey the dictates and admonitions of its higher, diviner self, by the influence and power of which it becomes daily strengthened, enlightened and purified and thus more and better qualified for ascension on to a higher plane of intellectual and spiritual thought and life.

After being unfrocked a second time and degraded, the doomed ones clad only in their vests and drawers· were led in front of the second platform occupied by the pope's commissioners and their retinue. Regarding them with stern and haughty mien, Romolino delivered a discourse, denouncing them in contemptuous terms as heretics, schismatics and despisers of the Holy See, and concluded by granting them absolution which though it might save their souls did not spare their lives and deliver them from death by the ghastly gibbet and the burning stake. Ere seating himself, he insultingly asked them whether they accepted of his hypocritical shriving; to which they gave no answer, but bowing in silence, were conducted before the Council of Eight or civil tribunal, who at once according to custom voted on the sentence of death which was as follows: "It is hereby decreed, after mature consideration of the depositions of the three friars and the atrocious crimes committed by them and therein laid bare and after considering the sentence pronounced by the papal commissioners who have now handed them over to the secular power to be punished, that each of them be hung from the gibbet and then burned so that their souls be entirely separated from their bodies."

This horrid judicial farce ended, Savonarola and his two companions were led up to the scaffold. The eyes of the vast multitude were turned towards them, bishops, commissioners, magistrates and citizens who stood in solemn silence regarding with bated breath the last act of the dread tragedy; their breasts throbbing with suppressed feelings and emotions they dared not and could not in that awful moment exhibit and express by voice or motion. As the doomed victims stood at the foot of the scaffold steps, the cynosure of all eyes, Savonarola appeared calm and unmoved; Sylvestro, with placid face upturned as though gazing on some heavenly object; whilst Domenico, fearless and joyous at the thought of dying along with the beloved master would fain have chanted forth the "Te deum" and only refrained from so doing by the entreaty of the Battuti whose duty it was to attend him up to the last moment of his life. "Sing it then with me," he said, "though it be in undertones." At its finish his last words were: Remember hereafter, that the predictions of Fra Savonarola will all be fulfilled and that we die innocent."

Sylvestro was the first called to mount the scaffold, but, ere the executioner after fixing the cord around his neck slung his body into mid air, he cried aloud, in the last words of the sufferer on Calvary: "*In manus tuas, Domine, commendo meam animam*" (into thy hands, thou Divine One, I commit my soul).

Domenico was the next to suffer and died as he had lived: to the last true and faithful, the bravest of the brave of his master's followers and adherents.

In silence the most intense and terrible, Savonarola mounted the fatal ladder. As he ascended its steps, a concealed and unknown friend standing near whispered a few words of strength and consolation, to whom he replied: "The Divine One alone can console men at their last hour." And now in presence of the executioner ready to receive him whose associates with torch in hand await his signal to fire the pile, Savonarola stands alone in the world, yet not alone, for as his gaze wandered over the vast crowd of upturned faces, it became fixed on high and in his eyes beamed forth a light that has never been seen on land or sea, for there invisible to mortal vision, he beheld, with palm of victory in hand a radiant and glittering form waiting to welcome him and lead him to her home of light and beauty, and there also on the lofty spheres on high surrounded by thousands upon thousands of angelic beings and the forms of seers and prophets, of apostles and teachers and martyrs in all ages, gathered together from out of all nations, stood the Great Master himself regarding and looking down upon him and speaking in tones and with a look of inexpressible love, "Well done, good and faithful servant, in as much as thou hast confessed me before men, so will I also confess thee before my Father in heaven and the holy angels."

A moment and the form of Savonarola dangled suspended over the devouring flames of the fiery stake. At that very instant a gust of wind blew the flames aside and a mighty shout burst forth from the vast multitude crying out, a miracle! a miracle! which was suddenly brushed into awful silence as the expiring form of Savonarola was seen raising its right hand as in the act of bestowing a final benediction, a last adieu. Thus finished and ended the tragedy of Savonarola's noble life and mission as a prophet of the Higher Life and Reformer of Florence whom he loved so deeply and well—giving up for her welfare and happiness all that he could give, and sacrificing everything to procure for her liberty and freedom, received from her as his guerdon a cruel martyrdom.

As the vast multitudes of citizens wended their way in silence homewards, a terrible feeling of apprehension of coming evil, a dread misgiving arose within them, a sense of blood-guiltiness they could not rid themselves of, seized hold of them, and at the bar of their own conscience convicted them as perpetrators of a most heinous and barbarous crime, unparalleled in the annals of history for its ingratitude and cruelty which though after the lapse of a few years they sought and endeavored to expiate by posthumous honor, in adopting again the constitution he had framed and following the wise counsels he gave them, they found out when too late, that no second Savonarola appeared and came forth to save them again from political ruin and deliver them from the rule and oppression of ambitious despots and selfish unprincipled tyrants. In slaying her prophet, priest and uncrowned king, Florence forfeited her liberty and freedom, and the city of the Lilies remains stained with the blood of the innocent.

During his lifetime and at the close of his wonderful career, Savonarola wrought no miracles either to enhance his prestige or save himself from a cruel death. Like John the Baptist, he was content to be a witness of the light of the divine life within the soul of man, in a darkened age when knowledge and experience of it as a fact and great reality had almost if not wholly become extinct in the church and the world. Political hatred and papal rancor concurred and plotted to undo and nullify his work as the reformer of Florence, but could not impair and annul his other greater mission as the exponent and revealer to humanity of the existence of the Higher Life. Henceforth he belongs not to Florence but to the human race through all ages of its existence on the earth plane and, if the value of a life be gaged not by length and number of years but by actions and deeds, then may it be truly said of Savonarola, "He lived not in vain and dying, left the world better than he found it."

Dante ennobled Florence by birth and poesy; Raffael and Fra Angelico painted and adorned her with frescoes of ethereal and almost celestial beauty; Michael Angelo and others embellished and decorated her with magnificent sculpture and works of art; but Savonarola made her glorious with the light of the Divine life in her midst. What they by pen, by chisel and brush, endeavored to embody in words and marble or depict on canvas and wall, he, by thoughts that breathed and words that burned, made actual and real and living in the soul of Florence; so that as on the day of the crucifixion, the dead came forth out of their graves and, bursting and casting aside their cerements of selfishness and swathes of worldly lust and desire, appeared and entered into the holy city. This was the great miracle performed by Savonarola, and this was the great object of his mission as an apostle and evangelist of the new and Higher Life, of which it is written for the ages to come:

And the Life was the Light of Men.

THE END.

THE INNER LIFE AND THE TAO-TEH-KING.

XIII.

By C. H. A. Bjerregaard.

YOU remember that "non-action" does not mean inactivity; doing nothing and expecting stewed chickens to come in through the windows, ready for the table. Wu Wei or "non-action" means having nothing to do with the incidental, the trivial, the "passing show," the phenomenal, and devoting oneself exclusively and with energy to the essential and the real. Wu Wei is simply the Chinese name from the Tao-Teh-King for the idea and teaching found among all kinds of mystics, namely, that the earthly, the temporal, is a prison, a chain, a hindrance and an obstruction on the Path, and must therefore be let alone and shunned.

How shall a Taoist attain results or do his duty to the world in which he lives? The doctrine of Wu Wei does not allow the use of means or efforts. Taoism teaches distinctly "avoid activity," "dispense with the use of means" and Tao, as you read in another chapter, is called "nameless simplicity"; it teaches:

> "Simplicity without a name
> Is free from all external aim.
> With no desire, at rest and still,
> All things go right, as of their own will."

And why should they not? The world is not ours! Who set us to manage the affairs of the universe? Surely nobody! We cannot manage our own affairs, how much less those of the world's!

The sage "takes no action" (XXIX.) because all efforts with a personal purpose are sure to fail. It is said (XXIX.) that "things" are spirit-like and cannot be got by active doing. He who would so win them, destroys them. He who would hold them in his grasp, loses them." That is the way a Taoist does his duty and avoids cutting his hands in the world's machinery. Things are "spirit-like," that is, they slip out of our hands like elastic rubber bands and spring back with pain.

Things, so called, are not so real as many of us think. They are merely centers of force and that is the reason we cannot "get hold of them by active doings." Things, so called, are time and space combinations of activities beyond our reach. We may and we do use these combinations, but they are only, so to say, loaned us; they are not subject to us.

We get things worth having without excessive efforts. Have you not observed sometimes that that which you got and which was of any real value to you came like a gift, not by an effort of yours? You called it luck, good luck, and let it pass. Was that quite right? You may have thought it was good karma. Was that enough? You may have said "God is good"; "this was providential." Was that a right attitude? Well, you may have said or thought thus, but you ought also to have withdrawn to solitude and silence and studied the law, which teaches that we get things worth having without efforts, by Wu Wei, and because things have their own way without regard to us; they crush us if we are in the way; they lift us if we are obedient. We live in a house not ours. We are tenants merely. If we adapt ourselves to the laws of this cosmic house, we call the world, it will be well with us. If we disobey, the landlord dispossesses us. Retirement will reveal many mysteries of Wu Wei, of "non-action," and you cannot afford to ignore that law. By "non-action" or by Wu Wei, all good things are gotten and brought about. Strange as it seems to all of us, till we have experienced the fact, it is nevertheless the moral law of our lives. And it ought not be hard to learn to obey.

This is the way we should live according to the Tao-Teh King, (LXIII.), "This is the way of Tao and Teh (or the true path) to act without thinking of acting; to conduct affairs without feeling the trouble of them; to taste without discerning any flavor; to consider the small as great and the few as many and to recompense injury with love and kindness." If we act that way, we are in Teh and follow Wu Wei. This for the present is enough about Wu Wei in the individual life. Now, about Wu Wei in the public life, in the state, in politics.

I shall now quote Laotzse and Kwangtzse on the paradisiacal state of early China, a state that was a result of Wu Wei, and, that you may be able to get some chronological idea of the time when that state existed, I will tell you what European scholars have found out regarding early Chinese chronology and history.

Chinese history, before 771 B. C, or up to about 150 years before Laotzse, is nothing but a record of internal feuds between many and various states or settlements, and, toward the end of that period, a record of striving for the establishment of an empire, which is finally established in 771 B. C. The next period of history, from 771 B. C. to 221 B. C., is a period of struggle for the total extinction of feudal power, which is finally extinguished totally in 221 B. C. by the first emperor of Tsin. Before all this lies a period of "paradise," if I may so call it, and most of that which Laotzse says about the "people of ancient days," relates to that period which, generally speaking, I should say was at least three to four thousand years ago, counting back from to-day.

We are told in the Tao-Teh-King that Tao, as Teh, ruled the world at first and at that time the world was in a paradisiacal state. Taoists do not tell us how long it lasted, but Laotzse says (XVIII.), it lasted till "Tao ceased to be observed," and "Kwang-tzse explains what this means. He calls that age "the age of Perfect Virtue" or "the age of Teh" and describes it as follows: "In that age, they attached no value to knowledge and did not employ men of action (soldiers or police). Superiors were no more than the higher branches of a tree; and the people lived freely in the Open. They were upright and correct, without knowing that to be so was to be righteous; they loved one another, without knowing that to be real goodness; they were honest, without knowing that to be loyalty; they fulfilled their engagements, without knowing that to do so, was to act in good faith; in their daily life they employed the services of one another without thinking that they were conferring or receiving gifts. Because they lived that way we cannot find any trace of their actions and no records of their affairs and that is all in their favor and to their glory." These people lived in Wu Wei and were full of Teh. Let me call them simple-minded in the best sense of that phrase. Kwang-tzse gives several other descriptions of "the age of perfect virtue," but this will be sufficient for the present. I will only mention that he tells us that people in those days did not form themselves into castes and classes of social distinctions; they were all alike and lived according to nature; they were, as he said, "on terms of equality with all creatures, as forming one family." Surely we are far remote from any such state of nature to-day!

Let me warn you! you must not take this description to

mean that the early Chinese were savages, as some scientists and sociologists will explain that state to be. These people were far from savagery, if ever their ancestors had been savages. They were tillers of the soil and knew the loom. Such people are not savages. The loom is sufficient evidence that they were not savages. Savages do not know the loom and cannot weave. They were simple. Theirs was the simple life; they did not talk it, they lived it.

The reason why "the simple life" was lost, says Kwang-tzse, as you heard, was that the people began to aim at "knowledge" rather than life, and at that which later was called "culture." (On this subject, of culture as a hindrance to spiritual life, I have already spoken in an earlier chapter.)

Laotzse and Kwang-tzse again and again repeat that the sage (I.) constantly tries to keep the people without "knowledge" and without desire, and, where there are those who have "knowledge," to keep them from acting their own will, and where there are those who have will, to weaken it. In chapter VII. Laotzse points to Heaven and Earth as patterns for the sage. They have no personal or private ends; they do not seek "knowledge" or cultivate desires. Nature in all movements is placid and contented (like water) and not self-conscious. Of this I have also spoken in an earlier chapter.

Kwang-tzse tells a grim story of how men came to lose themselves in culture, so called: "The ruler of the southern ocean was named "The Hasty" and he of the northern "Heedless." The ruler of the center was named "Chaos." "Heedless" and "Hasty" met often with "Chaos" and were treated well. They consulted together how they might repay his kindness and said: "Men have all seven orifices for purposes of the senses, such as seeing, hearing, but this poor ruler has none. Let us try and make them for him. Accordingly they cut one orifice in him every day and at the end of the seven days Chaos died." Fitting Chaos with senses and thereby with desires, they killed him.

About the government by the sage, the Tao-Teh-King (III.), says that it consists in "emptying the heart of the people," that is, of desires, and in "weakening the will of the people," that is, "the will to live," Tanha. By such "non-action nothing is ungoverned," and why? Because Tao and Teh then govern. It is the interference of the governor, be he imperial or democratic, in the affairs that hinders the actions of Tao and Teh. And this has been the general rule, for the better and the worse in the Chinese empire and elsewhere.

And so it is to-day. And Laotzse's advice (XIX.) is a good one to-day. It was: "Abandon your saintliness (that is a hint to preachers); put away your cleverness (that is a hint to so-called statesmen), and the people would be benefitted a hundredfold. Abandon your charity and put away your righteousness and people would become more brotherly and more kind; put away your riches and scheming and there will be no robbers or frauds (that is a hint to those who establish charities, like universities, hospitals, museums, after they have amassed enormous wealth by robbery of all kinds.)" Culture is insufficient for the highest purpose:

"Hold fast to that which will endure,
Show thyself simple; preserve thee pure;
Thine own keep small; thy desires poor."

If any of you would object and say that no progress is possible under such conditions, I am ready to answer you; first by the question: How do you know? Has it ever been tried? And next I will declare that that which we call "progress" is a sad caricature of that which your own ideas demand.

Thus far I have been speaking more or less abstractly. I must therefore bring this subject of Wu Wei or "non-action" down on a practical plane, down to our level. And I can do it by employing four forms of Tao, of which Laotzse speaks. The first form is called humility. How does the Tao-Teh-King itself explain humility? Here is the answer (LXI.), "When a great kingdom takes a lowly position, it becomes the place of concourse for the world; it is the wife of the world. The wife by quietness invariably conquers the man. And since quietness is also lowliness, therefore a great kingdom by lowliness towards a small kingdom, may take that small kingdom. And a small kingdom, by lowliness towards a small kingdom, may take that small kingdom. And a small kingdom, by lowliness towards a great kingdom may take that great kingdom. So that either the one stoops to conquer, or the other is low and conquers. If the great kingdom only desires to attach to itself and nourish (that is, to benefit), others, then the small kingdom will only wish to enter its service. But, in order that both may have their wish· the great should be lowly."

In the same vein it is said (XXXIX.) "princes and kings speak of themselves as orphans, lonely men and wheelless carts."

(2) In the 67th chapter Laotzse associates with humility what he calls his three "precious things or jewels," these are: gentleness, economy, and shrinking from taking precedence of others. "With gentleness," he says, "I can be bold; with economy I can be liberal; shrinking from taking precedence of others, I become a vessel of the highest honor."

These three, gentleness, economy and shrinking from taking precedence of others, together with humility, are the four forms of Tao or rather of Teh, which make Wu Wei possible for us in daily life. We are only too apt to say that the bad succeed in this world and that the good go down. I question the truth of the assertion. Look closely and you shall find as I have found, that it is not so. There is justice everywhere; karma rules.

To understand fully how Wu Wei or the principle of non-action can work as a principle in state government, it is necessary that I should explain the fundamentals of the Chinese state organism, which is so different from ours.

The life of Nature-peoples, as I call them, or of people who "live according to Nature," as we say popularly, is like that of a child.

I will take as an example a child four or five years old. How does it live? Does it know that it lives? Can it have any consciousness or reflective thought about its own existence? No! none! The moment it has reflective consciousness of itself it is no more a child.

Excepting the important fact, that the child lives outside its mother, and, that of course is most important, it is after all still so much dependent upon its mother that it can be said, that it is still in the womb, or in the mother's environment, and bound so closely that it depends upon her altogether. In the main it is merely a hereditary expression of the race, family or society, in which it lives. The child lives in generals, not in particulars, in Wu Wei, not in self-assertion.

The child does not live its own life, strictly speaking. The mother lives for it, thinks for it, plans for it, feeds it, clothes it. The child lives according to nature, at least in normal cases. It is not concerned in any way with the problems which it meets later in life. It does not even know that they exist, and could not be made to understand them if they were presented. The child may say "I" about itself and it may more or less selfishly assert itself in cries and volitions and be naughty, but it does not know what it is to be naughty except by being told, nor has it any shame, gratitude or any so called moral sense, except by drill. The child has neither intellectual nor moral pains or joys. It has no aesthetic feelings for the beautiful either. But the child is imitative. Imitation is the most characteristic thing about it and has been so since the second half of its first year of existence, and, the workings of imitation show the presence of will and becomes the beginning of learning and of individual development.

But if the child does not possess these ideas, it normally has all the joy and pains that come from the play of impulse and from feeding, sleeping and growing, including the pains that come naturally from teething and the like of children's troubles. Its little imagination entertains itself when the child hears stories told. And the child is a complex thing of personal pride, habits and self-consciousness. Spontaneously and without duplicity, formality or reserve, its mental life comes out in action. It has no prejudice and conventionality till these two are implanted by social formalities or by the parent's vanity.

In these, the positive sides of its life, the child is just as dependent as it is in the negative described before.

Under both conditions it can be said that the child cares for nothing; it takes life as it comes. The child born among poor people is no worse off for the moment than that born among the rich. Neither of them know what riches or poverty are.

The child has possibilities for growth, for intellect, for spiritual sense, but it is practically an animal in its life. The difference lies in the possibilities. The child is a possible human being, but no real one yet.

This criticism is by no means unfavorable to the child. On the contrary. For good and for bad the child is a dependent creature as I have described. It lives in generals, not in particulars; in Wu Wei, not in self-assertions. As it is, we say correctly that the child lives according to nature.

Hear how an old Tao-ist talks about a life according to nature. Huai-nan-tzu said:

"What is it that we mean when we talk about the natural or inherent? It is that which is homogeneous, pure, simple, undefiled, unvarnished, upright, luminous and immaculate, and which has never undergone any mixture or adulteration from the beginning. And what is the human or artificial? It is that which has been adulterated with shrewdness, crookedness, dexterity, hypocrisy and deceit; that which bends itself into compliance with the world, and defers to the customs of the age. For instance, the ox has horns and a divided hoof, while the horse has a dishevelled mane and a complete foot; this is the heavenly or natural. But if you put a bit into the horse's mouth and pierce the nose of the ox, this is human or artificial.''

The following is in the same vein: "If Nature has given you black hair, don't try to dye it yellow; if you have a sallow or pale complexion, don't daub it with pink paint; if your waist measures five and twenty inches around, don't try to squeeze it into eighteen. All such attempts are violations of Nature, and are sure to bring their own punishment along with them."

As you see, those old people knew perfectly well what it is to be natural. The principle of naturalness is the principle of the child's life and this principle may be attained by Wu Wei.

Now, all this about the child applies to peoples. It is for that reason that I have entered upon so many details. It applies directly to the conditions of Chinese life in which the Tao-Teh-King plays such an important part.

I must now describe the Chinese life and let me say to you that neither this description nor the one of the child is merely for your entertainment. The Chinese life of which you now shall hear, and, that of the child of which you just heard, are looking glasses that faithfully reflect conditions in which you and I now are, or, which you and I have just left, or are about leaving. Bear in mind that Tao and the early followers of Laotzse are not included among the Chinese I describe, nor is the village life as described in the Tao-Teh-King to be included.

The Chinese is an old man still in the cradle. When I say that, I have really given his characteristic in a nutshell. He is old; a very, very old race; he seems to be a remnant of prehistoric times; but he is still in the cradle, that is, he is still a child as far as historic life is concerned; just such a child as I have described. He is still living "according to nature." But as he has not passed through the evolution of mind and regeneration of spirit, he is still in the cradle, or nature's womb.

In this respect he is like a boy that never becomes a man. Go to China and you shall see that people of all ages play children's games, knowing nothing higher; that state officials are spanked, as are children where spanking is the custom. You shall find them so naïve that you cannot understand them, even when you know their language; exactly as it is with the true child. Read their books and you shall see that their writings are merely aphorisms and totally lack rational connection of sentences, and, that is because the Chinese mind lacks perspective. How funny a child's letter is! How funny a Chinese painting without perspective! You shall also notice that Chinese writings are mostly collections of traditions and lack the incentives to actions now or in the future. They live in the past. That, too, is the child.

In China you will see that agriculture is a religious and devotional cult. By toil, not by psalm singing or flattery they worship Mother Nature. Labor is to a Chinese a religious act. Nature is to him, as it is to other primitive people, the Mother. They kneel down and kiss the earth. Our farmers think only of crops, and they spread manures, plow and harrow for self-interest, not on account of any ideas of sacrifice, offerings, or like cults. The Chinaman's offering is work, hard labor.

The Chinese mind is natural history rather than psychology. It resembles the child described. Our education aims at new developments, but the Chinese object is preservation of results, reverence for tradition; quickening of memory rather than thinking. He imitates and does not care to create anything new.

His art is craft, artifice, and his language is monosyllabic, totally without grammatical reflective forms. What we do by grammatical forms, such as tense, or case, he does by modulation of voice. You will remember the curious mistakes of missionaries, which I mentioned in a former chapter, all caused by false intonation.

His music contains no inner note. It is merely sounds in succession, noise. His village life is merely an extension of a number of families living in one place and with a so-called governor appointed over them by the emperor. Somewhat like our territories; patriarchal government we call it in history. City life as we know it in theory is totally unknown. Where it has been attempted under foreign influence it even beats the outcast life of such places as London, New York, or Yokahama, in degradation and depravity, as might be expected. I need mention only Shanghai as an example.

Religion as a transcendental longing and spiritual regeneration is as incomprehensible to the Chinese as it is to the child. He knows only this life and thinks his departed ancestors live in the astral spheres, and he fears them. You should remember that this does not apply to Tao-ists.

We are able to make a tolerably clear picture of the state of things in the five centuries from 771 to 220 B. C. I shall speak of some of the points that relate to my subject.

Religion in a Western sense did not exist; even the word did not exist. Neither did notions or words for church or temple or priestly caste exist. "Gods" were known and offenses against "gods" were defined, but people had not yet sunk down to too much belief in "gods," and extravagant belief was called superstition. You see then that some purity or originality still existed. "Sin" meant no offense against a god, but an infraction of nature's general laws, such as these laws were defined by imperial command or by vassal princes delegated to define them. When the emperor defined these laws he was called "son of heaven."

Prayer was common enough. Here is an illustration. When the Chou conqueror fell ill, his brother, later regent, prayed to Heaven for the recovery of his brother and offered himself as a substitute; the clerk was instructed to commit the offer to writing, and this solemn document was locked up. Other similar instances are on record. It is even recorded that the emperor of Tsin, who was steeped in Laotzse's philosophy, in 210 B. C. prayed and offered sacrifices because of a bad dream, and was thus advised by his soothsayers.

But though the Chinese had to some extent sunk to sacrificial prayers, and the blood of the victim was constantly called for, they were yet ignorant of the occidental ideas connected with conscience, fear of God, mortal sins, repentance, absolution, alms-giving, self-mortification, charity, sackcloth and ashes, praise, glorification; all those notions which to Jews, Christians and Mohammedans mean so much.

Morally he is a materialist in the extreme; his manners and customs do not rest upon spiritual values, but upon extreme realities and the expedient. His ethics is Nature-life, both good and bad. That is childlike also.

All this applies to the Chinese in general.

In China, there are, as elsewhere three classes of people: (1) The mass; (2) the learned and (3) the ruling class. The relationship of the people and prince may be seen from a quotation from Mentgzse's works.

"The people are the most important and the prince the least important (because), the people can make the prince, but the prince cannot make the people." Further elucidation of this statement that the prince is of little importance you can find in the Tao-Teh-King.

In all of this you recognize the child. Some of it is childishness and some of it is child-likeness and the child-likeness is the condition we come into by means of Wu Wei or "non action," as it is called. The childishness of it is the result of activity or interference with Tao and Teh.

I have given you a faithful description of the psychological conditions of the child and of the Chinese people. In your opinion none of these conditions are desirable, because you naturally judge them from the modern point of view of history and from an advanced point of growth in evolution. I will not say that those conditions suit us to-day, that would be absurd and impossible to prove, but I will say that the principles back of the child's conditions and the principles back of the Chinaman's condition are most desirable, and moreover, I will say that they must be recovered. I will put some arguments before you to prove both of my assertions.

The principle that lies in Wu Wei and which is back of the child and of that condition I described the Chinaman in, is in occidental philosophical language called by various names, some of the most important of which I will mention. The first is immediacy. The term explains a condition which is original, or so direct and unconditioned that it comes without any efforts or means, and, which needs no proof. It means that which is natural to us; the heart's revelations; the truths implanted in man by nature and spirit and, in a broad way, that which is self-evident.

Upon this fact of an inner direct and immediate knowledge is built the doctrine that such knowledge, with the exclusion of all mediateness, is the truth.

Immediacy is also called (spiritual) instinct implanted, or innate ideas, "natural reason," common sense, "Faith."

When the sage says "I know I am I" he needs not give any proof. His knowledge is an immediate knowledge, or a know-

ledge without proof.   This phrase, "I know I am I" does not
mean that he can make a reasonable statement of that fact if
called upon to do it; it means simply that he has a sense of
identity, a sense of being an individual in contradistinction to
another individual.

As a mere elementary fact, the same truth applies also to
my dog who demonstrates his individuality on the street by
rushing for the first dog he sees and getting into a fight.   The
dog's case is also one of immediacy, but one on a lower plane.
The point of identity between the sage's immediacy and that of
the dog's is this, that both realize themselves and truth directly
and without proof or demonstration.   The two states are opposite
poles of intelligence, but within intelligence.   In the middle
lies our common everyday world with all its volitions, reasonings,
desires and quables.   People without realization of
the value of the sage's immediacy stay in the dog's condition;
they, like the dog, live their lives in desires, and take no thought
for higher things.   The thoughts they have are engaged in the
affairs of the day, for self-satisfaction and all other selfish ends.

The sage at the other pole has abandoned all such desires
and volitions and thinkings; yea, even more, he has become so
settled in the direct vision of truth and is so completely in the
company of the highest powers, that he even does not know
the lower conditions any more; they are not only forgotten, but
no more make a part of his mental, moral and spiritual condition.

Who and what the sage really is, I have described in earlier
chapters, in phraseology drawn from the Tao-Teh-King.   I will
now add thereto some of my own ideas in order to throw
further light upon immediacy, or the state we are in when we
live in Wu Wei or "non-action" and beyond.

The sage in the condition of immediacy seizes his point
with an intuition almost feminine, no matter what the point may
be, intellectual, volitional or perceptional.   And when he has
got his point, he realizes it with enthusiasm.   These realizations
are thoroughly individual, that is, when he presents a
philosophical idea, he does not do it in cool rationality, nay, his
presentation is thoroughly personal.   It is himself.   There is
no abstraction about it; it is his idea, and, we see and feel his
individuality.   In the occident we are disposed to throw contempt
upon such a man and his teachings.   We have become
so accustomed to the worship of words, or literary idols, that

we cannot perceive the life that comes to us through a sage, and our loss is consequently enormous. We get empty shells, and no more. The sage's immediacy contains a revelation, but we miss it. Immediacy as it works in the sage is the main characteristic of all Inner Life. Immediacy means feeling the truth, not reasoning it out. It lives in faculties of inner perceptions not cultivated in the Occident except among the mystics or Inner-Life-people. These people rest in their own subjectivity, and that subjectivity is moulded according to the eternal pattern, and all they need to do is to look and describe what they perceive themselves. An inner illumination is always present and that loosens the fetters of the mind and allows the mind, according to the degrees of its culture, to set forth the perceptions in words or deeds.

When we meet such immediacy we should not argue, but prefer insight to argument; subjectivity to objective forms. The insight allowed us will show the universe one glorious and eternally active whole. It will show us that mankind literally is divinity "in the making," that each one of us potentially is a living divine attribute. It will show us that we are not made by circumstances or by our environment, but from within. All this is gained by Wu Wei.

Immediacy discards or rather does not possess understanding as a degree of reason. It is like the child I have described; still a part of the whole and not claiming separate existence. It discards reasoning, but glories in its image-making power, a power which to it is everything and which does everything for it. In fact immediacy and the image-making faculty are twins, and between them they weave the real into individual forms. Immediacy is the loom and the image-making faculty is the weaver. Most of us cannot see, much less understand, the pattern that is woven, but when it is finished we see the sage.

I have said that when we meet immediacy we should not argue, but prefer insight to argument. Now I add, when we meet the sage we should not ask for a system of wisdom or an intellectual structure, but we should learn of him and through him as an individual; and relationship should be one of life, not one of thought; one of personal intercourse, not of distance. I think the true relationship is expressed by Jesu command to eat his flesh and drink his blood. In Tao and Teh all distinctions disappear and things are identical, universal, in unity.

Common people who regard the objective or the tangible

world as the only reality, will acknowledge existence is an unsolved riddle and a perpetual conflict. The sage understands the principle of identity of things.

Kwang-tze tells an anecdote to show how little value one ought to place upon distinctions. A keeper of monkeys ordered that their rations of nuts should be three in the morning and four at night; at this the monkeys were very angry and complained, and so the keeper ruled that the monkeys should have four nuts in the morning and three at night. And with this the monkeys were very well satisfied. They got no more nuts, but their whims or subjective views were satisfied. Another lesson can be drawn from that anecdote and Kwang-tzse draws it. It is this, that the sage cares not for distinctions; contraries to him are identical and by following what he calls "two courses at once" he follows the laws of heaven; what "two courses at once" is I will explain.

The real Taoist is "both-and"; not "this" or "that"; he is the reconciliation of opposites. Says Tao-Teh-King (XXVIII):

"Who his manhood shows
And his womanhood knows
Becomes the empire's river.—
All come to him, yea all beneath the sky,"

and he is

"The simple child again, free from all stains."

"Who his brightness knows
And his blackness shows
Becomes the empire's model.—
He in the unchanging virtue arrayed,
Man's first estate, the absolute.

"Who knows his fame
And guards disgrace
Becomes a specious valley.—
And men come to him from all beneath the sky,"

and in him

"They hail the simple infant."

Such a state is immediacy of the sage's kind and the very state we wish to attain and do attain by Wu Wei.

It was so in olden time, when mankind was still young. Then the sage was the leader of men and in undisputed possession of the truth. Alas! The age of innocence is lost—for good and for bad! We cannot recover what Mother Nature has taken back. The wheel of existence can neither be stopped nor made to revolve in the opposite direction. What Time has devoured cannot be restored, nor do we ask for the age of innocence or for the return of anything past. We have no need of these things, because the ages are still rotating and a new age of innocence is always possible; the wheel of existence is still revolving and offering the same possibilities as of yore, and time is everlastingly renewing all things. The mechanism of the universe is as young as ever. What we can do; what we must do; what we want to do is to learn Wu Wei of these ancient people, for it was by Wu Wei that they obtained happiness and immortality, and that is what we want.

Thus far I have been concerned with immediacy, and thereby with intelligence and knowledge as one aspect of Wu Wei. But there is also another and a most important side of our nature to be considered and that side also represents principles back of the life of the child and the Chinese as above described. That side is the side of conduct.

To perfect wisdom corresponds perfect goodness or love or affection. They correspond like masculine and feminine and like intellect and will. It is good practice to consider goodness, love, affection and will as the interior, and wisdom and intellect as the exterior, and in that respect we shall be in agreement with all Inner-Life-people. They all consider Love a direct form of Divinity, and say that when one acts from love he acts divinely. Love is to them divinity imminently present in the world and as such the principle that binds the world and its parts together. Plato might well and truthfully say "that love is the mediator and interpreter between God and men."

It is this principle that works at the root of the child's life and also back of the Chinaman's childishness and which is also in Wu Wei. They are both, the child and the Chinaman, wisdom and love, types of the power that binds things together. They both act intuitively and through the will. They are both flames of good, though unwittingly and often to the scorn of others.

These two principles of Wu Wei dominated in those ancient days of China, such as I have told you the Chinese Taoists reported them. Those ancient days they called "the age of perfect virtue" or Teh. They were, as I have said so often, a result of Wu Wei and worthy of our imitation.

To be continued.

THE CITY OF THE DEAD.

By Samuel Neu.

DURING a lull in the conversation, after several of us had told of remarkable experiences we had gone through, incredible scenes we had witnessed—all more or less truthful—a slight commotion was created by the rattle of a chair in the far corner of the room. Turning to find out the cause of the disturbance we discovered Captain McKanna straightening up and removing the pipe from his thin lips. He was a strange man, Captain McKanna; none of us had ever been able to discover where he had come from or who he was. One thing, though, we had come to regard as certain: that the signs he was manifesting foreboded, beyond all doubt, a story. And when the Captan told a tale all others held their peace. When, presently, he began inaudibly to mumble, the coming of the story was not only beyond doubt but an established fact.

His first utterances were, as usual, unintelligible. It was as though his mind had gone on to arrange the details of the story, leaving his tongue behind to make an introduction as best it might. We made out that he was trying to say something like: "Have any of you ever been to Paraknia, where all the inhabitants are dead men?"

Owing to the indistinctness of his mutterings, it was necessary for him to repeat his question before we could believe that we had heard rightly. Then, after each of us had solemnly assured him that the place was wholly unknown to us, and after each in turn had declared his eagerness to hear a description of it—we had found such assurances necessary—the Captain related the following tale, which I have written down in his own words, as nearly as I can recollect them.

It was during a journey in 1875 with my lamented friend, Dr. Kammera, that we happened upon a stretch of sandy country entirely devoid of vegetation or life of any kind, a veritable desert. Having traveled for three days through this dreary region, we were considering, toward sundown, the advisability of retracing our weary way. Then, on mounting a gentle rise of ground, we suddenly beheld on the horizon, about half-a-day's journey distant, the spires and domes of a city.

I was still for turning back, but the incorrigible Doctor, whose burning desire for adventure had led us into many remarkable—and oftentimes costly—experiences, would hear of no such thing. So, having still a fortnight's provisions, we camped where we were for the night and started before sunrise for the city, and we reached its gates just after noon.

Now, if the desert had been dreary and still, I know of no word to describe the stillness of this city. So thick was the silence that our very voices seemed muffled. It seemed as though the air had become so accustomed to quiet that it found difficulty in responding to the vibrations of our vocal cords. As for appearance, it seemed a deserted world. Houses, streets, stores, as far as the eye could reach, but not the slightest sign of life. Not even a blade of grass grew on the deserted pavements, nor any bird or tiny insect stirred.

"Well, Doc," said I, "what do you think of it?"

"How can I form my opinion," said he, "before I have seen the place? Come, let us look into some of these houses. Then perhaps we can arrive at some conclusion."

So we selected a particularly promising looking house, one that had probably belonged to a wealthy inhabitant, and entered. We had a little difficulty in getting past the door, but the few tools we always carried soon opened a way. We found that the door had been fastened with an ingenious contrivance of steel bars, evidently designed to keep out intruders, and therefore concluded that much valuable treasure must be concealed in the house.

A minute description of the interior would prove tiresome, so suffice it to say that the house consisted of three stories, as did most of the houses in the town; the lowest story, opening on the street, contained the working rooms, the second story the living and sleeping rooms, while the third or top story was vacant, as was the case in every house we visited. Our first surprise came when we entered what I have called the sleeping room. The Doctor entered first, but hardly had he stepped across the threshold when he recoiled with horror. For some moments I could get no intelligible answer from him, so pushing past him, I entered and found, lying on a pile of straw—a corpse.

I, too, was horror stricken for a moment, and yet, when I considered, it seemed only natural that we should find corpses in the place.

The Doctor had by this time recovered his usual nerve, and we approached the corpse to examine it. It was plain to see that the Doctor's professional instinct was aroused, and he at once tried to discover the cause of death. While he was thus engaged I explored about and discovered in an adjoining room another corpse. I called Dr. Kammera. Yes, it was surely dead.

"The hour," he said, "is getting late. Tomorrow I shall perform an autopsy and see what really put the city to sleep."

"And meanwhile?" I ventured.

"Meanwhile we shall eat our supper downstairs."

So we brought in our effects, got out our provisions and enjoyed a hearty meal. While the Doctor cleaned up the crumbs, I went on a search for the treasure we had expected to find. In a corner of the work room I found a wooden chest fastened with the same ingenious arrangement as the door. I had no difficulty, however, in cutting a hole in the top, and discovered four canvas bags, which, I found, contained huge lumps of yellow clay. This clay, we later discovered passed as money among the inhabitants, and often as food. Not knowing anything of this, however, I returned to the Doctor very much disappointed and reported the fruitless result of my search.

"And now, Doc," I said, "where to sleep?"

"Well, I suppose that vacant top loft ought to suit us. It is not often that we have a roof over our heads."

"But do you think it is safe?" thinking of the two we had seen.

"Yes. You see, my theory is that some poisonous gas swept over this city and wiped out the population. What that gas was I shall determine tomorrow. As for our present safety, we are here, and alive, hence the poisonous gas is gone."

I still retained some doubt, but as usual, relied on his judgment. So sundown saw us wrapped in slumber and our blankets, in the otherwise vacant loft.

Hardly had we reached the shore of sleep when we were recalled by something unusual. Neither of us could tell what it was that had awakened us, yet we felt, rather than heard, a commotion below. Hastily drawing on our clothing we descended hurriedly to the floor below, revolvers in hand. What we expected to find I do not know; what we found, we certainly did not expect. The two corpses were walking about! Were we surprised? Well, the Doctor surely was. I set it down immediately to another mistake of medical science.

"Well, Doc," I said, laughing, "that is one on you."

But Kammera shook his head and mumbled something about "impossibility," and wore a very mystified expression.

"They were surely dead," he said.

"No doubt about it," I agreed. "And it is a common thing for dead men to walk about. Next they will be telling tales. See, one is coming toward us."

I drew the Doctor aside just in time to escape the observation of the Paraknian, and hastily we reascended the stairs. There we remained throughout the night, fearing to descend lest we come to harm—from dead men! Evidently our presence had not been noticed, and therefore we felt safe in the deserted upper story and even managed to snatch a few hours of intermittent sleep.

At sunrise the sounds below ceased and we descended. The corpses were again lying on their straw beds, dead, apparently, and nothing we could do seemed to revive them. After a hearty breakfast, we gave the corpses a thorough examination to discover any latent life, but Dr. Kammera's original opinion was confirmed. He applied every known test at hand without result, and even discovered unmistakable evidences of putrefaction on both specimens. Before leaving the corpses, however, for further exploration, I suggested that we remove the clothing. This proved a rather difficult undertaking as the clothes were all fastened together with a network of fibrous material, metal clasps and pieces of bone, all interlaced in a most ingenious way. The Doctor ventured an opinion that it was the clothes and not a poisonous gas that had killed them, but this theory was hardly tenable. We finally did succeed in stripping one corpse, and discovered, to our amazement, a horrible looking reptile clinging to the abdomen of the deceased, with tentacles sunk deep into the flesh.

"There," said the Doctor, rising with the reptile and a self-satisfied gesture, "is the cause of death."

As we had not had much sleep on the preceding night, we decided to rest until sundown and then to investigate thoroughly any unusual phenomena that might occur.

Directly as darkness fell again we heard sounds as though someone was moving about, and we descended. Only one of the corpses had arisen. The one from who we had removed the reptile did not stir

"See, Doc," I said, "our friend, whose cause of death you removed, does not stir."

The Doctor was lost in profound thought for a moment. Gradually, a light broke into his mind and was reflected by his face.

"Do you know, Mac," he said, "I can hardly believe it— there is no such case on record—but I think that that 'cause of death' that I removed is really the cause of their life."

We suddenly remembered the presence of the other Paraknian and feared lest the sound of our voices might make him aware of us. But that individual had evidently neither heard nor seen us. He was just leaving the house. We followed, noiselessly, but soon found that precaution was unnecessary as almost all of these creatures were totally blind and deaf. As we emerged upon the street we found it crowded with corpses, all hurrying in one direction. They jammed and jostled and seemed entirely oblivious of each other, except when in actual physical contact. We noticed that each of the creatures carried a peculiar stick, shaped like a man. With these sticks they prodded each other, and at times appeared to be fencing together. It was the Doctor who first surmised that this was their mode of communication, which we later verified.

We followed the crowd, or rather, were carried along with it. None seemed to question our presence, and though one or two prodded me with their talk-sticks, trying to begin a conversation, yet, owing to their blindness we succeeded in escaping observation.

The course of the crowd led us to what we made out to be a vast eating house, and, of all surprises, here we had the greatest. About the floor were piled heaps of sand and stones of various kinds and sizes, while liquids were carried about by serving men who made cups of their hands. But the most astonishing about the place was the way in which the inhabitants partook of the strange food. Prostrating himself on the floor, the eater would open his mouth very wide. Then out would creep a form; from one, a reptile; from another, an insect; which would wander about the hall, make selections from its favorite gravels, and return to its home mouth. I may say in passing that we noticed later that these queer people performed very few acts themselves, and seemed to have no will or discrimination whatever; all their actions were performed by the insect and reptile creatures with which their bodies seemed infested.

But to return to the eating hall. There was one pile of brightly colored pebbles which seemed to attract the food-procurers (the appetites, the Doctor called them) more than any other, and this pile was soon demolished. Indeed, it seemed as though these creatures relished the food most for the brightness of its hue.

Not being able to eat any of the stones, I stopped one of the carriers of liquids and took a swallow. One swallow was enough. No health board would permit such a concoction to be dispensed for fifteen minutes, though I must confess that its effects on the Paraknians seemed to be exhilarating. I mentioned this to the Doctor. Before he could answer, the liquid dispenser was jabbing me with his talk-stick. Later, we found that he was asking payment, and had we known this at the time we should have avoided some trouble. But I did not know what he wanted and kicked his shins to keep him off. This upset him completely. He immediately told those about him, and, in a moment, the whole place resounded with the rattle of talk-sticks and there was a concerted movement in our direction.

The situation was serious. I look pretty robust, and Dr. Kammera was no weakling, but what would our strength avail against men who were already dead? Since death did not disable them what use would there be in inflicting any minor damage? Just as the crowd was about to close in on us a pair of strong hands grasped us and rushed us to a place of safety on the floor above. To the blind Paraknians below our disappearance must have seemed miraculous. Indeed, we considered it so ourselves, and before even stopping to regain our breath we turned to find out who our rescuer might be. Surprises were not yet at an end. For here was a corpse whose eyes were not entirely closed, and in whose finger tips, on our arms, we felt a distinct pulse. We were not long in finding, too, that he could hear slightly and emit vocal sounds. He appeared very friendly and immediately brought forward a large round wooden utensil filled with moss, which he offered to us to eat. We declined with thanks and he proceeded to make his breakfast.

We decided to live with this half live Paraknian and signified our intention to him. He was delighted. So we at once removed our camp to his lodgings.

In the course of two days we had arranged a complete sys-

THE CITY OF THE DEAD 173

tem of communication between our guide and ourselves. This consisted partly of elementary vocal sounds and partly of signs. We found him to be fairly intelligent, particularly in regard to subjects that came within the range of his observation. He was very unhappy about the condition of his people, most of whom, he told us, were totally dead at birth. Some few were born with a faint spark of life, but these were, in most cases, soon killed, either by their own people or by the reptilian creatures with which the race was cursed. After death they went on with existence until putrefied, animated by the very creatures that caused their decease. When nearly putrefied their talk-sticks were put aside and they retired to underground caves.

For three days we remained in seclusion with our friend, giving him at times a share of the food we had brought with us. This greatly improved his vitality. During this time we studied diligently the stick language, in which the Doctor became quite proficient. I did the best I could, but even after three days our guide said that my foreign accent was very noticeable. I have no doubt that I stuttered considerably, too. On the third day of our stay with him, our guide brought to us a number of other Paraknians, partly alive. We were warned and made to promise never to reveal to the dead ones the fact that we or the friends could see. They formed, as it were, a secret society in the city—Gonads they called themselves—being readily known to each other by their powers of sight and hearing, but undistinguishable by the others. Their secrecy in regard to their vitality was necessary, because death was the penalty if discovered. I have no doubt, though, that their powers of conversing without sticks, and predicting events, suc has rain, visitors and intruders, must have appeared miraculous to their unfortunate brothers. The Gonads recognized the malign influence of the reptile infection and exerted themselves constantly to subdue the creatures. Some of them even attempted to preach to the masses the doctrine of subjection of the reptiles, but were invariably greeted with derision.

The Doctor was greatly interested in the Gonads and tried to stimulate them with our food. In this he was, in a measure, successful, but our own food supply suffered in consequence. Noting this, the Doctor cut down his own rations, using, instead, some of the food of the Paraknians. To do this he had first to swallow an "appetite," after which the food agreed with him very well.

On the fifth day in the city the Gonads introduced us to the multitude of famous travellers. It was then that our knowledge of the stick language proved useful. We had wondered, before, how the Paraknians recognized and distinguished each other, but a few conversations showed us that different individuals spoke very differently. Their conversation, however, was anything but enlightening, often nauseating.

We were treated with great courtesy and shown all the wonders of the city. The prison was very interesting. Here we found criminals of all classes, confined by having their talk-sticks tied to iron rings. The greatest crime was considered to be the injury to another's talk-stick. This does not seem strange when it is considered that each citizen spent a great part of his life in perfecting his talk-stick and could not replace it, if injured, in a reasonable time. It often happens that, owing to some disease of the reptilian animator, one individual will steal another's talk-stick, although it is of no use whatever to the thief, he having his own. The penalty for such an offence is the loss of his own talk-stick. After this the thief is as though dead, to the multitude, and permitted to roam at large. We found a number of these "executed" criminals; drawn by their disease, they frequented the dens of vice, which the Paraknians also have, where the creatures infecting their bodies obtained gratification, infecting others with their malady. Frequently, the Gonads told us, these executed criminals stole sticks from those who had them and assumed their places in the city, while the poor losers, of peaceful disposition and unable to communicate with those around them, retired to the caves of putrefaction.

Among those confined at the prison were two Gonads who had committed trivial offenses against the laws. They excited considerable wonder by taking the chaining down of their talk-sticks very calmly. Little did the authorities know that they could communicate with each other and with their friends as easily if chained as when free.

We were shown the schools where the young Paraknians receive their education. The education centered about the talk-sticks, which they are taught to perfect so that they will be properly balanced and tuned to the use of each individual. In the highest classes they are taught how to change the shapes of their sticks, how to disguise their speech when necessary, and how to evade the laws. The education of some among the wealthiest class goes a little further. This consists in learning

THE CITY OF THE DEAD 175

a name for every object and experience that comes within the range of Paraknian perception. This was the highest knowledge among them, and those who possess it are held in high veneration and called the knowing ones.

We found that among the children the percentage of semi-animation was vastly greater than among the adults, for reasons already explained by our guide. The Gonads took great interest in the living children, but were badly hindered by the laws, which practically forbade life.

The chief man of the city was a very badly decayed specimen. So awful was the odor that emanated from him that the Gonads and ourselves could not approach him. We were informed that the Paraknians elected him because of this odor, which seemed to please their diseased olfactory nerves.

As may be expected, the mass of inhabitants knew very little of the history of their city. Indeed, beyond enumerating the names of the last five chief men and a few of their personal experiences, none of the Paraknians could enlighten us. From the Gonads, however, we learned an interesting tale. They told us that long ago a party of men and women set out to cross the desert and were halted by disaster at the place where the city now stands. Unable to proceed they made camp. Though a small spring bubbled near the spot, water was scarce, and they reserved it all for the humans, driving the animals off. Without horses and beasts they could not proceed, and therefore remained and turned their camp into a city. For a few generations they lived a life of want and privation, and, as the population grew, the water supply became less plentiful. One day, one of the inhabitants went down into the bowels of the earth to try to find a more plentiful water supply. When he returned, he was in the condition of the present day Paraknians, having probably swallowed some insect while below. His friends were alarmed at first, but when they found he could subsist on a diet of stones and gravel they, too, went into the earth and swallowed insects and reptiles. A few there were whose better judgment preserved them, and they remained, as they are to-day, the unknown guardians of the city. It is told that those whose wills are strong enough can resist the promptings of the reptilian "appetites" and finally free themselves entirely of the curse, but these are rarely found.

The origin and history of the talk-sticks is equally interesting, though I have almost forgotten it. It was one of the early

Gonads who invented this useful apparatus. It was necessary at that time to drive the unfortunate Paraknians to all their duties, as they were morbid and hopeless. Finding that the creatures were very sensitive to touch, this particular Gonad conceived a system of signals by which he communicated his wishes to them. After much labor he succeeded in teaching these signals to the Paraknians, so that they could communicate with each other. Long and patient study was necessary, however, to adapt the shape of the stick to the temperament and emotions of each. Even to-day the shaping of their talk-sticks is the chief care of the Paraknians, as a well-shaped talk-stick responds almost automatically to the user's thought, so wonderful is the system of signals.

A complete record of all we saw would bore you with its incrediblity, so I shall tell no more of the wonderful observations we made during the ten days of our stay. Our stay, I say, though the Doctor's stay was longer than mine, as you shall see. During this time he had been taking more and more to the indigestible Paraknian food, and his vitality had been constantly sinking. On the tenth day, in spite of all I could do, he died. In the night he arose as the dead Paraknians did. To my horror I found that one of the reptilians was fastened to his flesh. He still knew me, but only when conversing in the Paraknian way, and he shared their antipathy to life when the subject was mentioned, You can imagine how I grieved at this change, For a whole night I labored with him, but succeeded only in rousing his anger, I debated with myself whether it would not be better to remove the reptilian and allow the Doctor to rest peaceably dead. The Gonads, who appeared as much grieved as I, were all for doing this, but I could not bring myself to do it.

Only three days' rations now remained and if I did not wish to suffer a fate similar to Dr. Kammera's it behooved me to start at once. This I decided to do, resolving to return as soon as possible with ample provisions, with which I expected to work a social revolution. Calling together the Gonads I made known my intention and proposed to take our first found guide with me. To this they would not agree. Indeed, they all laid hands on me and tried forcibly to prevent my going. Seeing that force would not avail I resolved upon strategy. Apparently consenting to remain, I waited until high noon, when even the livest of them slept, and quietly stole away. Before leaving I had taken a promise from our faithful guide to watch over poor Dr. Kammera.

As I reached the hill from which we had first seen the city I looked back, and my heart was heavy. Here I stood, not a fortnight before, with a faithful and devoted friend who had been beside me through dangers of all kinds. Now that friend was fallen, through the fault of no wild beast or rushing torrent or leaden bullet, but by his own weakness. So goes the world, I meditated. But the journey before me was long, and the rations short, therefore time pressed. So picking up my baggage, less heavy than my heart, I resumed my journey across the desert to civilization.

And if there are any among you, gentlemen, who will join me in rescuing my dear friend and those other poor unfortunates from their horrible plight, be assured that the thanks of a grateful heart will be yours.

. . . .

As the Captain paused and relighted his pipe he was besieged with questions, but did not deign to reply. Only one question did he answer:

"Why did you never publish a report on this journey, in scientific papers?"

"I was afraid," said he, "that some of the Paraknians might find and read it and seek me out and kill me." After which he resumed his pipe, his thoughts far away.

After this answer, and even before, many of us, like you who hear it now, doubted the truth of this story, and Captain McKanna's reputation as a great traveller does not add to his credibility. Those of us who did not doubt it completely, advanced the suggestion that the Captain had perpetrated an allegory, that he was describing a land whose inhabitants were spiritually dead, possibly even our own beloved country. But this suggestion met with such hoots of derision that I hesitate even to set it down. Further doubt has since been added to the story by the fact that those who volunteered for the expedition of relief are still among us and maintain unbroken silence on the subject. On the whole I think the existence or non-existence of Paraknia must be left an open question until more conclusive evidence is forthcoming. Have you heard of any?

A DREAM OF ATLANTIS—THE LAND OF MU.

By Alice Dixon Le Plongeon.

(Continued from page 122.)

Among the maidens who had fled
From Mu, believing in its dread
Inevitable fate—foretold
By seers who could events behold
   Long ere these came to pass—
Was one of Princess Nalah's age,
Arona named—by parentage
   Derived from lowly class;
But dowered by beauty, precious gift!
And joyous smiles that could uplift
The heart by sorrow weighted down,
Or eyes o'ershadowed with a frown.
This maiden Kadimo beheld
   With favoring thought, and strove
To win the tender glance withheld,
   And stir her heart to love.
Responsive, sympathetic, gay,
Her mind to joy will ever stray.
Not lighter springs the agile fawn
Awakening at the blush of dawn
Than trip Arona's pretty feet
When forth comes she the morn to greet.
Her joy exhales upon the air
Like fragrance from a blossom rare.
What marvel then if Balba too,
Bold man-at-arms dares also woo
This damsel kind, whose modest mien
Must shield her as a sacred screen.

But, welcome as the dew of heaven,
Arona's virgin love is given
To Kadimo, whose reverie,
To sadness turned, she oft must see.

Dark Balba's rougher nature sought
Each pleasure life could bring,
His stubborn will and mind untaught
   Not brooking anything
That might his keen desire oppose
Whate'er the source whence this arose.

Sad Heppel chanced to hear one day
Rude Balba swear to have his way
By force if soft persuasion failed
   To win the maid for him;
And if another's suit prevailed
   He would have vengeance grim.
Arona shunned the eager gaze
Of Balba's eyes, whose ardent rays
   Seemed frought with ill intent—
As threatening cloud its flash betrays
   Ere by the storm 'tis rent.
Those eyes behold Kadimo place
A flow'ret where it most will grace
Arona's tresses, and her brow
Suffused become with rosy glow.
Thereafter as the days roll by
Kadimo's footsteps he will spy;
And soon it chanced one sultry day
When the physician strolled away
   Within the forest shade,
In silence Balba followed near
With stealthy tread, where daylight clear
   Deep foliage forbade;
And sudden forth a javelin hurled—
But missed his mark; then downward whirled
A shattered bough upon the ground:—
Kadimo, turning at the sound,
   Surprised beholds the glare
Of piercing eyes upon him bent
   In fixed and murderous stare,
Their charge of venom still unspent.
Impelled by jealousy and ire
   Another shaft of death
Is sped, but as the missile dire
Is aimed to still the breath

Of Kadimo, a rushing form
  Is there betwen the two,
And prostrate falls, his life-blood warm
  Soon welling into view.

"Ah! man of blood!" Kadimo cried,
  At Balba springing, "Rue this day
Shalt thou!" But as he reached his side
  The murderer lept and fled away;
While Heppel, dying, moaned, "Abide;
  Approach; a parting warning hear."
Kadimo gently staunched the wound
  And sorrowed, seeing death was near.
The victim faintly breathed each sound:—
"Beware! He loves Arona—I
Rejoice that duty bid me die.—
Great Atlas! unto thee I go;
Grant me at last myself to know
Forgiven of thee!" His parting sigh
Upon a zephyr floated by.

Far in the forest Balba went,
While curses on the air he sent;
In fear to turn his footsteps home,
Uncertain whither now to roam.
Here many dangers round him lurked
  In serpent-fang and leopard-claw,
And pits wherein the dwarfs had worked
  To delve for clay. But naught he saw
Beyond the shadows of his mind
That drove him to avoid mankind;
Regretting not the evil done,
But that no triumph had he won
In ending Heppel's harmless life
And rousing Kadimo to strife.

"I'll to the nearest coast," he thought,
And with the fishermen will earn,
The livelihood by others caught
  From out the waves; I'll not return
To find the very death I gave,
Unwilling, to a meddling knave."

Thus musing comes he to a dell
That slopes unto a spacious well
　By Nature fashioned there.
The fugitive his thirst to slack
Pursues à narrow winding track,
　Suspecting not a lair.
But panting leopards shelter found
In grottoes dim;—these with a bound
Upon him leap: Ravenous and strong
They mumble o'er his bones ere long.
No mortal tongue will ever tell
The fate of Balba in that dell.

Time wings its flight into the deep
Eternity of endless sleep.
While Life forever seeks a womb
Death points the way unto a tomb.

The Can, whose years have multiplied,
Exults, for he has lived to guide
The infant empire to a state
Of welfare; now its future fate
Unto his vision seems to grow
Most happily; afar will glow
Its wisdom; centuries first will fall
Asleep ere Death will drop his pall
Upon the nation's bier. Thus spake
The king to Itzat, who would take
To heart the good of high and low,
Now Can must from his kingdom go—
To learn what mystery farther lies
Beyond the reach of mortal eyes.

Three lustrums tranquilly have sped
Since Nalah was to Itzat wed.
The grandsire peaceful sees the end
　Of his most happy reign draw near,
Assured that Itzat will defend
　The *right*, with judgment true and clear.
That spirit of prophetic gift
Again his spirit doth uplift
　As in the days of yore,

And to the Land of Mu returns
   The gaze of Can once more;
While tenderly his heart now yearns
   For one upon that shore—
Manab who, faithful to her charge
Still lingers on destruction's marge:—
"And there," saith he, "will she remain
Till Mu by Homen shall be slain,—
Condemned to suffer fiery doom
Till overwhelmed by watery gloom.
Beneath the clear cerulean skies
A realm of beauty tranquil lies;
That country once to greatness nursed
By Wisdom, now by Folly cursed.
There, ruthless crime and evil power
Must reign until the destined hour
That surely comes, when ocean's bed
Will be invaded by the dead
Distorted forms of them who now
As tyrants lift their haughty brow;
While just below their strutting feet
The devastating forces meet
To overthrow what man hath wrought,
And bring proud Mu herself to naught;
Her mountain-tops alone may peep
Above the waters of the deep.

"From that dread scene I turn to thee
   My son, and Nalah dear—
Thou, ere tomorrow dawn, wilt be
   A queen. Weep not, but hear
What counsel may be granted ere
I go beyond all earthly care.
Thou, child, art mother of a race
That, east and west shall leave its trace—
By light of knowledge spread afar,
Not by the arts of ruthless war.
Behold on yonder Land of Mu
What tyranny the people rue.
Excesses, poverty, and crime
Undreamed of in the olden time,
Have sapped the virtue and the weal

A DREAM OF ATLANTIS

Of millions; but their woe shall end
When fire and sea the earth will rend.

"My son, forget not our request,
But follow in the footsteps blest
Of noble men. Let justice guide
Thy will. Keep ever near thy side
As councillors the good and wise—
Thus only can the nation rise.

Oppress no man. Example give,
Thy subjects; live as they should live.
Do thou and thy sons after thee
Fail not to urge *simplicity;*
For history shows that nations gone
Have found disaster, every one,
Thro' greed of wealth and luxury
While many suffered penury.
Be wise; thy people strive to lead
   Aright; that unto all
Who worthy prove in word and deed
   A just reward shall fall.
When sympathy forgets to glow,
The torch of Wisdom flickers low.
Far better miss each selfish aim,
And take defeat in life's brief game,
Than reach the goal by trampling o'er
Our fellow mortals frail and poor."

'Tis thus the Can, while life endures,
Entreats that son, who him assures,
That he will steadfastly fulfill
These last expressions of his will—
Till just before the break of day
The Lord of Death him bore away.

Dark sadness on the people fell,
And ululations loud would swell
The bosoms of the multitude
When they his flaming pyre reviewed.
But human sorrows quickly fly
When ready tears o'erflow the eye.
The populace expends its grief

In noise, and early finds relief
In noise again, their laughter high
Intruding on the sobbing cry.

But Itzat, now the ruling Can,
Mourns deeply for that noble man;
And Nalah long the loss bewailed
Of him whose wisdom never failed
To rescue her from threatened ill,
And with content her days to fill.
Her offspring were the only trace
Of Atlas, and her royal race
Long held its empire on the strand
By Egypt's sons called Kui-land;—
That "West," whose rulers, deified,
Were ever with the gods allied.

Not many moons have come and gone,
Since Can the First new life hath won,
When ships from yonder fatherland
Cast anchor with a goodly band
Of hardy men and women brave
Who venture forth upon the wave
To find new homes where tyranny
And evil plotters may not be.
Of Mu and what events befell
These new arrivals had to tell;
And so it chanced that Pepen's name
Unto the ear of Cho soon came.

Cho, grown to manhood's full estate,
Will seek, and save from horrid fate,
The one who was a generous friend
When he himself could not defend—
E'en tho' she be the courtesan
Of one who shames the race of man—
Her steps in tender girlhood strayed
To Folly's path, by Fate betrayed.
'Tis Gadeirus who holds her now,
Cho hears and, sad, inclines his brow.

A busy world left he behind
When forth he sailed with favoring wind;—

The blacks from distant Afric's shore
Mild servitude unmurmuring bore;
With burdens to and fro went they
From dawn until the close of day,
When every worker dropped his tool
And rested in the zephyrs cool.

Until the land of Mayach seems
  A shadow on the water bright,
Cho watches from the deck and dreams,
That soon again 'twill be in sight.
'Tis well that rarely mortal eye
May peer into futurity—
For while youth happily awaits
Dear Joy, on come the frowning fates.

BOOK FIFTH.

Part I

Awake! awake! the Mighty One
Triumphant hath his course begun
Arise! Receive the light that he
Again bestows on land and sea.

Thus call the watchmen from afar;
Sing too the sentinels of war;
While song-birds hail the morning bright
And prowlers slink away with night.

Now rapidly the broad highways
Are thronged—for on this day of days,
The greatest city of the earth
Must ring with victory and with mirth.
Ships laden with the richest spoils,
And capitves noble, in the toils
Of Mu's triumphant bands,
Lie at the docks, their hempen coils
Made fast by eager hands:—
The hands of stalwart, lusty, braves
Who spent their time with valor bold
In battling with the stormy waves,
Nor cared how high the billows rolled.

But when unto the land returned,
Restraint their ardent natures spurned,—
And wilder than the ocean spray
The sailors revelled night and day
Not far from where the shipping lay,
With those who lures attractive set
To make the hardy men forget
Themselves, their duty, and their pains,
Until deprived of all their gains.

But on this day both low and high
Must see the pageant passing by.
Each road and stately avenue
Presenting now a splendid view.
Great halls of justice and of state
Where wise and foolish share debate.
High temples sacred to the sun,
And famous towers that foes would shun;
Broad esplanades and shady groves,
Whose paths the dreamy student roves;
The courts where ardent youths compete,
That loud applause their ears may greet;
All these are now in grand array
To celebrate a joyful day.
But words could never serve to tell
The splendor and the magic spell
That made a scene of beauteous joy
With not a shadow of alloy.
   Perchance some sterner mind
Remembered that the surface fair
Removed, would lay dark misery bare,
   But vulgar souls are blind.

The pageant on its course rolls by
And not a tear bedews an eye
In that proud multitude at sight
Of captured heroes; they whose plight
May well evoke a smothered sob,
Or from some heart a quicker throb;—
Brave warriors, fair, and nobly built;
Charged not with any act of guilt,
But unto serfdom mean betrayed—
Against them all this host arrayed.
   To be continued.

THE SEPHER HA-ZOHAR—THE BOOK OF LIGHT.

BY NURHO DE MANHAR.

Containing the doctrines of Kabbalah, together with the discourses and teachings of its author, the great Kabbalist, Rabbi Simeon ben Jochai, and now for the first time wholly translated into English, with notes, references and expository remarks.

(Continued from page 127.)

SAID Rabbi Hiya, after listening to these comments of his fellow students: "These different expositions really amount to one and the same meaning. The generations of Noah signify the present human race in the world, the offspring and work of the Holy One."

Said Rabbi Simeon: "When the Holy One arrays himself, it is in the ornaments from both the celestial and terrestrial worlds, from the former with that heavenly light on high that no human being can approach unto; from the latter with the souls of the righteous who the more they approximate themselves to this divine light the more receptive and filled with it do they become, so that through them it expands in all directions and the world like a cistern or ocean is filled with it. It is written, 'Drink water out of thy cistern (meborecha) and running waters out of thy well' (beareche) (Prov. v., 15). Why does scripture use these two terms cistern and well, beginning with bar (cistern) and ending with bear (well or fount). Because the one contains; the other produces or sends forth water, and scripture wishes to teach us that the cistern will eventually become a well. Like a poverty stricken and poor man, the souls of the righteous or just are possessed of nothing in themselves, and are as a cistern into which water is poured. Every worldly minded and unjust man bears on him the mark of the letter D (daleth meaning poor) and is like a cistern without water. But the souls of the just become founts or wells sending forth water in all directions. Who operates and produces this change? It is he, the source and origin of celestial light, who causes it to flow into human souls on the earth plane as we have stated before. Another signification of these words is, that they apply to David, whom scripture makes to say, 'Who (mi) will give me to drink water of the cistern in Bethlehem?' The term 'running water' also designates Abraham, 'out of' (bethokh) Jacob and 'thy well' Isaac who is called a 'fount of springing or living water' (Gen. xxvi., 9). In this same verse is contained the holy and profound mystery of the patriarchs, amongst whom King David is included. The desire of union between the opposite sexes is only excited when the female becomes receptive and filled with the female spirit or principle which, becoming conjoined with the male principle from on high, causes fertility. So is it with the synod or congregation of Israel (or the pure and initiated in the secret doctrine). It experiences a desire after the Holy One only when it becomes filled with the spirit of righteousness and then is made fruitful in goodness and then union with the Divine is a source of the greatest joy and delight, that has been thus expressed by a writer. 'The Holy One then comes forth and takes delight in the company of the souls of just men made perfect.' Observe that the children of the garden of Eden, or the Edenic race of beings, became human only after Noah, the Just One, had entered the ark, or in other words had become incorporated. Until that happened, they were invisible and unmanifested as humanity which would never have been able to exist as at present on the earth plane unless Noah had entered the ark (of incarnation) and given birth and origin to offspring, subjected to the laws of evolution and development that generate alike both in the celestial and terrestrial worlds by which it was rendered competent to multiply and replenish the earth. Such is the occult meaning of the oracular words 'Drink waters out of thy cistern and running waters or streams out of thy well.' "

"And the earth also was corrupt before God" (Alhim) (Gen. vi., 11). Said Rabbi Jehuda, "Scripture states that the earth was also corrupt and then adds, 'before the Alhim.' Why so? It was in order to show the men of that generation then existent on the earth lived in violation both of natural and moral law,—that their wickedness was flagrant and open before man and God."

Said Rabbi Jose: "I think otherwise. The words signify, that men committed crimes secretly and known only to Alhim and that only by their enormity and heinousness did they manifest to everyone. The words 'these are the generations of Noah' apply equally to mankind who before the advent of Noah lived in open wickedness and to his posterity whose sin was in secret."

Said Rabbi Abba: "From the time of Adam's transgression of the divine commands all his descendents were called sons or children of Adam, not as a term of honor, but as a characteristic of birth from an ancestor who by his disobedience had broken the divine law. When Noah appeared in the world, men were termed the sons of Noah, an honorable distinction, as being the offspring of him who preserved the human race from extinction and not of Adam whose sin caused it to disappear by bringing death into the world to every soul.''

Said Rabbi Jose in objection to this statement: "If this were really true, wherefore is it written 'And the Lord came down to see the city and the tower which the children of Adam builded' (Gen. xi., 5), the sons or children of Adam and not of Noah and who were living after the time of the deluge.' "

Said Rabbi Abba in reply: "Through his disobedience it would have been better for Adam had he not been created, as all who like him become transgressors of the law are denominated 'sons of Adam,' not because deriving their birth from him but as being transgressors as he was, and such were the builders of the tower of Babel. Now may we gather why scripture uses the word Aleh (these are the generations) to distinguish the difference existing betwen the Adamic and Noachic races of mankind. The generations of Noah were now no longer termed the sons of Adam, but the sons of Noah who introduced into and brought them forth out of the ark in order to re-people the world. Adam did not bring forth children or sons out of the garden of Eden, for had he done so they would have been immortal or extra human. Then also would not the light of the moon have become diminished and the work of creation would have endured everlastingly. Even the highest angels themselves would not have equalled man in the endowment of celestial light, beauty of form and wisdom as it is written, 'In the image of Alhim created He him' (Gen. 1. 27). But the children of Adam, begotten after his expulsion from the garden of Eden, were both mortal and unworthy."

Said Rabbi Hezekiah: "How was it possible for Adam to beget off-spring in the garden of Eden, as it is certain, the tempter would have had no power over him and he would have remained childless in the world, even as Israel if they had not sinned by worshipping the golden calf, would have remained unique as a race and would not have given birth to another generation?"

Said Rabbi Abba in reply: "My contention is this. If Adam had not sinned he would not have engendered and begotten offspring under the influence of the tempter (sexual desire), but of the Holy Spirit (the Higher Self). After the fall, his offspring begotten under the influence of animal sexual propensities, were mortal, not being pure and unalloyed in their origin and constitution but compounded of the animal and spiritual. If however he had not fallen and remained in the garden of Eden, he would have begot offspring entirely spiritual and who in their constitution would have been as pure and immortal as the angels and other celestial beings. The children born after his expulsion from Eden enjoyed only a temporary and ephemeral existence up to the appearance of Noah who· after entering the ark (of incarnation) and by his righteous living becoming united with his Higher Self, was then able to produce off-spring that eventually spread themselves throughout all parts of the earth, leaving behind a posterity that will survive to the end of the world.

Said Rabbi Hiya: "It is written, 'And God saw their works, that they turned from their evil way' (Ion. III. 10). Observe, when men become upright and obey the dictates of the good law, the earth itself changes and acquires a virtue to administer to the enjoyment and happiness of mankind, as then the Schekina or that divine something termed life that operates in all organic and inorganic creatures and by its attractive power binds together the mundane and heavenly sphere, the harmony between which, results in peace and joy. On the contrary, when sin and wrongdoing prevail, this divine life and influence is banished from the earth, which becomes itself infected and desolate and infertile through the evil influence that then pervades it. But if Israel sins, which God forbid, scripture states that then Alhim quits the earth and ascends into heaven (Ps. LV. II. 6) and also gives the reason thereof, 'because they have prepared a net for my feet. My soul is bowed down through their iniquity; which words are expressive of a degree of wickedness similar to that of the antediluvians. If it be asked, do they apply equally to Jerusalem? Doth the Schekina forsake it when men become corrupted? for we have been taught that it is under the special care and protection of the Holy One who has chosen it for his habitation, so that no other spirit or celestial chief reigns and rules in the land of Israel. Notwithstanding this, we affirm that it comes to pass that an evil spirit or influence visits it and corrupts the dwellers therein. How know we this? From King David of whom it is written, 'And David beheld the angel of the Lord standing between the earth and the heaven· having a drawn sword in his hand stretched over Jerusalem' (I. Chron. XXI. 16), owing to the land of Israel having become corrupted by evil." *To be continued.*

MOMENTS WITH FRIENDS.

Is it possible and is it right to look into the future and predict future events?

It is possible but seldom right to look into the future. That it is possible is attested on many pages of history. As to its being right that must be determined by one's own fitness and good judgment. A Friend would not advise another to try to look into the future. One who looks into the future does not wait to be advised. He looks. But of those who look into the future, few know what they are looking at. If they look and do see, it is only when the future has become the past that they know what they saw when they looked. If one sees into the future naturally, there is no particular harm in his continuing to look, though few are able to derive any benefit from the operation. Harm comes almost invariably from predicting what the looker thinks he sees.

If one looks or sees into the future he does so with his senses, that is, his astral senses; or with his faculties, that is, the faculties of the mind; and there is no particular danger in doing so, providing he does not attempt to mix the world in which he sees with this physical world. When he attempts to predict future events in this world from what is seen in another world, he becomes confused; he cannot relate what he has seen and fit it into its place in the future in this physical world; and that is so even though he did see truly. His predictions cannot be relied on when applied to future events in this physical world, because these do not occur as predicted in time, nor in manner, nor in place. He who sees or who tries to see into the future is like an infant seeing or trying to see objects about it. When the child is able to see, it is quite pleased, but it makes many mistakes in its understanding and judging of what it sees. It cannot appreciate relation nor distance between objects. Distance does not exist for the infant. It will try to grasp the chandelier with as much confidence as it lays hold of its mother's nose and does not understand why it does not reach the chandelier. One who looks into the future sees events and fancies that they are about to occur, because he has no judgment as to the relation between what he sees in the world in which he sees it, and the physical world, and because he is unable to estimate the time of the physical world in which it may occur in relation to the event at which he is looking. Many predictions do come true, though not always as predicted. It is unwise, therefore, for people to depend on the predictions of those who try to look into the future by use of clairvoyance or other of the inner senses, because they cannot tell which of the predictions will be correct.

Those who depend on predictions coming from what are usually called "inner planes" or "astral light," lose one of their most valuable rights, that is, their own judgment. For, however many mistakes one may make in attempting to judge things and conditions for himself, he will judge correctly only by learning, and he learns by his mistakes; whereas, if he learns to depend on others' predictions, he will never have sound judgment. One who predicts future events has no certainty of their coming true as predicted, because the sense or faculty by which the prediction is made is unrelated to the other senses or faculties. So one who sees only or hears only, and that imperfectly, and who attempts to predict what he saw or heard, is likely to be correct in some respects, but to confuse those who rely on his prediction. The only sure way of predicting future events is for the one who predicts to have his senses or his faculties intelligently trained; in that case each sense or faculty will be related to the others and all will be so perfected that they can be used with as much accuracy as that with which a man is able to use his senses in his action and relation to this physical world.

The much more important part of the question is: Is it right? In man's present condition it is not right, because if one be able to use the inner senses and relate them to events and conditions of the physical world, it would give him an unfair advantage over the people among whom he lives. The use of the inner senses would enable a man to see what has been done by others; the seeing of which would as surely bring about certain results as the tossing of a ball in the air would result in its fall. If one saw the ball tossed and was able to follow the curve of its flight, and had experience, he could estimate accurately where it would fall. So, if one could use the inner senses to see what had already been done in the stock market or in social circles or in matters of state, he would know how to take unfair advantage of what was intended to be private, and could so shape his actions as to benefit himself or those in whom he was interested. By this means he would become the director or ruler of affairs and could take advantage of and control others who were not possessed of powers such as his. Therefore, before it can be right for a man to look into the future and predict future events correctly, he must have overcome covetousness, anger, hatred and selfishness, the lust of the senses, and must be unaffected by what he sees and predicts. He must be free from all desire of possession or gain of wordly things.

A FRIEND.

THE CANDIDATE FOR TRUTH.

God offers to every mind its choice between truth and repose. Take which you please—you can never have both. Between these, as a pendulum, man oscillates. He in whom the love of repose predominates will accept the first creed, the first philosophy, the first political party he meets,—most likely his father's. He gets rest, commodity and reputation; but he shuts the door of truth. He in whom the love of truth predominates will keep himself aloof from all moorings, and afloat. He will abstain from dogmatism, and recognize all the opposite negations between which, as walls, his being is swung. He submits to the inconvenience of suspense and imperfect opinion, but he is a candidate for truth, as the other is not, and respects the highest law of his being.

—EMERSON, *"Intellect."*

THE
WORD

A MONTHLY MAGAZINE

PUBLISHED AND EDITED BY
H. W. PERCIVAL, 253 West 72d Street, New York City

LONDON—KEGAN PAUL, TRENCH, TRUBNER & Co., 43 Gerrard Street

CONTENTS FOR JULY, 1910

ADEPTS, MASTERS AND MAHATMAS, . .	EDITORIAL	193
THE INNER LIFE AND THE TAO-TEH-KING,	C. H. A. BJERREGAARD	218
TALES OF AN ANCIENT TRAVELLER, . .	SAMUEL NEU	227
A DREAM OF ATLANTIS—THE LAND OF MU,	ALICE DIXON LE PLONGEON	236
THE SEPHER HA-ZOHAR—THE BOOK OF LIGHT,	NURHO DE MANHAR	247
MOMENTS WITH FRIENDS, ...	A FRIEND	255

Yearly Subscription - - - - - -	$4.00 or 16s.
Single Copies - - - - - - -	.35 or 1s. 6d.
Six Months' Subscription - - - - -	2.00 or 8s.
Three Months' Subscription - - - - -	1.00 or 4s.

BOUND VOLUMES OF THE WORD
Vols. I-X in Cloth and Half Morocco
Cloth, $21.00; Half Morocco, $26.00

The ten completed volumes of The Word are a valuable addition
to any Library
They are a library in themselves

[Entered as Second-class Mail Matter, May 2, 1906, at the Post Office at New York, New York, under the Act of Congress of March 3, 1879.]

NEW
THE MAGICAL MESSAGE
according to
IÔANNÊS
commonly called
The Gospel according to [St.] John
A verbatim translation from the Greek done in modern English, with introductory essays and notes

BY

JAMES M. PRYSE
Price, Cloth, $2.00

The root of Mr. Pryse's claim is that the Gospel by John is altogether mystical in intention and that the mystical eanings of the words should never be distorted. According to Mr. Pryse the fourth gospel is much more than an account of the physical career of Jesus. He sees in it the history of the purification of the soul and so well does he buttress his claim that the best exponents of biblical criticism and Greek scholarship will be hard put to it to find anything to say in disproof.

The Theosophical Publishing Company of New York, 253 W. 72d Street

---

A Book of practical Development
is
WILLIAM J. FLAGG'S
Yoga
Or Transformation.
It gives the Facts.

It shows the true Magic which underlies the Akkadian, Hindu, Taoist, Egyptian, Hebrew, Greek and Christian Religions.

It gives a comparative statement of the various Religious Dogmas concerning the Soul and its Destiny.

It is a religious Education to read this Book carefully.

Price, cloth, $3.00.
Send for Descriptive Catalogue.

Charles G. Leland,
The well-known writer, has written a fascinating volume, called,
HAVE YOU A
Strong Will?
Or How to develop and strengthen the Will-Power, Memory, or any other Faculty or Attribute of Mind.

It is written, so all will grasp it.
Brilliant, so you will enjoy it.
Powerful, so you will not forget it.

It will help you to do what you want.

Price, cloth, $1.50.

Send for a booklet, "Books for the Higher Life."
It will tell you all about this Book.

The Theosophical Publishing Company of New York, 253 W. 72d Street

When ma has passed through mahat, ma will still be ma; but ma will be united with mahat, and be a mahat-ma. —The Zodiac.

THE WORD

Vol. 11   JULY, 1910.   No. 4

Copyright, 1910, by H. W. PERCIVAL.

ADEPTS, MASTERS AND MAHATMAS.

(Continued from page 137.)

FIGURE 33 is here given to show the nature of each of the races which contribute to the making of man, how and under what dominant character and sign each race begins and is developed and ends, and how each race is related to and affected by those which precede or which follow it. A few suggestions will indicate some of that which may be found in this symbol.

The Figure 33 shows the great zodiac with seven smaller zodiacs. Each of the seven surrounds one of the seven lower signs of the great zodiac. Within the lower half of the great zodiac are drawn lesser zodiacs, one within the other, in the proportions heretofore given in figure 30, and symbolizing respectively the physical man and the physical world, the psychic man and the psychic world, the mental man and the mental world and the spiritual man and the spiritual world.

The horizontal diameter from ♋ to ♑ of the great zodiac is the line of manifestation; above is that which is unmanifested, below is the manifested universe. In this figure are shown seven races on four planes, the planes being the spiritual plane which begins with ♋ and ends with ♑, the mental plane which begins with ♌ and ends with ♐, the psychic plane begins with ♍ and ends with ♏, and the physical plane of ♎, which is the pivotal plane for the upper three planes in their involutionary and evolutionary aspects.

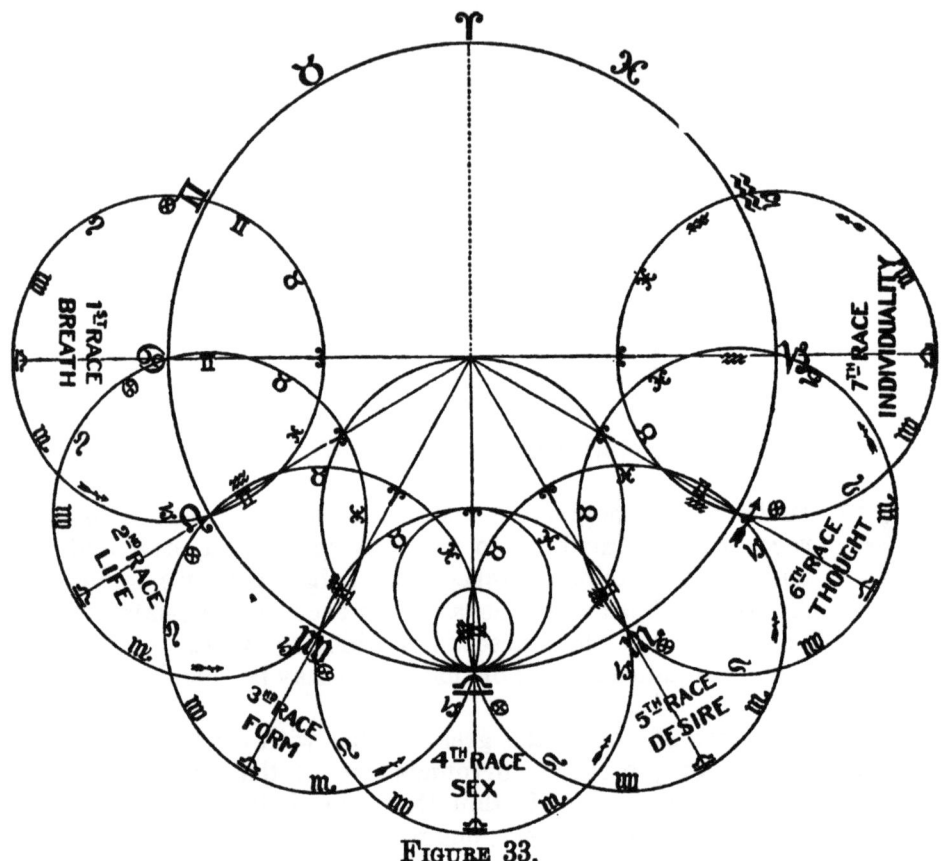

Figure 33.

The vertical diameter, from ♈ to ♎, symbolizes consciousness; this extends throughout the unmanifested and the manifested. These two lines, the vertical and horizontal, apply in the sense here used to the great zodiac; not to the seven lesser zodiacs representing here the seven races. In the fourth race, the race of ♎, the line symbolizing consciousness is vertical, as to the horizontal diameter of the great circle, and identical and coincident in part with the line symbolizing consciousness in the great zodiac. This is not a matter of accident.

The lower half of the great circle symbolizes the horizontal diameter or line of manifestation of the seven races unfolded, involving and evolving. From the center, the point at which matter (that is, spirit-matter, the dual manifestation of substance) becomes conscious, radiate seven lines which, extended, coincide in part with the diameters of the seven lesser zodiacs.

These vertical diameters, each from ♈ to ♎ in the lesser circles, symbolize the line along which each race develops consciously. The horizontal diameter in each zodiac of the seven from ♋ to ♑, is a curved line, coincident, in figure 33, with the periphery of the great zodiac.

Each race begins its development at the sign ♋ in its own zodiac, reaches its middle point at ♎ and ends at ♑.

The second race began at the middle or ♎ of the first race and at ♋ of its own zodiac, and ended at ♑ of its own zodiac and in the middle of the third race, which was the beginning of the fourth race. The third race began at the end of the first, the middle of the second and ended at the middle of the fourth race, which was the beginning of the fifth race. The fourth race began at the end of the second race, which was the middle of the third race, and ends at the middle of the fifth race, which was the beginning of the sixth race. The fifth race began at the end of the third race, which was the middle of the fourth race, and will end at the middle of the sixth race, which will be the beginning of the seventh race. The sixth race began at the end of development of the fourth race which was the middle of the fifth race, and it will end at the middle of the seventh race.

The first race began with the beginning of the universe, which came out from the unmanifested. The first race began at its sign ♋ and became consciousness only at its middle period, when it reached its ♎, which was the beginning of its line of consciousness. The line of its consciousness was and is also the line of manifestation of the great zodiac. The first race has not ended. It does not die throughout the period of manifestation.

The development of the seventh race will begin at the end of the fifth race which is the middle of the sixth race and will be completed in its sign of ♑, which will be in the unmanifested. Its line of consciousness completes the line of manifestation of the great zodiac. More could be written in elucidation of Figure 33, but the foregoing is sufficient to explain the symbolism relating to the matter here treated.

There is a great difference between one who becomes an adept before he becomes a master and the adept who is born after his master. The difference is that the first kind of adept has an unborn mind, whereas, the master, the mind, has a fully developed adept. The adept of the master can at all times act in accordance with the laws of the mental world, because the master, acts through him and he responds to thought more readily than the brain responds to the action of the mind. The adept whose mind is unborn, acts under the laws of the desire world, but he cannot or does not know clearly the law above him, around him, which is the law of time, the law of the mental world. He cannot control it nor can he act in perfect accordance with it. He acts according to the law of the astral world, the world of the inner senses, which world is a reflection and reaction from the physical world and from the mental world. The adept with his unborn mind will most likely remain unborn in the mental world at the close of the manifestation of the cycle of worlds. The adept of the master has been raised and born legitimately of the mind, and his heritage will be the mental world into which he will pass after the master has become a mahatma.

The adept with the unborn mind does not have the independent use of the mental faculties, though these faculties are used by him in a greater or more pronounced degree than the intelligent man of the world is able to use them. The independent and intelligent use of the mental faculties belongs exclusively to the disciple of the masters, who learns to use them fully only when he becomes a master.

The independent and intelligent use of the focus faculty causes the self appointed disciple to become and constitutes him an accepted disciple in the school of the masters. The free use of the image and dark faculties belongs to the adept who is made adept by his master. The free use of the time and motive faculties is had by the master only. But the master cannot fully and freely use the light and the I-am faculties, though he knows of them and they act through his other faculties. The free use of the light and I-am faculties is had by the mahatma only.

The master has full possession of and uses his time and image and focus and dark and motive faculties, independently of the inner senses, such as sight, hearing, taste, smell, touch, moral and I senses, or their action into the physical world. Instead of a dreary waste or a world of darkness and confusion, the master knows that the physical world is a place where heaven may reign. He sees the physical world to be more beautiful than eye can see, a place where harmonies prevail that the ear cannot detect, and where forms are grander than the mind of man can imagine. He sees it as the place of change and trial where all beings may be purified, where death must be overcome by all in turn, where man will be able to know and discriminate the true from the false, and where he will some day walk as the lord and master of his forms, the conqueror of illusion, while he still uses it for those beings who are nursed through it into the real.

From the mental world, the heaven world, the master acts through the inner world of the senses into the physical world and while using the inner senses and the physical body he controls them by his faculties. By his mental faculties through his senses and in his physical body, he can interpret the illusion of matter in the three worlds of its transformations. By means of his focus faculty he can bring into the physical world and make present there the thoughts of the mental and forms of the astral worlds. He can perceive the astral and mental through the physical. He sees the harmonies and beauties of the combinations of the physical, astral and mental. Through his time faculty the master can hear and see the atoms of time as they constantly flow through the physical matter and on, and he knows the measure and duration of a form made physical, because he knows the tone to which it is set and sounds. By this tone which is the time limit and measure, he knows the period the form will last until the physical matter in the form is borne on and into the time world from which it came. By his image faculty the master can create a form and cause it to be made visible by the flowing into and through it of the units of time, the time atoms. Through the image faculty he can cause forms to appear infinitely great or infinitely small. He may magnify or enlarge a molecule to the size of the world, or cause a world to appear as small as a molecule. This he does by holding the form in his image faculty and increasing or reducing its size by means of his focus faculty.

By means of his focus faculty the master enters or leaves the physical and psychic worlds or any portions of them. By means of the focus faculty, he relates and adjusts the faculties to each other and to the senses through which the faculties may act.

By means of the dark faculty he can cause to disappear or to be transformed any of the forms which he has called into existence. Through the dark faculty he can produce sleep in any being that breathes. By exercise of the dark faculty the master may prevent the minds of men from entering the realms of the mental world before their time, and he sometimes does it when an entrance would cause their becoming unbalanced, or he may give them power to subject other minds to their own and he does it to check men who train their minds with the object of controlling others. By exercise of the dark faculty, on a man's mind he may cause the man to be confused, bewildered, and forgetful of the object he had in view. By means of the dark faculty a master may befog the senses and prevent curious and inquisitive people from discovering that to which they have no right. By exercise of the dark faculty the master checks the inquisitive from sensing, reading or knowing the thoughts of others. By means of the dark faculty the master prevents those who seek for selfish ends, from learning of words and their power.

By use of his motive faculty the master knows the motives of men which prompt them to action. The master knows by the motive faculty that man's motives are the mainsprings of his life and that they, though often unknown to man, are the causes of all occurrences of importance in his life. Through his motive faculty he knows that motives are the causes of thought, which creates all things in the three manifested worlds. Through the motive faculty the master knows the kinds and classes and degrees of all thoughts of which men are capable, and of thoughts as beings of the mental world. Through the motive faculty he knows of the nature of his own master body and of his own motive by which it has come into fullness. By his motive faculty he can follow the trains of thought which have been worked out in the coming into fullness of his time in the mental world. Through his motive faculty he looks into the other motives which he might have but did not act from. By comparison of his motive with other motives he may judge and does judge his own motive, which is the cause of his action in the three worlds. Through his motive he knows what is and so chooses his work as a master. Through his motive faculty he knows that his work is not yet done, if he would pass into the spiritual world as a mahatma. By his motive faculty he knows that he has outgrown life, overcome death, that he is immortal and has worked out the karma of the life of the body through which he has attained, but that he has not completely exhausted the karma of each and of all the personalities through which the mind has incarnated, or else that he has obligations, duties, of which he could not acquit himself in the present life because those others to whom he owes a debt or is obligated are not in human form. He knows that even though he may have worked out all his own karma, exhausted the karma of all his lives, it may still be necessary for him to take another human form or many human forms, as a duty to which he may have pledged himself to the world and as decided by the motives which caused the taking of his pledge. By his motive faculty the master knows the causes which have determined his work.

By the time faculty he will know of the periods and appearances and the cycles of his own work and, of the periods of those with whom and for whom he will work. By his image faculty, he may know the forms in which they will appear. He knows that his own form and features will be about as they now are in physical outline. By the dark faculty he will know how and under what conditions the forms or races with whom he will work, shall die or be changed. By the focus faculty he will know where those are for and with whom he will act and the conditions under which they will appear.

The mental faculties of the master do not act separately nor entirely independently of each other. Similarly to the senses of man they act in combination or relation to each other. As a man may anticipate the taste of a lemon by hearing its name, or by its odor, or by touching it, so a master would know the nature and duration of a form through his motive faculty, and would find any of the transformations of that form by use of his focus faculty.

So the master carries on his work and assists in the completions of the cycles of time. When his physical body is worn out and he needs another, he takes it from the early and pure stock of humanity previously mentioned. If his work leads him among men he appears usually as an unknown and obscure person and does his work as quietly and inconspicuously as the requirements will permit. Men who see him see his physical body only. They cannot see him as a master body, though they may see his physical body, which gives evidence of the presence of the adept within it, and the master around it and through it, by the quiet power which it carries, the benign influence which it imparts, the love which it engenders and the simple wisdom in his words.

A master does not often come among mankind because it is not well for men. It is not well for men, because the presence of a master about and through his physical body prematurely quickens men. The presence of a master is like one's own conscience. A master's physical presence quickens the conscience in man and causes him to be aware of his shortcomings, vices and untruthfulness, and, although it also wakens all of the good qualities and encourages the virtues in him, yet man's knowledge of his virtues, side by side with his being conscious of his evil tendencies and untruthfulness, brings almost overwhelming remorse and regrets, which sap his strength and make his path seem hopelessly dark with insurmountable obstacles. This is more than his egotism can stand and he withers under the influence which were he more mature would quicken and assist him. The presence of a master does not make the fight in man's nature unequal; it causes the nature and its qualities to become manifest and apparent. This is so not by the will of the master, but because of his presence. His presence gives life to the inner nature and tendencies and makes them apparent, as sunlight makes visible all forms on the earth. Sunlight does not will the trees to bear fruit, birds to sing, nor flowers to bloom. Trees bear fruit, birds sing, and flowers bloom and each species manifests itself according to its nature because of the sun's presence, not because the sun wills that they should. The sun increases in strength as winter is passed and the season of spring advances. The gradual advance and increasing strength of the sun is borne by the tender plants as they shoot out upward in response to the warmth. They cannot stand and flourish under the sun's strength, until they are fully grown. Were the sun to shine suddenly and continuously on the young plants they would be withered by its strength. So it is with big and little men of the world who, like young plants, are unable to grow under the powerful influence of a master. Therefore a master does not come among men in his physical body, if the needs of the time will permit being cared for by a disciple of the masters. The influence of the masters is in the world at all times and surrounds it; but this influence affects the minds of men only who are susceptible to it. Their physical bodies and their desires are not in touch with the influence, and therefore do not feel it. Not the bodies, but the minds only of men can be affected by the masters.

Removed from the world of ordinary men, the master still is aware of and acts upon it; but he acts through the minds of men. The master does not consider men as they consider themselves. Men in the world are known to the master in his mental world when and as they are there represented by their thoughts and ideals. A master knows a man by his motive. When a man's motive is right he assists him in his thoughts toward the attainment of his ideal, and though men may say that they are promoted by right motives and have unselfish ideals, they cannot know because they do not know their motives and, therefore, cannot judge their ideals. A master is not affected by whims nor sentiments. These do not appear in the mental world as thoughts or ideals. Whims and sentiments and idle wishes never reach the mental world; they remain in the emotional astral desire world and are moved or blown about by the impulses as heavy smoke is blown about or shifted by gusts of wind. When a man has worked earnestly and assiduously and with devotion to his ideal, and his motive shows that he is entitled to it, the master thinks and his thought reaches the mind of the assiduous devotee who then sees the way of attainment of his ideal. This seeing comes after effort, and there is a mental joy and happiness which follows it. Then the man who had strained and struggled sets himself about his work confidently and with assurance and because he sees the way in which it is to be done. In this way a master may and does help man. But a master does not assist man by proclamations, nor by sending messages or issuing edicts, because a master wants men to use their reason as their authority for action, and not to take as authority the word of another. Those who issue edicts, send messages and make pronouncements, are not masters. At least they are not masters as are here described. A master may cause a message to be given to the world, but the message must be taken on its own merits, on the nature of the message and the principle involved. To say that a message is from a master will cause the believer to accept it without judgment, and will cause the unbeliever to ridicule its pretended source. In either case the message will fail in its purpose. But if the message is given inconspicuously without pride or pretense by the channel through whom it comes and on its own merit, the reasoning unbeliever will accept it without prejudice and the believer will take it because it will appeal to him with power and because it is right.

With an accepted disciple in the school of the masters, a master acts through the one thought by which he becomes consciously an accepted disciple. The master speaks to men through their ideals. He speaks to the disciple through thought. He speaks to other masters by motive and by his presence.

Though a master has not a human form, his form is quite as individual as that of a physical man. Were it possible for human eyes to see the forms of masters, they would, though all the same in principle, seem less alike than those who are daily met on busy streets.

For a man of the street, or a man of action, there is a great deal to be done. He is busy, and others of his kind are busy, and all must hurry. To the busy man, a master without human form, without senses, with mental faculties only, living in the mental world where night and day do not exist, where there is nothing of the senses present, to the busy man, such a picture would be inane, flat, perhaps less interesting than a picture of a sense-heaven where angels flutter over rivers of milk and honey or pass lightly over jasper streets and float around the great white throne.

The man of hurry cannot be blamed if he thinks such description flat. But ideals toward the masters will not always be flat, even to the busy man. Some day the claws of his desires will scratch and awaken him, or his mental growth may reach upward beyond his desires and his busy play in life, and then on his mental horizon there will come a thought he had not before had, and he will awaken to the ideal of the mind. This ideal will not leave him. He will continue to dream of his ideal and the dream will become gradually a waking dream and, at some day, most likely in a future life, the waking dream will become reality to him; then what was reality will be a dream, a dream of the childhood of his lives from which he has passed, as the days of children pass when they become men. He will then look back on the busy life of his childhood, with its momentous questions, with its burdens and responsibilities, its duties, sorrows and its joys. He will then look back on it as another busy man looks back on his early childhood with its important play, with its serious lessons, its merry laughter, bitter tears, and all of the wonderful exploits and things which make a child's atmosphere and world and shut it in from those who are older than it.

Masters are engaged with the ideals and the thoughts of men, as parents are with the play of their little ones. Like the prudent mother or kind father who look on at the play of their little ones and listen patiently to their dreams, so the masters look on at the little ones in the nursery, and in the school of life. Masters are more patient than parents, because they have no ill temper; they are not peevish nor dyspeptic, and can listen and understand as parents never can. The busy man has no time to learn to think, and he does not think. A master always does. Masters have much to do and do much and do all that they have to do. But it is a different work than that of the busy man.

The masters are the elder men of the race. Without them there would be no progress for man, because men, like children, if left to themselves before their maturity, will die in childhood or else revert to the animal state and condition. As children are drawn out and acquainted with life by their elders, so masters lead on and draw upward the minds of men.

As men approach their ideals and are ready for higher ideals, the masters direct their minds to the eternal verities, here called ideas, in the spiritual world. Their thought of an idea is the ideal held in the mental world by the master, and the minds of the leaders of men in the world of men, who are ready, catch glimpses of the ideal and by their thoughts bring it into their world of men. As the leaders of men speak the thought, the new ideal, into the world of men, those who listen to them are impressed by the thought; they take it up and look up to it as their ideal. In this way man is ever lead on and educated by his ideals if he will only think upward rather than downward. In this way, by giving to men new ideals as teachers give their scholars new lessons, mankind is lead onward in its growth by the masters who, though not seen, are ever present.

According to the ideals of humanity as a whole or the race in part or a few leaders, the masters think, and time arranges itself and flows according to their thought. The power of the masters is their thought. Their thought is their speech. They think, they speak, and the time flows on, bringing into fullness the aspirations of man. The word of the masters keeps the world in balance. The word of the masters keeps it in its form. The masters' word causes the revolution of the world. But though the masters' word sounds through and supports the world, few ears can hear its tone, few eyes can see its form, few minds can comprehend its meaning. Yet all minds are trying to understand the meaning of the age, which the masters' word has spoken into being. Many eyes look forward to see what it will bring, and ears are strained to catch the note, which the new age sounds.

From age to age in the time world, in the mental world, in the heaven world of man, the master works until he works out all measures of time. His cycle of necessary incarnations ended, his physical, psychic and mental karma long since exhausted, with his physical and adept desire bodies in their respective worlds acting with and for the law, the master thus acting from the mental world is ready to become a mahatma, to enter the spiritual world.

The passing of a master as mahatma into the spiritual world is not attended by the difficulties nor preceeded by the darkness that attend the birth of the disciple through its womb of darkness into the day of the mental world. The master knows the way, and knows how to enter the spiritual world. But he does not enter before the measures of time are run. Standing in his physical body and through his adept body, the master speaks the word of birth. By his word of birth he is born. By his word of birth the master's name passes into or becomes one with his name as mahatma. The word of his birth as mahatma is called into being by the use of his light faculty and his I-am faculty. As he gives his name by these faculties, he enters the spiritual world. There he has always been, but could not perceive it, could not realize it, until the use of the light and the I-am faculties realized it.

In becoming a mahatma all faculties are blended into one being. All faculties become the I-am. I-am is the mahatma. I-am no longer thinks, for thinking ends with knowledge. The mahatma, I-am, knows. He is knowledge. As mahatma, no one faculty acts alone. All are together as one, and all are the end of all thinking. They are knowledge.

To the mahatma, the physical, buzzing world has disappeared. The inner desire world of sensation is stilled. All thought in the mental world has stopped. The three manifested worlds of time have disappeared into and blended with the spiritual world. The worlds have gone, but they are comprehended in the spiritual world by the mahatma. In the worlds of time, which were made up of indivisible particles which are the ultimate divisions of time, each world was distinct in itself, but at the fulling of time, when time runs into its sources from the mental world, all the individual units run together like drops of water, and are blended, and all make up the eternity, the spiritual world which is one.

He who has entered and knows eternity is the eternity. He knows that he was and is ever and always I-am. All things are present in this knowledge. As I-am knows itself, limitless light abounds, and though there are no eyes to see it, the light knows itself. I-am knows itself as light, and light is I-am. If the mahatma wills to be throughout eternity only as he knows himself, I-am, as being, he shuts out from his light the manifested worlds, and remains I-am, his light, the light throughout the eternity. In the ancient eastern philosophies, this state is spoken of as entrance into nirvana.

ADEPTS, MASTERS AND MAHATMAS

The becoming of mahatma and such entrance into nirvana is not determined at the time or after he becomes a mahatma; it is decided by a master through his motive faculty, and that decision or the causes of such decision have been determined by and made up of all the motives which have prompted man in his efforts in overcoming and toward attainment. This choice is that of those ascetics who do not love the world, and leave it that they may attain their own deserved bliss. The choice results from the beginnings of man as he sees and thinks of himself as distinct and separate from others and does not relate himself to others.

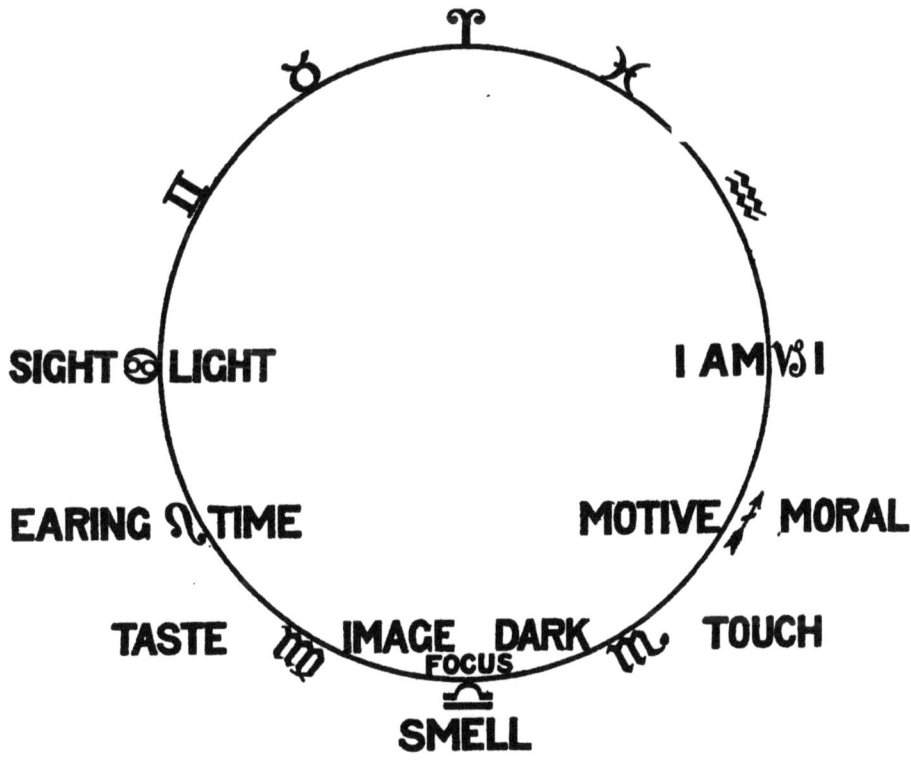

FIGURE 34.

The Faculties of the Mind and the Senses Which Correspond to Them.

The master who thinks of the welfare of mankind for the sake of mankind, and not that he shall advance, does not on becoming mahatma remain in the quiet bliss of nirvana. The mahatma who remains in his bliss knows I-am, as I only. He who knows beyond and within the I, knows I-am, as I; but he also knows I-am, as Thou. He does not remain in the knowledge of his own light. He speaks the knowledge of his light, which is the light, into the three manifested worlds. When one on becoming mahatma speaks his light, all the worlds respond and receive new power, and the unselfish love is felt through all beings. One who has grown into the one light, one who knows the spiritual identity of all beings, will always speak into the world the light which he has become. The light thus given lives in the world and cannot die, and though it may not be seen by men, still it will shine, and the hearts of men to whom it is spoken will find it at the ripening of their time.

The mahatma who has chosen to remain as an eternal light through the manifested worlds retains his physical, adept and master bodies. One cannot become a mahatma without his physical body, but not every mahatma keeps his physical body. The physical body is necessary for the development and birth of all bodies. The physical body is that in which spiritual and mental and psychic and physical matter is transmuted, balanced and evolved. The physical body is the pivot of the worlds.

The mahatma who remains through the worlds and in the worlds uses the faculties which relate to the worlds on which he acts. But a mahatma uses the faculties differently from a master. A master uses his faculties by thought, a mahatma by knowledge; a master knows as the result of thinking, and knowledge follows thought. A mahatma knows before he thinks, and thought is used only as the working out and applying of knowledge. The faculties of the mind are used by mahatmas and masters in any of the worlds, but only a mahatma may have full and free use of the light faculty and the I-am faculty. A mahatma uses the light and I-am faculties singly or together, with or apart from the other five faculties.

Each faculty has a special function and power, and is represented in each other faculty. Each faculty has not only its own function and power, but may be empowered by the other faculties, though all the others are dominated by the faculty to whose power they contribute.

The light faculty is the giver of light through all the manifested worlds. But the light of one world is not the light of another world. In its own world, the spiritual world, the light faculty is pure and unmixed intelligence, or the faculty through which intelligence comes and through which intelligence is expressed. The light faculty of the mind is the faculty through which the universal mind is perceived, and the faculty by or through which the individual mind becomes united with the universal mind.

By the aid of the light faculty, the time faculty reports truly the nature of time. The light faculty enables the time faculty to conceive and report matter truly in its ultimate and atomic combinations. By the light faculty acting with the time faculty all manner of calculations may be made. In the absence of the light faculty, the time faculty cannot truly conceive nor report the changes of matter, the mind is inaccurate and cannot make any calculations nor have any true notion of time.

The light faculty acting with the image faculty enables the mind to give shape to unformed matter, to picture mentally an image or combination of images and forms in harmonious relationships, according to the power of the light which is perceived and by which light the forms are harmoniously shaped.

By the light faculty acting with the focus faculty, the mind is able to direct its attention to any subject or thing, to bring into range of consideration any mental problem, and by the light faculty the focus faculty is enabled to hold steadily and estimate truly all forms, subjects or things. By the light faculty, the focus faculty is enabled to show the way to any attainment. In proportion to the absence of the light faculty the focus faculty cannot truly show to the mind the subject or thing to which it is directed.

The light faculty of the mind acting on the dark faculty, causes the mind to become conscious of its own ignorance. When the dark faculty is used under the light faculty, falsehoods and all untruthfulness are brought to light and the mind may find all imperfections, absurdities and disproportion, concerning whatever subject or thing it is directed to. But if the dark faculty is used without the light faculty, it produces confusion, ignorance and mental blindness.

By the light faculty acting with the motive faculty, the mind can know the causes of all events, actions or thoughts, and may decide or predict truly what will result from any thought or action. By the light and the motive faculties, the guiding principle of one's life and action, the causes of anyone's actions and the results which will accrue therefrom may be known. By the light and the motive faculties acting harmoniously together, one is able to find his own motives and is able to decide and choose which motive shall be the guide of his future thoughts and actions. Without the light faculty, the motive faculty will not truly show the motives in one's self which prompt thought and action.

By the light faculty acting with the I-am faculty, the I-am-I becomes conscious of and may be known to itself. By the light acting with the I-am faculty man impresses his identity on all surrounding things and charges his I-am faculty on and into the atmosphere and personalities with which he comes in contact. By the light and I-am faculties, the mind is able to see itself throughout nature and to see all things evolving toward self-conscious individuality. In the absence or in proportion to the absence of the light faculty, the I-am faculty is unable to distinguish itself in matter, and man is undecided and in doubt as to whether man has any future existence apart from his body.

The light faculty should act and be always present in the action of the other faculties. When the light faculty is absent or has ceased to function, man is spiritually blind.

The time faculty is the recorder of changes of matter in manifestation. By the time faculty the differences and changes in matter and phenomena are known. Time or the change of matter is different in each of the worlds. By the time faculty, time in any of the manifested worlds is comprehended in the world in which it is acting.

By the time faculty acting on the light faculty, the mind is able to look into the world to which it is directed and to perceive the proportion in which particles or bodies are related to each other and what is the period of their action in combination. By the time faculty acting on the light faculty, the light faculty may make clear to the mind, according to its power and purity, the duration of a cell and the relation and changes of its indivisible particles, and the mind may comprehend the relation and changes of the worlds in the duration of eternity. Without the function of the time faculty, the light faculty can show to the mind no changes in anything.

By the acting of the time faculty on the image faculty, the image faculty shows rythm and meter and proportion in form, whether the form be considered as an etheric wave or ideal image to be chiselled from a marble column. When under the influence of the time faculty, the image faculty will reveal the succession of forms, how one form follows that which preceded it and ends in the one which follows it, throughout involution and evolution. In the absence of the time faculty, the image faculty can show no relation between forms, and the mind will be unable through the image faculty to make or recall or follow melody, meter, and harmony, or to see color in or give it to any subject.

The time faculty directed on the focus faculty shows the difference and proportion and relation of subject and object. By the aid of the time faculty the focus faculty can group and show the relation between things and events of any particular period. If the time faculty does not lend aid, the focus faculty is unable to gather all the matter relating to the subject to which it is directed and the mind is unable to estimate the subject in its true light.

Acting with the time faculty, the dark faculty may declare the succession and nature of desire, the measure and intensity of desire, and the transformations of desire. Under the influence of the time faculty, the dark faculty may show the different states and changes of sleep, its depths and their periods. If the time faculty does not act with the dark faculty, the dark faculty can have no regular action and is unable to follow any order in action.

By the action of the time faculty with the motive faculty, the cycles and their changes may be known in any of the worlds, the causes of the groupings and actions of atoms, of international wars, or the peaceful combination and co-operation of nations. By use of the time faculty, the motive faculty will make known to the mind the effects which will follow the thinking of any thought and the action of that thought in the different worlds and the periods in which the events will occur. If the time faculty is inactive, the motive faculty cannot show the relation of cause to effect, and without the time faculty the mind will be confused and the motive faculty will be unable to distinguish cause from effect.

The I-am faculty acting under the influence of the time faculty spins and weaves out of matter webs and conditions and environments for the mind through the manifested worlds in, under and according to which it acts. By the use of the time faculty, the I-am faculty is able to trace the conditions and environments through which the mind has acted in any period of time. According to the inactivity of the time faculty, the I-am faculty is unable to recall its relation to any period or event and is unable to see itself as existing in the past or the future. The time faculty must be present in all mental activities and operations of men.

The image faculty is the matrix in which matter is held and given outline and form. Through the image faculty, forms last.

The image faculty acting with the light faculty causes the mind to picture forms in color and in the quality of the world in which it acts. Without the image faculty the light faculty can show no distinction in outline, nor difference in form.

By the image faculty acting on the time faculty, time, matter, is shaped and precipitated into form in the world in which it acts. With the image faculty the time faculty shows to the mind the forms which have been related or associated in the past. Without the image faculty the time faculty is unable to take and to come into form, in any of the three manifested worlds.

By the use of the image faculty the focus faculty can bring into view any of the forms of the past and show to the mind any form of the future which has already been outlined and determined. Without the image faculty, the focus faculty is unable to show forms to the mind.

By action of the image faculty on the dark faculty, the dark faculty causes to appear to the mind and take form, its fears, doubts, appetites and passions. By use of the image faculty the dark faculty causes the mind to see forms in the dream state. Without the image faculty, the dark faculty is unable to give shape to any fear or to see any forms in dreams.

By the image faculty the motive faculty makes the mind aware of the types and species of forms which result and how they result from different thoughts. Without the image faculty the motive faculty is unable to make known to the mind the forms which thoughts take, or to give form to ideals.

By the use of the image faculty, and through the I-am faculty, the mind may know the forms of its past incarnations, see the forms through which it had passed, or the form in which it now is in the psychic world, and its form in the mental world, and may comprehend what it as form is at the time in the spiritual world. By aid of the image faculty and through the I-am faculty, the mind is able to conceive its form in its own state as distinct from the form of the physical body.

In proportion to the absence of the image faculty, the I-am faculty is unable to picture to the mind any forms or designs relating to any of the worlds, or to have any form or style of expression. Without the image faculty acting with the other faculties the mind is unable to describe or picture to itself or other minds, other forms or its own in any of the worlds except that and at the time in which it is then acting, and it will be unable to see the beauty of form in figure or speech or grace in movement.

The focus faculty balances and relates the other faculties to each other. It gives a mental grasp of any subject and is that faculty by which the mind rises and descends from world to world. By the focus faculty the other faculties are drawn together and blended from world to world until they enter into the spiritual world where they all become one. When all the faculties are blended into one, the mind is knowledge and power, radiant and immortal.

When the light faculty is directed or induced by the focus faculty the mind is illuminated on any subject in the world to which it is directed. As the light faculty is aided by the focus faculty, the mind is able to surround itself with a body of light other than that of the world in which it is acting. By aid of the focus faculty the light faculty brings light to a center and makes a body of light. In the absence of the focus faculty, the light faculty diffuses light without relation to subjects or objects.

The time faculty acted on by the focus faculty enables the mind to find any event in the world of its action and to trace the consecutive periods of time, matter, in its revolutions, and to calculate the succession of changes from world to world. With the aid of the focus faculty the time faculty may be made to increase or decrease the flow of time and to show how time passes from one world into the other and becomes the time of that other. Without the focus faculty the time faculty is unable to report to the mind any occurrence of the past, and the mind is not able to see any change that may come about in the future, and the mind is unable to calculate concerning the past or future.

Acted on by the focus faculty the image faculty may reproduce any form that has existed anywhere. By the focus faculty acting on the image faculty the mind is able to magnify infinitely the minutest forms, and reduce those of greatest magnitude to the infinitely small. In the absence of the focus faculty, the image faculty cannot show to the mind any distinct objects or forms, nor can it give mental perspective to figures.

Under the influence of the focus faculty, the dark faculty may suspend the activities of the mind on the physical plane of action, and produce sleep, or it may produce a hypnotic sleep of other minds, or it may keep one's self awake and awaken others from a hypnotic sleep. Under the influence of the focus faculty the dark faculty can make known to the mind, darkness and the nature of sleep, what death is, and the processes of death. Under the direction of the focus faculty, the dark faculty can be made to report each of one's desires and what one's ruling desire is, what the appetites are, what passions, anger and the vices are, and how they affect the other faculties of the mind, and it can show the manner of the action between the faculties and the senses. In the absence of the focus faculty the dark faculty suspends the action of the other faculties of the mind, and produces sleep. When the focus faculty ceases to act with the dark faculty, the dark faculty produces death.

By directing the focus faculty on the motive faculty, one is able to know the governing principle of his own life or in the lives of others. With the focus faculty the motive faculty will make known the motive which caused any thought, action or result and judge the consequences resulting therefrom. By aid of the focus faculty, the motive faculty will show what thought is, what prompts it, and where it dwells. Without the focus faculty motives cannot be known, thought cannot be discovered and the mind cannot know the causes of its action.

The I-am faculty by the correct use of the focus faculty makes known to the mind who and what it is. It is able to know and preserve its identity in any of the worlds, irrespective of the conditions under which it might act. But according to the inability of the I-am to use the focus faculty the mind will not know itself in any of the worlds. In the absence of the focus faculty, the faculties cannot act in combination, and insanity follows. The focus faculty preserves a unity in the action of the faculties. If the focus faculty is not used in connection with each and all of the faculties no one singly or in combination can give true reports concerning any subject or thing.

The influence of the dark faculty extends through all the worlds and affects all other faculties of the mind. The dark-faculty is the cause of all doubt and fear in the mind. If not dominated, checked or controlled by one or all of the other faculties, the dark faculty will produce riot and confusion in the mind. The dark faculty is negatively strong and resists control or domination. It is under control only in so far as it is made to perform its functions in the service of the other faculties. The dark faculty is a necessary and valuable servant when mastered, but a strong, ignorant and unreasoning tyrant when it is not controlled.

When acted on by the dark faculty, the light faculty is unable to make known to the mind any subject or thing in proportion to the strength of its action or resistance, and in proportion to its dominance the mind is blinded. In the absence of the dark faculty, all things could be seen by the mind, but there would be no periods of rest and activity, or day and night.

Under the action of the dark faculty, the time faculty can not report orderly changes and is unable to make calculations concerning periods or events. In proportion as the dark faculty ceases to control or influence the time faculty, the time periods are lengthened and when the dark faculty does not act at all, time disappears into eternity and all is a day of negative bliss, because there would be no shade or contrast to the light which would then prevail and the mind would make no calculations.

The image faculty acted on by the dark faculty is unable to give form to anything or it will reproduce all the forms of darkness of which the mind had ever been aware, and the dark faculty will cause the image faculty to produce new images, new forms of ungainly or hideous and malignant aspects, representing the phases of desires and passions and sensuous vices. In the absence of the dark faculty, the image faculty would show forms of beauty, and picture to the mind those things which are pleasing to the mind.

In proportion to the influence of the dark faculty, the focus faculty is unable to present to the mind any subject or thing, cannot draw into view or relate to each other thoughts and the subjects of thought, nor co-ordinate or relate the action of the faculties to each other. In the absence and quiescence of and control over the dark faculty, the focus faculty can group and co-ordinate objects, thoughts and the subjects of thought, and present them clearly and concisely to the mind. In the absence of the dark faculty the focus faculty is unable to temper and strengthen the mind. But while quiescent and controlled, the focus faculty enables the mind to be continuously conscious.

When dominated by the dark faculty, the motive faculty is unable to acquaint the mind with its motives or the causes of its action, and in proportion as the influence of the dark faculty prevails, the motive faculty is prevented from enabling the mind to understand the relation between cause and effect, the manner and method of thought and the mind is unable to distinguish between its faculties and the senses, and the causes of the actions of either. In the absence of or its control over the dark faculty, the motive faculty can make known to the mind its own nature and enables the mind to choose and decide without doubt the best course of action.

In proportion to the influence and prevalence of the dark faculty, the I-am faculty is unable to give the mind identity, and the mind ceases to be conscious in any or all of the worlds of its action. When the dark faculty prevails against the I-am faculty it causes the mind to become unconscious of and produces death in that world; in the absence of the dark faculty the I-am faculty becomes all-conscious in the world of its action; light prevails, but the mind has nothing to overcome, and having no resistance, by the overcoming of which it could gain strength, it can not become fully self-conscious and immortal. By the mastery of the dark faculty, the I-am faculty gains immortality and learns to know itself. In the absence of the dark faculty the faculties do not learn perfection in function, and their operations would become slower and finally cease; the mind would be simply conscious without individuality and without being conscious of consciousness.

By means of the motive faculty, the mind causes all action and the results of action; and starts action of the other faculties. The motive faculty is the cause of their acting and determines their power. By the motive faculty, the mind decides upon its ideals and what its attainment shall be.

By the motive faculty the mind decides on what subject or object the light faculty will illuminate it. In proportion to the absence of the motive faculty the light faculty cannot inform and the mind cannot understand the spiritual world, the nature of light.

By the motive faculty, the time faculty makes known to the mind the nature and action of time, or matter, in any of the manifested worlds; it shows the causes of its circulations, determines the periods of its action and decides the quantity and quality and proportion of its action. With the aid and according to the development of the motive faculty, the time faculty can report to the mind any occurrence or event of the past, however distant, understand the present and predict the events of the future, in so far as they have been determined by a motive. By the motive faculty the time faculty can show to the mind the nature of thought, the method and manner of its action on other matter, and how and why it guides or directs matter into form. When the motive faculty is inactive, the time faculty is unable to report or make known to the mind the nature of matter, the cause of its changes and how and why it comes and goes and changes in regular periods.

By the motive faculty through the image faculty are decided the various kinds of figures, forms, features, colors and appearance in any of the manifested worlds, or what these will be in the spiritual world, and whether they will or will not be according to proportion of the ideal. By the motive faculty acting through the image faculty, figure and color and form is given to thought, and thought takes form. Without the aid of the motive faculty the image faculty of the mind cannot give form to matter.

When the motive faculty acts on the focus faculty there is determind when, where and under what conditions the mind will incarnate, and it is decided and regulated what one's karma will be. By the motive faculty is determined birth in the physical world and how and under what conditions the mind will be born into any of the other worlds. By aid of the motive faculty, the mind is able to find through the focus faculty its motives and to know causes. In the absence of the motive faculty, the worlds cannot start into operation, matter has no impetus to action, the mind has no purpose in effort, its faculties remain inert and the machinery of karma cannot be set in action.

According to the action of the motive on the dark faculty, the dark faculty is aroused into action; it resists, beclouds and confuses the mind; it is the cause of inordinate appetites, and produces passion and all phases of desire; it suggests and stimulates all longings, wishes and ambitions. On the other hand, it is the means of controlling the appetites and passions, and is the cause of noble aspirations, according to the motive which governs the dark faculty. With the motive faculty acting through the dark faculty, the mind is cut off from the physical world and death is produced; and, according to the motive, the mind is detained by the dark faculty of desire, after death. According to the motive, the mind is born from its physical body through the dark faculty into the mental world. In the absence of the dark faculty the mind would have no means of overcoming resistance and it could not achieve any attainments nor self-conscious immortality.

By the motive faculty acting on the I-am faculty, the mind decides of what it will become conscious, and by being conscious what it will become, determines what the quality of its reflective powers will be and what it will reflect.

The motive faculty acting on the I-am faculty decides what the mind will do and sense and think and know when acting in the physical and the other worlds. The motive faculty determines why and for what purpose the mind seeks immortality, the method by which immortality will be attained, and what the mind will be and do after immortality. According as the motive faculty guides the I-am faculty, the mind will or will not misunderstand or mistake itself for its bodies, will or will not know right from wrong action, will or will not be able to judge circumstances and conditions at their true value, and to know itself as it is at any time in any of the worlds, and also what it may become in this and in future periods of manifestation. If the motive faculty is absent, there is no self action of the mind. The motive faculty must be present in all mental functions and action. Only by learning its motives can the mind know its true self.

The I-am is the self-conscious, self-identifying and individualizing faculty of the mind.

The I-am faculty gives individuality to and individualizes light. By the I-am faculty acting with the light faculty, the mind becomes a sphere of splendor and power and glory. By the I-am acting with the light faculty, the mind may remain in the spiritual world, or may appear as a superior being to any of the beings of the worlds in which it may enter. In the absence of the I-am faculty, light remains universal and not individualized, self knowledge is impossible and mind can have not identity.

The I-am faculty of the mind acting through the time faculty impresses matter with identity, gives to the mind continuity and preserves identity of self through change. In the absence of the I-am faculty, mind cannot assimilate simple matter, and matter can not become self-conscious.

By the action of the I-am faculty through the image faculty the mind dominates, holds and gives distinctness to form. It impresses the idea of I-am-ness on forms and shows the way by which forms evolve and by which progress toward individuality can be made; it determines species and type; it numbers, names and preserves order and species of and in form. Through the image faculty, the I-am faculty determines in one physical life what the form of its next physical body shall be. In the absence of the I-am faculty, the image faculty can give no distinctness nor individuality to form; matter would remain simple and uniformed and there would be no forms.

Through the focus faculty the I-am faculty gives power. The I-am faculty acting through the focus faculty speaks itself out of, through and into each of the worlds.. By the I-am acting through the focus faculty, the mind is equilibrated, balanced, adjusted and related to its bodies and can be in and act and know itself through all the worlds and as distinct from its body of each of the worlds. By the I-am acting with the focus faculty, the mind may locate and find itself in any of the worlds. By the action of the I-am with the focus faculty, the mind has memory. In the absence of the I-am faculty the human form would be an idiot. Without the I-am faculty the focus faculty would become inactive and the mind would be unable to leave the world in which it is.

By the I-am faculty acting on the dark faculty, the mind resists, exercises, trains and educates desire and overcomes ignorance, regulates its appetites, silences and transmutes its vices into virtues, dominates darkness, conquers and overcomes death, perfects its individuality and becomes immortal. In the absence of or without control by the I-am faculty, the dark faculty would control or suppress and crush out or cause to become inactive the other faculties of the mind, and the mind would suffer mental and spiritual death.

By the action of the I-am on the motive faculty, the mind becomes impressed with the idea of egotism, which is the dominant motive of its action. As I-am dominates the motives, the mind will have an uneven development and imperfect and inharmonious attainment. As motive decides the action of the I-am faculty, the mind will become evenly developed, harmonious in its action and have perfect attainment. Without the I-am faculty acting with the motive faculty, the mind would have no comparison for action and no idea of attainment.

The I-am faculty should act with all other faculties of the mind. It conveys the idea of permanence to the other faculties and is the end of attainment as mind. Without the I-am faculty, there would be no continuity, permanence nor individualty of the mind.

(To be continued.)

THE INNER LIFE AND THE TAO-TEH-KING.

XIV.

By C. H. A. BJERREGAARD.

IN this chapter I will give a few hints to the understanding of the Shawnee tale told before. A full interpretation I have given elsewhere. The present hints will help to an understanding of Teh and conclude the exposition of the subject. Waupee and his life may be looked upon from the standpoint of the three gunas and that view will show how great he is. The introductory description of him in the story shows the two gunas: Tamas, the fundamental quality of bigness in rest, both in activity and in passivity; it shows him in nature's primary state of preparation or "inertia," if this word be properly understood. The same description also shows him in the guna of Rajas or as a youth full of energy and motion. He is always in action, hunting, fishing, exploring and studying his surroundings. These two qualities, for good and bad dominate him until the time he weds the celestial sister. Her advent, the story tells us, makes him perfectly happy and that is an evidence of the sattwa quality, the force and power of harmony, of truth. The three taken together show him as no mere specimen of a man, but as a species of man.

You know that the three gunas are modified in seven kinds of ways or in a sevenfold way. All of these I also see in Waupee. Let me show them in the seven steps in his life. We hear first a description of the simple minded Waupee who, to begin with, is without any special development in any direction. The first step is his first day's discovery and the rise of selfhood in him, caused by the marvels of the open plain and his first vision of the sisters. The second is his assertion of selfhood in deceit, when he "plays the possum." The third is renunciation of self, at the time he became a mouse. The fourth is his marriage to his own Higher Self, represented by wedding the celestial sister. The fifth is his "fall," described as his being "absent," and the loss of the sister as a result of these "absences." The sixth is his condition of suffering because of his loss and his resultant "penances," represented by his "returns" to the haunted spot or the condition in which the Celestial had come to him in the beginning. And finally his seventh degree is his restoration by the "celestial marriage," at the time he comes up on the heavenly plains.

His return to earth has nothing to do with his development. That represents a new feature of what I will call a second series of development. The story of the return may also be looked upon as Indian folk lore to account for the origin and character of the White Hawk.

It is curious, but it is a fact, people will rather walk that Path, which is Teh, positive, than the Path, which is Teh, negative. It appears that we will rather stand a strenuous life than a negative, and yet, the negative, Wu-Wei, would quickly give us the fulfillment of all legitimate desires. We will rather be killed by overwork than by non-action. That appears to be the condition of mankind in general.

Yet a closer examination will easily show that no one can live positively without being "hammered" from time to time. Death is a necessary element in the universe. Nobody likes a cross. Yet, Teh, positive, is not finished before we learn to love the cross and approve of afflictions. The reason is this, that only submission produces genuine simplicity. The eternal "No!" that follows some people, finally frees them. The closed doors are closed to prevent side-tracking. The ball that some drag after them fastened to the foot hinders hastiness. And all the endless chains that hold so many of us in conditions we call prison life are so many ropes that connect with bells that hang in the tower of conscience. And these bells are always sounding the alarm, when evil desires set us on fire,—still we will not listen or obey!

Crosses are set against all kinds of lawlessness and place us in conflict with ourselves; conflicts that always end in victory for the eternal Self. The last thing we discover is that it is always justice that cuts down the tree for our cross, and, that it is justice which nails it together and hangs us upon it.

No cross, no crown! But as little as you or I can manufacture the eternal crown with our hands, as little can we manufacture crosses of eternal value. Saints, so called, have done it. They have tortured themselves, and some have even calculated the value of the coming crown in proportion to the manufactured cross.

Do not manufacture crosses. Those that come to us in the natural course of life are quite sufficient. It sounds paradoxical, but it is true. Suffering, or the negative in life, has no power to hurt us if we live in Wu-Wei, that is, in non-action. It is my own action that makes suffering what it is. Teh, negative, is of our own making and that is why we walk the road. Nobody compels us.

Who and what is this celestial sister? I claim she answers to Teh. You have read what I have said about Teh, and, rather abstractly at that. I must therefore add to my foregone statements a view of Teh, hitherto held back. I have purposely ignored the view which I now present, in order to avoid confusion, and, to connect the conception Teh with Tao, which I, in earlier chapters, explained to be Nature, without qualifying the term. The connection is now easily made and seen by you; when I recall to your mind that all goddesses in the various mythologies are no more than personifications of forces or nature-powers. I take for granted, that my readers know this. That, too, is the case in folklore, and my story is folklore. The heroines of folklore are no more than similar personifications. This celestial sister of the Indian tale, I have related and now endeavor to explain, is such a personification of the Higher Self, which reveals itself to Waupee. All heroines and supernatural personalities that appear in folklore, folk-songs and old religious legends, have no meaning for us unless understood that way. Psychology as studied now-a-days endorses this statement. It says that the human mind cannot express itself (whatever it may feel) or give form to its ideals except by images taken from its own subjectivity, nor can we human beings commune with another human being except through mind or the Higher Self. In no other way can we possibly blend. Mind or the Highest Self is the alembic for the smelting of human personalities and the extraction of the pure metal, called Entity. Many mystics, however, deny this and claim direct communion with the Highest.

I will offer a few thoughts on the subject of Teh or Mother Nature as a personality and then apply these thoughts to an understanding of this celestial sister. Mother Nature is not a person like you or I; yet we cannot liberate ourselves from a realization and the feeling that at times we are guided, checked, even pushed; that at times "the voice of the silence" has something in it akin to us; that at times we long so intensely for what we call "the heart of nature," that we intellectually cannot escape the conclusion that there must be an essential affinity between the spirit of man and the life of nature. Our feeling asserts a personality, something akin to ourselves. But we never can get an intellectual verity before us. We are never directly approached. The whole activity is going out from us. It is so with most of us.

Mystics of all ages and all lands however tell us that they have been spoken to, have walked with and otherwise met such a personality. And they have a surety against deception in their "inner sense," so they say. Most of us must leave that assertion to them. We cannot follow, though we will not for that reason deny.

This is a fact: we have a sense of the infinite, the boundless, the eternal, and, though that sense will not tolerate any limitation of this conception, yet that infinite, that boundless, that eternal seems to be something like ourselves. In reason, we cannot account for the sense, but in feeling we are perfectly at rest. And if we are not spoiled by reflective logic, we even become eloquent or poetic, as Plato would say. That again is the case with most of us, yet mystics assure us of their union with that Infinite! It cannot be verified for us. Who has or is in the Truth?

We have a sense of beauty which responds to the beauty of the universe. At times our response is so powerful that we are lifted out of our temporary self and perceive ourselves in a strange mingling with Nature's beauty, a mingling that bears witness to a close relationship. That, too, is for mystics far more than mere perception. They are translated beyond themselves and their visit yonder leaves them transfigured. Again, I say, ordinarily for the mind, it cannot be proved. But that is no reason for a denial of such high perception. Some one is deceived, mistaking appearance for reality! Is it the mystic or the common mind? Is Nature merely appearance? May Nature not be the same as that great Personality the mystics speak of?

But it is not merely emotional people and poets who realize the relationship. Greek philosophers were overcome when they realized the ordered arrangement of the universe, and the classical people all agreed that that which they saw was not confusion, but an universe, that is, an existence of one idea, one aim, one kind, a One. Of moderns, we know of Kepler's outburst: "Oh, God, to think thy thoughts—that is my religion." It was the uniformity of what astronomy showed him, and its response within that created this perception of a personality! And the Greek realization of the same caused the famous line of Aratus and that of Cleanthes: "For God's offspring we are."

Laotzse, if he had heard it, would have said: "men! Yes Nature, Teh, is the queen and goddess of mortals."

But Laotzse would never have clothed his thought in anthropomorphic forms. He felt Her, Mother, Nature, Teh, both positively and negatively, but no terms of language or art would exhaust his idea and he refrained from use of personifications.

As is well known, Christianity asserts a family relationship to the Highest, and that doctrine involves a communion far deeper than one of thought merely.

Yes! cried Goethe, "We are surrounded and encompassed by Nature; unable to step out and unable to enter deeper into her."

It is, however, a fact, she has never lifted her veil and no man has ever seen her face to face, yet it seems to us, that ever and ever she creates new forms, and, ever and ever she rushes them out of life again, acting like a person. She is ever sacrificing her own product, and, death seems her method for getting more life. We see a system resembling thought.

This fact, that Mother Nature leaves a red trail after her, is often enough, and only too often observed and criticised in such a way that the critics only hurt themselves. But those of us who have spent a life-time with nature and in close observation, study and meditation, think differently. To us Nature is no slaughterer or murderer; no slayer or assassin; no Moloch or Thug, as is only too often said by the ignorant. The truth is that she herself is blind and is the sacrifice; she is the one slaughtered and slain; she is the one who is offered to Moloch and the Thug. She herself wonders why, and has never answered her own riddle, and could not lift the veil if she wanted to. She herself would like to know the answer to the everlasting flux and transmutation which is her life and being. Well has William Harbutt Dawson (N. Y. *Sun*, Aug. 24, 1901) sung about this mystery.

> Giant of old am I,
> The rock-ribbed earth is my body;
> The mountains that rise on high,

These are my hands, my fingers;
The snow is my hair, and the clouds
Gather around at my breathing;—
I whisper in wandering winds,
But the avalanche crash is my calling.
When I raise myself anon
And shake my limbs in the sunlight
The sweat flows forth in rivers.
Sons and daughters of man
Roam at will upon me,—
Climb to my utmost hand-tips,
Hide in the hair on my shoulders,
Glide in the blue of my eyes,
In cor'acles made of the corn husks,
But I heed not their coming and going.

Mystery am I to myself.
Knowing not why, whence, whither,
Knowing not purpose or end,
Or the things that were or shall be;
Only faintly surmising
That I was by another fashioned;
A being vaster than I,
Stronger in thew and sinew
Mightier in body and arm-girth:
"Giant of eld, thy child,
I greet thee Unknown, Great Maker!"

But a wonder stranger is mine,
From age to age enduring:
As I lie in the night's deep silence,
(When the light-giver rests in his chamber),
And gaze in the firmament o'er me
Far from my utmost arm's reach,
Far from the sound of my calling,
And watch in the solemn distance
Of infinite space overshadowing
Those pale fires burning yonder,
Never farther or nearer,
Never brighter or dimmer,

Burning forever and ever:
This is the wonder unceasing
This is the light that appals me!

It is the light, the counterpart that seems so far off that becomes "the wonder unceasing."
You hear the melancholy all through this confession of self-conscious earth-nature: "Giant I am—yet I am as naught!" And why? Because the light is so far off! The cry of the poem is the cry of life for light, a cry that can be heard everywhere, not only where the moose calls across the lake, but in the roll of the thunder, when lightning leaps from cloud to cloud; not only where human souls sigh in pain, but also when and where the angels, who have no body, look into the mysterious garment of men and wonder. And why this wonder? Why "this wonder unceasing?" Because, Nature, ever in pain, ever bearing and reproducing is also self-sacrificing, and it is the cry of the victim and the smoke of the offering that throws the melancholy veil over her, preventing her from understanding the mystery of which she herself is the wonder. She is a sublime no-thing. Nature is like Teh. Teh is life and Tao is structure. They cannot exist apart. In the poem just read, Nature is life, and Light is the counterpart; and, the two are inseparable and mutually call for each other, and are in pain when separated.

Look into the eye of a dog or a bird and the melancholic question stands there is large letters! There is life seeking light. Look over the landscape, be it ever so smiling, you think; look long enough and the mystery shall be seen.

Wherever she is, she is incarnate and manifested in a form of sacrifice. She does not live for her own sake, she is part of another. As you heard it in the poem, she wonders! she suffers!

Now, see how this Mother Nature, is a savior, an ever present deliverer: Whenever things have come to an extreme and balance is lost—there is an explosion and things readjust themselves. That is deliverance, salvation.

When the day has been excessively hot and we are about to succumb for lack of air fit to breathe, Nature in the evening either provides a thunderstorm in which all the miasma of the air eats itself up and we are set free under a clear sky and to new hope and life, or she sends a cool night to redeem us. Is she not thus a deliverer, a savior?

If she robs the shore on one side of the ocean, she gives

freely on the other and the whole does not lose, but is set free from stagnant conditions. Is she not saving from death? Real death! She has no speech or language, but she takes care of me and saves me from fall by the tongue and the voice she creates in another for that purpose! Is that not redemption? Men do not see Salvation nor understand their own redemption, because the mother never betrays the mystery. She never betrays it openly, but she whispers it to her darlings.

Another way of putting it would be to say that it is the essential character of Nature to sacrifice self, to consume self and to rise again from the ashes like the fabled bird Phoenix. This is something we see daily, hourly, always and everywhere in organic life and in a little slower process, but none less certain, in inorganic existences. Change and transmutation everywhere!

Nature in us is that wonderful, strong and sharply drawn pattern according to which your separate individuality is built up in a personality. It is the throb of the blood and the excitability of the nerves that do the work of building, repairing and improving. It is that master-power Will which holds the rudder firmly and prevents your ship from wreck and ruin. It is the navigator, Intelligence, studying the charts and keeping the course straight. It is that quick and living perception which intuitively finds the way in darkness, distress and in all growth. It is that urge and those longings which restlessly call you, and invite you to search the depths and to scan the latitudes. It is those images of Eternal Beauty which stand as beacon lights in your life; and it is that intense wish to be good which from time to time enthuses you; it is also the dawn and the full daylight of understanding that leads you on and on. Everywhere it is motion, birth, rebirth and it never tires nor comes to an end; it is immortal; dreadfully immortal. All these phenomena we imagine to be the glories of existence—yes! they are that!, but they are also subtle falsities, shadow plays and impermanencies! They are positive while on the early stages of the Path; they are negative later on. Two sides of Nature! Some of the wise men declare they have seen this power beyond the universe and themselves, but have left no records of the vision!

I will now gather together these various thoughts, opposites and contradictory as some of them are. When gathered and seen at one point, they represent to some extent that stupendous power and moving force called Teh in Laotzse's book, and also those personifications which we in mythology call goddesses, and in folklore hear of as celestial visitors, like the young sisters in the American Indian story about Waupee and the other visitors I referred to in a former chapter, which came to Boëthius and to that poor copyist who died saying, "I lost what I never possessed." In a summary the characteristics are somewhat like this:

There is about us a power, infinite and mighty; we feel it to be personal like ourselves, and, fail to express our feelings unless we choose anthropomorphic terms. Mystics assure us this power is personal, but common mortals have no experience by which to prove it. Ancient philosophers also expressed themselves and declared there is a close relationship between ourselves and that power. Laotzse felt the same, but used no personal terms for his feeling. Keen intelligence and pure emotional souls look upon this power as sacrificing its own product in order to create more life, and, they also see this power, which they call Mother-Nature as self-sacrificing, though it appears to them that she does not herself know the aim and end of her self-sacrifice. But they see her self-sacrificing to have the same aim and end as her sacrificing her own product, namely, the production of more life. These deeper seeing minds and more sensitive souls see in all this sacrificing both of her Self and her products the salvation or deliverance of man from thraldom and the earth from death. They see her as the fabled bird, Phoenix, as change and transmutation; they feel her as nervous force; as masterwill; as intelligence and quick perception; as unceasing longings and as an image of Eternal Beauty; as the wish to be good and the enthusiasm to be it; as birth, rebirth and immortality.

The principle of all this is embodied in this mysterious Celestial Sister that comes to Waupee. She is to him both heavenly and earthly. She comes like a sacrifice to him, that he may be lifted into the higher plane and she sacrifices him in order to be his salvation.

Teh acts in the same way with us all.

To be concluded.

TALES OF THE ANCIENT TRAVELLER.

Translated from an Obscure Source.

By Samuel Neu.

Prologue.

AT the Court of Omee, most noble King and Sovereign of the Great Middle Country, dwells an ancient man whose only duty and occupation is and for many years has been to tell to our beloved and all-wise king and his courtiers tales of his strange adventures in many lands; and I, Lipo-va, the Scribe, have been honored far beyond my feeble worth in being chosen by our gracious sovereign to record and preserve in the archives of the state, as they are told, these mystic tales.

By the same royal decree that has honored me, I am commanded first to set down upon my record all that is known about the individual whose historian I am to be. I give not his name because I know it not. No name or title have we ever called him but the Ancient Traveller. Even I doubt, if I may be forgiven to doubt the wisdom of our noble king, even I doubt if the king himself knows what the name of the ancient man may be.

His origin is shrouded in the mystery of the ages. Nought is known save tradition. And even tradition, forever stretching to the utmost bounds of credulity, in the case of the Ancient Traveller, far oversteps those bounds as though they never were. It would be folly, indeed, to record here what future generations needs must scoff at, and therefore of traditions I will set down that one only that the least defies reason; yet how incredible is even this sanest tradition those who read may judge.

And what says this, the most credible, yet belief-defying story? That the Ancient Traveller formerly lived upon the moon! That by some unknown or long-forgotten passage he arrived upon the earth, and, after many strange wanderings among many peoples, became the counsellor and story-teller of our illustrious king. For ages, says this tradition, ever since the reign of the great king Atlaes, this Ancient Traveller has sat beside kings, has watched them come and go, watched dynasties rise and fall, while only he remains. And it is further said that when he leaves a land, to travel on, that kingdom falls apart; and when a new king comes, even of another race, from a far-off land, behold, beside him again sits the Ancient Traveller.

Such tales as this posterity will not believe, nay worse, they will smile and jeer. Nor can we indeed all-believe them now. Yet, as this of all the fanciful traditions is the least fantastic, I record it here to fulfill the duty put upon me by our beloved king. And perhaps even in it may lie some truth.

And now, by that same august decree that so honors me, I must describe his appearance. Yet here again I fail, for looks he has none! So, indeed, it seems must be, for although all the court have seen him many times sitting before the king, yet, except for a vague memory of a great gray beard and kindly eyes, not one of all of us can say like what he looks. Oh, mysterious man, what wonder you have caused us! His voice, too, none can remember, though I have often asked of others at the court, princes, warriors and scribes: a certain sweet, kindly tone, clear as the song of the lute, with the force of the roar of the clouds, the benevolence of the silver-throated bird singing its morning blessing, and through all, the ring of truth that sounds from a golden bell,—these we hold as impressions rather than memories.

For years this venerable man sat in the court, near the king, and spake no word. None ever gave him heed or paid him notice. He simply sat among us, a relic of by-gone days; with us, yet ever apart. But when the war with the barbarous tribes of the South Country was at its height, when the news of a great defeat to the armies of Omee in the field had stricken the king and all the court silent, dumb with despair, then for the first time in the memory of men now living the Ancient Traveller spoke. His words: "Conquer, but do not kill; teach, do not destroy." Wonder struck the gracious noblemen assembled, and of a sudden the dumbness of despair was loosed and a great hubbub arose. Counsellors here laughed and jeered at the strange advice, counsellors there who had the welfare of the merchants much at heart approved, saying the country needed slaves; captains proclaimed plans to destroy, and priests asked explanations of the doctrine. The king, having heard the strange and startling words and finding much of wisdom in them, silenced the throng, and, turning to the man of hoary mien, he said:

"Worthy father, your words sound much of truth, therefore I ask you give me words of counsel."

The new made counsellor answered not but signed the court to withdraw, and the counsel he gave the king is not known to this day. But the history of the realm, compiled by abler hands than mine, sets forth in ample form the great victory of the king over the South Country, a victory whereby the barbarians were conquered, yet not slain; were taught, but not destroyed.

Not until the end of that great war, when peace reigned at last within the realm, did the Ancient Traveller speak again. Then to while away the time and uplift the minds of the courtiers he would join the bards and story-tellers in their tales, and in time became the chiefest of them. For, of all the tales the bards sang and told, many of which were without doubt true, none had the golden ring of those the Ancient Traveller told, incredible as some were.

It is many years since the tales began and some of them are lost beyond recall, though on our hearts they have wrought their work. It was to save for future generations what may still be saved that our most noble and beloved king has decreed that I set down the tales as they are told.

Perchance that among those who read this record in ages yet unborn there may be some who also have been permitted to meet the Ancient Traveller and to whom these tales may be known. If I, Lipo-va, the Scribe, err as mortal must do, I, from out the dim yet living past, ask them freely to criticise, correct and pass them on.

THE ROMANCE OF SVARAT'S KING.

To a Tale of The Ancient Traveller, as told at the Court of Omee, noble King of the Great Middle Country, and by him called The Romance of Svarat's King set down by Lipo-va, the scribe, give ear:

KNOW thou, most noble king, that he, the great and powerful one named Mahm, who sits on Svarat's throne, ruling o'er all, was not born thus to Svarat's throne as you were born to this, but once a poor and humble slave, he rose to that estate. The tale of how he won the princess Buthima, of Svarat, and the throne Svarat, too, is one of wonder and romance.

Once on a time a humble artisan, named Apadrach, who

lived in Svarsa, had an only son, of whom 'twas augured at his birth that he would wed a princess and rule all the land. Old Apadrach paid little heed to these old women's tales, but the young son, Osiso, having a mind impressionable and credulous, used oft to dream that it was really true; and often when his daily work was done he wandered in the cool of eventide upon the road that led up to the gate of Svarat's gorgeous palace, and, arrived, peer through the gate within (for at this hour the gates were always left ajar), and peering thus, dream dreams that were to be.

And so it came to pass one fair evening as he was peering through the palace gate and viewing all the gorgeous throng within, arrayed in fine and costly clothes of silk, bedecked with costly lace and precious jewels, that Svarat's princess, Buthima, passed by that very gate; and, seeing Osiso earnestly regarding what took place, she smiled, blushed, paused and then passed on. But though her form had passed, poor Osiso with popping eyes could still behold her there: for, with that instant's smile and blush, the heart of Osiso had left forever more, and never to return, its proper seat.

And so it passed, Osiso came to love.

Being young, Osiso did not stop to think on difference of state and rank and caste between himself, a humble workman's son and her, the noble princess of Svarat. But, ah! too soon he was to be awaked.

The youth, with thoughts full of his new-born love (if such a love is truly born anew), walked boldly forth and inward of the gate. But now his time of wakening has come. The captain of the palace guard, aroused at seeing pass a man in leather garb (for it is known to you that in that land all artisans in leather garb are clad) pass inward through the gate, detains him now, saying in voice that sounds like thunder:

"Knowest thou not, oh lowly artisan, that none in leather garb may pass this gate?"

Whereat Osiso now remembered well: one of the kingdom's strictest laws was this. And then his heart, erstwhile so full of hope, sank in him and he turned his humble steps unto his humble home, and all that night sat sorrowing, sunk in tearful, dark despair.

But on the morrow, rising with fresh life and hope, he vowed that humble though he be, a dress of silk and jewels he would have and then go wed the princess Buthima.

Oh, simple vow to make! How hard the task! For when

he calmed and thought how this great feat which he had set himself should be performed, once more his spirits fell; for where should he procure the means to buy a better than the garb he wore. For many days he sat and pondered this, and as each evening fell, despaired the more. But on the fifth day hunger smote him hard, and rising from his fruitless, dark despair he fared forth to labor and returned at evening with three silver pieces earned. Two of these silver pieces bought him food, the third he laid aside and said: "Each night I shall lay by one silver piece to buy a dress to woo the princess in."

And so it passed, Osiso loved his work.

Now, after many days, in all one year, Osiso had laid by a goodly sum, wherewith he sought the merchant Probostra. Said he:

"Behold, O Probostra, here have I many silver pieces, which are yours. Give me, I pray of you, a suit of silk, that I may go and make the princess mine."

Probostra first would fain have laughed aloud; and then his anger rose, with threatening scowl. But looking at the young man's hopeful face a pity took him and he held the words his angry tongue would speak, and said thus softly:

"Knowest thou not, O artisan, that such as thou may not within the kingdom's law procure a dress of silk? For it is clearly writ: 'No silk within this kingdom shall be sold to him who pays in silver, but in gold.'"

At this Osiso's spirits fell once more, and long he felt the sting of deep despair, until Probostra, noting his sad plight, took pity once again and kindly said:

"Be of good heart, my son. You wish to raise your lowly born condition? Take, then, this warrior's dress of finest wool and join the warriors fighting for the king. There perhaps you may earn gold."

And so it passed that Osiso cast off the leather garb his ancestors had worn, and donned the warrior's dress of woolen cloth.

Once more Osiso sought the palace gate, and as the evening fell he passed within; and so it chanced that on this very night and at this very hour and very gate the princess Buthima passed once again. She noted Osiso, his woolen dress, then stopped and smiled and spoke these words to him:

"Go forth, O valiant warrior of the king. Uphold the law and quell all evil deeds; succor the gentle when they need thy aid, for thou art they if thou but knewest; and when thy task is done thou shalt be paid in gold, for such the kingdom's law my father made."

She kissed her hand to him and smiled and went. Osiso's heart then beat with glad acclaim, and grasping fast the sword the captain gave he fared forth with other warriors. He upheld the law and quelled all evil things, succored the gentle when they needed aid, and came in time to know that he was they. Each day he did receive from the great king a piece of gold which each day he laid by.

But many of his brothers squandered theirs in buying luxuries and poisoned drink, which made Osiso sad, until he said:

"My brothers, why do you thus spend and waste the gold the good king gives to you?"

To which they answered:

"Why dost thou hoard thine?"

To which in turn, Osiso answered them:

"I keep my gold to buy a dress of silk that I may wed the princess Buthima and bring great good upon this land of ours. Do you the same, and you may wed her too."

At which they laughed, and asked him:

"Thinkest thou the princess Buthima will even look at thee because thou wearest a dress of silk? Ho! Ho!"

But Osiso marked well her words and smile and turned away and murmured to himself:

" 'Tis not because my dress shall be of silk the princess will consent to wed with me. It is because I worked and fought and won."

It came to pass that as the year grew closed Osiso had saved many golden coins, with which again he turned towards Probostra and asked again what he had asked before. The worthy merchant, seeing he was clad in wool and paid in gold, welcomed him gladly, clad him all in silk, from sandals, robe, to turban; for behold! Osiso had saved gold enough for all.

And for the third time Osiso repaired before the gate that led to Svarat's throne, and this time no one bade him stop, for he was one of them. And when he passed within, behold! there stood the princess waiting him with open arms: and they were wed that day.

And when the good king's earthly work well done, he went his way beyond, they made him king. Turning to Buthima Osiso said:

"My princess, I take this, thy kingdom, in thy right."

But Buthima laid fingers on his lips to silence him and spoke to him these words:

"No, noble prince, this vast domain is thine by right, for it is thou who hast attained."

And then the populace and courtiers cried and greeted him with shouts of praise:

"Long life unto the mighty Svarat's king, king Mahm."

And so he rules, oh noble king Omee, thy king and mine. And he has brought many blessings on the land.

And then the mighty king arose and thus addressed the court:

"This tale the worthy story-teller has unfolded I do believe right and true."

But he told them not that the gold and silver which Osiso saved are not the gold and silver of this realm. And therefore none of his courtiers, ignorant of this, although they hoard their silver, gold and precious stones, will thus attain. For so the Ancient Traveller whispered to me, Lipo-va, the scribe, and I have set it down.

THE RIVER OF LIFE.

To a Tale of the Ancient Traveller, told at the Court of Omee, noble King of the Great Middle Country, and by him called the tale of The River of Life, set down by Lipo-va, the Scribe, give ear:

KNOW, most noble king, that through this land there is a river, flowing east and west and onward to the peaceful sea beyond. The journey thither would take many days, and few would make it, but in ancient times I once approached that river from the North, and there beheld the Carnival of Spring. Few were permitted to look on the sight, save those who took part in the Carnival; but having travelled all over the earth it was not difficult for me to make the guards to let me view the spectacle.

As I approached the river from afar I saw its surface covered with black dots, which bobbed about and drifted with the stream as bits of cork will bob and drift about. As I approached more closely I beheld these bobbing dots were human heads. Far up and down the stream as eye could reach, the waters floated drifting human forms, all battling, struggling, rising but to sink, with here a bare arm for a moment raised, and there a foot uplifted in the air, all drifting, drifting, onward to the sea.

Beckoning the servant who attended me, I hastened on and soon came to the bank. The sight that there met my astonished gaze first bade me laugh, but then my pity rose. And surely one who saw that struggling stream must pity those who wrested in its flood. A million human beings struggled there. They struggled with each other and the stream. Not one of them essayed to reach the land, but only fought each other, thinking thus that each would save himself a watery death. They climbed upon each others' slippery forms; they grasped at straws that floated on the tide; they clambered upon rubbish in the stream. And if one reached a temporary hold upon some drifting log then those about would try to tear him off until at last, spluttering and bawling like a new born babe, he sank again beneath the river's wave; and as his refuge on the log was high so would his plunge beneath the wave be deep. Some dived beneath and built them mounds of mud upon the river's bed, but others came and snatched the mud for theirs, and so they sank. Truly it was a pitiable sight.

A few there were who counselled peace and help. But no one heeded them, or those who did turned for an instant to hear what they said, splashed water in their faces and swam on with mockery and laughter. And the stream carried them, drifting, drifting, onward, all.

I walked along the bank, following the stream, and presently I came upon a man who also walked and held fast in his hand a silken cord. I stopped and asked of him why helped he not the struggling swimmers there. He smiled a sad, compassionate, tender smile and answered me:

"It is against the law. For help must not be given them until they learn. Each year at this same season must our people enter the river at its source and drift or sink until they learn. If they drift on into the sea they are drawn out and after some short rest thrown back again."

"And why this throwing back again?" I asked.

"That they may learn to swim," he said, and smiled again his sad, compassionate, tender smile.

"And in the end, how do they learn," I asked, "and finish finally this cruel test?"

He answered: "That you shall see presently."

"Tell me," I asked, "what is this silken cord, one end of which you hold here in your hand."

He pointed to a swimmer in the stream, to one who glided quietly along, who followed steadily the river's swing yet ever ready to render others aid. I knew him in a moment to be one of those that I had seen before among the few who counselled peace and help.

"He has been down the river many times," said he upon the bank; and as he spoke he jerked the silken cord within his hand. This I had seen him doing many times.

"He swims quite well," I said. "Why do you not draw him to safety here upon the land?"

"Such as he is are always safe," said he. "We watch and guide them, though they often think it is an undercurrent in the stream that draws them safe from danger. But he has not yet learned all, therefore he cannot land."

"And are there others, then, like him?" I asked.

He pointed down the stream. I hastened on.

I passed many watchers on the bank, all holding silken cords of different hues, jerking upon them now from time to time. And always those who thus were fastened safe were those who helped their brothers in the stream and counselled peace and help. Yet they must learn.

And now I came upon a point of land and sat me down to watch the spectacle. I watched the noisy, bustling, struggling mob; I watched the quiet swimmers who were fast; I watched the watchers watching on the bank. And as I watched, one swimmer who was fast turned suddenly as his silken cord was jerked, and grasped it: then the silken cord grew taut and he was drawn safely to the land, and so became another watcher there. For he had learned the lesson of the stream, had found the tie that held him safe and turned and grasped it. No more need he learn to swim.

And then the king arose and said:

"I do believe much truth is in the tale the worthy storyteller has just told. And if you, noble courtiers, will grasp the silken cords when next you swim you will be drawn safe."

But he told them not, because he knew it not, how they must turn, nor in what river this might be done. And unless he station watchers on the bank none of his courtiers will be drawn safe. For this the Ancient Traveller whispered to me, Lipo-va, the scribe, and I have set it down.

A DREAM OF ATLANTIS.—THE LAND OF MU.

By Alice Dixon Le Plongeon

(Continued from page 186.)

O heart of man! how dark a scroll
Thy history must to view unroll!
But in the stern Athenian breast
Hope keeps alive its ray most blest,
That future days will make them free,
And they once more their home may see.

On winds the long and glittering show,
The triumph swelling with its flow;
While trumpet, flageolet, and lyre,
Shrill pipes, and clashing cymbal, higher
  Their brazen voices send
Unto the heavens; yet wilder dance
The bacchants, and the horses prance
  As voices loudly rend
The air with shouts, from lusty throats
Not tuned to give melodius notes.
The whitest elephants, revered,
And sacred bulls, here, too, appeared,
With garlands woven round their horns,
While cloth of gold the back adorns
Of they whose trumpet tones are said
To rouse the souls of mortals dead.

From every vantage ground sweet flowers
Are tossed by lovely hands from bowers;
And if a blossom chance to light
Upon a hero te'en in fight,
A searching glance now upward turns
To meet a fleeting look that yearns
With sympathy for valiant foe
Who into servitude must go.

Perchance the Lady Nenuphar
May save this blue-eyed son of war.

As hotter fall the ardent rays
Of Kin upon the broad highways,
More boisterous grow the surging crowd,
While swells the music, ever loud,
And no one in the multitude
Perceives the rumblings that intrude
  Below their restless feet—
The earth, that palpitating oft,
Its menace sendeth up aloft
  All triumphs to defeat.

As now the king of day ascends
His lofty dome, in homage bends
The human mass, whose footsteps turn
To temples many, wherein burn—
On altars of the purest gold
And ruddier orichalcum old,—
The sacred fire, from out the sky
Procured each year, ne'er left to die.
For now in every holy place
The priests a multitude will face,
And empty sound, to still enslave
  And strive with gorgeous show
The devotees whose gold they crave,
  Pretending all to know.

The temple dancers, too, must aid,
And each seductive, beauteous maid
Her pretty hands will clap, to beat
The measure for her agile feet.
With voices musical are blent
The tinkling sistrums whose ostent
Is rich and beautiful to see,—
Clear bronze inlaid with ivory.
The rumbling of the tunkul drum
Makes every lesser voice seem dumb,
But agitates and re-inspires
The dancer who of motion tires.

Now brazen gongs, resounding loud,

Make known to all the host within
That expiation of their sin
Is granted, since the culprits vowed
Rich offerings to the gods who heard,
For them, the priests petitioning word.
From those whose lives have been effaced
Some spoils are on the altar placed;
While to the lofty arch goes up
Sweet incense from the sacred cup;
And priests in gorgeous robes intone
Their ritual, while the tunkuls moan.

Now drowsing vapors slowly creep
Above the dancers till they sleep
Where they have drooped, and must remain
Till they from dream-land come again.

Surpassing other temples, one
Was consecrated to the sun,—
Magnificent its roof of gold
Whose worth was often proudly told.
As now the populace withdrew,
The priestess Manab passing thro'
This temple vast, emerged before
The portal, on a marble floor
Which led by spacious steps below;
Here, lighted by the midday glow,
   The priestess paused to gaze
Upon the agitated throng
As back and forth they surged along
   The streets, with light ablaze.
The while she stands so pensive here,
Upon the steps are gathering near
Observant ones who see her white
And slender figure on the height—
For Manab lives revered by all;
And soon a voice is raised to call:—
   "Behold! th' Exalted One!
To Atlas sister; Good and Great
Was he. Alas! that cruel fate
   His life too briefly spun."

This hearing, Manab thinks a sign
From *him* hath come. Her smile benign
Is turned to those who look her way.
The will of Atlas to obey,
She now exhorted these to strive
To keep some virtues yet alive
Within this city soon to fall,
When none may rescue great or small.
But most she pleadeth for the poor
Petitioning at every door.
"Behold this show of wealth that stares
Upon the face of ¡Want, and dares
Withhold the pittance it entreats
Wherever want with luxury meets:
Regaled are those who feel not need;
Begrudged are they who hunger plead.
O ye, who reap the earth's full fruit,
Brief now the time ye may dispute
Upon the meagre dole bestowed
Where charity once broadly flowed.
Go! seek the dens starvation haunts—
Where constant need the bravest daunts.
Relent! give freely of your store;
The end is near, for rich and poor."

This theme is touched and that, while all
Seem spellbound at her earnest call.
Of war priestess too now spake,
And of the mothers' hearts that break—
"¡While thousands die and thousands slay
But soon the gods will join the fray,
To crush this power degenerate
That aims to overthrow each state."
She pauses, and a man of years
Cries out, "Yea, yea, the climax nears—
At last, great priestess thou hast come
To voice the truth too long kept dumb."

Another begs they may be told
If she could in the stars behold
The awful fate she now foretold;
And Manab's swelling word rings out
To find the ear of all about:

THE WORD

"Say I the stars this thing declare?
Nay, then! 'T is even I who dare.
The days are few!—Do we our best
To make our fellow creatures blest."

From out the throng a man approached
Who matters doctrinal thus broached:
"My faith goes not, Exalted One,
To bow to yonder glowing sun;
How small a cloud its face can hide!
A storm its fullest powers deride."

But she: "When Light abandons earth
No form will ever come to birth.
The sun is our sustaining force—
We live in its unerring course.
The least and greatest, high and low,
Must die without its ardent glow.
The watchful bird within her nest
Obedient yields to Life's behest,
Productive force, whose quickening flame
In bondage holds her tender frame
While there she broods with wings outspread
To guard Creation's mystic bed:—
The fire-god breathing from above
Awakens constant mother-love.

"The lofty tree whose shielding arms
Protect the nest from rude alarms,
Draws in thro' every swaying bough
The beaming rays that will endow
With buds and blossoms. Year by year
The tree drinks life; in winter drear
It sleeping bides the spring, still fed
By warmth yon mighty orb hath sped.
In Time's abyss the ages glide;
The trees in silent darkness hide
In mines profound, till virile hands
Restore them to the upper lands
Where, yielding, all its treasured rays,
The tree a final joy conveys—
The fire-god, preserver, smiles,
And from dull care man's sense beguiles.

"The sower drops within the earth
Ripe grain, to find in death rebirth;
The clouds life-giving rains bestow;
The god of day sets all aglow.
The corn attains its stately height,
And mortals, gladdened by the sight,
The fire-god praise with heart and voice,
While in his bounties they rejoice.

"The mighty orb unceasing leads
Its circling worlds thro' starry meads—
But when the parent of our sky
Shall fade, its offspring too must die.
Resistless power in earthy deeps
Forever surges, roars, and leaps;
The bellows of a mighty force
Impel destruction on its course
To fire the mounts and shake the plains
Till nothing living there remains
The fire-god's all-consuming hand
Proud Mu will scourge, till o'er the land
The seas will rush, and every breath
Be strangled in the grasp of Death."

As from the height turns she away
Comes Cho, entreating her to stay.
With eager gaze and bowing low,
   He says: "I do thy pardon crave;
But thou did'st aid us forth to go
   When Can and Itzat went, to save
The princess Nalah, now our queen—"
The look bestowed on him is keen
And swift, but fails to find a trace
Of any well-remembered face,—
   As he perceives, so ventures yet
To take the word, "Twere strange indeed
   If thou my face did'st not forget.
For I, a little child in need
Was rescued from the dreadful haunts,
Where children suffer blows and taunts:—
Of those days only gratitude
Upon my memory must intrude."

THE WORD

Said Manab: "Yea, I saw thee go
With that young student, Kadimo,
And I adjure thee, turn once more
To find that safer, distant shore;
For here should none abide who love
This earth-life. Coming from above
Destruction will submerge this land
With all upon it, small and grand."

Now he: "Exalted One, I came
For that our wisemen know this same;
And I would save one friend at last
From watery grave and fiery blast;
The first and tenderest friend to bless
My helpless childhood and distress."

At this a glorifying tear
In Manab's eye springs pure and clear—
Then: "Hasten! Well dost thou, I ween,
To save thy friend, or great or mean.
Be not like yonder swarm who doubt
Our word and every warning flout.
The time is brief, most brief, we feel;
But vainly unto fools appeal.
So perish they! all deaf and blind,
Till ocean waves their bodies grind.
Delay not! Seek thy friend and go
Before the billows overflow."

But he: "I know not how to seek
The way with that kind one to speak.
In palace walls abides she now,
And kingly favor wreathes her brow.
Her path to come anear, perchance
Would be to dare the monarch's glance.
Ah! if thy wisdom would advise
Some measure that might safe disguise
The purpose treasured in my heart,
To venture I would now depart."
"Let not thy spirit be depressed,"
Thus she, "The simplest ways are best."

Soon comes he to the palace ground
Where many servitors are found;
And, questioned why he enters there,
Replies that for a lady fair
A message he hath brought; so past
This questioner and that. At last
He enters thro' a door where stand
The sentries in their armor grand
   And sternly bar the way—
Some other entry must thou find,
For we our orders closely mind,
   And none pass here this day."

"I care not if within I go,"
Cries he, "But Pepen is to know,—
For 't is her wish—that one she sought
Hath come, and of poor Cho hath brought
Good words; most gladly she'll repay
The messenger who this will say."
The sentries not a word reply;
But just within a maid goes by,
Who quickly has the words retold
And carried further by a bold
And handsome page, with promise sure
To share the recompense secure.

Can this most lovely woman be
The Pepen he hath come to see;—
The hungry girl in tatters mean
Transformed into a dazzling queen;
His Butterfly in film of gold
And gems whose worth must be untold!

Himself to manhood nobly grown
To her could nevermore be known
   Save by his word declared.
His face she eagerly doth scan
While maidens ever gently fan
   Her beauteous form, half bared.
"Of Cho, thou bringest word?" she asks;—
While one, who in her sunshine basks,
Another questions by a sign,

And both their laughter must confine,
To think that mortal man can bear
A name unwelcome to their ear.

The guest in quiet tones now spake—
"Kind lady, I alone would make
The story known to thee; could these
Thy favored maidens, have release?"
　She smiled half bitterly—
"In grand estate no freedom lies:—
Go further off, my pretty spies,
But keep me yet beneath your eyes
　Lest Pepen strive to flee."

"And now, thy tale, of that poor lad
Who with me often wandered glad
In yonder ways where freedom wild
Seems joy unto the homeless child
　Till hunger breaks the charm,
And pain close follows on the track
Of him who everything must lack,
　And cruelty oft alarm."

He then: "Behold in me the boy
Whom Pepen kindness gave, and joy"—
Exclaims she now: "Thou, little Cho!
Ah! glad am I once more to know
Thy face," and from her couch would rise,
Her orbs alight with glad surprise.
But he: "Your courtiers on us gaze;
Not here as on the broad highways,
　May each the other greet.
To save thee I from countries far
Have journeyed; there my friends all are;
　And there a safe retreat
Thy presence waits. These hands of mine
Its walls have beautified as thine;
There, too, warm hearts will welcome thee,
All eager thy kind face to see,—
For I have told how in my woe
To Pepen might I ever go."

A DREAM OF ATLANTIS

Within her eyes the tear-drops welled,
As quickly too were they repelled,
While he, unhesitating, still
Her mind with his desire must fill:
"I know not if unto thine ear
Have come those rumors of a fear
Long held in faith by those who can
Within divining mirrors scan
What signs and portents there unfold,
That Fate may give, and what withhold.
But I from boyhood days have heard
The scholars tell, and none demurred,
That Mu itself and all which here
Exists, was soon to disappear.
Our king who late in Mayach died—
For there since childhood I abide—
Beheld, when life was ebbing fast,
This land within the ocean cast,
  And that with brief delay.
This morn the same hath Manab voiced
While crowds triumphantly rejoiced;
  She bade me haste away
To seek thee and to save with speed,
Since thou did'st rescue me in need.
The land beyond this Sacred Height
In timid hearts awakens fright;
For scarce a day now finds its close
Without this earth betraying throes.
Perchance to-night or early dawn
May find us into havoc drawn."

He paused to eagerly await
The words that would decide her fate—
Nor waited long: "My life," she said,
  "Unto myself and every one
  Is worthless. All that I have done
Were best forgotten with the dead!
So vainly have I lived my day,
'T were pity to prolong my stay.
The Power that moulded me and cast
Me in this net will hold me fast
Beyond, or loose the trammels. What

Matters it—bide I or not?
In chains of gold I live.
Choice had I none, of what my path
Should be, but if the present offer wrath,
The future may forgive."

Entreating her he lingered yet:
"To plead once more I will return
Ere long; thou surely wilt not spurn
My services, and brand regret
Upon my life. Consent to flee,
For overwhelmed this land will be.
By every token"— "Hark! they call"
Exclaimed Pepen, "Thro' yonder hall
Gadeirus comes this way. Depart!
This portal take,—and cease to grieve
That thraldom I can never leave
Till Death release me by his dart.
But haste! I pray thee disappear—
My tyrant-slave is very near."

To be continued.

TRUE ART IS SINCERE AND DIRECT.

I remember when in my younger days I had heard of the wonders of Italian painting. I fancied the great pictures would be great strangers; some surprising combination of color and form; a foreign wonder, barbaric pearl and gold, like the spontoons and standards of the militia, which play such pranks in the eyes and imaginations of school-boys. I was to see and acquire I knew not what. When I came at last to Rome and saw with eyes the pictures, I found that genius left to novices the gay and fantastic and ostentatious, and itself pierced directly to the simple and true; that it was familiar and sincere; that it was the old, eternal fact I had met already in so many forms,—unto which I lived; that it was the plain *you and me* I knew so well, I had left at home in so many conversations.

EMERSON, *"Art."*

THE SEPHER HA-ZOHAR—THE BOOK OF LIGHT.

By Nurho de Manhar.

Containing the doctrines of Kabbalah, together with the discourses and teachings of its author, the great Kabbalist, Rabbi Simeon ben Jochai, and now for the first time wholly translated into English, with notes, references and expository remarks.

(Continued from page 190.)

SAID Rabbi Eleazar: "What David beheld at that awful moment was not an angel but a manifestation of the Holy One. The scripture uses the words 'The Angel of the Lord' as a metaphoric appellation of the Divine Being, as did also Jacob when blessing Ephraim and Manasseh saying, 'The Angel which redeemed me from all evil bless the lads.' And furthermore, in Exodus XIV. 19. The Almighty is referred to and designated as 'The Angel of the Lord that went before the camps of Israel removed and went behind them.' Whether Israel acts uprightly or not, the Holy One is still its ruler and governor in order that it may not become subject to other nations, and that its good works may put them to shame. It may however be said, yet it is written, 'The adversary hath spread out his hand upon her pleasant things, for she hath seen the heathen entered into her sanctuary' (Lam. I. 10). If the Holy One governs Israel as stated, how was it that the heathen entered her sanctuary and destroyed it? Scripture itself gives the reason, as it is written, 'Thou hast done all these things (Jer. XIX. 22). The Lord hath done that which he hath devised. He hath fulfilled what he proposed in days of yore (Lam. II. 19). From these words we conclude and affirm that notwithstanding the occurrence of all these calamities, the Holy One is still ruler of Israel and that only by his permission could they have happened. Observe, scripture states, 'And Alhim looked upon the earth, and behold, it was corrupt,' because the Schekina had deserted it as we have said. Moreover it is stated, 'And God saw their works that they turned from their evil way' (Ion. III. 14). The cry of the earth is always ascending heavenwards and desirous of union with the celestial world, enrobes itself with raiments of beauty and splendor, as doth a maiden expecting the arrival of her lover.

When its children are upright and virtuous, they become its ornaments. Far otherwise was it when the deluge came, for then they were vile and depraved and corrupted, so that the earth blushing with shame at their deeds of wickedness hid itself, as doth an unfaithful wife from her husband. When, however, they became brazen, openly lewd, obscene and sensual, then like an immodest courtisan casting aside her veil, it also became unclean and corrupted, as it is written 'The earth is defiled by the inhabitants thereof, because they have transgressed the laws, changed the ordinance, broken the everlasting covenant' (Is. XXIV. 5). Then corruption both moral and physical prevailed throughout the world, for all flesh had corrupted its way upon the earth."

Rabbi Eleazer was once on a visit to Rabbi Jose the son of Rabbi Simeon and grandson of Lakunya, who on beholding him spread a sumptuous couch on the floor in order to recline and rest himself. After engaging a while in silent meditation, his grandfather said: "Have you ever heard your father explain the meaning of the words, 'The Lord hath done that which he had devised. He hath fulfilled his word that he had commanded in the days of old?'"

Said Rabbi Eleazar: "Initiated students have interpreted them thus, the words 'fulfilled his word' (bitza emratho) signify that God hath rent his purple robe of glory and light with which he had arrayed himself from the beginning of creation, and contributed to the beauty and perfection of his sanctuary."

Then asked his grandfather again: "Does a king think or devise punishment before his son has acted wickedly?"

To this Rabbi Eleazar replied; "A certain king possessed a most costly and precious vase. Fearing the loss of it, he caused it to be continually placed before him. At length his son came to visit him and on a dispute arising between them, the king in a moment of anger seized hold of the vase and dashed it to pieces on the ground. Such is the signification of the words, 'The Lord hath done what he had devised.' Observe, from the day the sanctuary was finished and completed, the Lord regarded it with continuous joy and delight, yet fearing that Israel would act wickedly, he determined it should be destroyed. Whilst Israel kept the good law and lived in obedience to its dictates, purely and uprightly, there was the sanctuary the glory of God on the earth, but when Israel fell with idolatry and forsook his worship it was destroyed. At its destruction then only did the Holy One feel grief at the punishment of the guilty. On all other occasions it is a source of delight to him when the wicked through their misdeeds are swept out of the world, as it is written, 'When the wicked perish there is shouting.' (Prov. XI. 10). If, however, it be objected, we are taught that the Holy One never rejoices at the punishment of the evildoer observe that punishment is twofold in its character. There is the punishment of those who, despite the admonitions and long-suffering of God, continue in their wickedness. The suffering of these causes joy to the Holy One. There is also the punishment of those whose perversity in crime has not attained its climax. Far from being a source of joy to him, their suffering causes the Holy One to sorrow and grieve over them. There are wretches who are afflicted before their wickedness has reached its culmination, as it is written, 'For the iniquity of the Amorites is not yet full' (Gen. XV. 16). If, again, it be asked, wherefore God chastises sometimes those whose iniquity is not full? We answer, evildoers whose bad deeds injure only themselves are punished only when the measure of their iniquity is filled, whilst the unrighteous who attach themselves to Israel with the object of afflicting and injuring it are punished before their evil intentions are realized. It is the chastisement of this class of evildoers that causes grief to the Holy One. Amongst such were the Egyptians that were drowned in the Red Sea, and the enemies of Israel in the time of Ichosaphat. . . . . It is written: 'For yet seven days, and I will cause it to rain upon the earth, forty days and forty nights, and every living substance that I have made will I destroy from off the face of the earth' " (Gen. VII. 4).

Said Rabbi Jehuda: "Wherefore this limit of forty days and nights? It was because this number is always found in connection with the infliction of punishment, as it is written, 'Forty stripes he may give him and not exceed' (Deuter. XXV. 3). This number is fixed to correspond with the four cardinal quarters of the world, each of which is divided into ten parts or degrees as man was created to correspond with them in a manner, for the commission of crime he must not be beaten with more than forty stripes. For a like reason, this number forty was equally necessary in the punishment of the world."

Rabbi Isaac was sitting in presence of Rabbi Simeon, and in course of conversation asked the question: "What is the real meaning of the words, 'And the earth was corrupt before the Alhim.' Though man commit crime how can it affect the earth and make it corrupt?"

Rabbi Simeon replied: "Scripture informs us that the earth and all flesh upon it had together become corrupt. There is found another and similar expression or statement, 'And the land is defiled and therefore I do visit the iniquity thereof upon it.' Now, if it be said, though men sinned, how could their crimes cause the earth to be corrupt, so that along with them it is subject to punishment? Observe that the sins of mankind that corrupt it are effaceable by repentance except that of self-defilement; and so scripture states, 'Though thou wash thee with nitre and take thee much soap, yet thine iniquity is marked before me saith the Lord God' (Jer. II. 22); and again, 'For thou art not a God that hath pleasure in wickedness, neither shall evil dwell with thee' (Ps. V. 5). Only by extraordinary penitence can this heinous sin be expiated, respecting which it is written, 'And Er the elder son of Judah was wicked before the Lord, and the Lord slew him' " (Gen. XXXVIII. 7), which verse has already been commented upon.

Again Rabbi Isaac questioned Rabbi Simeon: "Wherefore did God punish the antediluvians by a deluge of water rather than by fire or some other scourge?"

Rabbi Simeon replied: "Therein is involved a deep mystery. In indulging in the heinous sin of self pollution man impeded and prevented the union of the waters above with the waters below, or in other words, the male and female principles, and as therefore punished by a watery element; so that in their case the punishment fit the crime. Scripture states, 'All the foundations of the great deep were broken up and the windows of heaven were opened.' (Gen. VII. 4). The fountains of the great deep refer to the waters below, and the windows of heaven to the waters above."

Rabbi Hiya and Rabbi Jehuda when traveling, passed near some great and lofty mountains, in the gorges and fissures of which they observed bleached skeletons of the remains of men who had perished in the deluge. They measured two hundred feet as they extended on the rocks. Overcome with astonishment, they said: "Now we comprehend what the masters have told us, why the antedeluvians feared not the divine punishment, as it is written. 'Therefore they say unto God, depart from us for we desire not the knowledge of thy ways (Job XXI. 14).' But their haughtiness and pride of strength availed them nothing, for they perished, swept off the face of the earth by the waters of the deluge."

"'And Noah begat three sons, Shem, Ham and Japhet'" (Gen. VI. 10), said Rabbi Hiya to Rabbi Jehuda, "Come and I will make known unto thee what I have learned as to the occult meaning and sense of these words. The life of Noah was similar to a man entering into a cavern from which after a certain time, come forth two or three sons, each of them different in character, habit and temperament, one being upright, one unjust, whilst the third is void of any special trait of disposition. The same peculiarity and distinction between individuals obtain alike in the three worlds. Observe when the soul descends from the celestial sphere or plane in heaven it becomes as it were entangled in mountain ravines, and meeting with its lower intellectual self, they take on the animal bodily life, and thus blended form one individual."

Said Rabbi Jehuda, "The mind and the lower nature depend the one on the other, but the spirit (the higher or real self) is independent of both of them. They are located or inhere in the physical organization, but not it, which as yet has never been discovered or seen by any individual. When a man leads a pure life, his higher self is present and aids him in his endeavors, and by its purifying and enlightening influence enables him to attain to and enter into the enjoyment of the higher life of peace and bliss unspeakable. If, however he is careless and unwilling to live the higher life, then though he may become intellectual, he can never become pure and one with the Divine. Furthermore, whoso lives impurely depraves his nature, and by ignoring the dictates and admonitions of the spirit within him renders himself more and more receptive of and swayed by objects of sense in following the bent of his animal appetites and inclinations."

It is written, "And God said unto Noah, 'the end of all flesh is come before me'" (Gen. VI. 12). Said Rabbi Jehuda: "David says, 'make me to know mine end and the measure of my days, what it is, that I may know how frail I am.' From these words addressed unto the Holy One, we learn that there are two ends, one on the right hand, the other on the left, which man must choose to walk in during his life on earth. Of that on the right it is written, 'Go thou thy way until the end be, for thou shalt rest and stand in thy lot at the end of thy days' (Dan. XII. 13). Of that on the left it is said, 'He setteth an end to darkness and searcheth out all perfection, the stones of darkness and the shadow of death. He considereth the depth of all things.' (Job XXVIII. 3.). When by affliction and suffering the stones buried in darkness become manifested and the shadow of death hovers over, then the end of darkness becomes visible, or in other words, the angel of death or the serpent. Thus 'the end of all flesh' has the same meaning as the words 'the end of darkness,' that is, the death angel or the serpent. 'He considereth the depth of all things' refers to the same being who, when judgment falls upon the world, constitutes himself the satan or accurser of mankind and strives to disparage and blacken the characters of all creatures. With reference to the end on the right, the Holy One said to Daniel, 'Go thy way till the end come, for thou shalt rest.' Thereupon Daniel turned and said, 'In which world shall my rest be, in this or the world to come?' 'In this world,' replied the Holy One, "where rest is necessary, 'as it is written, 'He who walks in the right way shall rest in his bed' (Is. LVII. 2). Then asked Daniel again of the Holy One, 'Shall I be of the number of those who will rise again at the end of the world?' The Holy One replied 'Thou, shalt rise.' Said Daniel then· ' I know that amongst these who shall rise, there will be upright and just men who during their lives on earth walked in the path of truth, and others there will be who have done wickedly, but as yet I know not amongst which I shall rise again.' Said the Holy One, 'In thy lot or state in which thou diest.' Again Daniel spake and said, 'Thou sayest unto me, 'Go thou thy way to the end (lekh lecetz). There is an end on the right and an end on the left, which of these meanest thou?' 'The end on the right,' answered the Holy One. David also said unto the Lord, 'Make me to know my end,' and found no rest until he knew which it would be, and it was said unto him, 'Sit thou on my right hand.' Observe, the Holy One also spake unto Noah, 'The end of all flesh has come before me.' What does the word 'end' here mean? It is that which causes the faces of all creatures to become pale and darkened. Hence we learn that the worldly minded and impious attract to themselves this end or state that causes the hue and complexion of their visages to become dark and gloomy. This unknown something or terror called 'the end' does not seize hold of anyone except by permission from on high. When God spake to Noah, it was present before him, waiting for his word of authority to seize hold of the antediluvians, and then he added, 'I will destroy them with the earth,' at the same time saying unto Noah· 'Make thee an ark of gopher wood,' in order to protect himself and ward off the attack of the death angel that he may have no power over him. Observe, we have heard that when death invades a city or enters into the world abroad, a man should not walk in the public streets and thoroughfares if he wishes to avoid the death angel, who then has the power to afflict and destroy anyone whom he meets and encounters. Therefore, was it the Holy One said unto Noah, 'Thou must conceal thyself within the ark and so avoid meeting the destroying angel and thus be secure from his lethal power.' If it be said, there was no such being existing at the time of the deluge whose waters caused the destruction of the human race, observe that no judgment has ever overwhelmed the world but what this malefic angel has been present to inflict it. At the time of the Flood, he was present in the water which was an instrument used by him, and so God warned Noah and counselled him to avoid his presence by building and entering into the ark. But if it be furthermore asked, what advantage could accrue to the patriarch by so doing? How could that prevent the entrance into it of the destroyer? Our reply is, that he has no power over anyone so long as he keeps himself out of his sight. We gather this from what happened to the Egyptians, since God commanded, 'Let none of you go out of the door of his house until the morning.' (Ex. XII. 22). What was the reason of this prohibition? That he might avoid meeting the destroying angel who had the power of inflicting death. Therefore was Noah admonished to include and hide himself in the ark and thus escape destruction.''

Rabbi Hiya and Rabbi Jose, whilst traveling in Armenia, and passing by some great and lofty mountains, observed in them vast gorges and deep ravines resulting from the action of the waters of the deluge. Said Rabbi Hiya, ''These have existed from the time of the flood and, by the will of the Holy One, will endure unto the end of the world as tokens or reminders of the great wickedness of the antedeluvians, even as it is his will that by their good deeds, the memory of the righteous should abide before him and never be effaced. And even with those who delight not in his service, their evil works are transmitted and become manifested throughout all generations, as it is written, 'Though thou wash thyself with nitre and take thee much soap, yet thine iniquity is marked before me, saith the Lord God' '' (Jer. II. 22).

Said Rabbi Jose ''We read, 'Lift up thy voice, Oh daughter of Gallim, cause it to be heard unto Laish, Oh! poor Anathoth'

(Is. X. 30). These words already explained apply really to the congregation of Israel. The daughter of Gallim besides designating the daughter of Abraham our father, refers also to Israel who in another part of scripture is termed 'a closed fountain:' The term 'Gallim' also signifies rivers, which all flow towards the garden they fill and irrigate, as it is written, 'Thy plants are an orchard of pomegranates with pleasant fruits' (Cant. IV. 13), cause it to be heard at Laish has the same meaning as 'the lion (laish) perisheth from lack of prey' (Job. IV. 12). Laish denotes the male and laishah the female. Wherefore so, is it because scripture states, 'The lion is strongest amongst beasts and fearless of any it meets' (Prov. XXX. 30) or 'The lion is dead through lack of prey.' The true interpretation is in the word laish, an occult term of that mundane virtue which emanating from on high manifests itself on the earth plane. When the affluents of the celestial virtue cease descending and are no longer transformed into the lower mundane power, 'laish' then takes the name of 'laishah'; that is, it manifests itself as female. The words *aniah anathoth* (oh, poor anathoth) signify the same as those (in Jer. I. 1), namely 'Jeremiah, son of Hilhiah, of the priests who lived in poverty (ba-anathoth), and also those I Kings II. 26'. And unto Abiathiar, the priest, said the king, 'get thee to Anathoth, or, rather, live thou in poverty in thine own fields; the signification of which words is as follows: During the life of David Abrathar lived in wealth and opulence, but after David's decease Solomon condemned him to live in poverty on his own land or property."

(*To be Continued.*)

TENDERNESS A BOND OF FRIENDSHIP.

The other element of friendship is tenderness. We are holden to men by every sort of tie, by blood, by pride, by fear, by hope, by lucre, by lust, by hate, by admiration, by every circumstance and badge and trifle,—but we can scarce believe that so much character can subsist in another as to draw us by love. Can another be so blessed and we so pure that we can offer him tenderness? When a man becomes dear to me I have touched the goal of fortune. I find very little written directly to the heart of this matter in books.

—EMERSON, *"Friendship."*

MOMENTS WITH FRIENDS.

Is it possible to put a thought out of the mind? If so, how is this done; how can one prevent its recurrence and keep it out of the mind?

It is possible to keep a thought out of the mind, but it is not possible to put a thought out of the mind as we would put a tramp out of the house. The reason why so many are not able to keep away undesirable thoughts, and are not able to think on definite lines, is because they believe in the prevalent notion that they must put thoughts out of their minds. It is impossible to put a thought out of one's mind because in putting it out attention must be given the thought, and while the mind gives the thought attention it is impossible to get rid of that thought. The one who says: Go away you bad thought, or, I will not think of this or that, keeps that thing in his mind as securely as though it were riveted there. If one says to himself that he must not think of this or that thing, he will be like the ascetics and hermits and fanatics who make a list of things they are not to think about and then proceed to go over this list mentally and to put those thoughts out of their mind and fail. The old story of "The Great Green Bear" illustrates this very well. A mediaeval alchemist was pestered by one of his pupils who wanted to be told how to transmute lead into gold. His master told the pupil that he could not do it, even though he were told, because he was not qualified. On the continued pleading of the pupil, the alchemist decided to teach the pupil a lesson and told him that as he was going on a journey the following day he would leave him the formula by which he might succeed if he were able to follow all instructions, but that it would be necessary to pay the closest attention to the formula and to be accurate in every detail. The pupil was delighted and eagerly began the work at the time appointed. He followed the instructions carefully and was accurate in the preparation of his materials and instruments. He saw that metals of the right quality and quantity were in their proper crucibles, and the temperature required was produced. He was careful that the vapors were all conserved and passed through the alembics and retorts, and found that the deposits from these were exactly as stated in the formula. All this caused him much satisfaction and as he went on with the experiment he gained confidence in its ultimate success. One of the rules was that he should not read through the formula but should follow it only as he proceeded with his work. As he proceeded, he came to the statement: Now that the experiment has proceeded thus far and that the metal is at white heat, take a little of the red powder between the forefinger and thumb of the right hand, a little of the white powder between the forefinger and thumb of the left hand, stand over the glowing mass which you now have before you and be ready to drop these powders after you have obeyed the next order. The young man did as ordered and read on: You have now reached the crucial test, and success will follow only if you are able to obey the following: Do not think of the great green bear and be sure that you do not think of the great green bear. The young man paused breathless. "The great green bear. I am not to think of the great green bear," said he. "The great green bear! What is the great green bear? No, I will not think about the great green bear, but, confound it, I *am*, thinking about the great green bear." As he continued to think that he should not think about the great green bear he could think about nothing else, until finally it occurred to him that he should go on with his experiment, and although the thought of a great green bear was still in his mind he turned to the formula to see what the next order was, and he read: You have failed in the trial. You have failed at the crucial moment because you have allowed your attention to be taken from the work to think about a great green bear. The heat in the furnace has not been kept up, the proper amount of vapor has failed to pass through this and that retort, and it is useless now to drop the red and white powders.

A thought remains in the mind as long as attention is given to it. When the mind ceases to give attention to one thought and places it on another thought, the thought which has attention remains in the mind, and that which has no attention gets out. The way to get rid of a thought is to hold the mind definitely and persistently on one definite and particular subject or thought. It will be found that if this is done, no thoughts which do not relate to the subject can intrude themselves upon the mind. While the mind desires a thing its thought will revolve around that thing of desire because the desire is like a center of gravity and attracts the mind. The mind can free itself from that desire, if it wills. The process by which it is freed is that it sees and understands that the desire is not the best for it, and then decides on something that is better. After the mind decides on the best subject, it should direct its thought to that subject and attention should be given to that subject only. By this process, the center of gravity is changed from the old desire to the new subject of thought. Mind decides where its center of gravity will be. To whatever subject or object the mind goes there will its thought be. So the mind continues to change its subject of thought, its center of gravity, until it learns to place the center of gravity in itself. When this is done, the mind withdraws into itself its ramifications and functions, through the avenues of sense and the sense organs. The mind, not functioning through its senses into the physical world, and learning to turn its energies into itself, finally awakens to its own reality as distinct from its fleshly and other bodies. By so doing, the mind not only discovers its real self, but it may discover the real self of all others and the real world which penetrates and upholds all others.

Such realization may not be attained at once, but it will be realized as the final result of the keeping undesirable thoughts out of the mind by attending to and thinking of others which are desirable. No one is at once able to think only of the thought which he wishes to think of and thus to exclude or prevent other thoughts from entering the mind; but he will be able to do so if he tries and keeps on trying.

A FRIEND.

VALOR NEEDED TO FIND TRUTH.

Valor consists in the power of self-recovery, so that a man cannot have his flank turned, cannot be out-generalled, but put him where you will, he stands. This can only be by his preferring truth to his past apprehension of truth, and his alert acceptance of it from whatever quarter; the intrepid conviction that his laws, his relations to society, his Christianity, his world, may at any time be superseded and decease.

—EMERSON, *"Circles."*

THE
WORD

A MONTHLY MAGAZINE

PUBLISHED AND EDITED BY

H. W. PERCIVAL, 253 West 72d Street, New York City

LONDON—KEGAN PAUL, TRENCH, TRUBNER & CO., 43 Gerrard Street

CONTENTS FOR AUGUST, 1910

ADEPTS, MASTERS AND MAHATMAS, ... EDITORIAL	257
IMMORTALITY AND MODERN SCIENTISTS, . BY EDUARD HERRMANN	265
THE INNER LIFE AND THE TAO-TEH-KING, BY C. H. A. BJERREGAARD	278
TALES OF THE ANCIENT TRAVELLER—THE TWIN CITIES, SAMUEL NEU	284
A DREAM OF ATLANTIS—THE LAND OF MU, ALICE DIXON LE PLONGEON	288
EXPERIENCE AND ITS RESULTS, ... J. B. GRAY	302
THE SEPHER HA-ZOHAR—THE BOOK OF LIGHT, BY NURHO DE MANHAR	307
MOMENTS WITH FRIENDS, ... A FRIEND	316

Yearly Subscription - - - - - - $4.00 or 16s.
Single Copies - - - - - - - .35 or 1s. 6d.
Six Months' Subscription - - - - - 2.00 or 8s.
Three Months' Subscription - - - - - 1.00 or 4s.

BOUND VOLUMES OF THE WORD
Vols. I-X in Cloth and Half Morocco
Cloth, $21.00; Half Morocco, $26.00

The ten completed volumes of The Word are a valuable addition to any Library
They are a library in themselves

[Entered as Second-class Mail Matter, May 2, 1906, at the Post Office at New York, New York, under the Act of Congress of March 3, 1879.]

NEW
THE MAGICAL MESSAGE
according to
IÔANNÊS
commonly called

The Gospel according to [St.] John

A verbatim translation from the Greek done in modern
English, with introductory essays and notes

BY

JAMES M. PRYSE

Price, Cloth, $2.00

The root of Mr. Pryse's claim is that the Gospel by John is altogether mystical in intention and that the mystical meanings of the words should never be distorted. According to Mr. Pryse the fourth gospel is much more than an account of the physical career of Jesus. He sees in it the history of the purification of the soul and so well does he buttress his claim that the best exponents of biblical criticism and Greek scholarship will be hard put to it to find anything to say in disproof.

The Theosophical Publishing Company of New York, 253 W. 72d Street

---

A Book of practical Development
is
WILLIAM J. FLAGG'S

Yoga

Or Transformation.

It gives the Facts.

It shows the true Magic which underlies the Akkadian, Hindu, Taoist, Egyptian, Hebrew, Greek and Christian Religions.

It gives a comparative statement of the various Religious Dogmas concerning the Soul and its Destiny.

It is a religious Education to read this Book carefully.

Price, cloth, $3.00.

Send for Descriptive Catalogue.

Charles G. Leland,
The well-known writer, has written a fascinating volume, called,

HAVE YOU A
Strong Will?

Or How to develop and strengthen the Will-Power, Memory, or any other Faculty or Attribute of Mind.

It is written, so all will grasp it.
Brilliant, so you will enjoy it.
Powerful, so you will not forget it.

It will help you to do what you want.

Price, cloth, $1.50.

Send for a booklet, "Books for the Higher Life." It will tell you all about this Book.

The Theosophical Publishing Company of New York, 253 W. 72d Street

When ma has passed through mahat, ma will still be ma; but ma will be united with mahat, and be a mahat-ma.
—The Zodiac.

THE WORD

Vol. 11   AUGUST, 1910.   No. 5

Copyright, 1910, by H. W. PERCIVAL.

ADEPTS, MASTERS AND MAHATMAS.

(Continued from page 217.)

THE faculties do not act singly and independently of each other, but in combination. When one attempts to use one of the faculties exclusively, the mind is inharmonious in its action and will not be even in its development. Only when all act together and in their proper functions and capacities, will the mind have the best and fullest development. The faculties are as organs to the mind. By them, it comes in contact with the worlds, takes in, changes, assimilates, transforms matter into itself and acts on and changes the matter of the worlds. As the senses serve the body, so the faculties serve the mind. As sight, hearing, and the other senses aid each other, and contribute to each other's action for the general welfare, economy and preservation of the body, so the faculties should act with and contribute to each other's action in the exercise, training and development of the mind as a whole; and as the well preserved and well ordered body is an important and valuable servant to the mind, so is the mind, with well trained, developed and articulated faculties, a valuable and important servant to humanity and the worlds. As great care through long years of effort must be exercised in training and perfecting the senses of the body, so also should great care be

258   THE WORD

exercised in the use and development of the faculties of the mind. As loss or impairment of any of the senses affect the value and power of the body, so will impairment of the action of the faculties limit the action of the mind.

All men use their senses, but only by training and development can the greatest or best use be made of them. All men use their faculties, but few consider differences and distinctions between the faculties themselves, and between the faculties of

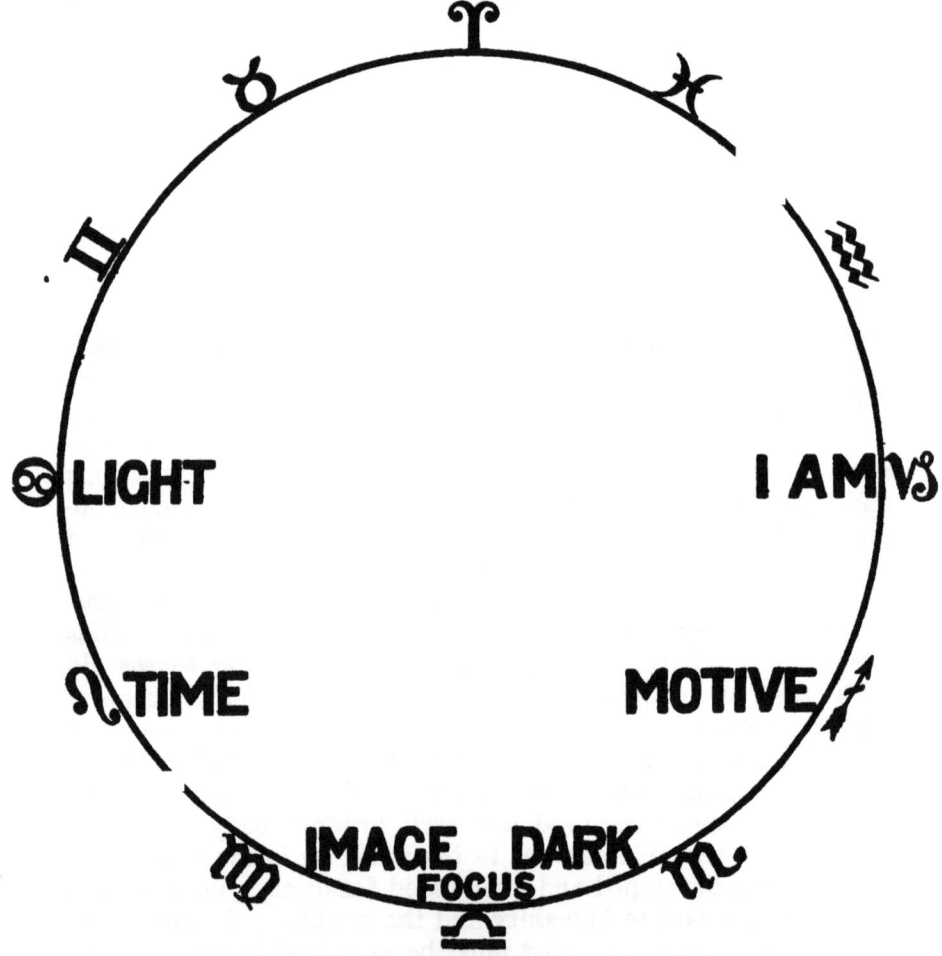

FIGURE 35.
The Faculties of the Mind and the Signs of the Zodiac to Which They Correspond.

the mind and the senses of the body. An artist becomes great in proportion to the ability to use his senses. A mind becomes great and useful to the degree that it develops, and co-ordinates its faculties.

A man becomes a master when he has learned how to use his faculties. A master alone is able to use his faculties at all times intelligently and to know them as distinct from his senses, but every man uses the faculties of his mind in some degree. From the time one begins to exercise and develop his faculties and to control by them his senses, from that time, consciously or unconsciously to himself, does he begin to become a master. A man's body has special organs through which the senses act, so also are there centers and parts of the human body through which and from which the faculties of the mind act and are operated while the mind is in the body.

One who would become an artist knows that he needs and must use the organs of the senses, upon which his art rests. He knows that he must care for that part of his body through which he develops his sense; yet he does not give his eye or ear special treatment; he trains it by exercise. As he measures tones and distances and compares colors and forms and estimates proportions and harmonies, his senses become keener and answer more readily to his call, until he excels in his particular art. Though it may not be known to him, he must, to be proficient in his art, exercise his faculties. He is using his faculties, but in the service of the senses, which is what those do who are in the school of the senses. Rather should he use his senses in the service of his mind and its ministers, the faculties.

The eye does not see, nor the ear hear shades of color and tone, form and rythm. The senses, through the eye or ear, sense the color or form or sound, but they cannot analyze, compare nor reason about them. The light and time faculties do this and they do it under the name of the senses of sight or sound, and not under the name of the faculties of light and time. So that the senses gain honor not due to them and they masquerade as the faculties, but these serve the senses. By training the faculties to serve the senses and by recognizing the senses as the things to be honored, the way is found which leads to the school of the senses, that of the adepts.

Considering the faculties as distinct from and superior to the senses, and training one's self to know the faculties and their working as distinct from the senses, and letting the faculties control the senses, is the way leading to the school of the mind, which is the school of the masters.

The faculties of the mind can be trained in a way similar to the way in which the senses are trained. As with the senses, the way to train the faculties is by exercising them. They must be exercised independently of the senses. While the faculty is developed which corresponds to the sense of sight, the eye and the sense of sight should not be used. Only after the practice in the training of the light faculty has met with enough success to warrant assurance in its independent use, only then may the eye be used in connection with it. But even then the organ of sight as well as the sense of sight must be considered and understood as subordinate to the light faculty. One does not exercise nor develop the light faculty by sitting with his eyes closed and trying to see things. If one sees things with his eyes closed, he is developing his inner, clairvoyant or astral sense of sight, and not the light faculty. The faculties are trained by mental processes and not by the senses or their organs. The senses should not be keyed up as by gazing fixedly with the eyes closed, or by straining the ear to hear. The senses should be relaxed, not keyed up.

One should begin to train the faculties by a certain attitude of mind. To train the light faculty, the attitude should be of attention, confidence, sincerity and good will.

The light of the light faculty is intelligence, which comes and illuminates the mind according to one's progress. To develop this faculty of the mind, one may direct his mind to the subject of light and try to perceive and understand what is light in each of the worlds, spiritual, mental, psychic and physical. As one becomes proficient in the exercise, he will find that intelligence is a light and will illuminate the mind when the light faculty is able to perceive it.

The attitude of mind to exercise the time faculty is of patience, endurance, exactitude and harmony. All the faculties should be directed in thought to the subject of time and the time faculty. As one develops in the practice of these four virtues, the mind will become enlivened, stimulated, and a change will come in the understanding of things, and change itself will have new meanings.

To seek co-ordination, proportion, dimension and beauty, should be the attitude of mind when one wants to exercise the image faculty. The energies of the mind should be directed to the idea of the image faculty, but no pictures or forms should be created by the mind while the image faculty is being called mentally into operation. If pictures or colors or figures are outlined and seen, the clairvoyant sense of sight is being developed and not the image faculty. To assist in the calling of the image faculty into independent use, words, names and numbers should be conceived and their beauty and proportion, dimension and co-ordination should be seen, as the names, numbers and words are formed or imaged.

Seeking balance, justice, duality and unity is the mental attitude or condition in which one should be for the exercise of the focus faculty, and with this attitude he should bend all his faculties to know that which he values above all things. The subject which is taken must, however, not be anything connected with the senses or possible to be reached by sensuous perception. As he advances in his practice his mind will become clearer, the mental fog will be removed and he will be illuminated on the subject of his search.

Strength, service, love and sacrifice should constitute the attitude in which one should attempt the exercise and training of the dark faculty. He should try to be informed concerning the secret of death. As he preserves the right attitude of mind and continues the exercise, he will understand it.

Freedom, action, honesty and fearlessness, should be the qualities making up the mental attitude necessary for the exercise and training of the motive faculty. All of the energies of the mind should be centered on knowing the action of right thought. With this purpose in mind the exercise should be continued and the success will be announced when one's true nature is revealed to him. All of these qualities are necessary to face one's true nature. But the man exercising this faculty should determine and have the earnest desire and firm resolve to right wrongs at any cost. If this intention is certain and persistent in his mind, he will not fear.

Permanence, knowledge, self and power, form the attitude in which the mind can, with all faculties bent on the subject of self, try to call into independent, conscious being, the I-am faculty. In proportion to the success achieved, the mind will receive an accession of power, and man a confidence in his persistence through death, and he may at his will stand forth as a column of light.

The parts of the body through which the focus faculty operates during normal activities have been given. In order to exercise and discipline the faculties, it is not actually necessary to know all correspondences of the parts of the body with which they are connected, nor the centers from which they are operated. The parts and centers will become apparent to those who are able to use them. As the faculties are understood and their action becomes clear to one's thought, he will of himself find the way to exercise, discipline and use them as naturally as he learns to speak and think and give expression to his thought. It is not necessary to have a teacher or a master. One learns by aiding himself and he is assisted in his efforts to the degree that he finds the means to aid himself.

Outside his own heart, there is no place at which an aspirant to discipleship in the school of the masters may apply for admission, and no person is able to receive or accept such aspirant, nor is anyone able to introduce him to a master. The school of the masters is the school of the world. There are no favorites. Each disciple must depend on his merits and is accepted by no preference nor because of credentials. The only speech which the masters can hear and respond to are the thoughts and aspirations of the heart. One's thoughts may be hidden to one's own view, but they speak their true nature in no uncertain notes, where thoughts are words.

The age is ripe for those who will to appoint themselves disciples in the school of the masters. The appointment can be made in no other way than by one's resolution. Most people are willing to be masters, as they are willing to be great men and leaders of civilization, but few are willing to fit themselves and comply with the requirements. Those who make rash promises, who expect much in a short time, who look for results and advantages within some fixed time, who think that they may practice on other people and who promise the world to give it an uplift, will do others little good and be themselves the least benefited. One cannot appoint himself as disciple to another whom he opines to be a master, nor to a society or group of people, and have the appointment result in permanent good to any concerned. Masters do not hold their lodges with men. There are lodges, societies and groups of people who do accept pupils and do give secret instructions and who do have occult practices, but these are not the masters spoken of in the preceding pages.

When one appoints himself a disciple in the school of the masters, he shows that he does not understand what this means if he sets a time for his acceptance. His self appointment should be made only after due consideration and in a calm moment, and when he has an understanding that he is in eternity and that he makes the appointment for eternity, and not subject to time. When one so appoints himself, he will live on confidently, and although the years may roll by without his seeing any other evidence than his moral improvement and increase of mental strength, still he knows he is on the way. If he does not, he is not made of the right stuff. One who is of the right stuff cannot fail. Nothing will daunt him. He knows; and what he knows no one can take away.

There are no great things for one to do who would be a disciple, but there are many little things to do which are of the greatest importance. The little things are so simple that they are not seen by those who look about to do great things. But no great thing can be done by the disciple except by nurture of the small.

Cleanliness and food are simple subjects and these he must understand. Of course he will keep his body clean and wear clean garments, but it is more important that his heart be clean. Cleanliness of heart is the cleanliness here meant. Cleanliness of heart has been advised for ages. In every sphere of life it has been advised. If a student of occult lore makes light of it, let him know that a clean heart is not a metaphor; it is a physical possibility and may be made a physical fact. A self appointed disciple becomes an accepted disciple in the school of the masters, when he learns how and begins to cleanse his heart. Many lives may be needed to learn how to begin to clean the heart. But when one knows how and begins to clean his heart, he is no longer uncertain about it. Once he has learned the work as an accepted disciple, he knows the way and he proceeds with the cleansing. The cleansing process covers the entire period of discipleship.

When the disciple has his heart clean, his work as disciple is done. He passes through death while living and is born a master. His heart is needed for his birth. He is born out of his heart. After he is born out of it, he still lives in it, but is master of it. While he lives in his heart he lives with the laws of time, though he has overcome time. A strong heart is needed. Only a clean heart is strong. No drugs, sedatives, or tonics will avail. Only one specific, one simple, is needed. No apothecary, nor any cult or organization, with or without quick cures or sure ones, can supply it. This simple is: Simple Honesty.

One must be his own physician and he must find it. It may have been long unnoticed, but it can be found in the heart. It may take a long search to find it, but when it is found and used, the results will repay the effort.

But honesty in the gross, the kind which the legal and even moral codes of the world demand, is not the simple which the disciple needs. Much of the gross is needed to get a little of the essence, in the simple. When honesty is applied to the heart, it changes the heart. The treatment will be sure to hurt, but will do it good. Only one who tries, knows the difficulties and obstacles encountered and the strength needed to find and use honesty. Those who are already honest, and are always offended at having their honesty questioned, need not try.

When a little of the specific of honesty is by an aspirant applied to his heart, he begins to stop lying. When he begins to stop lying, he begins to speak truly. When he begins to speak truly he begins to see things as they are. When he begins to see things as they are, he begins to see how things should be. When he begins to see how things should be, he tries to make them so. This he does with himself.

To be concluded.

A THINKER, THE TRANSFORMER OF FORMS.

Beware when the great God lets loose a thinker on this planet. Then all things are at risk. It is as when a conflagration has broken out in a great city, and no man knows what is safe, or where it will end. There is not a piece of science but its flank may be turned to-morrow; there is not any literary reputation, not the so-called eternal names of fame, that may not be revised and condemned. The very hopes of man, the thoughts of his heart, the religion of nations, the manners and morals of mankind are all at the mercy of a new generalization. Generalization is always a new influx of the divinity into the mind. Hence the thrill that attends it.
—EMERSON, *"Circles."*

IMMORTALITY AND MODERN SCIENTISTS.

By Eduard Herrmann.

THE burning question of the day is as it has always been: "Is or is not, man immortal?" The influence of this question on our social and moral well being is immense. The great thinkers of the past, as well as those of the present, knew of its importance and have devoted much of their time to the solution of it; for thousands of years the churches have taught the immortality of the soul; philosophers have fought for and against it; the innate feeling of man seems to confirm it; and still there are few people who can truthfully say that they know it to be true.

There was a time when humanity was satisfied to be led by their priests, and the priests pretended to have all the knowledge necessary for the solution of questions which were too difficult for ordinary minds. In those days the immortality of the soul was made a dogma of the churches; very few men dared to question it and those who did were severely punished for their heresy—no other answer was ever obtainable from the priests.

Even the old christian philosophers were in the power of the church and they tried their best to prove the truth of the dogmas by reasoning. But this was not easy, since dogma and reason could not always be made to harmonize. The difficulties became greater and greater until there was an entire separation between philosophy and the theology. Now while theology tried to prove immortality by means of revelation, philosophy expected to do it by an analysis of Consciousness; but, unfortunately, both are proofs insufficient for the man who does not believe in immortality as long as he has no evidence for the existence of a soul apart from his physical body.

The progress of natural science has so far been very disturbing to the belief in immortality, for it sees in the soul nothing but a function of the body. Science has destroyed many a teaching of the church, and thereby undermined its authority.

In short, the belief in the immortality of the soul is failing because neither religion nor philosophy is able to furnish those proofs which our twentieth century humanity is asking for. The center of gravity of our endeavors has entirely changed, for instead of it being directed towards the future life, the christian heaven, it now inclines towards the sensual life, this earth. We are getting more learned and less moral; more learned because it helps us to win in the battle for existence, less moral because we believe only in this life and its pleasures. Morality can only get a firm footing when it is based on the belief in the immortality of the soul; a few great minds may be moral without this belief, but the masses cannot be so. It is to be apprehended that our civilization with all its great acquisitions in knowledge, in art, in discovery, is doomed if we cannot convince the masses that the immortality of the soul is a fact, a demonstrable fact. For only with the proof that we are immortal, can they understand that our terrestrial life is not the main thing, the only thing, to be cherished. If they have proof that life continues after death, their terrestrial egotism will at least be changed into a transcendental egotism, which would bring about an entire change in all our social conditions; for anybody can understand that only he who gives love in this life, can expect to be loved in the next one.

But how is it possible to regain this lost belief in immortality, to regain that great moral influence which is so necessary for the well-being of humanity and which is in danger of being entirely lost by religion, philosophy and natural science?

It is only possible if it can be proven that man has a soul and that this soul can be separated from the body without losing its essential faculties. Our religions and many of our philosophical systems emphatically declare, and the greater part of human beings instinctively believe, that we have a soul; but what it is and what its possibilities are, only few of us know. Those few firmly believe in it because they know; the belief of all other men is easily shaken, because they do not know but simply believe what others say; they repeat what their authorities say. Until lately the church has been that authority, but with the greater learning of the masses, with the general distribution of knowledge, the change of authorities is unavoidable, especially if they teach a doctrine which allows man to do as he pleases, to gratify all his sensual desires and appetites, and to be only careful not to come in conflict with the public prosecutor. Such a doctrine is: "that man has no soul which is immortal."

This teaching is on the point of becoming generally accepted, and we can already see how its degrading influence manifests itself, not only in the lower classes but even in so-called good society. It is therefore absolutely necessary that the belief in immortality becomes again firmly established among the sceptics of the western world, and this can only be done by showing that the soul can be separated from the body of living man, and that it does not lose the power to understand and to act in this exteriorised condition. The mystics of the middle ages, especially Paracelsus, and in our time Theosophy, have always maintained that such is the case, but of modern scientists there are only few who dared to experiment along these lines. Though it must be admitted that in recent years several eminent men of science have courageously taken up the study of the soul and of its marvelous powers. These men have placed the new science (called psychic science) on a firm basis and have furnished important, if not conclusive evidence, of the existence of the soul and of the strange powers which have always been regarded either with ridicule or with superstition. Psychic science has also furnished abundant proof of the truth of the theosophic teaching that the soul is not only able to detach itself from the living body and return to it, but also to manifest its continued consciousness after the death of the physical body. I cannot, in the short space at my disposal, speak of all these men of science, who, by their experiments and researches, have come to the firm conclusion, that the soul of man is immortal, but I will mention the names of a few, whose works can be recommended as a most interesting and useful study of this subject matter.

Thompson J. Hudson wrote a book, "A Scientific Demonstration of the Future Life," which, in its logical reasoning, is excellent. His principal theory is, that man has a dual mind; this fact he says lies at the foundation of the science of the soul, for it is in a sense demonstrative of the fact that man has a soul; that is to say, if man has a soul, its mental organization must necessarily be supposed to be identified with one or the other of his two minds—the subjective, or the objective. Now the facts of hypnotism and of experimental surgery demonstrate that the objective mind is a function of the brain and necessarily perishes with that organ. That fact therefore excludes the objective mind from consideration as a possible heir to a future life and clears the way for the consideration of the facts relating to the subjective mind, which facts must of necessity either prove or disprove its claims to immortality.

And now he shows by relating the experiments of well known men of science, that the subjective mind of man (what is here called the soul) does not necessarily perish with the brain; that there is no faculty, emotion or organism, of the human mind that has not its function, use or object; then he finds that some of the subjective powers, as for instance intuitional perception, telepathy, clairvoyance, clairaudience, absolute memory, perform no normal function in earthly life and are only observed in abnormal conditions. Then he puts his argument in the syllogistic form:

"Every faculty of the human mind has a normal function to perform either in this life or in a future life. Some faculties of the human mind perform no normal functions in this life.

"Therefore: Some faculties of the human mind are destined to perform their functions in a future life."

The book is worth while reading and must give pleasure as well as valuable information to every seeker after truth.

Another important book dealing with this subject is Myers'; "Human Personality, and its Survival of Bodily Death." This book might be called an encyclopaedia of all the important experiments, researches and experiences, of a man well known in science and literature who by his great learning and fine character, as well as by his position as president of the Society for Psychical Research in London, has had great influence on modern psychical science.

His belief in the immortality of the soul was absolute and could not be shaken by anything; this was acquired through life long endeavor and research. He says: "The central claim of the soul's life manifested after the body's death, can less and less be supported by remote tradition alone; it must more and more be tested by modern science and inquiry. . . . Now our researches have shown, that amid much deception and self-deception, fraud and illusion, veritable manifestations do reach us from beyond the grave. The central claim of Christianity is thus confirmed as never before. . . . I predict that, in consequence of the new evidence, all reasonable men, a century hence, will believe the resurrection of Christ, whereas, in default of the new evidence, no reasonable man, a century hence, would have believed it."

About the necessity for our belief in the immortality of the soul, he says: "If we believe that endless life exists for all, with infinite possibilities of human redress and of divine justification, then it seems right to assume that the universe is either already wholly good, or is at least in course of becoming so . . . through the very ardour of our own faith and hope. Spiritual evolution is our destiny in this and other worlds . . . and the passion for life is no selfish weakness, it is a factor in the universal energy."

There is another well known man of science, who has just published a book with the title, "The Survival of Man." I am speaking of Sir Oliver Lodge, the English scientist and former President of the Society for Psychical Research.

In this work as in his former "Science and Immortality," Sir Oliver is very careful not to assert a thing as absolutely true which is not proven by science; but all through both works, you feel that he is personally satisfied that the question of continuity of life after death has been proven by the most careful observations and experiments of well known scientists. He says that "Objection is sometimes taken against any attempt being made gradually to arrive at what in process of time may come to be regarded as a scientific proof of immortality. . . . An objection of this kind can only be felt by those who think that knowledge is the enemy of belief, instead of its strengthener and supporter. . . . Whatever science can establish, that it has a right to establish: more than a right, it has a duty. If there be things which we are not intended to know, be assured that we shall never know them. Let us study all the facts that are open to us, with a trusting and an open mind; with care and candour testing all our provisional hypotheses and with slow and cautious verification making good our steps as we proceed."

This is the attitude of a true scientist, whose testimony must be of great weight to any impartial observer, and his testimony is to the fact that "Death and decay are interesting physical processes, in which there is nothing to suggest ultimate destruction—since there is in nature no real waste, no real loss, no annihilation." That there is a permanent element in man, he tries to prove with arguments, from telepathy, from praeternormal psychology, from automatism, from the subliminal faculty, from mental pathology. That this permanent element in man continues to exist after death is fully proven to Sir Oliver Lodge because "Intelligent co-operation between other than embodied human minds than our own, has become possible."

Then there is a German scientist, Dr. Carl du Prel, who devoted his whole life to similar researches, because he recognized the great moral influence which would necessarily follow if the claims of mystics and theosophists could be experimentally proven. Shortly before his death he wrote a book embodying his experiments and experiences regarding the separation of the so-called astral body from the physical, by living men; from this book, whose title is "Der Tod, das Jenseits, das Leben im Jenseits." I will now quote, to show how far experimental science has progressed in the inquest of this most important question. He says: "Man is a complicated product of nature, a microcosm so to speak, in which all the powers of the macrocosm are densified; consequently he must possess (although unknowingly) the same magical or occult power, that is, hidden forces and laws, which are always working in nature whether we discover them or not."

Modern science makes the mistake not to recognize those magical powers, but only those of which we are conscious and which we can voluntarily use. But our ordinary consciousness is cerebral and extends by means of the nervous system over our body; it is not capable to say whether a soul exists and what it is. In other words: the soul, if it exists, lies outside of the cerebral consciousness; for this reason the latter can define only one half of man. Our magical powers do not adhere to the body—they need a special carrier, a magical man (or as Theosophy teaches the astral body) and it is this magical man who has to be considered if we talk of immortality. There is a transcendental world, for the recognition of which we do not have organs, and a transcendental man which exceeds our self-consciousness; this transcendental man encloses our soul and brings forth those remarkable phenomena which Occultism tries to explore and to explain. We, as terrestrial men, are a combination of soul and body. Now although the cerebral consciousness embraces as a rule only the bodily half, yet there are certain abnormal states possible, when the threshold of consciousness might be removed or enlarged, so that we could learn something of the nature of our soul, as well as of the manner in which it exists in the transcendental world.

This happens in Somnambulism, for which reason we must

not neglect to study its remarkable phenomena if we ever want to get a knowledge of the psychic and hidden powers latent in man. Somnambulism, and in fact all sleep, may justly be called the brother of death; let us now consider what happens in both these phenomena. If a man dies we do not see anything like a separation of the soul from the body. We see that life becomes extinct, that a perfect anaesthesia of the body takes place and that the body is resolved into atoms. But this process might be accompanied by another one which, if we could see it, would guarantee the further existence of the individual. It is true that we perceive the anaesthesia of the body, but we do not know if this is a complete annihilation of the power to feel, for in sleep also we become anaesthetic to a certain degree and, in the hypnotic sleep, even so much so that the most difficult operations can be performed without pain; but the power to feel is not annihilated by all that, for it returns when the person is awake. Now we have to find out where that power goes to when a person is in the sleeping or hypnotic or somnambulic state. This problem has been solved by several scientists, but especially by Prof. de Rochas in Paris, who made the anaesthesia of somnambulists his special study. He pointed out that the power to feel is not annihilated in the state of anaesthesia, not even suppressed, but simply transferred—to the outside.

In 1848, Baron Reichenbach affirmed that every living organism, and especially that of man, exhales a certain fluid, invisible under normal circumstances, but visible in the hypnotic, somnambulic and clairvoyant state. He called this fluid the Od. Now de Rochas finds that in somnambulism layers of od come out of the sleeping person's body, and these layers of od retain the power to feel, so that a needle, when applied to the body of the sleeper, was not felt; but when applied to the exteriorised layers of od the needle was felt keenly. Many such cases are cited in de Rochas' interesting work, "L'extériorisation de la Sensibilité." It is therefore proven that the temporary oppression of bodily life is connected with a transcendental occurrence, namely, the stepping out of a soul principle which continues to exist, although separated from the body. This very important phenomenon gives us a right to suppose that a similar occurrence takes place when natural death overtakes a person: the separation of the inner, odic, man from the body.

If this should be the case, it would bring us much nearer to the solution of the question of immortality, for then we would have the bearer of consciousness separable from the body and independent of the bodily organs. It is true that exteriorised layers of od cannot be called the soul, but they may contain other powers besides that of feeling. For instance, it is well known that in the process of magneting life power is transferred from the healer to the patient by means of this same mysterious fluid called od. Scientific proofs for this assertion may be found in G. Defosses work: "Le magnetisme vital." Furthermore, it is proven by many exact experiments that thought transference between magnetizer and patient is a common occurrence, which could not take place without a medium that carries thought from one person to another, and again this medium is, od.

If the principle of life can be exteriorized, we may expect the same from the power of formation; that is, the exteriorized layers of od must be able to take the shape of man to form the so-called astral body of the mystics. This happens so frequently that the Society for Psychical Research in London has been able to collect 700 cases which (Gurney, M. D. Phantasms of the Living) prove that strongly excited and especially, dying persons are able to send out their astral body and make it visible to others, sometimes at a very great distance. The fact that the double of still living persons has the greatest semblance, in regard to its apparition, activity and disappearance, with ghosts and materialisations, makes it probable that in the process of dying the same thing happens, namely, the stepping out of the astral body, but with this difference that it is then a lasting exteriorisation, while with the double it is only a temporary one.

The experiments of de Rochas show that the exteriorisation always begins with still unformed layers of od, and in spiritistic seances, the same has been observed. It always takes some time until the human form is developed out of the od particles. One of the best illustrations of this peculiar process is given in Aksakow's book "Animism and Spiritism"; "There the progressive formation of the phantom out of a ball of od particles, about as large as a hand, is distinctly visible by means of photographic pictures."

Now the orthodox believers, as well as the spiritists, will probably not be satisfied to hear that the soul has an odic body; they hold the soul to be pure spirit, while the naturalist cannot think of a pure spirit, nor of a force, without a material foundation. The old Greek writers never mention a spirit without a

IMMORTALITY AND MODERN SCIENTISTS 273

body. Gods, good and bad demons, like the souls of the departed ones, were thought to be in a body of some kind. Plato gives expression to this general belief when he says in his Phaedrus, that the soul takes a somatoic (an etherial body) over into the next world; and even the christian fathers held to that belief. Origen says that no being is without a body[1]) and Tertullian even believes this of God,[2]) St. Paul teaches that, besides the physical, man has a spiritual, undying body,[3]) and the philosophers, Leibnitz, Fichte, Hellenbach, teach the same. With the old Egyptians the astral body was named "ka," with the Kabbalists, "nephash," Paracelsus calls it "evestrum."

In fact the belief in the astral body has always existed and only our modern natural science denies it and with it also immortality. But it is not worthy of science to deny a thing which it has not inquired into; science has to prove by actual experiment that the astral body does not exist, and the actual experiment will lead, or has already led, to its rediscovery, and with it to the experimental proof of the immortality of the soul.

It is true that the artificial exteriorisation of the astral body is a transcendental process which cannot be directly observed by the scientist. But it can be brought under control, as de Rochas proved; and the observations which he made, well deserve our attention. If a person, A, is put in the somnambulic sleep, he is able to see the odic emanations of another person, whom we shall call B. If B is now somnambulized, A describes the layers of od which ooze out of B's body as a mist which later becomes shining. The experimentor cannot see it, but he can verify the power to feel, which is inherent in those layers of od, by touching, stinging or pinching them, when told by A, where they are. If B's sleep becomes deeper, more layers of od come out of his body which surround him for a distance of about 10 feet. Then they condense and form a phantom—half of blue color on his right side, which is about three feet distant, has the form of B's right side body and takes on all his power to feel; and also imitates the movements of B. In the same way there is half a phantom of red color formed on B's left side. These polarized radiations Reichenbach has also observed on plants, crystals, and magnets. The two phantom halfs unite in the course of time and form one whole phantom, but without losing their

---

(1) Origen: de princ. I-F.
(2) Tertullian: adv. Ivox.
(3) Paulus 2. Cor. 4, 16.

peculiar color. If the sleep of B is deepened he cannot move, but through his will he can cause the phantom to move; he can send it to distant places in order to make observations there.

The astral body, for it is nothing else, being of an ethereal nature is able to penetrate other bodies and all obstacles. De Rochas believes that a total suppression of consciousness of the medium would make the astral body visible for everybody, and not for sensitives only. But this being dangerous for the medium, he never went so far; he however tried diverse experiments in order not to depend entirely on the evidence of the clairvoyants. A sting in the finger of the blue half phantom, caused a drop of blood on the corresponding finger of B. He also took photographs of the phantom; then he caused the phantom to divide itself again and return into the body of the medium.

If we now consider what happens in the process of dying, we find first: anaesthesia of the body; the same as in artificial exteriorisation. Knowing that the power to feel is confined to the astral body, it is correct to infer that anaesthetic symptoms are the result of odic exteriorisation. Then we find the same magical functions with the dying as with the somnambules, esspecially the appearance of the astral body at a distance, many verified examples of which are to be found in "Phantasms of the Living." All these magical functions can be explained only through the externalisation of the astral body, or at least through its radiations.

Death is in fact the odic essentification of man; for od is not only the carrier of the life power, but also of the formative power and the power to feel; it is also the carrier of consciousness and of thought. The whole psychic man is externalized in death.

Now natural science, which excludes the supernatural but concedes the supersensual, will certainly contest that man continues to live as pure spirit; but it need not deny the existence of spirits which are clothed in bodies of some kind of matter. It all depends on experience. It is possible that there are beings who never become so densified that they can be optically seen; and it is also possible that there are beings who do not see man, although he is densely materialized. The naturalist will deny that death transforms man into a supernatural being; but he can concede that we become supersensual. He may deny that we get something new in death, the astral body; but he cannot deny

---
(1) Le Lotus Bleu. May, 1894.

IMMORTALITY AND MODERN SCIENTISTS 275

that we have it already in life and preserve it in death. Here he has to experiment and his experiments will furnish him the proofs for immortality; for as soon as he has seen the phenomenon of exteriorisation, he cannot deny the double with its possibility of stepping out of the body; and then he has to concede that the same process is possible and actually happens in death. Materialism, which teaches that the spirit of man develops out of the human organism, must lose all ground; for externalisation shows that the spirit uses the body as a means for its manifestation, and that our terrestrial life is not the only possible kind of life, since the externalized astral body is able to think and to feel without the physical body.

The question of immortality has now become a problem for natural science; which is very good, since neither philosophy nor religion have been able to guard humanity against theoretical and practical materialism. The phenomenon of exteriorisation alone is able to remove materialism, and to make the proof of immortality independent from religion, philosophy, and even from spiritism.

The sending out of the double is a process of odic externalization; death is the same. To die does not mean to disappear altogether, but only from our physical eye, through the laying aside of our body and through odic exteriorisation. Birth and death are not opposites, because every birth is a relative death as every death is a relative birth. In terrestrial birth our astral being disappears for the cerebral consciousness; in terrestrial death it becomes free; enriched or impoverished, according to the use which we made of our physical life. We shall certainly die poor if we have only taken our physical well being into consideration, and the consequences must show themselves after death.

The metamorphosis of the physical existence into the etherial (or magical, as du Prel calls it) brings changes with it, which we are hardly able to grasp. "We do not have to expect an eternal heaven nor hell, both of which would be undeserved, but we will be freed from all the evil and sufferings connected with our physical body. Our power of cognition, now greatly hampered by the sensual consciousness, must then be immensely enlarged; our activity not anymore limited to the use of corporeal organs, must receive a very large sphere of work, and equipped with the astral or ethereal power of locomotion, we shall lead an existence which is difficult to describe. But from all these causes we have to expect that the communion of spirits is there much more intimate than here among men, and the significance of morality must be much greater than here. For this reason it becomes imperative for us, to live now a life of purity, honesty and brotherly love; to seek for that knowledge and wisdom which alone will enable us to commune after death with those exalted beings, who, although denied by many, must exist if evolution is true and if immortality is not an empty word."

But there is a still higher aspect of this question. Man has to understand that his soul is a tangible reality, which not only connects him with the outer or sensuous world, but also with the super-sensuous. Just as his soul forms the outer or physical body, so it moulds the inner or spiritual, as St. Paul calls it; and if we inquire what it is that forms them, then we answer: his thoughts. A seer has said: "All material things created by man are forms of his thoughts; and these are the offspring of the soul. The form of man is a likeness, a type, a representative of the cause or soul, which animates and unfolds it to the outer world. The outer senses are typical of the inner ones; for they are unfolded from the corresponding parts of the interior essence." The process of evolution proves this. Wherever we turn our eyes we see that the outer unfolds from the inner; that the real creative force which works in a plant, an animal, a man, is hidden in it—or in himself. But we can also see that while plants and animals seem to have reached a stationary point in their evolution, that is, a point where they cannot develop any further, man seems not to know any such limitations. He evolves new thoughts continually and consequently develops new powers, new forces.

Just now man seems to be all absorbed in thoughts about the physical universe and consequently he must reach great perfection in this line of thought and action. Much good for humanity can come out of those efforts, but undoubtedly, also much evil. The greatest danger lies in the possibility of his forgetting that he is a spiritual being and only temporarily engaged to this physical world; that it is really a great loss to spend his whole life in the exploration of material things, when by doing this he is unable to develop the higher soul powers, those which relate to immortality and connect him with the spiritual world. We ought not to forget that the real man is the internal man, "the invisible one which animates the material form in order that it may perfect its constitution and preserve its identity, and also establish an inseparable connection between the material and spiritual world."

If man were always conscious of this truth and better educated, his thoughts would not be so far removed from the higher or spiritual world and he would develop those soul powers which can connect him with the invisible world and beings which, to-day, are denied by so many. He would get an understanding of the relations existing between the two worlds and feel himself to be a citizen in both. He would be able to receive higher impressions and glimpses from the better world, and materialize them here on earth, in the form of art, poetry, the sciences, inventions, or in social betterments and everything that tends to make life happier to all; he would banish misery and crime, poverty and evil, from this globe of ours. Man is bound to react this glorious state of being, to become a true Lover of everything that lives, as soon as he is firmly convinced that he continues to live after death and that immortality is no idle dream. For this reason, let us appreciate the efforts of our scientists who want to solve this greatest riddle of the universe, and who try to do it in a way that entails no suffering to human beings. The truth is one only, but many ways lead to it.

WHO IS A FRIEND?

We can seldom go erect. Almost every man we meet requires some civility,—requires to be humored; he has some fame, some talent, some whim of religion or philanthropy in his head that is not to be questioned, and which spoils all conversation with him. But a friend is a sane man who exercises not my ingenuity, but me. My friend gives me entertainment without requiring any stipulation on my part. A friend therefore is a sort of paradox in nature. I who alone am, I who see nothing in nature whose existence I can affirm with equal evidence to my own, behold now the semblance of my being, in all its height, variety and curiosity, reiterated in a foreign form; so that a friend may well be reckoned the masterpiece of nature.

—EMERSON, "*Friendship.*"

THE INNER LIFE AND THE TAO-TEH-KING.

XV.

AN APPENDIX ON JEAN JACQUES ROUSSEAU'S IDEAS OF "A RETURN TO NATURE."

By C. H. A. BJERREGAARD.

Concluded from page 226.

I HAVE made so many references to "A Return to Nature," that, to avoid misunderstandings, I now append a few words on Jean Jacques Rousseau's famous sentence, "The Return to Nature," a sentence my reader may easily suppose that I have had in mind and refer to.

In my use of the phrase "return to Nature" there is no other reference to Rousseau than the one that naturally arises when great men like Laotzse and Rousseau both draw from the great wells of the Inner Life, which as a Finnish proverb well says, "*Diupa brunnar torka icke*: Deep wells never dry up." The well they both drew from was Nature, and it is to Nature that both, in their own peculiar way, recommend a return.

Both Laotzse and Rousseau understood by Nature: immediacy, simplicity, freedom and goodness, and they set Nature in those senses against culture by which they understood that which makes life complicated, constrained, evil and too reflective. By culture they meant the formalism, social and ecclesiastic, of their day. Their general tendencies were therefore the same and very much like those of the reformers of various times. It is in such senses that Rousseau and Laotze agree.

Their methods and expressions naturally differed widely. Laotzse lived many centuries before our era and in a country of so much ceremonialism and formalism that we hardly can imagine its condition. Everything was overdone, in religion, ethics and societary order, though these were not evil or corrupt as we understand such terms. Order had become a tyrant and was no more a help to live rationally. Regulations or customs crushed expansion and competition. Men did not think for themselves, but observed rules laid down by others as ignorant and narrow as themselves, but in power of government. This state of affairs was a result of the former age's struggles for mental, moral and spiritual life and freedom. In that age, it was a living state of things, and it was a high form of civilization and culture and useful for progress, but it was not taken over by the next age in its original vitality and progressive power, but as mere matter and form, and for that reason it became a curse. It was this curse and burden, that Laotzse labored against.

Rousseau lived many centuries after the beginning of our era and in an age which he declared, in his Dijon-Prize essay on the effect of the progress of civilization on morals (1750), had lost its soul and substituted corruption in the same measure as it had progressed in the sciences and arts. His age had denied a state of happy ignorance with its original spontaneous way of living and immediate relations to nature. It had allowed itself to be suppressed by externalities; it had tolerated restlessness to supplant the inner peace, that comes from a contented life. Rousseau's charges were set forth with much warmth and enthusiasm and it was felt that he was a new power. He became famous but, like Laotzse and all men of his stamp, in his old age a lonesome and deserted man. His enemies and the enemies of naturalness did not like originality, natural energy and the fresh and healthy aroma that comes from a life in the Open. Such people shun the cool and clear waters fresh from the springs. They prefer the compound drinks of intoxicating liquors and the rich sources of flattery offered at societies' testimonial dinners.

As they were in Rousseau's day, so they are to-day, and right here among us. We have to fight them if we wish to help our age to truth and liberty. They are the real hindrances to all Inner Life and true social order. They are the associates of Kali, the dark and dreadful goddess, who has given the name to this age.

I shall not need to review Laotzse's principles and system, if any "system" can be attributed to him. Enough has been said in the foregone chapters. But I will give a resume of Rousseau's ideas and teachings and invite the reader to make comparisons.

One special difference between Laotzse and the Inner Life on one side, and Rousseau on the other, must be noted at the outset. It colors all Rousseau's utterances and it places him apart when we speak of the Inner Life. He is a literary man, and neither religious nor philosophical.

The fundamental type of Rousseau's thinking is the opposition he sees between the immediate, the original, the self-centered, the totality of the soul on the one side and the relative, the partial, the dependent and the mixed, on the other side. In the first he sees life as its own cause and effect, born of its own energy and endeavor, and in the second he sees limitations, compulsions and inner diremption. The first is the Absolute; the second is the Relative. The first is Nature, the second is what he calls Culture.

Rousseau uses the word Nature in three senses. The first sense, the theological, appears when he speaks of the world as God's creation and the "heavenly and majestic simplicity with which its creator adorned it." That divine condition he calls Nature and contrasts it with the distortions, twists and obliquity introduced by man, which he calls Culture. Rousseau also says that all things proceed pure and good from their natural origin.

The second sense, the "natural-history" sense, appears when he describes "the primitive condition" and explains how inequalities arose. In man's original "zoological" nature-condition there was perhaps no marked "majestic simplicity." It was an instinctive life. Man had no reflection nor imagination. He had but few necessities; they were physical and easily satisfied. While Rousseau is not blind to the "primitive man's" low and brutal state, and seems to have seen its contradiction to "the majestic simplicity" elsewhere described, he laments its loss. The loss of the life of instinct is to him a sort of "fall" from a paradisaical state.

The third sense of the word Nature appears in Rousseau's psychology. When he speaks in this sense he ignores the two others and plunges into introspection, that he may find man's original (natural) and fundamental powers and being. The result of his examination is that he declares that the original Man, or, Man according to his nature, is good and sound, though men may be bad. He wants men to return to this, the original good and sound nature, to heart-life, and shun all external relations which blurr the vision and contaminate morals. He thinks that silence and solitude make it possible for mankind to find the original nature. By "being good" Rousseau meant that "we express our nature" and he himself in moments—*sans diversion, sans obstacle*—thought himself to have been so good such as Nature intended him to be. And he declares emphatically that all men have fundamentally a desire to be as they should and ought to be. There is in everybody a natural tendency to maintain his selfhood, an *amour de soi* as he calls it. But this *amour de soi*, the healthy self maintenance, has to meet and fight an *amour propre*, selflove, something our surroundings develop, something not ourselves. The *amour propre* does not exist in a society where man has to do with himself alone. Such a society does not create a desire for distinction, preferment. In the *amour de soi* there is an abundance of energy, and it is all spent in natural self-development, while the *amour propre* paralyses man's energy by shattering his self-centredness. To be directed by Nature and to live according to Nature means a life according to *amour de soi*, and, moreover, such a life creates sympathy with other beings, the very opposite of *amour propre* which sets distinctions of separateness against other beings. In the *amour de soi* only are we free beings and may feel ourselves as gods: *on se suffit à soi-même comme Dieu!* In the *amour de soi* we have few needs and make no comparisons. In the *amour propre* we multiply desires and defer to other people's opinions.

Like Laotzse, Rousseau also thinks that much learning is a hindrance to a natural life. By self-rest, on the other hand, we open ourselves to all the natural influxes which correspond to our own nature.

Our best and true teacher in the natural life is feeling, and Rousseau has the merit of having placed the feelings in their right position in psychology, and, he has that merit in spite of previous work done by such men as Spinoza, Shaftesbury, Hutcheson and Hume. We have (all of us) an inherent liking or disliking; and these are Nature's monitors; they act instinctively and speak clearly, where they are not corrupted. Feeling and reason are really two sides of the same nature. If we follow feeling we live in unity. By feeling is of course not meant our sensations, or what psychology generally calls the feelings. By feeling is understood broadly, the Inner Man.

By feeling or which is the same, by inner perception or immediate knowledge, we get religion. City people who have no feeling except when they run against stone walls; who have no perceptions except when tired out by the length of their streets;

who have no immediate kowledge, but are full of reports of crimes and the like from their newspapers,—city people have no religion. How could any ecstacy strike them! Their hearts are not sensitive; their eyes do not know the wide views; their ears hear only noises, but never the rhythm of the winds sighing at sunrise. Let them withdraw from that unnatural existence. It never generated religion or mystic longings for the greatest, the Infinite. Rousseau never tires of calling to us to close our books and ecclesiastic conventions and retire to open-air-nature, there to find our own soul, who is our true god.

In the first stages of education, says Rousseau, it is of prime importance that the original nature of the child has full and free play of its feelings for and against that which it wants or does not want. Only by so doing does it become possible to regulate the child's growth according to its own inherent character or nature and not—according to somebody else's notions. This idea is the prevailing one in Rousseau's handling of the problem of education.

In the history of the development of human thought and life, Rousseau represents a revival of the ancient naturalism which placed instinct above reflection. A little before him there had already been an awakening of the Hellenic sense of Nature, with all its acceptances of objective joy in natural facts and natural simplicity and impulses. But Rousseau is the man whom history names as the father of the movement in Europe in a general way, and, in France in a special way, and as the opponent to abstract ideological notions.

With Rousseau, feeling comes into the history of philosophy as an independent and absolute principle and in no way subject to the intellect. From feeling is henceforth derived religion, poetry and romanticism, represented by such famous names as those of Schleiermacher and Novalis, for instance. Everywhere humanity seems to "find its own" by turning against the dry intellect, and alas! humanity also finds itself tied by the new errors and sins!

Ever since Rousseau's time genius has spread its wings as never before; common man, who before was not even supposed to be able to think, broke out from his social and mental prison, borne by the new overflowing life and images and thought, and combinations of these now made possible have enriched the human mind most marvelously. Never before had men directly from the soil come forth as leaders in life and thought. The New Age culture, such as it is known in the United States, could never have seen the day except for Rousseau.

A sensible study and intelligent application of the ideas and methods of Laotzse and Rousseau will go far to refresh individual souls and develop true self-reliance. It will create true will power and work, and, wealth both of mind and pocket. It will do away with our boastful self-complacency and the intolerable strain of trust associations, and also place these in their position as public servants rather than as tyrants. In my opinion the new ideas for our age and the coming age, ideas, we all long for in the name of religion, philosophy and social organization, lie slumbering in the teachings and methods left us by Laotzse and Jean Jacques Rosseau.

In the confidence that I have done something to draw these teachings out of their unmerited obscurity, and in the hope that they sooner or later may be made useful, I conclude these chapters on

THE INNER LIFE AND THE TAO-TEH-KING.

THOUGHT SPEAKS THROUGH ALL TIME.

We are often made to feel that there is another youth and age than that which is measured from the year of our natural birth. Some thoughts always find us young, and keep us so. Such a thought is the love of the universal and eternal beauty. Every man parts from that contemplation with the feeling that it rather belongs to ages than to mortal life. The least activity of the intellectual powers redeems us in a degree from the conditions of time. In sickness, in languor, give us a strain of poetry or a profound sentence, and we are refreshed; or produce a volume of Plato or Shakespeare, or remind us of their names, and instantly we come into a feeling of longevity. See how the deep divine thought reduces centuries and millenniums, and makes itself present through all ages. Is the teaching of Christ less effective now than it was when first his mouth was opened? The emphasis of facts and persons in my thought has nothing to do with time. And so always the soul's scale is one, the scale of the senses and the understanding is another. Before the revelations of the soul, Time, Space and Nature shrink away.

—EMERSON, "*The Over-Soul.*"

TALES OF THE ANCIENT TRAVELLER.

The Twin Cities.

Translated by Samuel Neu.

TO a tale of the Ancient Traveller, told at the court of Omee, King of the Great Middle Country, and by him called the Tale of the Twin Cities, set down by Lipo-va, the Scribe, give ear:

Where enters mighty Aya to the sea there is a harbor, famed in all this land, whence all the ships that ride the sea sail forth, and where again, deep laden, they return. From all the earth, rich merchandise they bring. All things that thou hast here that thou hadst not, were brought upon the ships and through that port. And mighty though thy power, gracious king, yet can thy people never travel forth nor e'er return, except they pass that way and ride in ships that in that port are home.

In Aya's harbor, one on either shore, there stand two cities, as thou knowest well. In one, Shyinka, are the building yards, where forest kings, laid low, are brought in state and, ere the day-god once has run his round, are grouped and built by Shyinka's great host into the man-made monsters of the sea. Yet are the men of Shyinka but slaves, for naught can they accomplish of themselves without the warrant and the food and gold that from Yinkara's king are sent to them. While in Shyinka all the ships are built, yet in Yinkara is Shyinka ruled. One half the ships fly proud Yinkara's flag, their pilots from that city's king is sent; while Shyinka's adorns the other half, their pilots from that city's prince come forth.

Thy people, when their time to sail the sea has come, float down on Aya's peaceful waves and with their warrant from Yinkara's king, wait in Shyinka for their ships to build. In ancient days, when knowledge was not hid, thy people ordered from Yinkara's king the ship they wanted, and in Shyinka they showed the plan on which the builders built. But in the modern day there is complaint that they must bide in Shyinka and wait until the caprice of the lawless men shall build for them a ship

THE TWIN CITIES

that fits them well. And so it happens often, in this day, that ships sail forth without a mariner, and others are but half built when they sail, and others leak so badly that they sink ere they have buffetted the first fierce gale. Yet blame not this, oh King, on those who build, but blame it rather on thy men who err, as I shall show, who oft have passed that way.

In ancient days, ere came thy men, there was one city only at great Aya's mouth, and all who lived there dwelt in joy and peace. The land about them fed them, and their king, Karaku, ruled them wisely in their way. All that was needful had they, and they knew naught of those things they wished but needed not, for none had come to speak to them of such. Then came thy people's warriors, rich in arts, conquerors of the land and all therein.

"Fools," said they, "why in idleness thus dwell while all the world beyond this ocean's shores awaits your coming. Wake, and build you ships, and we will teach you how to ride the sea, that you may bring the riches of far lands. Here, on the East shore, stands a forest land wherein great giants swing their leafy arms and beckon you to take them for your use, that they may carry you beyond this sea. There, on the West shore, lies a silent bay whose very silence cries to be awaked by sound of axe and mallet, adze and wedge."

Thus spake thy country's warriors, and they heard. And some departed to the Eastern shore and in the forest set themselves to work and after they had felled and hewed and split, within the silent bay began to build. Crude ships, at first, these unskilled workmen built; some ships that would not float upon the tide, and some that floated well but would not sail, and some that were too small to hold a crew, and some that were too large to handle well. Then Karaku, the king, bade labor cease, and, that the work might well be brought to pass, he gave to each his proper labor-share. He first divided all his willing men into two bands, and placed them East and West on either shore of Aya's harbor. Then he placed a city on the Eastern shore where those who felled and hewed should have abode, and this he called Yinkara. On the Western shore he built Shyinka, where the ships to bear thy country's people should be built and those who built them might in comfort dwell. And Karaku went into Shyinka, and Karaku into Yinkara came; in both of these he has his dwelling place, for anciently the cities two are one. But Amarak, the son of

Karaku, in Shyinka, is prince. In Yinkara Amarak's half brother, Marak, whose mother was a daughter of this land, is king, and Karaku proclaimed the law that Amarak should by Marak be ruled, in honor of thy people's ancient race.

Then ordered Karaku that when one came from this the Middle Country, seeking ship, first should he in Yinkara seek the king, and, making known his wants, lay down the plan and from the king receive a royal grant, a warrant and a senopa of food, and, waiting his return, a loan of gold, or, if the traveller had passed that way before, the gold that he received was but his own. Then, with the warrant and the food and gold, the traveller should cross to Shyinka in royal state and seek Shyinka's prince and tarry with him till the ship was built. Then should he take as crew Karaku's men and under one or other of the flags and pilot furnished by the king or prince should sail with them wherever led the sea.

So did it come to pass through many years, and warriors crossed the sea to distant shores, and after sailing far returned again rich laden with the splendor of the earth. They tarried for awhile at Aya's mouth then journeyed homeward, there remained awhile, and then set forth again for further voyage.

The gold they gathered made Yinkara rich with richness far beyond its earth-found wealth and those who in Yinkara dwelt in turn made glad Shyinka's people, those who built. They came to love thy people's warriors well, who taught them how to live as merchantmen, and glad their hearts when any traveller came to order ships and hire them for a cruise. So glad they came to be in course of time that Karaku, to aid them in their joy, proclaimed a fete whenever warrior came. A carnival there was when royal grant was carried from Yinkara to the bay and great rejoicing on the other shore when pageant brought it to Shyinka's prince, and songs that made all nature pause to hear.

Thy people, too, soon came to love the fetes and listened far too often to the tales and dreams Karaku's people whispered them, whence came the evil that at Aya's mouth exists to-day, where ships have gone to ruin. Too often, when no ship a traveller needs, the king proclaims a carnival to please the citizens who clamor for it loud with shouts and cries. Then with all royal pomp a royal grant is carried to the bay and to Shyinka's prince, with food and gold; but ere the workmen start upon their work the wood is thrown upon the ocean's tide, the warrant is destroyed, the gold is lost, the food is given to the scavengers. Small wonder, then, the workmen are confused and build unworthy ships, or none at all. Small wonder is it that the forest land is oft devoid of trees when need is great. Woe, now, unto the wayward traveller whose ear has listened oft to Aya's song, whose ships aforetime have gone forth to sea captained by pilot, not by him who sails, to plunder, burn and pillage distant shores or other ships ill met upon the sea. For him unworthy monster will be built that leaks or founders or is rudderless. And woe unto the wayward traveller, yea, thousand woes, if, for the false parades, his name it was the royal warrant bore, for often will he find the forest bare, and often will he find no men to build, until he swims the ocean's tide alone and gathers back the timbers cast adrift. For thus the evil Karaku doth rule.

Yet even while this evil rides the land those travellers who know the ships they want and how to use them well, still hold respect, and even Karaku will honor them, and Amarak and Marak will bow low; and, though the last tree has been felled and hewed, will find the timbers ready for their need and skillful workmen who can build of old, yea, even ships to sail on Aya's stream. This know I well, for often have I sailed.

The king and all the Court heard this tale in silence, and as the Ancient Man finished, many there were who hung their heads, and these were those who loudest had complained against the evil of Karaku. Then rose the king and commanded them to heed well and never more to bring complaint concerning the manner of their treatment at the Aya's mouth, but heed instead the laws of Mahm, whose law rules the kings of all the land. And this, too, have I, Lipo-va the Scribe, set down.

A DREAM OF ATLANTIS—THE LAND OF MU.

By Alice Dixon Le Plongeon.

(Continued from page 246.)

PART II.

Atlantis! Who thy praise would breathe,
Surpassing beauty must inweave
With glories never dreamed before,
Or only dreamed on heavenly shore;—
Of valor which the sun-god loved
To watch, where his devout ones roved,
E'er guarding them within his ray,
To vanquish foes day after day;—
Of riches never seen on earth
Till Cleito brought her sons to birth,
And they by magic arts despoiled
Those treasures where the gnomes had toiled;—
Of wisdom wrested from the soul
Of all that is—mighty scroll
That future ages may unroll.
Then sing, O sing, great Mamiké!
While yet the sun can send his ray
Upon that wonder of the world,
Ere back to chaos it is hurled.

In mirage we behold a day
Whose light, with tender radiance gay,
Reflects upon a scene of joy
(In seeming free from all alloy)
  To gladden youthful hearts;
A lake whose perfumed slopes are set
With flowers the eye would not forget;—
  And, culled from distant parts,
Exotics too here smiled to know
How warm the sun of Mu could glow;
How balmily the zephyrs fell;

A DREAM OF ATLANTIS

While birds melodious must tell
   Their love to listening mate.
Here every pulse of nature beat
With all the joys that earth may give;
Enchanting dreams in this retreat
Must move the heart to love and live
   Where only pleasures wait.
The lilies on the water ride
All upward looking, golden-eyed;
Sweet lotuses, white, blue, and pink,
That naiads may together link,
Unseen below,—while water sprite
May revel there in soft delight;
And on the broad leaves silent creep
The midget tortoise, half asleep.
Bright warblers too alight and dip
Their beaks, the water cool to sip.

The Lake of Joy, called Pepen this—
   For sadness ne'er could stay
With one who knew the dreamy bliss
   Of yielding to its sway:
Its air entrancing, perfume-filled,
Had caught the breath of flowers that thrilled
The senses with their radiance sweet—
From heaven sent down, the earth to greet.
And everywhere soft laughter floats
In ripples, from the pleasure boats
That follow in kind Pepen's train—
Her court whose gaiety would wane
Not till the sun could nevermore
Reveal the broad Atlantean shore
Nor glorify those peaks of snow
That blushed beneath his ardent glow.
E'en now the city, long fore-doomed,
Might see afar, where grimly loomed
Volcanoes old, a column high
Of threat'ning smoke that sought the sky.
Her lovely eyes had Pepen raised,
And said, "'T were grander if it blazed."

Surrounded was the floating nest

Of Butterfly, who in her breast
Was pondering deeply once again
On him who yesterday in vain
  Had pleaded for her sake:—
Familiar with luxurious ease,
She felt no poorer life would please;—
  And not a word she spake
To gay attendants seated by,
Until at last with pensive sigh,
She turned unto a maiden near,
Exclaiming: "Sing thou, Alil dear,
  That plaintive olden lay
Brought here from over seas of late—
Anent the mockery of fate—
  That I forbade one day
When thou its sadness had bemoaned."
The maiden softly thus intoned:

SONG.

Dark Fate! thou mockest with thy sombre brow
The hopes of mortals, be they high or low;
While seeming yet to leave a choice of way,
Thy goad is ever there to urge or stay:
But if one go, on him thou worketh ill;
And if he stay, thy frown is darker still.

"Enough! No more! I like it not,"
Cried Pepen, "It were best forget.
Thou, Alil, banish from thy mind
This sad lament, for it would bind
  With thongs of fear, and stay
Endeavor on the road of life
Where man should mingle with the strife,
  Each active call obey.

"Sing ye, my boatmen, sing of war;
Sing loud! Awake the echoes here.
Proud Victory crowns us near and far;
Your voices blend, and let us steer
Away from thoughts of craven Fear."

SONG.

Beat, beat the sacatan;
Louder thrill the drum.
Clash the cymbals; blow the trumpets;
Warriors eager come.
Shrill the pipes and strike the plectrum;—
Cowards linger, dumb.

Gird thy heart to win the battle;
Forward ever stand.
Give not back before the onslaught,
Nor withhold thine hand.
Die! but never homeward turn
To bear the coward's brand.

The beauteous Pepen now exclaimed—
While her imagination flamed—
"What awful sights must one behold
On battle fields when all is told!"
But Nenilich, seductive maid,
At once would chase the gathering shade,—
"Dear mistress, as the golden spray
Within this lily hides with day,
Yon wondrous orb of power divine
Its heart must kiss to make it shine
each morn; and on the banks of Nile,
Where once I dwelt a little while,
A pleasing melody I heard,
And took to memory with each word."

The lily Nenilich beheld,
Lay where her bosom gently swelled;
Her slender fingers were inlaced
About the arm of Pepen, graced
With raiment beautiful and rare,
And precious gems beyond compare;
Her boat of pleasure, too, was made
As gorgeous as her fancy bade:—
But never one who with her dwelt
Dependent, ever harshness felt.
With love she smiled on Nenilich,

Exclaiming: "Clever little witch!
Sing now, for us, that song
About the lotus—for, behold!
The tender petals will enfold
Its heart to sleep ere long."

SONG.

Fragrant chalice! alabaster
On a stem of jadeite-green;
A golden spray its beauteous center—
Earth no lovelier flower hath seen.
A poet sang—The sun-god sleeps
Within the lotus pure and white;
The drooping lily fondly keeps
Till Morn awake, its god of light.
Faint at last with love's emotion,
Heart of gold vibrates no more—
But wafted from creation's ocean,
Back to heaven its love will soar.

"A pretty, tho' a vain conceit,"
The Pepen cried, "But thou, my sweet,
Shalt be rewarded for the lay,
And for that thou art ever gay,"
Thus saying, from her smooth round arm
She took a rich and valued charm
To clasp it round the singer's wrist,
Who bent her head, and softly kissed
That hand which ne'er had done a wrong
To aught that lived—nor weak, nor strong.

"Klemena! Be not sleepy-eyed:—
Come, sing of love," now Pepen cried.
A slave from Athens sighed: 'My thought
Had drifted far away and sought
The one whose absence I bewail—
My mother who, without avail,
I long to see; since harsh defeat
My valiant countrymen still meet.

O Hellenes! thy shame to learn
Is anguish!—Yet would I return"—
Her mind but half expressed, she ceased
When Pepen—"Be thy heart appeased.
  My promise unto thee,
To ask thy freedom from the king,
Deliverance unto thee will bring,—
  Thou art a guest with me;
And of thy courtesy we pray
Of love now sing for us a lay."

SONG.

Ah! Love, deceitful sprite,
  Why comest thou to halt my hurrying feet?
  With eager joy I pass thee by to meet
What things my heart delight.

Ah! Love, here at my side
  I now entreat thee stay; for wanting thee
  No happiness life giveth unto me;—
In thee will I confide.

Ah! Love, thou witching light,
  Whose beams enticing led to many a net;
  My heart thou fillest now with keen regret,
Departing from my sight.

Now Pepen"Boyhood, prime, and age,
In turn against the passion rage,
But life without it barren seems
Of joys that fill the poet's dreams."

Gay song and mirth resumed their sway
  Beneath the rosy hue
Of silk that softened every ray,
  And more enchantment threw
Within that bower, where everything
Must to the senses pleasure bring—
While lotus-wine and dainty sweet
Were served, the rosy lips to meet.

O'erbrimmed with joy the days that sped
  Where Pepen ruled her court;
But ghastly were the fields of dead
  Where stubborn heroes fought.
Who had the worst, and who the best?
Pelopa, in such splendor dressed,
Or they for triumph all athirst,
And eager on the foe to burst?—
Those hardy, ruthless, men of arms
Who suffered torture and alarms,
Were surely wearied less than she
Who glitter constantly must see—
The dame was thinking, and her mind
Beheld again that visage kind—
  If he perchance would come
Once more—So earnest grew her look
That many on her gazed. She shook
Her meditations off, and said,
"Who hath a spell upon us shed
  To turn these maidens dumb?"
Then laughter on the air rang out,
While from the shore a watchman's shout
Was heard. Said Pepen: "Homeward now
Let those who follow turn each prow;
Bid, too, the oarsmen in our train
Rejoice us with a rowers' strain."

SONG.

We glide, we glide,
Above the lake's unruffled tide.
We row, we row,
And smoothly o'er the surface go—
    Echo! echo!
We sing, we sing,
And lilies from the water bring.
We love, we love,
The golden radiance from above—
    O love! sweet love!
We dip, we dip
Our oars, and thro' the water slip.

A DREAM OF ATLANTIS

  We sigh, we sigh,
  For life is swiftly flitting by—
   Goodbye! goodbye!

So came unto the landing place
The pleasure craft. The populace
 May not intrude too near.
Where courtiers in their fine array
Stand waiting ready to obey
 The whims of Pepen dear—
Who now must be conveyed in ease
Within the palace gates, by these
Swift coursers; like the wind they race,
Their gilded hoofs devouring space.
Thus sees the friend from far away,
Yet waiting for a future day
Departure once again to urge
Away from Death's engulfing verge.
But Cho loves not the noisy street,
And he hath found a still retreat
 Beyond the city's vale;
His simplest needs are there supplied
And there he roams in country wide,
 Till he shall homeward sail.

A mountaineer who tills the soil
Beyond the city's mad turmoil,
Speaks thus to Cho who comes his way:
"This mountain wakes; but yesterday
Its horrid serpents came below
To die from many a vigorous blow.
Look up and see that crooked gap
Extending far adown its lap.
Old Homen oft hath stirred and rumbled
While we have labored on and grumbled.
This time he seems to settle not,
But aims to make his stronghold hot.
Long tremors move the earth since last
The moon her fullest orb hath past.
As now we near the month of Zac
Lord Homen may arouse his pack—
A mischief-breeding horde! And Ppa,

The Breaker, may not be so far
Away; if once set loose then he
Will havoc play, as all will see."

But ever rambling, pensive went
The disappointed friend, intent
On pleading ardently again;
Still hoping that not all in vain
Would be his journey to this land
From Mayach, the ancient strand.
While strolling on he chanced to meet
A hermit, sandals on his feet.
From Cho he learned about the land
Where Can had led his little band
In years gone by, and how the race
Of Atlas there would hold the place
Of rulers, and the sceptre wield
With wisdom, and their subjects shield.
Can's dying view of what must fall
On Mu, destroying great and small,
Was also told,—when thus the sage
Attention wholly would engage:
"A sulphurous fume offends the breath
Of him who nears that mount of death
To cull a certain flower the dame
Pepen, kind wench of evil fame,
Demands. The king, who naught denies
To her, gives him who thus supplies
    The flower, a generous pay.
This man, named Ruto, hesitates
To scale again the crater's height,
Where luring death perchance awaits
To launch destruction and affright
    At no far distant day.
Yon brooding monster heaves and snores,
While like a mist his hot breath soars;
And terrifying rumbles sound
Below, a tempest in the ground.
Great Homen's cauldron boils and bubbles,
And warns us of approaching troubles;
For, look you! late the venomed snake
That breeds aloft, where it doth make

A DREAM OF ATLANTIS

Its home quite undisturbed, hath left
Those haunts in search of lower cleft
Where gliding to and fro are seen
Their gleaming coils of black and red.
Above, rich berries thick abound
To tempt adventurous feet; but dread
Of serpent-fang forbids the ground.
The shifting vipers show, I ween,
Disaster soon will leap from there—
Let those who nearby dwell beware.

"Yon peaks that to the clouds aspire
We glory in; 't is said none higher
Are known to be upon the face
Of earth; they lend a stately grace
To this most favored land; more yet,
The lovely hamlets therein set,
The meadows, streams, and lakes, found there,
Attract the wealthy and the fair.

"Yon city o'er the plain outspread
Looks not aloft wth thought of dread,
But pleased beholds on every hand
The towering peaks which guard this land,—
Upon the north from Winter's breath,
That brings the blossoms early death.
Behold those giants east and south,—
Once they, from out each flaming mouth
Disgorged their inwards parts which spread,
Transforming Mu into a bed
Of death. So very long have they
In silent grandeur stood, to-day
None think they might again belch forth
Foul smoke, like Hakol on the north.
But they who sometimes lend an ear
To those for whom the future's clear,
Distrust this slumber long and deep
Of craters out of which may leap
Destruction that within doth lie,
Increasing as the time goes by."
He ceased, and left the flowery spot
To rest within his favorite grot.

THE WORD

Like smiling lips that silence keep
While treachery dark behind them sleep,
Those rounded cones by sunbeams kissed
Stood mutely where the valley mist
Reached not; but hid within them lay,
Awaiting their exultant day,
The brooding forces, storing fast
Great furnaces that would at last
Assert their awful, mighty birth,
By devastating all the earth.

Not many days had drifted by
When Cho went cityward to try
If he might now persuade the dame
To chance her life upon the sea,
Before the doom of promised flame
Should burst, as prophets could foresee.
But Fortune turned away averse
To his intent; he might not reach
The friend whose ear he would beseech
Gadeirus frequent must converse
With her. Cho waited patiently,
But 't was decreed that never he
Again would reach her side to plead
That she from coming death might speed.
Here pause we, that tradition's page
A moment may our thought engage.

Athena, in the days long past
A state had founded, to outlast
The little nations that must die
Ere grown, and soon forgotten lie.
This daughter of great Zeus then
Her name bestowed upon the men
To her heart dear, and Athens throve
Protected by her power and love.

Of years a thousand rolled away
Ere she—upon the banks of Nile
Called Neith—again on earth would play,
Eternal leisure to beguile;
So founded Sais at the head

A DREAM OF ATLANTIS

Of Egypt's Delta, whence the flow
Of Nilus to the sea must go.
Thereafter these fine cities both
Extolled her in each sacred oath;
While those who dwelt in Sais, claimed
Affinity with Athens famed.
The noblest and the fairest race
Were those of Athens. Every grace
The gods to mortal man could lend
Was theirs; for these could none transcend
   In excellence of laws;
In noble and in valorous deeds;
And in the wisdom that concedes
   Full justices in each cause.
In arts of peace triumphant they;
In war to none they yielded sway.
Their prodigies of valor set
A record time would not forget.

But greatest of these all, was told
Their action, marvellously bold,
When from the vasty deep beyond
Came forth a power to all oppress,
Enslave, and grant to none redress,
To cries for pity ne'er respond.
That empire vast o'er islands spread,
E'en to a distant continent;
In Lybia too and Egypt, dread
Seized those who 'neath its force were bent.
Athenian courage, skill, and arms,
Must quell forever these alarms—
Tho' allies their alliegiance broke,
A sterner valor this awoke;—
What hero recked of loss or gain
When Athens triumph would attain—
Extremities of cruel woe,
Calamities and deathly throe;
None faltered of those legions bold;
And never were their names enscrolled.
But in Olympus rang their praise
When out of overwhelming frays
They wrested triumph from defeat,

And saved from tyrant thrall
The hosts that waited awful fate;—
Those too with Heracles Gate
　Were freedom given, all.
Alas! that in the Deluge near
These heroes were to disappear.

Atlantis aimed to overthrow
Athens and Sais at one blow;
That all the wealth within the Strait
Victorious greed might satiate.
And while triumphant pageants trod
Atlantean soil, on foreign sod
Untired legions, rank on rank,
Harassed the foe upon the bank
Whose slopes had oft been dark with blood;
Cleansed ever by the ocean flood.

Atlantis still would onward rush,
Nor pause until her power must crush
What nations dwelt within the gates
Of Hercules, whose wealth awaits
To gratify the lustful greed
That gorges while its victims bleed.

Atlantis, blessed with means untold,
And harboring within its fold
The sturdy ones of many lands,
Could muster countless willing bands.
The city crowned by sacred height
Gave nobly of its wealth and might;
For now combatants would be led
By princes whom the foe must dread.

Unstinted was the substance spent
To furnish those who seaward went.
Each city gave its generous share;
While Maya, chiefest one, had care
Ten thousand chariots to provide
With steeds, and others to bestride.
Unnumbered bows and arrows, slings,
Whose stones the victim earthward brings.

Swords long and short, broad axes, spears,
Are stored in every ship that clears;
Long javelines stack on stack were piled
By seamen who this task reviled.
Great catapults were safely stored
Within the vessels going abroad—
By hundreds these would plow the wave;
And triremes many, manned by brave,
Intrepid, toilers of the main—
All hoping to return again.
One great ship bore the dregs of earth—
Sent forth to die, or prove their worth:
From out the prisons of the land
These felons, on a distant strand,
Would be vouchsafed a chance to win
Their life, or perish for their sin.
Thus sailed afar the prince, the knave
And warriors:—most would find a grave,
Or sink beneath the ocean wave.

DEGREES OF KNOWLEDGE.

There are all degrees of proficiency in knowledge of the world. It is sufficient to our present purpose to indicate three. One class live to the utility of the symbol, esteeming health and wealth a final good. Another class lives above this mark to the beauty of the symbol, as the poet and artist and the naturalist and man of science. A third class live above the beauty of the symbol to the beauty of the thing signified; these are wise men. The first class have common sense; the second, taste; and the third, spiritual perception. Once in a long time, a man traverses the whole scale, and sees and enjoys the symbol solidly, then also has a clear eye for its beauty, and lastly, whilst he pitches his tent on this sacred volcanic isle of nature, does not offer to build houses and barns thereon,—reverencing the splendor of the God which he sees bursting through each chink and cranny.

—EMERSON, *"Prudence."*

EXPERIENCE AND ITS RESULTS.

By J. B. Gray.

IF a philosopher were asked: "What of all the riches of earth and Heaven do you covet for your own?" his answer would probably be: "Wisdom above all else."

What is Wisdom? It is the right use of knowledge. And what is knowledge? It is the result of experience. And, again, What is experience? *It is living.* It may be likened to the sparks emitted from the friction of the fast moving emery wheel on the steel bar held in the hand of the mechanic. Every act of living calls forth experience of one kind or another. The first trial of anything is an experience, though it may make no lasting impression, though it may not be converted into knowledge now; and yet, each experience, faint though its effect may be, is stored away in the mind to be later brought out and reviewed. How many of us have lived through some period of life that was rich in lessons for us, without in any way profiting by them. Perhaps years afterward we again go through the same experience, and like a flash it comes to us—the lesson that was meant for our betterment. We cry out: "How foolish we were not to have seen it then and saved ourselves all this pain and suffering."

The mind, *manas,* is the principle in man that profits by experience, but we may pass through the same experience many times before the mind does profit by it. The thing itself may not be recognized by the mind to such an extent that it becomes a lesson. For instance, one may stand by a window and see various vehicles passing on the street, and yet if he were asked to mention what he saw, would say: "Oh, I don't know; I wasn't paying attention " In the same way, the mind is not always on the alert, not always in the watch tower ready to take down the message. Why is this? "Why," you ask, "do not we profit by each and every experience that comes our way?" I will tell you: *"Because it does not hurt enough."* If some one throws a ball of cotton at you, striking you, you laugh. Suppose it should be a stone of the same size that struck you. This does not arouse any mirth on your part; furthermore you make up your mind to keep out of your antagonist's way in the future. If the balls had all been cotton, you might have stood the fusillade for an indefinite time with a smile, but the fact that it hurt, changed the situation.

Man is so constituted that he either will not or cannot learn without pain and suffering. As we look around us and see the different personalities, we are sometimes aroused to envy this one and that one their disposition. Even-tempered, generous, self sacrificing, noble; we say: "Why could we not have that delightful personality. Life would be so much easier." Think you that that very disposition was a gift or an inheritance from their parents? An inheritance it was surely, but their own. In the past ages they were working at it, hewing it out, while perchance you were idle, or working to produce the personality which you now have. The experiences which came to that soul were stored up; the mind, ever alert, ever watchful, pointed out the approaching danger, saying: "You have been there before, take care how you act, don't get hurt again." And the personality obeys, passes the dangerous point, and is master of the situation. That is what it means to be a conqueror; that is what it means to have character, to be a power in this world—to possess knowledge. Knowledge gained only by having been through the difficulty, or facing the danger or temptation, whatever it may be; meeting that same danger or temptation again and saying: "No, I know you, I have fallen once, I have paid the price. You no longer have any power over me."

Can we learn by another's experience? No, never. Theosophy teaches that the soul must at some time pass through the gamut of human experiences. It is not a pleasant thought to contemplate that any of us, so comfortable and well-dressed, so satisfied with ourselves and our surroundings, might possibly have committed crimes, or picked pockets, or have been drunkards; but how else can we account for the fact that these things do not allure. We might lay it to environment and heredity, and in scorn refuse to believe it possible that we were ever a thief or a drunkard; but there have been many who were born of just as good parents as we, whose lives were just as tenderly sheltered as ours and whose future was just as assured, who have fallen from the path. There is but one logical explanation, and that is, that the soul was ignorant of that phase of life, that in its everlasting thirst for knowledge it stumbled upon that experience in the dark and fell. And the great lesson to be learned from this is, Do not judge too hastily.

How dare we stand in judgment unless we are willing that we shall be dealt with for our every wrong thought and act as it deserves, or unless we know that we have risen above that sin, or all sin. And if we have risen above all sin, we shall like the Leader of us all, be the last to cast the stone.

How often must an experience along a certain line of action be repeated before knowledge therefrom results?

Until the mind takes note of it. As the man at the window looked without seeing, so the mind can live through experience after experience, but unless there is a mental note taken, no warning sign will be posted up, and the traveler will probably stumble in the dark the next time.

If we are kept in after school for our mis-spelled words, if we are punished for our mistakes in life, we will probably remember next time. You will say: "We always do pay, sometime." Yes, that is true. No one escapes the payment, and the more bitter the experience, the quicker the payment, the sooner school is out, and the soul is free.

What shall determine the right use of this knowledge gained through experience? Whence comes wisdom? What part of man is it that exercises the judgment so as to use this knowledge rightfully? It is the ray from above, called in Theosophy the divine spirit. It is the Divine Intelligence, of which there is but the faintest spark in man. Our purpose here in life is, whether we are aware of it or not, to increase that spark, to so garner from the passing days and years experiences that mean something that will lead to the full development toward ultimate consciousness.

HAPPINESS.

Speculative gentlemen we have seen more than once almost forget their wine in arguing whether Happiness was the chief end of man. The most cry out, with Pope: "Happiness, our being's end and aim," and ask whether it is even conceivable that we should follow any other. How comes it, then, cry the Opposition, that the gross are happier than the refined; that even though we know them to be happier, we would not change places with them? Is it not written, Increase of knowledge is increase of sorrow? And yet also written, in characters still more ineffaceable, Pursue knowledge, attain clear vision, as the beginning of all good? Were your doctrine right, for what should we struggle with our whole might, for what pray to Heaven, if not that the "malady of thought" might be utterly stifled within us, and a power of digestion and secretion, to which that of the tiger were trifling, be imparted instead thereof? Whereupon the others deny that thought is a malady; that increase of knowledge is increase of sorrow; that Aldermen have a sunnier life than Aristotle's, though the Stagyrite himself died exclaiming, *Foede mundum intravi, anxius vixi, perturbatus morior;* etc., etc.: and thus the argument circulates, and the bottles stand still.

So far as that Happiness-question concerns the symposia of speculative gentlemen,—the rather as it really is a good enduring hacklog whereon to chop logic, for those so minded,—we with great willingness leave it resting on its own bottom. But there are earnest natures for whom Truth is no plaything, but the staff of life; men whom the "solid reality of things" will not carry forward; who, when the "inward voice" is silent in them, are powerless, nor will the loud huzzaing of millions supply the want of it. To these men, seeking anxiously for guidance; feeling that did they once clearly see the right, they would follow it cheerfully to weal or to woe, comparatively careless which; to these men the question, what is the proper aim of man, has a deep and awful interest.

For the sake of such, it may be remarked that the origin of this argument, like that of every other argument under the sun, lies in the confusion of language. If Happiness mean Welfare, there is no doubt but all men should and must pursue their Welfare, that is to say, pursue what is worthy of their pursuit. But if, on the other hand, Happiness mean, as for most men it does, "agreeable sensations," Enjoyment refined or not, then must we observe that there *is* a doubt; or rather that there is a certainty the other way. Strictly considered, this truth, that man has in him something higher than a Love of Pleasure, take Pleasure in what sense you will, has been the text of all true Teachers and Preachers, since the beginning of the world; and in one or another dialect, we may hope, will continue to be preached and taught till the world end.

Carlyle, *Schiller*.

TRUTH APPEARS AFTER THOUGHT ONLY.

What is the hardest task in the world? To think. I would put myself in the attitude to look in the eye an abstract truth, and I cannot. I blench and withdraw on this side and on that. I seem to know what he meant who said, No man can see God face to face and live. For example, a man explores the basis of civil government. Let him intend his mind without respite, without rest, in one direction. His best heed long time avails him nothing. Yet thoughts are flitting before him. We all but apprehend, we dimly forebode the truth. We say I will walk abroad, and the truth will take form and clearness to me. We go forth, but cannot find it. It seems as if we needed only the stillness and composed attitude of the library to seize the thought. But we come in, and are as far from it as at first. Then, in a moment, and unannounced, the truth appears. A certain wandering light appears, and is the distinction, the principle, we wanted. But the oracle comes because we had previously laid siege to the shrine. It seems as if the law of the intellect resembled that law of nature by which we now inspire, now expire the breath; by which the heart now draws in, then hurls out the blood,—the law of undulation. So now you must labor with your brains, and now you must forbear your activity and see what the great Soul showeth.

—Emerson, "*Intellect.*"

THE SEPHER HA-ZOHAR—THE BOOK OF LIGHT.

By Nurho de Manhar.

Containing the doctrines of Kabbalah, together with the discourses and teachings of its author, the great Kabbalist, Rabbi Simeon ben Jochai, and now for the first time wholly translated into English, with notes, references and expository remarks.

(Continued from page 254.)

SAID Rabbi Hiya "Since the day that Adam transgressed the command of God, the world became affiliated with poverty until the advent of Noah, who, through the sacrifice he offered up, caused it to regain its normal fertility."

Said Rabbi Jose, "the earth recovered its fertility, but did not become freed from the infection of the serpent until Israel stood at the foot of Mount Sinai and was united with the Tree of Life. And if they had not broken the law, there would have been no death in the world, Israel having become purified. When they sinned through their idolatry of the calf, the first tables of the law that freed it from the power and influence of the serpent or 'the end of all flesh' were broken. When the Levites rose up to slaughter and kill, the Israelites engaged in idolatrous worship the serpent who is the same as the destroying angel, placed himself at their head, but was unable to inflict any injury on them, as they were protected by certain amulets that made them impervious to his attacks. And only when God said unto Moses, 'Put off thy ornaments from thee' was the serpent able to smite them as it is written, 'And the children of Israel stripped themselves of their ornaments by Mount Horeb' (Ex. XXXIII. 5). Why is the word here used *vaithnatzelon* (they were despoiled) and not *vainatzelon* (stripped off). It is in order to show that the Israelites. deprived and despoiled of the protecting ornaments (amulets or pentacles) they had affixed on themselves at Mount Sinai when receiving the law, fell under the influence of the serpent who had now the power to afflict them."

Said Rabbi Hiya: "Why, if Noah was just and upright did not death disappear out of the world? It was because it was not altogether purified and freed from the infection of the serpent. Moreover, the antedeluvians had lost all faith and belief in the existence of the Holy One and were really atheists and given up to the worship and service of the evil one, who after the deluge caused men to sin in a similar manner to those who lived before it, for the holy law that constitutes the Tree of Life was not revealed on earth by the Holy One until Israel stood at the foot of Mount Sinai. Noah was, therefore, unable to suppress death in the world, but rather, after his exit from the ark contributed to its continuance and perpetuity therein, as it is written, 'and he drank of the wine and was drunken; and he lay naked in his tent'' '' (Gen. IX. 21).

Kabbalistic Explanation of the Feast of Tabernacles and The Loulab.

As Rabbi Hiya and Rabbi Jose travelled onwards, they beheld a stranger approaching them whom they judged by his appearance, to be an Israelite. After saluting him they asked "Who art thou?" "I am," he replied, "a resident of the village of Ramin and as the feast of Tabernacles is coming on I have been specially deputed to prepare the Loulab and am therefore on my way to cut down palm branches and prepare them according to ancient and legal custom. After walking a little together, the stranger turning to them said, "Do you know why the Loulab must consist of four different objects in order to secure the blessing of rain upon the earth?" "With Students of the Secret Doctrine," they answered, "it has often been a subject of much discussion, but if you know anything that will further enlighten us, we pray you to impart it unto us."

Then spoke again the stranger and said, "The village in which I live, though small and in an obscure locality, is distinguished by the residence of students of the Secret Doctrine and also of a master, Rabbi Isaac, son of Jose of Melrozaba, who daily gives discourses and lessons on occult subjects from which we always gather knowledge new and most interesting. Once when conversing with him, he stated that during the Feast of Tabernacles the Israelites are exalted and pre-eminent above all other people and nations of the world and therefore we carry

---

[1] The theosophical meaning of which words is, that through indulgence in sensual delights or pleasures of sense, he lost and became bereft of that bright aural halo resulting from harmony and close union between the higher and lower selves and which had once distinguished him from the rest of mankind.—N. de M.

the Loulab in hand as a trophy of victory over them, inasmuch as only from Israel, do the great chiefs of idolatrous nations receive and participate in the blessings that descend from heaven. These chiefs or governing angels are called in scripture "hamayim hazzedonim' (the proud waters) as it is written 'Then had the proud waters gone over our soul. Blessed be the Lord who hath not given us as a prey to their teeth.' (Ps. CXXIV. 5.) The four components of the Loulab (the palm, willow, myrtle and citron) correspond to the four letters of the sacred name I H V H by which Israel is exalted above all other nations and to whom is owing the descent of water to serve as libations upon the altar of sacrifice. From the beginning of the Feast of Tabernacles to Cippur or day of expiation, the Holy One sits and judges the world, during which period, the Serpent no longer appears before Him as man's accuser, being attracted to the goat that is offered unto him and therefore heedless of anything of a sacred character. So is it with him when a goat is offered to him at the time of new moon. For this reason, the children of Israel pray then the Holy One to grant them remission and forgiveness of their sins."

The Occultism of Sacrifices.

There is yet another subject the knowledge of which is only imparted to those who are conversant with the teachings and wisdom of the Secret Doctrine. From all others I am prohibited and forbidden to discourse thereon. "What may that be?" asked Rabbi Jose. "I cannot," said the stranger, "divulge it unless I am assured of your fitness to receive it." Travelling on together in silence, he turned to them and said: "When the moon approaches the sun, the Holy One by his power revives the North and attracts it to himself in love; whilst the South revives itself. When the influences of these two combine and blend together; then occurs the conjunction of the two luminaries. When the sun rises in the east it attracts the influences of these two cardinal quarters and reflects them upon the moon at full. The approximation and conjunction of the sun and moon are analogous to that of the male and female. The law of attraction prevails throughout the universe, in the world above as in the world below and is expressed in the aphorism—"as above so below." As the right side of the sephirotic tree stands for love, the attractive principle, so does the left stand for rigour or the principle of repulsion personified by the serpent from whom emanate all impurity and corruption and death. It draws and attracts all who are receptive of its evil influence.

Now when the North is not revived by the Holy One, the moon becomes drawn to the left side and in order to prevent this, Israel is obliged to sacrifice a goat in which the serpent delighted, lets go his hold of that luminary that then begins to shine and daily increase in light and splendour. Thus on the day of atonement when the serpent or Evil One is engaged with the goat offered unto it, the moon freed from its evil influence undertakes to defend and protect Israel as a mother watches over the safety and welfare of her child. Then it is that the Holy One grants his blessings with remission and pardon of sins. During the Feast of Tabernacles the influence of the right side of the Sephirotic tree so attracts the moon that she attains its fulness and heavenly blessings are showered upon the tutelary guardians of pagan nations on earth in order to preclude them from imagining they have any right to share in those that are reserved and allotted to Israel. During its rise and fall the visible disk of the moon symbolises those blessings that are bestowed upon Israel, but the obscured part, those of idolatrous nations. When the moon however is at the full, Israel receives and profits from the full tide of blessings from heaven and therefore it is written "On the eighth day there shall be an "abzereth" amongst you (Num. XXVIII. 15) the word abzereth here meaning as the Targum translates it "a reunion" in order that the divine in all their fulness and extent may descend upon Israel as a whole. On this day, Israel prays to the Holy One for the blessing of rain not only for themselves but also all other nations. This feast peculiar to Israel is referred to in the words of scripture "My beloved is mine and I am his" or its attendant blessings are shared in by no other nation; in the dispensing of which the Holy One is like unto a King who invites his friends to a banquet on a certain day. After reflection, the monarch says to himself, "I wish to enjoy myself with the company of my friends but in sending invitations to my governors, and chiefs and rulers of provinces I am afraid these will be so numerous as to interfere with and lessen my enjoyment." What did the King do? He first regaled his official guests with the usual meats and vegetables, and after their departure well filled and satisfied, he sat down at the table laden with the best and most delicious viands and after his friends had feasted thereon, he further added to their pleasure by granting the requests they made unto him and so the banquet passed off pleasantly and without any exhibition of ill-feeling or discontent. In a similar manner the Holy One acts with Israel and therefore scripture saith, "on the eighth day shall be your abzereth (coming together) that is, for the reception of blessings to be participated in only by yourselves." Amongst the requisites used during the Feast of Tabernacles, were the palm and the citron. During every day of the feast, Jews with a citron in their left hand and in their right a bundle of branches viz: one of the palm tree and two of the willow and myrtle, pass around the altar exclaiming seven times, in memory of the conquest of Jericho and hence called the Great Hosanna. In preparing the Loulab, the stem of the branches was covered over with palm leaves. If it was dry or withered, crooked or split in the least, it was considered worthless. It must be fresh and green, smooth and without burr or blemish. It was encircled with sprigs of willow and myrtle each of which must have three leaves otherwise the Loulab was Posoul.

Then said Rabbi Hiya and Rabbi Jose to the stranger, "This has indeed been a most pleasant and interesting journey; blessed are they who delight to study the Secret Doctrine." Then embracing him, Rabbi Jose exclaimed, "Surely thou art of the number of those referred to in Scripture "And all thy children shall be taught of the Lord and great shall be the abundance of their peace" (Ps. LIV. 14). Proceeding on their way, they at last sat down and rested themselves.

"A VEXATA QUESTIO IN BIBLICAL PHILOLOGY."

The stranger began speaking again. "Know you," said he, "why the sacred name I. H. V. H. is found mentioned in the verse, "Then Jehovah rained upon Sodom and Gomorrah brimstone and fire from heaven" (Gen. XIX. 24) instead of the divine name Alhim which is exclusively used in connection with the account of the deluge? Listen to the explanation handed down by tradition through the masters of the Secret Doctrine. Wherever the name Jehovah is found in Scripture it designates the Holy One sitting and presiding over the members of his executive tribunal of justice. But when Alhim is used, it refers to his tribunal only. At the destruction of these two cities involving but a small part of the world, Jehovah acted along with his judicial executive whilst at the deluge when the whole world perished only the members of it were concerned in carrying out the divine decrees. If it is objected, that the whole world of human beings was not destroyed, inasmuch as Noah and his family were preserved from perishing, what differentiates the punishment of the deluge from that inflicted upon Sodom and Gomorrah. Our reply is, that Noah by his entry and inclusion in the ark became sequestered from mankind as a whole which was destroyed by the operation of the Alhim, whilst the overthrow of the cities of the plain was accomplished openly by Jehovah in concert with His celestial tribunal.

The mystery of this difference is referred to in the words "The Lord was seated at the time of the flood" (Ps. XXIX. 10). What does the word yeshab (was seated) really mean? but that He was alone and by Himself at the time the deluge occurred; which interpretation unless corroborated by other texts in scripture, we would not have dared to apply to the Divine Being and therefore conclude that the Holy One was not conjoined with the members of his justiciary tribunal, the Alhim in the destruction of the world by the deluge. That this view is correct is further proved by the use of the word yasheb in Lev. XIII. 46. "He shall dwell alone (yasheb) without the camp shall be his habitation." Thus it was that Noah hidden in the ark, escaped the general destruction and after divine justice had been appeased, we read that then the Alhim remembered or thought of Noah (Gen. VIII. 1). From these remarks we infer that the Holy One punishes sometimes openly and sometimes in secret,—openly when acting with and through the Alhim whose jurisdiction extends over and throughout the world—secretly when sitting in that celestial sphere whence descends all the blessings of heaven. Knowing this we can understand why the precious goods a man hides are sources of blessings whilst those that are visible and perceived by all excite envy and covetousness through the influence of the demon known as *Ra-ain* (evil eye)."*

As the stranger ceased speaking Rabbi Jose was delighted and exclaimed, "blessed are we students of Rabbi Simeon through whose teachings and instruction we have been able to understand and comprehend what has just been imparted to us. Truly this stranger has been divinely directed and sent to instruct us in the Secret Doctrine concerning truths and teachings

---

*This opinion is frequently expressed in the Talmud; see Gract Bathra fol. 6.

the most ennobling and sublime." On reaching the dwelling of Rabbi Simeon they related to him all that the stranger has said unto them whereon after listening to them he replied, "well and truly hath the stranger spoken."

"Kabbalistic Explanation of the Goat Azazel."

Rabbi Eleazar whilst sitting in presence of his father Rabbi Simeon, spake and said, "the demon called 'the end of all flesh' doth it take pleasure and receive any advantage from the sacrifices of Israel or not?"

Whereupon Rabbi Simeon replied "Yea truly, both heaven above and earth below are benefited. Observe that priests (cohanim) Levites and Israel are collectively termed Adam when imbued with the same holy will and desire to, offer up a sacrifice either of a sheep, an ox or any other animal. Before so doing, however, they must make confession and expiate their sins of word, thought and deed, for then only are sacrifices of any avail and become charged with the sins confessed as was the case with the Azazel or scapegoat driven forth into the wilderness bearing the sins of the congregation of Israel, as it is written—'and Aaron shall lay both his hands upon the head of the goat and confess over it all the iniquities of the children of Israel and all their transgressions, putting them upon the head of the goat and shall send him away by the hand of a fit man into the wilderness." (Lev. XVI. 21). It is the same with other sacrifices. When placed upon the altar they become charged with the good deeds and thoughts, as also of the sins and evil thoughts of the sacrificer, each of them ascending to its own appropriate place on high and distinguished as emanations from a man's higher self and denominated Adam or from his animal or lower nature and called "behemoth" (beastly). This distinction is referred to in scripture, "Thou savest both man (adam) and beast." (Ps. XXXVI. 6). Offerings of unleavened cakes and all other comestibles are for attracting the Holy Spirit and inducing it to operate through the service of the priest, the chanting of Levites and the prayers of the worshippers. In the oil and wheat of such offerings, none of the expeditive angels of retribution can participate so that they are unable to add to the severity of their afflicting judgments, being attracted for the time being by the offerings of animals. This is why sacrifices of both kinds take place at one and the same time, in accordance with the injunctions of the Secret

Doctrine that gratitude and thankfulness the true elements of every oblation and sacrifice may ascend on high pure and sincere before the Almighty and thus obtain responsive blessings.

"Rabbi Simeon's Reflections on the Supreme and its Union with Human Souls."

Said Rabbi Simeon, during prayer, I raise my hands on high as a token and expression of the gratitude of my will nature that goeth up to the almighty supreme Being whose essence is Will infinite and beyond all human comprehension. He is the great Beginning, the mystery of all mysteries. All created things in the universe are but emanations from Him who is the height of height that neither man nor angel can approach unto, nor hath ever seen or can see its origin and source. In vain the mind of man attempts to fly towards the omnipotent Will Being of which it is a fraction infinitesimal and infinitely small. Vain are all efforts to grasp and comprehend Thought Supreme and eternal, as we sink confounded, overwhelmed with feelings of awe ineffable. Yet though the height Divine remains eternally invisible to human vision, it manifests its presence and operates within the minutes and hours chiefly within the soul of man with whose natural light it blends whenever its aspirations and thoughts tend towards and are centered on the great source of all being and creation, the primal light that enlighteneth every man that cometh into the world. Between the enlightened human soul and the great Beginning are nine palaces or grades of evolutionary development two Kabbalah are designated Sephiroth whose culmination is Kether or The Crown. These grades, palaces or sephiroth call them as we may, are not entities but modes or stages of ascent towards union with the Divine Will and their respective lights are but the luminous reflection of the Divine Thought. Though nine in number, they are really one in this sense, they are derivations of the great Thought without which they could not exist and can never be but imperfect and obscure representations of the Divine Entity that must remain always unknown in its sublimity and transcendency beyond all human comprehension. Through these palaces the enlightened soul enters by continuous aspirations and thus they become the intermediaries to it between the known and unknown, between the comprehensible and the incomprehensible. Within them are hidden all the great spiritual mysteries and realities that to humanity as at present must remain objects of faith rather than of reason and intellectual perception. Only by the enlightened soul can they become cognised in its gradual ascension through them on its way to the great and transcendent Being termed The Eternal, The Everlasting One. But this cannot be effected only as it becomes receptive of and imbued with the light and splendor of the Sephiroth Binah (Doctrine Intelligence) by which it is brought into union with the Divine and enters into the enjoyment of the Beatific Vision. From these observations we are better able to understand and penetrate into the meaning and mysteries of sacrifices in general which as mere rites and ceremonies have no intrinsic efficacy. Only when they are the expression of the soul gradually becoming purified and enlightened by and through its higher self are they a means of spiritual ascension in the divine life which is the true light of mankind assimilating and bringing it into closer relationship with the divine, Eternal I Am in whose presence there is fulness of joy and at whose right hand there are pleasures forevermore.

This union and harmony between the finite and the infinite, the human and the divine, God and man is the highest and deepest of mysteries, the mystery of all ages since the creation of the world. Happy are they in this world and the world to come who have attained unto a knowledge of it. Observe furthermore that the destroying angel known as "the end of all flesh" derives benefit and pleasure from acts of charity in this sense, that as such acts and deeds of charity and gratitude are a source of joy to the angels on high, so the material part of sacrifices symbolising the element of the impurity and imperfection of human nature becomes a source of strength and enjoyment to the inferior orders of spirits and this being the case, the Holy Spirit Israel's Watcher that neither slumbers nor sleeps, provides against their troubling her children and preventing their good deeds from becoming perfect and freed from impure thoughts.

To be continued.

MOMENTS WITH FRIENDS.

"Does the belonging to Secret Societies have the effect of retarding or advancing the mind in its evolution?"

Membership in a secret society will prevent the mind from or assist it in its development according to the nature and development of that particular mind and the kind of Secret Society of which that one is a member. All secret societies may be classed under two heads: those whose object is to train the mind and body for psychic and for spiritual purposes, and those whose object is physical and material benefit. People sometimes form themselves into what may be said to be a third class, which is made up of the societies which teach psychic development and claim communication with spiritual beings. It is said that strange phenomena are produced in their circles and sittings. They also claim to have and to be able to confer on whom they see fit, physical advantages over others. All these should come under the second class, because their object will be found to be sensual and physical.

The secret societies of the first class are few as compared to the second class; of these few only a small percentage really help the mind in its spiritual development. Under this first class are included societies of religious bodies who try to assist their members in spiritual awakening and unfolding—who have no such objects as political training or military instruction or instruction in business methods—and also organizations of a philosophical and religious basis. Those who are of particular religious faiths may be benefited by belonging to a secret society within that faith if the objects of the society do not allow the mind to be kept in darkness and do not prevent it from acquiring knowledge. Before one of any faith joins a secret society of his faith he should inquire well into their objects and methods. There are many secret societies within each of the large religions. Some of these secret societies keep their members in ignorance concerning the knowledge of life, and they prejudice their members against other faiths. Such secret societies can do great harm to the minds of their individual members. Such prejudicial training and enforced ignorance may so warp, stultify and cloud the mind that it will require many lives of pain and sorrow to rectify the wrongs which it may have been lead into committing. Those who have religious convictions of their own regarding a religion, may be benefited by belonging to a secret society of that religion if the objects and methods of that society meet with the approval of that mind, and as long as that particular mind belongs to or is being educated in that particular religion. The religions of the world represent the different schools in which some minds are trained or educated for spiritual development. When one feels that a religion satisfies the spiritual longings of his mind, he belongs in the class of spiritual life which that religion represents. When a religion no longer supplies what is generally called the spiritual food of the mind, or when one begins to question "the truths" of his religion, it is a sign that he no longer belongs to it or that he is being separated from it. If one doubts, if he is dissatisfied with and denounces the teachings of his religion without having other reasons than dumb and ignorant discontent, this is a sign that his mind is being closed to spiritual light and growth and that he is falling below his class in spiritual life. On the other hand, if the mind feels that his particular religion or the religion in which he was born is narrow and cramped and if it does not satisfy or answer the questions of life that his mind yearns to know, this is a sign that his mind is unfolding and growing out of that class which is represented by that particular religion and it shows that his mind demands something which will supply the mental or spiritual food which it needs for continued growth. All secret societies under the first class, which have as their object the development of psychic tendencies, will retard the mind because all things of the psychic nature have to do with the senses and bring the mind under the dominion of the senses.

The secret societies of the second class are made up of those organizations whose objects are the attainment of political, social, financial and mercenary advantages. Under this class come the fraternal and the benevolent societies, those who are secretly organized to overthrow a government, or those who band themselves together for purposes of blackmail, murder or sensual and vicious indulgences. One may easily tell whether or not any of these will assist or retard the development of his mind if he knows its aims and objects.

The idea of secrecy is the knowing or the having of something which others have not, or in sharing knowledge with a few. The desire of this knowledge is strong and is attractive to the undeveloped, the youthful and the growing mind. This is shown by the desire which people have to belong to something which is exclusive and hard to enter and which will excite the admiration or envy or awe of those who do not belong. Even children like to have secrets. A little girl will wear a ribbon in her hair or on her waist to show that she has a secret. She is the object of envy and the admiration of all the other little girls until the secret is known, then the ribbon and secret loses its value. Then another little girl with another ribbon and a new secret is the center of attraction. Excepting the political, financial and the vicious or criminal societies, most of the secrets of the secret societies in the world, have as little worth or are of as little importance as the secrets of the little girl. Yet those who belong to them may be furnished with "play," which is as beneficial to them as the girl's secret is to her. As the mind matures it no longer wishes secrecy; it finds that those who wish secrecy are immature, or that their thoughts and deeds seek darkness to avoid the light. The maturing mind wishes to spread knowledge broadcast, though he knows that knowledge cannot be given alike to all. As the race advances in knowledge, the demand for secret societies for the development of the mind should decrease. Secret societies are not necessary for advancement of minds beyond the school girl age. From business and social and literary sides, ordinary life has all the secrets necessary for the mind to solve and by which the mind will be advanced through its youthful stages. No secret society can advance the mind beyond its natural development nor enable it to see through the secrets of nature and to solve the problems of life. A few secret organizations in the world may benefit the mind if the mind will not stop on the surface, but will penetrate the real meaning of their teachings. Such an organization is the Masonic Order. Comparatively few minds of this organization derive other than business or social benefit. The real worth of symbolism and the moral and spiritual teaching is almost entirely lost to them.

A truly secret organization which is of benefit to the mind in its development is not known as a secret society, nor is not known to the world. It must be as simple and plain as natural life. Entrance into such a secret society is not by ritual. It is by growth, through self effort of the mind. It must be grown into, not entered. No person can keep a mind out of such an organization if by self effort that mind continues to grow. When a mind grows into the knowledge of life that mind endeavors to dispel ignorance by removing the clouds, uncovering secrets and by throwing light on all problems of life and to help other minds in their natural unfoldment and development. Belonging to a secret society will not help the mind who wills to grow into its own.

MOMENTS WITH FRIENDS

"Is it possible to get something for nothing?" "Why do people try to get something for nothing?" "How do people who appear to get something for nothing, have to pay for what they get?"

Everyone inherently feels that no one can get something for nothing and that the proposition is wrong and the attempt unworthy; yet, when he thinks of it in connection with some object of *his* desire, good judgment is ignored and he with willing ears listens to the suggestion and deludes himself into believing that it is possible and that *he* may get something for nothing. Life requires that a just return or account be made for everything received. This requirement is based on the law of necessity, which provides for the circulation of life, the maintenance of forms and the transformation of bodies. He who tries to get for nothing something which would not otherwise come to him, interferes with the circulation of life and the distribution of forms according to natural law, and he thereby makes of himself an obstruction in the body of nature. He pays the penalty, which nature as well as all law-governed bodies exacts and is made to return that which he took or else is he altogether suppressed or removed. If he objected to this by arguing that what he got was only what would have come to him anyway, his argument fails because if what he got for nothing, apparently, would have come to him without his effort, then he need not have made the effort which he did to get it. When things come to one without apparent effort, such as what is called accident and chance or by inheritance, they come because of and according to the natural working out of law, and in this way it is legitimate and according to law. In all other cases, such as receiving physical and sensual benefits by wishing only, or by thinking only, or by making demands according to phrases known as the law of abundance or the law of opulence, it is impossible to get something for nothing even though one does appear to get something for nothing. One of the reasons why people do try to get something for nothing, is because although they feel that this cannot inherently be true, they see that others have obtained what those others do not seem to have worked for, and because it is said by other people that they do get things by simply wishing for them or demanding them and claiming them until they have them. Another reason is because the one's mind is not sufficiently matured and experienced enough to know that it cannot get something for nothing notwithstanding all allurements, inducements or pretences that it can. Another reason is because the one who thinks that he can get something for nothing is not truly honest. In ordinary business life the biggest rogues are those who believe they can outwit the law and can get something for nothing, but this is because they intend to make the people less crafty than themselves supply their wants. So they provide a get-rich-quick-scheme or some other scheme and induce others as dishonest but with less experience than themselves to come into it. Most of those who are taken into the scheme are often shown by the schemer how he is going to get the best of some other people and which explains how they also can get rich quick. If these were honest they would not be taken into the scheme but, by appealing to the avarice and covetousness in his dupes and through his own dishonest methods, the schemer gets what his victims provide. When one is truly honest he will know that he cannot get something for nothing and he will not try, though he may accept that which lawfully comes to him when it comes by natural means.

People who get something have to pay for what they get. If people get things which seem to come out of the air and to fall in their laps as the result of a call on the law of abundance or the universal storehouse or on the law of opulence, or what not, they are like the short-sighted ones without means who make lavish purchases on credit, unthinking of the time of settlement. Like those without resources who buy on credit, these sanguine temperaments often get what they do not really need; like these thoughtless purchasers, the demanders of "the law of abundance" dream and fancy they will do much with what they get—but they find themselves near bankruptcy when the time of settlement comes. A debt may not be acknowledged, but the law exacts its payment nevertheless. One who asks physical health and physical wealth by claiming and demanding these from "the law of abundance," or from "the absolute," or from anything else, and who obtains something of what he demands, instead of getting it legitimately in the realm where it belongs, must return what he has obtained plus the interest demanded for the use.

One may correct nervous disorders and restore the body to health by an attitude of mind; but it will be found that nervous disorders are in most cases brought on and continued by a troubled mind. When the right attitude is taken by the mind the nervous trouble is corrected and the body resumes its natural functions. This is a legitimate cure, or rather a removal of a cause of sickness, because the cure is effected by treating the trouble at its source. But not all diseases and poor health is due to a troubled mind. Ill health and disease is usually brought about by the eating of improper foods and the gratifying of morbid appetites and unlawful desires. Physical conditions and possessions are provided by seeing that they are necessary to one's work, and then by working for them according to the recognized legitimate physical means.

It is possible to cause diseases brought on by improper feeding to dis appear, and it is possible to obtain money and other physical advantages by claiming and demanding these from whatever phrase the mind is pleased to invent or adopt. This is possible because the mind has power to act on other minds and cause them to bring about the conditions which it desires and because the mind has power and may be able to act on the state of matter of its own plane, and this matter in turn may act upon or bring about the conditions demanded by the mind; it is possible because the mind may exert its power over the body and cause a physical disease to disappear for a time. But in every case where the mind goes against natural law to bring about physical results the law demands a readjustment, and the reaction is often more severe than the original trouble. So when health is claimed and when the physical requirements for physical health are not provided, the mind may compel the disappearance of an unhealthy growth, such as a tumor. But for such apparent cure payment is demanded by nature for trying to prevent the exactment of her laws. By forcing the dispersion of the tumor the matter of the tumor may be—as when lawless people are compelled to leave their haunts by meddlesome and foolish reformers—driven to seek residence in another part of the community, where it will do more harm and be more difficult to locate and treat. When dispersed by mental compulsion the tumor may disappear from one part of the body as a tumor and reappear in another part of the body as a loathsome sore or a cancer.

When one insists on and is provided with physical possessions by demanding them from "the absolute" or "the storehouse of the absolute," he will enjoy them for a time as a gambler enjoys his ill-gotten gains. But the law demands that not only shall he restore what he did not get honestly, but that he shall pay for the use of that which he had. This payment is called for when the demander has actually worked for a desired object—and which is lost when just within his reach; or the payment may be made after he has earned certain possessions and loses them in some unforeseen way; or he may have them taken from him when he feels most sure of them. Nature requires payment in the coin or its equivalent of the debt contracted.

When a mind attempts to make itself a servant to the body by illegitimate means, and prostitutes its powers from its own plane to the physical, the laws of the mental world require that mind to be deprived of power. So the mind loses its power and one or many of its faculties are obscured. The payment required by law is made when the mind has suffered the deprivation of power, the suffering and trouble which it has caused others in obtaining the objects of its desires, and when it has struggled through the mental darkness in which it is, in its efforts to correct its wrongs and restore itself as a mind to its own plane of action.

Most of the people who appear to get something for nothing do not have to wait for another life to be compelled to pay. Payment is usually called for and exacted in their present life. This will be found true if one will look into the history of people who have tried to get something for nothing and who have appeared to succeed. They are mental criminals who are self-imprisoned in jails of their own building.
—A FRIEND.

BE TRUE TO YOUR LIGHT.

The characteristic of heroism is its persistency. All men have wandering impulses, fits and starts of generosity. But when you have chosen your part, abide by it, and do not weakly try to reconcile yourself with the world. The heroic cannot be the common, nor the common the heroic. Yet we have the weakness to expect the sympathy of people in those actions whose excellence is that they outrun sympathy and appeal to a tardy justice. If you would serve your brother, because it is fit for you to serve him, do not take back your words when you find that prudent people do not commend you. Adhere to your own act, and congratulate yourself if you have done something strange and extravagant and broken the monotony of a decorous age. It was a high counsel that I once heard given to a young person,—"Always do what you are afraid to do." A simple manly character need never make an apology, but should regard its past action with the calmness of Phocion, when he admitted that the event of the battle was happy, yet did not regret his dissuasion from the battle.

—EMERSON, *"Heroism."*

THE
WORD

A MONTHLY MAGAZINE

PUBLISHED AND EDITED BY
H. W. PERCIVAL, 253 West 72d Street, New York City

LONDON—KEGAN PAUL, TRENCH, TRUBNER & Co., 43 Gerrard Street

CONTENTS FOR SEPTEMBER, 1910

ADEPTS, MASTERS AND MAHATMAS, ...	EDITORIAL	321
THE MARVELS OF THE HAND, ...	C. H. A. BJERREGAARD	330
TALES OF THE ANCIENT TRAVELLER—THE PEARLS OF KHOR—THE BHAHDISHIH, ...	SAMUEL NEU	345
A DREAM OF ATLANTIS—THE LAND OF MU,	ALICE DIXON LE PLONGEON	353
THE SEPHER HA-ZOHAR—THE BOOK OF LIGHT,	NURHO DE MANHAR	368
MOMENTS WITH FRIENDS, ...	A FRIEND	378
OUR MAGAZINE SHELF, ...	B. B G.	382

Yearly Subscription - - - - - - -	$4.00 or 16s.
Single Copies - - - - - - -	.35 or 1s. 6d.
Six Months' Subscription - - - - - -	2.00 or 8s.
Three Months' Subscription - - - - - -	1.00 or 4s.

BOUND VOLUMES OF THE WORD
Vols. I-X in Cloth and Half Morocco
Cloth, $21.00; Half Morocco, $26.00

The ten completed volumes of The Word are a valuable addition to any Library
They are a library in themselves

[Entered as Second-class Mail Matter, May 2, 1906, at the Post Office at New York, New York, under the Act of Congress of March 3, 1879.]

NEW
THE MAGICAL MESSAGE
according to
IÔANNÊS
commonly called

The Gospel according to [St.] John

A verbatim translation from the Greek done in modern English, with introductory essays and notes

BY

JAMES M. PRYSE

Price, Cloth, $2.00

The root of Mr. Pryse's claim is that the Gospel by John is altogether mystical in intention and that the mystical meanings of the words should never be distorted. According to Mr. Pryse the fourth gospel is much more than an account of the physical career of Jesus. He sees in it the history of the purification of the soul and so well does he buttress his claim that the best exponents of biblical criticism and Greek scholarship will be hard put to it to find anything to say in disproof.

The Theosophical Publishing Company of New York, 253 W. 72d Street

---

A Book of practical Development is

WILLIAM J. FLAGG'S

Yoga

Or Transformation.

It gives the Facts.

It shows the true Magic which underlies the Akkadian, Hindu, Taoist, Egyptian, Hebrew, Greek and Christian Religions.

It gives a comparative statement of the various Religious Dogmas concerning the Soul and its Destiny.

It is a religious Education to read this Book carefully.

Price, cloth, $3.00.

Send for Descriptive Catalogue.

Charles G. Leland,

The well-known writer, has written a fascinating volume, called,

HAVE YOU A Strong Will?

Or How to develop and strengthen the Will-Power, Memory, or any other Faculty or Attribute of Mind.

It is written, so all will grasp it.
Brilliant, so you will enjoy it.
Powerful, so you will not forget it.

It will help you to do what you want.

Price, cloth, $1.50.

Send for a booklet, "Books for the Higher Life."
It will tell you all about this Book.

The Theosophical Publishing Company of New York, 253 W. 72d Street

When ma has passed through mahat, ma will still be ma; but ma will be united with mahat, and be a mahat-ma. —The Zodiac.

THE WORD

Vol. 11　　　　SEPTEMBER, 1910.　　　　No. 6

Copyright, 1910 by H. W. PERCIVAL.

ADEPTS, MASTERS AND MAHATMAS.

(Concluded from page 264.)

WITH the subject of cleanliness, one learns about the subject of food. One who would enter the school of the masters must learn what are his needs of food, and what the kind and quantity which should be taken. The kind of food which he needs, to begin with, will depend upon his digestive and assimilative powers. Some get only a little nurture from much food. A few are able to get much nurture from little food. A man need not bother whether uncracked wheat, flaked rice, meat, fish or nuts, is the proper food for him. Honesty will tell him what he needs to eat. The kind of food needed for one self appointed in the school of the masters is of words and thoughts.

Words and thoughts are too simple for most people, but they will do for the disciple. They are what he needs. Words and thoughts are the food which one can make use of in the beginning and words and thoughts will be used ages hence, when he is more than human. At present, words are of little value and are only empty sounds, and thoughts can find no lodgment, and pass undigested through the mind. As one studies words and learns their meaning, they are to him as food. As he is able to see new things and old things in the words, he takes new mental-life. He begins to think, and delights in thought as his food. He has new uses for his mental digestive tract.

At present, the minds of men are unable to digest words and assimilate thoughts. But to do this is incumbent on one who would be a disciple. Words and thoughts are his diet. If one cannot create them himself he must use such as he has. The mind takes, circulates, digests and assimilates its food by reading, listening, speaking, and thinking. Most people would object to take drugs and poisonous and indigestible stuff as food with their soups, salads and meats, lest that might cause injury and require the doctor; but they will read with avidity the latest yellow novel and family paper, with its rapes, murders, crookedness, corruption and abject worship of wealth and fashion's latest excrescence. They will listen to slander and slander others, enjoying gossip over the tea or card table, at the opera or after church, and they will spend odd moments in planning social conquests, or think out new business ventures just inside the limits of law; this through the greater portion of the day, and at night their dreams are of what they have heard and thought and done. Many good things are done and there have been many kind thoughts and pleasant words. But the mind does not thrive on too mixed a diet. As a man's body is made up of the food he eats, so a man's mind is made up of the words and the thoughts which he thinks. One who would be a disciple of the masters needs simple food of plain words and wholesome thoughts.

Words are the creators of the world, and thoughts are the moving spirits in them. All physical things are seen to be words, and thoughts are alive in them. When one has learned somewhat of the subjects of cleanliness and food, when he is able to distinguish somewhat of the difference between his personality and the being who inhabits it, his body will have a new meaning for him.

Men are already in a measure conscious of the power of thought and they are using it, though rashly. Having found the giant power, they delight in seeing it do things, not questioning the right. It may cost much pain and sorrow before it is realized that thought can work harm as well as good, and more harm than good will be done by using thought as a moving power unless the processes of thought are known, the laws governing them obeyed, and those using that power are willing to keep a clean heart and tell no lie.

Thought is the power which causes man to live from life to life. Thought is the cause of what man is now. Thought is the

ADEPTS, MASTERS AND MAHATMAS 323

power which creates his conditions and environment. Thought provides him with work and money and food. Thought is the real builder of houses, ships, governments, civilizations, and the world itself, and thought lives in all these. Thought is not seen by the eyes of man. Man looks through his eyes at the things which thought has built; he may see thought living in the things which it has built. Thought is a constant worker. Thought is working even through the mind that cannot see the thought in the things which it has built. As man sees thought in things, thought becomes ever more present and real. Those who cannot see the thought in things must serve their apprenticeship until they can, then they will become workers and later masters of thought instead of being driven blindly by it. Man is the slave of thought, even while he thinks himself its master. Huge structures appear at the command of his thought, rivers are changed and hills removed at his thought, governments are created and destroyed by his thought, and he thinks he is the master of thought. He disappears; and he comes again. Again he creates, and again disappears; and as often as he comes he will be crushed, until he learns to know thought and to live in the thought instead of its expression.

The brain of man is the womb in which he conceives and bears his thoughts. To know thought and the nature of thought, one must take a subject of thought and think about it and love it and be true to it, and work for it in the legitimate way which the subject itself will make known to him. But he must be true. If he allows his brain to entertain subjects of thought unfavorable to the one of his choice, he will be the lover of many and will cease to be the real lover of the one. His progeny will be his ruin. He will die, for thought will not have admitted him into its secret. He will not have learned the true power and purpose of thought.

One who will think only when and as long as he pleases to think, or one who thinks because it is his business to think, does not in reality think, that is, he does not go through the process of forming a thought as it should be formed, and he will not learn.

A thought goes through the process of conception, gestation and birth. And when one conceives and carries a thought through gestation and brings it to birth, then he will know of the power of thought, and that a thought is a being. To give birth to a thought, one must take a subject of thought and must ponder over it and be true to it, until his heart and his brain give warmth to it and arouse it. This may take many days or many years. When his subject responds to his brooding mind, his brain is quickened and he conceives the subject. This conception is as illumination. The subject is known to him, so it seems. But he does not yet know. He has only a germ of knowledge, the quickened germ of a thought. If he does not nurture it the germ will die; and as he fails to nurture germ after germ he will at last be unable to conceive a thought; his brain will become barren, sterile. He must go through the period of gestation of the thought and bring it to the birth. Many men conceive and give birth to thoughts. But few men will bear them well and bring them well formed to the birth, and fewer still are able or will follow the process of the development of thought patiently, consciously and intelligently to its birth. When they are able to do so, they can sense their immortality.

Those who are unable to conceive a thought and follow it through all its changes and periods of development and watch its birth and growth and power, should not weaken their minds and keep them immature by useless regrets and idle wishes. There is a ready means by which they may become mature for thought.

The means by which one may make himself mature and fit for thought is, first, to procure and apply the cleansing simple to the heart, and at the same time to study words. Words mean little to ordinary man. They mean much to those who know the power of thought. A word is an embodied thought. It is a thought expressed. If one will take a word and fondle it and look into it, the word which he takes will speak to him. It will show him its form and how it was made, and that word which before was to him an empty sound will impart to him its meaning as his reward for calling it to life and giving it companionship. One word after the other he may learn. Lexicons will give him a passing acquaintance with words. Writers who can make them will put him on more familiar footing. But he himself must choose then as his guests and companions. They will become known to him as he finds delight in their company. By such means a man will become fit and ready to conceive and bear a thought.

There are many subjects of thought which should come into the world, but men are not yet able to give them birth. Many

ADEPTS, MASTERS AND MAHATMAS 325

are conceived but few are properly born. Men's minds are unwilling fathers and their brains and hearts are untrue mothers. When one's brain conceives, he is elated and the gestation begins. But mostly the thought is still-born or abortive because the mind and the brain are untrue. The thought which was conceived and which was to have come into the world and been expressed in proper form, suffers death often because the one who was carrying it has turned it to his selfish ends. Feeling the power, he has prostituted it to his own designs and turned the power to work out his ends. So that those who might have brought into the world thoughts which would have been great and good, have refused them birth and brought forth monstrosities in their place which do not fail to overtake and crush them. These monstrous things find fruitful soil in other selfish minds and do great harm in the world.

Most people who think that they are thinking do not think at all. They cannot or do not give birth to thoughts. Their brains are only the fields where are prepared still-born thoughts and abortive thoughts or through which pass the thoughts of other men. Not many men in the world are really thinkers. The thinkers supply the thoughts which are worked over and built up in the fields of other minds. The things that men mistake and which they think they think, are not legitimate thoughts; that is, they are not conceived and given birth by them. Much of the confusion will cease as people think less about many things and try to think more about fewer things.

One's body should not be despised, nor should it be revered. It must be cared for, respected and valued. Man's body is to be the field of his battles and conquests, the hall of his initiatory preparations, the chamber of his death, and the womb of his birth into each of the worlds. The physical body is each and all of these.

The greatest and noblest, the most secret and sacred function which the human body can perform is to give birth. There are many kinds of birth which it is possible for the human body to give. In its present state it is able to give physical birth only, and is not always fit for that work. The physical body may also give birth to an adept body, and through the physical body may also be born the master body and the mahatma body.

The physical body is developed and elaborated in the pelvic region and born from the place of sex. An adept body is developed in the abdominal region and passes through the abdominal wall. A master body is carried in the heart and ascends through the breath. The mahatma body is carried in the head and is born through the roof of the skull. The physical body is born into the physical world. The adept body is born into the astral world. The master body is born into the mental world. The mahatma body is born into the spiritual world.

People of good sense who have seriously questioned the probability whether there are such beings as adepts, masters or mahatmas, but who now believe that necessity demands them and that they are probable, will indignantly object when being told that adepts are born through the abdominal wall, masters are born from the heart and that the mahatma is born through the skull. If there are adepts, masters and mahatmas they must get into existence in some way, but in a grand, glorious and superior way, and one becoming to beings of their power and splendor. But to think of their being born through the body of a friend or one's own body, the thought is shocking to one's intelligence and the statement seems unbelievable.

Those to whom this seems shocking cannot be blamed. It is strange. Yet physical birth is as strange as other births. But if they will go back in memory to the years of early childhood, perhaps they will recall that they then experienced a shock quite as severe. Their minds were little concerned with views of themselves and of the world around them. They knew that they were living and that they came from somewhere and were content in the thought until some other child explained, and then they were taunted or dared to ask mother. Those days have passed; we live in others now. Yet, though older, we are children still. We live; we expect death; we look forward to immortality. Like children, we suppose it will be in some miraculous way, but concern our minds little about it. People are willing to be immortal. The mind leaps at the thought. The churches of the world are monuments to the heart's desire for immortality. As when children, our modesty, good sense and learning feel shocked at hearing of births of immortal bodies. But the thought becomes easier as we grow older.

The disciple of the masters regards his body differently than when he was a child of the world. As he cleans his heart with honesty, and will not lie, his heart becomes a womb, and in purity of thought he conceives in his heart a thought; he conceives the master thought; that is the immaculate conception. At an immaculate conception the heart becomes a womb and has the functions of a womb. At such times the organs of the body bear a different relation to each other than at a physical conception. There is an analogous process in all manners of birth.

Physical bodies have seldom been conceived in purity. They have usually been—because conceived in unrighteousness—born in pain and fear, afflicted by disease and succumbed to death. Were physical bodies to be conceived in purity, carried through the period of gestation to birth in purity, and were then intelligently bred, there would live in them men of such physical might and power that death would find it hard to overtake them.

For physical bodies to be conceived in purity, both the man and woman must pass through a period of mental probation and bodily preparation before conception should be allowed. When the physical body is used for legitimatized or other prostitution, it is unfit to usher worthy human bodies into the world. For some time yet bodies will come into the world as they now do. Virtuous minds seek worthy bodies in which to incarnate. But all human bodies fashioned are for minds awaiting their readiness to enter. Different and worthy physical bodies must be ready and await the superior minds of the new race to come.

After physical conception and before the foetus has taken new life, it finds its nurture within its chorion. After it has found life and until birth, its food is supplied by the mother. Through her blood the foetus is fed from the heart of its mother.

At an immaculate conception there is a change in the relation of the organs. At the immaculate conception, when the heart has become the womb for the preparation of the master body, the head becomes the heart which feeds it. The master thought conceived in the heart is sufficient to itself until the growing body takes new life. Then the head, as the heart, must furnish the food which will bring the new body to birth. There is a circulation of thought between the heart and head as there is between the foetus and the heart of its mother. The foetus is a physical body and nourished by blood. The master body is a body of thought and must be nourished by thought. Thought is its food and the food by which the master body is fed must be pure.

When the heart is sufficiently cleansed it receives a germ fashioned of the quintessence of its life. Then there descends a ray through the breath which fecundates the germ in the heart. The breath which thus comes is the breath of the father, the master, one's own higher mind, not incarnate. It is a breath which is clothed in the breath of the lungs and comes into the heart and descends and quickens the germ. The master body ascends and is born through the breath.

The body of the mahatma is conceived in the head when the male and the female germs of the same body are there met by a ray from above. When this great conception takes place, the head becomes the womb where it is conceived. As in foetal development the womb becomes the most important organ in the body and the entire body contributes to its building up, so when the heart or head are acting as a womb the entire body is used primarily and principally to contribute to the support of the heart and head.

The heart and head of man are not yet ready to be the centers of operations for the body of a master or a mahatma. They are now centers from which are born words and thoughts. Man's heart or head are as wombs in which he conceives and gives birth to things of weakness, strength, beauty, power, love, crime, vice and all that is in the world.

The generative organs are the centers of procreation. The head is the creative center of the body. It can be used as such by man, but one who would make of it the womb of creation must respect and honor it as such. At present, men use their brains for purposes of fornication. When put to that use, the head is incapable of giving birth to great or good thoughts.

One who appoints himself as disciple in the school of the masters, and even to any noble purpose of life, may consider his heart or head as the fashioners and birthplaces of his thoughts. One who has pledged himself in thought to the immortal life, one who knows that his heart or head is the holy of holies, can no longer live the life of the sensuous world. If he tries to do both, his heart and head will be as places of fornication or adultery. The avenues leading to the brain are channels along which illicit thoughts enter for intercourse with the mind. These thoughts must be kept out. The way to prevent them is to clean the heart, choose worthy subjects of thought and to speak truthfully.

Adepts, masters and mahatmas may be taken as subjects of thought and they will be of benefit to the thinker and his race. But these subjects will be of benefit to those only who will use their reason and best judgment in the consideration. No statement made concerning this matter should be accepted unless it appeals to the mind and heart as true, or unless it is borne out and substantiated by one's experience and observation of life, and seems reasonable as in harmony with the future progress, evolution and development of man.

The preceding articles on adepts, masters and mahatmas may be of benefit to the man of good judgment, and they can do him no harm. They may also be of benefit to the rash man if he will heed the advice given and not attempt to do things which he infers from what he reads but which have not been written.

The world has been informed about adepts, masters and mahatmas. They will not press their presence upon men, but will wait until men can live and grow into it. And men will live and grow into it.

Two worlds seek entrance or recognition into the mind of man. Mankind is now deciding which of the worlds it will prefer: the astral world of the senses or the mental world of the mind. Man is unfit to enter either, but he will learn to enter one. He cannot enter both. If he decides for the astral world of the senses and works for that, he will come under the notice of the adepts, and in this life or those to come he will be their disciple. If he decides for the development of his mind he will as truly in time to come be recognized by the masters, and be a disciple in their school. Both must use their minds; but he of the senses will use his mind to get or produce the things of the senses and obtain entrance to the inner sense world, and as he tries to think of it and holds the thought in his mind and will work to gain entrance, the inner sense world, the astral world, will become more and more real to him. It will cease to be a speculation and may be known to him a reality.

He who would know the masters and enter the mental world must devote the power of his thought to the development of his mind, to calling into use the faculties of his mind independently of his senses. He should not ignore the inner sense world, the astral world, but if he senses it he should try to use his faculties until it disappears. In thinking and even by trying to think of the mental world, the mind becomes attuned to it.

Only a slight partition, a veil, divides man's thought from the mental world, and though it is ever present and his native realm, it seems strange, foreign, unknown, to the exile. Man will remain an exile until he has earned and has paid his ransom.

The End.

THE MARVELS OF THE HAND; "THE INSTRUMENT OF INSTRUMENTS."

By C. H. A. Bjerregaard.

MY subject is the hand. It suggests an essay on palmistry and chiromancy and character-reading in some form, but I will not write on those subjects. I shall not even speak of the hand in its occult, theosophic or mystic aspects. I shall speak of the hand as "the instrument of instruments," a name given it by Aristotle. The occult signification of the hand is too deep for me, and worthy of a better pen than mine.

I shall go back to first principles, to the soul and its tool, the hand, in such a way that I shall hope to awaken in my readers not only a realization of what a marvel the hand is, but lead them to inquire into its mystery, especially as an image of the soul. My essay will simply go to show what a marvel we possess in the human hand, and, that all that which we call culture and civilization depends upon the hand, is made by the hand. My essay will not be a string of arguments, but a series of illustrations to prove this and no more.

In the third paper on "The Inner Life and the Tao-Teh-King" (printed in "The Word" March, 1909) I spoke of the human hand as an absolute necessity for human life. I argued for a more rational view of the senses, than that commonly held. I said at the time, "Mind is the interpreter and the fashioner of the music that the Divine plays upon us, and I may say without fear of contradiction, that the senses are the mechanics, who mould the divine fire into acts, into deeds. They are the hands of the mind. Can you realize what our world would be if we had no senses? Have you ever thought of it? If mind only existed, and no senses, the Word might be spoken, sounds might thrill the vacant spaces and colors might dash from pole to pole or illuminate the night, but there would be no human world. The human world is made by the human hand, or, which is the same, by human deeds, and there can be no human deeds without the senses, the flesh. That is a fact! . . . The human hand is the most marvelous organ we have, none other excepted. Without the hand, no human society."

At the time I promised to prepare an essay on the hand and its marvels. It is this promise I am now trying to redeem.

I mean to raise the hand to the dignity of the face and call it "the second face." I shall certainly not deny that the hand primarily is a "grasper"; on the contrary, I shall illustrate that fully, but I will claim with Anaxagoras of old, that man owes his wisdom, knowledge and superiority to the use of his hands, and say with him, that if oxen had hands, they would be men. Aristotle likewise held that man is the wisest of creatures because he has hands. Galen, on the other hand, a little later, thought that the hand was given to man because he was the wisest of creatures. It is reason that has taught us, not our hands, he said. The hands are the organs of reason. But, no matter if Galen differ from Anaxagoras and Aristotle. All three raise the hand to great dignity and would say as I have said, the hand is the most marvelous organ we have, none other excepted. You may think of other organs as superior and equally valuable as the hand, but I beg you remember that those organs are limited to special uses and therefore cannot compete with the hand, which is not thus limited. I will now demonstrate my assertions by descriptions of the hand's manifold abilities.

Of what use would sweet lips or the tongue be, if the faithful hand did not verify the lip's or tongue's actions? It is very well to have teeth, but the food must be brought to them. The hands do it. The hands in both cases are the mediators; they execute the desires of the lips and they are the instruments for the passing in of all that which enters man through the mouth.

Surely, we could not press our friend or child to our breast without the hand; nor swear upon the heart without laying hand upon it; nor could lovers plight their faith by joining hands as they did it in olden times over a running stream. How would we be dressed without hands? Perhaps clothes would be unknown amongst us and we would have no other covering but natural hair. It would be possible to go into water and be wetted, but we should have no bath, nor all the romanticism connected with it. We might sing without hands, but the drama would be unknown and impossible and so also all instrumental music. Some of us have the Pascinian corpuscles developed in our fingers and elsewhere. By means of these we feel like the bats.

Ordinarily, even without specially developed Pascinian corpuscles, the finger tips are four times as sensitive as the palms of the hand and ten times as sensitive as the back of the hands. Without these corpuscles no sense of space. Why is it that all praying people supplement their prayers with hand gestures? Think of Belshazzar's fright when he saw that terrible finger write judgment on the wall! And why do we applaud an act by clapping the hands? How characteristic that we lay the finger upon our lips, when we command silence or when we do not wish to utter ourselves. How well it would be with many people if they followed the proverb: "If thou hast done foolishly or thought evil, lay thine hand upon thy mouth." Why do we do all these things by the hand and not by other members? Because the hands lend themselves so readily to be the heart's instruments, and, from the heart come all our vital acts, our inward life, all that which the soul realizes in its surrounding world.

If our heart is hard, the hand clenches its fingers tightly into a fist and threatens, defies or condemns. If our heart is false it stretches out a cold, clammy and weak hand. If our heart is raging, the fingers of the hand tear like talons of a hawk. A foxy heart uses a hand sharp as a razor, yet of pleasing aspect; if our heart is humble it kisses the hand that slays. Indeed, "the alphabets upon the fingers" spell out the condition of the heart! In short, is there any moral, immoral or unmoral act in which the hand does not take a part? "Hand" and "doing" are synonymous terms when we talk about the mind's activity and utterances. There is no doing, nor can there be any without the hands. In English we are limited in our expressions, but in German and the Scandinavian languages we say handlung (noun) and handling (noun) for our doings, our acts; and the words directly show that they relate to the hand, that they express what the hand does. For that reason it was that in former days they cut off a man's hands before they cut off his head; they dishonored him, before they killed him.

It is true, the head, and the glory that rests upon and over the head is a man's crown; but the glory of an erect position are the arms and the hand. You get no perfectly straight figure out of a man standing with his arms bent like handles on a pitcher. It is the hand and its position that makes the figure straight. Stretch the arms and hand and the figure of itself becomes straight.

The nexus between the hand and the eye, or the tongue, has been made the study by several eminent men in the past. I shall give you the results of those studies as far as I have traced them.

The nexus between the hand and the eye is this, that generally "a good eye" for things and "a good hand" go together; really hand and eye are in partnership and may be called the directors of a company called "the human faculties." Such a partnership is as evident as that expressed by the term "head and heart." When you play croquet or billiards you measure the line for your ball and the distance it has to traverse by the eye, and the hand of the practiced player immediately translates these impressions into muscle power and into energy, and, it is done. How, we do not know. But it is done. David could not have told us how he managed to hit Goliath in the forehead; no slinger can tell, but their eyes and their hand know how to do. Their hands and their eyes are in company.

Most of us have not eye enough to see when the artist has failed to draw the hands correctly, and it is fortunate for him. To draw the hands is most difficult, because the hands are so full of our life, our character and our occupation, that it requires years of study to learn how to draw them. Well drawn hands on a painting or chiseled on statuary are therefore most significant. You know the famous statue, the Milesian Venus, has no arms and hands. I, for one, am glad of it. Arms and hands might destroy the happy illusions that now hover over her, in the same way as arms and hands entirely disillusion us in the Medicean Venus. Leonardo da Vinci discovered many mysteries in the hand, such as only an artist could discover, and has laid down his observations in a pamphlet of great interest.

An American writer, Dr. Burt G. Wilder, in the American Naturalist, Vol. 1, holds that the tongue and the hand are in a teleological sense (not anatomically or morphologically) the most characteristic organs of man and that they correspond to his peculiar endowments of rationality in thought and freedom of action. And he points out that these two organs are not only capable of much good, but also, by perversion, the most potent for evil, and that the hand ought to be called "the unruly member" as well as the tongue, because both of them, either singly or together cause man to be the most unruly member of the animal kingdom. I think the charge is well founded.

Washing of the hands is a common ceremony with wild

races, and was so with many of the ancients. It was a sign of purification of the soul and a sign by which an accused or suspected declared his innocence. The act of Pontius Pilate is well known and needs no comment. Washing of hands also was done in antiquity, and today in many churches before the priest officiates in any of the sacred acts. Perhaps the wisdom buried in these ceremonies may be discovered in this bit of English rhyme "to the maidens':'

> "Wash your hands, or else the fire
> Will not tend to your desire;
> Unwashed hands, ye maidens, know,
> Dead the fire, though ye blow."

I shall not claim to be able to unravel the occult sense of this doggerel, but I believe there is one in it. There is a relationship between innocence and fire, the same as between truth and power, cleanliness and godliness; look into the Zend Avesta and some of this will be understood.

Among the numerous symbols on monuments from the time of the ancients there are many and various signs that represent authority. For the present I shall only mention from among them that of the hand, a sign very common. For a thousand of years the Christian church has represented God by a hand extended from the clouds, and it is still common for painters to represent the act of creation by God's finger pointing upon some kind of matter. As if to taunt Job and to assert the divine omnipotence, a voice cries out of the whirlwind: "Canst thou bind the sweet influences of Pleiades, or loose the bands of Orion? Canst thou bring forth Mazzaroth in his season?"

In zodiacal astronomy the hand, together with arm and shoulder, holds mystic communion with gemini.

It is a very old belief that there is a connection between prophetic inspiration and the hand. The fact is that the two are related is numerous instances mentioned in the Bble and elseiwhere.

Henry Schoolcraft says that the figure of the human hand is used by the North American Indians to denote supplication to the Deity or the Great Spirit, and that it stands in the system of picture writing, for instance that of the Mayas, as the symbol for strength, power and mystery and that the hand everywhere in ceremonial observances has a sacred character. The hand in the most varied forms, clenched or extended, grasping or open, fingers pointing or held in curious positions shows that American Indians, especially those of Mexico, employed it extensively as a glyph. It will interest my readers to look at Maya manuscripts or Mexican monumental remains in museums. They will undoubtedly discover something of interest to themselves. (Plate illustrating such hands can be seen in the American Antiquarian, vol. 19.)

Other Americanists tell us that the red hand, or a hand dipped in red paint and slapped on the walls of caves, or high cliffs, dwellings, buffalo skins, is very common in Arizona, New Mexico, Utah, Colorado and Yucatan.

On the authority of J. G. R. Forlong, the well known archeologist and mythologist, I state that the hand as the special "weapon" or power of man represents solo-phallic gods throughout Asia, as well as the two Americas. And he tells us that the "blood red hand" of Siva can be seen on thousands of Hindu shrines, and especially on the doorposts because the god Siva is "the god of the door" of life—the Dvarkanath. Forlong also tells us that the solar "hand" is also in sun and moon on many old sculptures in Great Britain and Germany. The Teutonic god Tyr corresponds to the Vedic Savatar; both are "onehanded," and numerous other gods, and prophets, can be mentioned, all of which are characterized in some way or other by the hand, and, the hand in all these cases is a solo-phallic symbol. In many cases of mythology, the hand and the pillar are synonyms. Any one desirous of more details in these matters will find them in "Notes and Queries," sixth series, vols. 11 and 12.

Folklore is o fcourse full of hand-lore, but I must pass by it all. There is only one point I shall touch upon, and that is the question of right and left hand, but I shall not do it because it is folklore, but because Laotzse mentions the subject. He says: "The superior man, the sage, makes the left hand, which is the weak side, the place of honor; but, he who goes forth to war places his weapons in the right hand, the strong hand. Weapons are instruments of evil omen. They are not the tools of the superior man, the sage; he uses them only when he cannot help it. Peace is the highest aim." It is interesting to notice this, because Laotzse represents Turanian ideas. With the Semites, on the contrary, the right hand was the place of honor. With the right hand Jahveh destroys his enemies, and," the Lord said unto my Lord, sit thou at my right hand until I make thine enemies thy footstool." The Aryans also honored the right hand.

Apollo, for instance, was placed on the right hand of Zeus by Callimachus. This change of symbol from left hand to right hand is in itself of profound occult signification and shows cyclic evolution.

The following is a very curious piece of folklore, and something of interest to chirosophists.

In Hone's "Everyday Book" you will find his descriptions of two old prints in the British Museum and learn how the saints are kept busy with the affairs of the human hand. The top joint of the thumb on the right hand is dedicated to God; the second joint to the Virgin; the top joint of the forefinger to Barnabas; the second joint to John; the third to Paul. The top joint of the second finger to Simeon Cleophas; the second to Thaddeus and the third to Joseph. The top joint of the third finger to Zaccheus; the second to Stephen and the third to Luke. The top joint of the little finger to Leatus; the second to Mark and the third to Nicodemus. The top joint of the thumb of the left hand is dedicated to Christ; the second joint to the Virgin; the top joint of the forefinger to James; the second to John, the Evangelist; the third to Peter. The first joint of the second finger to Simeon; the second to Matthew; the third to James the Great. The top joint of the third finger to Jude, the second to Bartholomew; the third to Andrew. The top joint of the little finger to Mathias; the second to Thomas; the third to Philip." It is tedious and without profit to read such stuff. How much more useful would this monk have been if he had gone ploughing the fields or woven clothes for the poor, instead of wasting precious time upon such nonsense, much to the discredit of his intelligence and that of his monastery.

While I was copying this classification of the joints and the respective assignments of the saints to do duty, it occurred to me how easy one could control heavenly influences and carry them in one's pocket, if the above classification was real and true, by simply sticking the hands into them. The idea of carrying the heavenly clergy in one's pocket: how ludicrous!

I shall go no further into palmistry of that sort, but tell you of another kind of chirosophy: the value of the human hand as estimated by the Miner's Accident Insurance Company of Germany. The loss of both hands is estimated at one hundred per cent., or the whole ability to earn a living. The loss of the right hand depreciates the value of an individual as a worker seventy to eighty per cent.; while the loss of the left hand represents from sixty to seventy per cent of the earnings of both hands. The value of the thumb is estimated to be from twenty to thirty per cent. of the earnings; the loss of the other fingers is valued but little. That is much better knowledge and chirosophy than that of the monk.

The ancient Egyptians called man's life principle ka, and, as all of my readers know, who have peeped a little into the life of the Egyptians, everything was done for the welfare of the ka in this life and hereafter. This ka is in the hieroglyhics represented as a pair of hands and arms uplifted. In other words, to the Egyptians, hands and uplifted arms were identical with life. How that symbol arose, I think a little guessing on your part, will reveal. The hand in general with them was a symbol of strength and propagation of life. On the Egyptian monuments there are representations of a ceremony called "the imposition of the sa." The sa, according to Egyptian belief, was a mysterious fluid which circulated through the members of the gods and gave health, life and general vigor. Some gods had more of it, others less; as a rule the gods communicated sa to each other and to men. Maspero tells us that even statues of the gods could communicate the sa, and that it was done by placing the right hand upon the nape of the recipient's neck and making passes, which caused the fluid to flow. The supply of sa could be exhausted; and in that case it could be renewed from "the Pond of Sa," a mysterious lake in the northern sky. The occult teaching of this you can easily guess.

New Zealanders to-day maintain that sacred persons hold a similar spiritual essence within them and that it is communicated to any object or person that touches them. This essence is generally supposed to be derived from an ancestral spirit. In some form or other the same idea of the essence and its origin is known to most peoples. Until very recently, royalty in Europe was supposed to possess that spiritual essence. It is beyond the scope of my essay to discuss what this sa really was. Your own imagination will probably give it many names and a meaning, and, in a general way you will identify it with the life and active principle in man, and, you will be correct in your guessing.

It is a biological fact, that as soon as life has emerged from its lowest or rudimentary conditions and manifestations, then the nerves of touch, which before were distributed over the whole surface of the body, now become collected in force at convenient points, so that the body readily and quickly can sense danger or that which is good for it. The nerves or the sense of touch are not removed entirely from the other parts of the body, but they are in the main gathered on specific points. We have feelings all over by the skin, but certainly not the same intensity of perception, say on any part of the arm, as that which we have on the inside of the hand and fingers, where are gathered sensitive nerves.

Of convenient points for active investigation of the surrounding world, I would mention the antennae of the insects, the tongue of the fly, the lips of the horse, the snout of the hog, the trunk of the elephant and man's superior tactile organ, the hand.

Our hand is an exploring instrument, more sensitive than the needle that records an earth tremulation thousands of miles away. Our hand with its five fingers is like complex compasses that measure their own movements. If you would understand the marvels of the hand go to some place where those born blind work, and you shall see what the hand can do both in registering and in reflecting. Hand a broken basket to one born blind and who is a basket maker and you will see how quickly his fingers will find the dilapidated and torn place. His fingers do it as quickly as your eye can do it. His hand will readily measure the work to be done, cut the osiers and run them in at one side and out at an other and in short time finish the work. A blind man will do that without being told. Even if he is both deaf and dumb, he can do it. His hand both discovers the break and reasons out what is to be done and does it. The mind of the blind seems to be concentrated in the hands. You see the same thing i ntheir feeling the way on the streets.

I beg you study a little biology; not only for the interest the study awakens, but as a help to spiritual life and as a key to much that is otherwise obscure; and, also because the Inner Life is largely unintelligible without some knowledge of biology. Man is a microcosm and reflects the universal and corresponds to that macrocosm we all seek to unite with. Study a little biology, especially the anatomy of the hand, to learn how the twenty-seven bones and forty muscles of the hand operate. The twenty-seven bones and forty muscles of the hand are allied to the brain and the interpreters of the will. And the numerous nerves and blood vessels are the operators who work these bones and muscles.

It is a fact, that most animals come into the world with a physical frame which quickly develops and is ready for use in an astonishingly short time. Man comes into the world utterly helpless, feeble and unprotected. What saves him? The hand! First the hand that receives him, nurses him, and next his own hand. Clearly, his existence depends upon the hand!

Again, it is a fact that animals come into the world well equipped for the battle of life. The eagle, the vulture, the falcon have strong beaks and talons; lions, tigers, bears, have powerful claws and teeth. Other animals have tusks, horns, quick motions. What has man? None of these arms. No natural arms at all. What has he? He has a mind, that develops by and by and this mind invents arms; but of what use would the invention be, if his hands could not make the arms and use them? His existence depends upon his hands.

We invent and dream of heavenly habitations; the prisoner dreams of freedom, but neither has the ability to construct the heavenly habitation nor to unlock the bars. They have no hands adapted for that use and consequently are entirely at the mercy of circumstances. So would we be if we did not have hands wherewith to manufacture the tools that give us our freedom.

Like her work in so many other cases, Nature knows how to vary her design so that by some slight change she creates radical distinctions among her creatures. A careful study of the anterior limbs of the vertebrate animals shows that they are all built upon one general plan, but varied in form and proportion to suit the special needs of man, the beast, the bird and the reptile. It is such a varied form which has placed man in superiority among other creatures; in short it is the variation we call his thumb which gives him his superiority. About that later. At the time of the creation of Adam, the old legend tells us that God said "Let man have dominion over the fishes of the sea, and the fowls of the air, and the beasts of the whole earth, and every creeping creature that moveth upon the earth." Think what we may about God speaking and directing that man become master in the animal realm of nature, the fact is there; man has gradually become such a master. It is true he has become master largely by exterminations, though also by subduing wild animals to his use, for instance, the dog has come out of the wolf and both the ox and the horses have been tamed from wild conditions. However, be man's dominion won by extermination or by cunning, it was and is by the hand that that dominion was won and is maintained.

But man's dominion on earth extends further than that over organic creation and he is not master alone by his brute power or his cunning, but also by arts and sciences; and none of these could be such realities as they are without the hand. Pythagoras could not have transmitted the number values he discovered if he had not had a hand wherewith to write down the figures. It is true that much of the ancient tradition was handed down by oral repetition, but it is also commonly believed that much valuable knowledge possessed by the most ancient people is lost, because it was not written down. That which was written down has come down to us, thanks to the hand.

We cannot conceive of musical instruments being invented and constructed if man had had no hand. Certain it is that animals have not music, though some have song and others know the notes that mean fear, joy, calling. Animals have nests, lairs, dens, caves, and various other places for hiding, breeding and general resorts, but they have no architecture. A house can only be erected by a hand that has a thumb. And moreover that which the hand builds is architecture, viz., a home, a domicile or a temple, a council chamber, a palace, in which man as Man rules in virtue of his highest and noblest character. Architecture is not the same as a stall, a barn, a kennel, a pen or a kraal. Nay, architecture is in the true sense man's real handicraft. Architecture, or the science of building, is a fine art and is not the same as engineering which erects a skyscraper, though, of course, the hand is also indispensable in building such iron monsters. Go through the list of the sciences and arts and you shall find how intimately they connect with the hand. "The thousand soul'd Shakespeare" has said, "What a piece of work is man! How noble in reason! how infinite in faculties! in action, how like an angel! in apprehension, how like a God!" Singularly he does not mention the hand. What would a drama be without the hand? Can any of us imagine a drama without the hand and its gestures? It seems to me the drama would be an impossibility. Perhaps I am not saying too much, that if man had had no hand, there would have been no Shakespeare, no drama.

Now, all these wonders of the hand depend upon the thumb, as I already mentioned, when I said that mother Nature can create miracles by very slight changes in her handicraft. She performed a miracle when she turned one of man's fingers into a thumb. And the miracle she performed, I have pointed out by descriptions of some of the marvels of the hand. But the story is not half told, I believe. The marvels and miracles of the hand are not fully known, I think. There is for instance, in all probability, a reason for our five fingers. Why are there five? If we did not have five fingers and five toes we would not count by fives; there would be no decimal system of reckoning; I wonder what our number system would be—and I think of all the forms of culture which are fivefold in their essence. The thought is amazing in its power!

Now, something about the thumb, which is really the main thing about the hand. A hand without a thumb is no hand. All the marvels I have spoken of in relation to the hand may properly be attributed to the thumb. "The remarkable peculiarity that distinguishes the hand (or paw) of the chimpanzee from the human hand is the smallness of the thumb; it extends no further than to the root of the fingers. It is upon the length, strength, free lateral motion, and perfect mobility of the thumb, that the superiority of the human hand depends. The thumb is called pollex, because of its strength; and that strength, being equal to that of all the fingers, is necessary to the perfection of the hand. Without the fleshy ball of the thumb, the power of the fingers would avail nothing; and accordingly the large ball formed by the muscles of the thumb is the distinguishing character of the human hand, and especially of that of an expert workman."

Albinus, a famous anatomist of old, characterises the thumb as the lesser hand, the assistant of the greater, and it is no exaggeration to say so. The thumb is the lesser hand. The thumb is the sign and symbol of life in many senses. I am now writing an essay on the hand in general and have collected numerous facts to show how marvellous it is and what it symbolizes. I might do the same for the thumb. It would be easy to talk for an hour on the thumb alone and to show its power dynamically and symbolically. I will mention one interesting point. We usually call the little finger the fifth finger. I do not do it. I call the thumb the fifth finger because it is the center of the square.

You know man is built in a square. The hand (bending the thumb inwards) looks like a square and the thumb bends naturally into the middle of it and as you shall hear is really the hand; the jack in the box. "The loss of the thumb amounts almost to the loss of the hand; and were it to happen in both hands, it would reduce a man to a miserable dependence." In olden time it was common to deprive important prisoners of war of the thumbs by cutting them off! and to do the same with the great toe. Adoni-bezek, we are told, cut off the thumbs and great toes of three-score and ten kings, and said contemptiously "they gather their meat under my table." It is also recorded that Judah and Simeon mutilated him in return in the same manner. By cutting off the thumb and its corresponding member on the foot, they deprived their enemies of everything, except life, and made them most miserable.

While I am extolling the excellency of the human thumb and the hand, it might be well that I also mention that when the distinguishing marks between man and the ape are spoken of, it must not be forgotten that the great toe (the hallux) is perhaps even more characteristic of man in his difference from the ape, and that certainly man's erect posture and gait mainly depends upon it. But this has no real or direct bearing upon the value of the thumb and of course does not relate directly to culture. I am speaking of the hand not of the great toe. I merely mention the fact. Scientists hold that the hand must be said to belong to man exclusively, because in its sensibility and motion it is the counterpart to mind, especially to that ingenuity which through and by the hand makes the weakest being on earth the ruler of animate and inanimate nature.

In short, "the hand's superiority consists in its combination of strength with variety, extent, and rapidity of motion; and furthermore in the power of the thumb, and the forms, relations and sensibility of the fingers, which adapt it for holding, pulling, spinning, weaving, and constructing, properties which may be found separately in animals, but combined only in the human hand." All these qualities correspond to man's superior mental capacities and they can therefore obey the mandates of the mind. The hand was not always a hand says evolution. It has followed and is a result of the general evolution by means of which the animal body became transformed to be what it now is in man.

Originally, the limbs were the means of two functions, locomotion and prehension, and when the use of the limbs became more specialized in course of time, and, the hind limbs were used principally to sustain an erect position, the forelimbs gradually extended their sphere from mere prehension in the direction of what we now call arts and crafts. The extended sphere depended upon and also caused the transformation of the thumb into the position of an opposite to the fingers, the position which conditions the arts and crafts. There could be no arts and crafts if the thumb could not meet the fingers. The monkey form of hand, the form immediately prior to the human hand, is adequate for seizing and climbing branches, but deficient for mechanical purposes. It cannot grasp nor pull, nor dig, nor tear, nor handle stones or sticks, nor employ weapons, nor construct defenses against attacks, be they by man or beast, all of which the human hand with its thumb can do in a superior way.

In the nature of the act and the purpose for which the hand acts, lies the whole significance and meaning of man's character.

I said in "the nature of the act" and "the purpose for which" we use our hand, one may read our moral, mental and spiritual value. I have not laid emphasis upon the shape of the hand, because I know, that that is illusive, just as much as the facial expression. Socrates could not change the shape of his nose and we know that his character belied the nose. He was not the bad man the nose would indicate. I have, however, duly regarded the shape of the hand, as you will perceive. But I pay more attention to what the hand can do, than what it is. I know of people coming from what is considered low stock, who are far superior to others, I know, of so-called fine and noble stock. Nature cares more for uses than for form. Nature cares not so much for a handsome body as for a useful body. In my anatomical and occult studies, I do not overlook structural characteristics; I know perfectly well that they mean much cosmically; but for the present, I am not talking about cosmic mysteries, but about moral values, of life on the Path, hence I pay most attention to functional characteristics, and I want my essay understood from that point of view. When I speak of Nature, I mean function. I take the standpoint of Aristotle, that the mind is as much an instrument of the body as the body is an instrument of the mind. The logic of that standpoint is unassailable. With him I also hold that the hand is man's most primitive instrument and the instrument of instruments. And now in conclusion, I claim that my descriptions of the hand have fully borne out the assertion, I made, that the hand is the most wonderful organ we have, none other excepted. I know that some may think of other organs, but I beg them to consider that those other organs they think of are limited in their activity to some special uses, hence cannot compete for eminence with the hand, which has numerous spheres of activity, a multiform plan,

THE WORD

and, as far as we can judge now, must remain mind's executive officer long after certain other organs must have ceased to be of importance to man in his evolution towards spirituality.

If I have not already said enough, let me quote what another has said:

"The instrument of instruments, the hand;
Courtesy's index; chamberlain to nature;
The body's soldier; and the mouth's caterer;
Psyche's great secretary; the dumb's eloquence;
The blind man's cradle, and his forehead's buckler;
The minister of wrath; and friendship's sign."
—(*Lingua.*)

THE SOUL IS THE WHOLE THROUGH ITS PARTS.

We see the world piece by piece, as the sun, the moon, the animal, the tree; but the whole, of which these are the shining parts, is the soul. Only by the vision of that Wisdom can the horoscope of the ages be read, and by falling back on our better thoughts, by yielding to the spirit of prophecy which is innate in every man, we can know what it saith. Every man's words who speaks from that life must sound vain to those who do not dwell in the same thought on their own part. I dare not speak for it. My words do not carry its august sense; they fall short and cold. Only itself can inspire whom it will, and behold! their speech shall be lyrical, and sweet, and universal as the rising of the wind. Yet I desire, even by profane words, if I may not use sacred, to indicate the heaven of this deity and to report what hints I have collected of the transcendent simplicity and energy of the Highest Law.

EMERSON, "*The Over-Soul.*"

TALES OF THE ANCIENT TRAVELER.

Translated by Samuel Neu.

THE PEARLS OF KHOR.

To a Tale of the Ancient Traveler, told at the Court of Omee, Noble King of the Great Middle Country, and By him called the Tale of the Pearls of Khor, set down by Lipo-va, the Scribe, give ear:

MOST noble King, those precious pearls of Khor which from the far South Country have been brought and laid before thy feet, are truly precious, and wonderful their luster to behold. But if thine eyes could see the many years of misery and pain and toil and sacrifice, by which those pearls were gained, then wouldst thou give thy very throne itself to hold a handful of them in thy hand. And, beautiful and lustrous though they are, they look but common sea stones when compared with those the great King, Mahm, wears in his crown.

Though bright and pure these pearls, the land of Khor, from whence they came, reeks with vile filth and muck, though those that dwell there seem to know full well the way to keep themselves above the mire. It was not always so. In ancient days the people of the land worked in the fields. They plowed and harvested, and plowed again, their only thought to sow and reap and live. One man among them harbored many dogs, on which he fed himself. One fateful day, within the carcass of his oldest dog, he found a shining pearl of countless worth. This dog, the legend says, was wont to play and gambol in the city's offal filth. So thereupon he dug among the filth in hope to find another wondrous pearl; but, though he labored hard, no pearl found he. But while he labored all his other dogs were playing in the filth, and as he killed them, one by one, for food, he found within their bellies, shining pearls of countless worth.

This man, whose name, the legend says, was Kwan, gave to each son of his one of his dogs. And his six brothers also got them dogs and gave them to their sons to gather pearls. And Kwan and his six brothers and their sons polluted all the land of Khor with filth, that their dogs might seek in it after pearls; so all the other people left the land and left it to the dogs that served the sons of Kwan and his six brothers, and their sons.

For ages long these dogs dwelt in the mud, the while their masters watched them, each his dog; and after many days were past the dog would die, and in his entrails was the pearl.

But Nakoru, a grandson of old Kwan, discovered, most by chance the legend says, that if he fed his dog upon a pearl the day that he was born, then in the years to come that pearl would grow, and when the dog died there were two more shining pearls. His brothers, then, which were the men of Khor, did likewise, and thereafter, it is told, each dog is fed one precious pearl at birth.

But, now, strange though it may seem unto you who know not dogs that glean for pearls in mire, the pearl-fed dogs no longer hear the voice of masters calling them, or if they hear they heed it not, but go their way alone. Something within the pearl they hold within impels them ever on to gather more; they feel this, but not knowing what it means they gather colored stones to call their own, and shut themselves in mud-piles, walled around, where they may sit and count their stones alone. Some think it is for place and power they seek, and fight each other. Others sink still more, but these are they whose masters have grown weary and give them but small pearls at their birth, who fill themselves with poison and vile stuffs. And so the Land of Khor has come to stink. And so the pearls of Khor today are scarce.

And yet the masters in the land of Khor do not desert the dogs they send to dig. They give to each a pearl when he is born and watch him ever as he treads the earth, and call to him incessantly, to guide, and do all things they may to turn aside their workers in the mire from evil ways. And once in many days one of the dogs will heed his master's call and turn aside and labor for the making of fine pearls. Then is the master thankful, and when dies the dog the master takes the pearls that he has made and gives them to his next and that one labors on for more, and more.

Then, after many dogs have labored so and many pearls are made, enough to form the "Formless Casket," then that lucky dog becomes a man, and labors on until he shall receive from Mahm his great reward, the pearl of priceless price, which once was made by dogs of Khor. All this, O king, I saw.

The King, having heard, spoke: "Yea, it is true that dogs make pearls in Khor, and, more strange still, the dog that makes enough shall become a man."

But the Ancient Traveler whispered to me what the king told not—that the dogs of Khor are those that we call men; and I, Lipo-va, the Scribe, have set it down.

THE BHAHDISHIH.

WHENCE came, oh noble king, the Bhahdishih? Wherefore, oh king, the awful Bhahdishih? So have the men of all the ages asked; so ask they now, and so they ever shall. Men said the Bhahdishih was good, divine, and gave him honor, burnt the perfumed oil and living sacrifices at his feet; and plagues and evil things beset the land. Men said the Bhahdishih was evil, foul, and banished him from out their huts and land; and then the people ceased to live or be. And yet men ask: whence came the Bhahdishih? And yet men ask: wherefore the Bhahdishih?

This is the tale of Uht, the King of Bhor, and what befell the Bhahdisih in Bhor.

Oft came the awful Bhahdishih to Bhor, as oft he comes to other of thy lands, and in the guise of strolling charlatan he drew the people's gaze and raised their joy and pleased their senses mightily, until, bereft of sense, they blindly did those things that ages of salt tears could not wipe out. Oft did they burn the city of their king while maddened by the sweetly poisoned gifts by which the Bhahdishih enchanted them. Oft in his spell they even were so mad to fall upon the palace of the king. And it is said that numbers count the times when Uht must need to flee from their distress.

Then came a day when fell the King of Ghol, Uht's brother, in the land near to his west, beneath the hands of those the Bhahdishih had wrapped within his net of poisoned charms. Yea, that fair king was slain by those he ruled, by those who hearkened to the Bhahdishih.

Then rose the wrath of Uht, and he was stern, and forth there went an edict from his hand that bade the gates of Bhor be closely sealed against the entrance of the Bhahdishih. And many men rejoiced that this was so, for now might peace reign in the land of Bhor.

But came the Bhahdishih before the gate and pleaded that he might gain entrance there, to show the men of Bhor by wondrous arts the things that pleased their senses and made glad the children and the foolish and the wise. And as he pleaded rose a mighty shout from those within the land. They prayed the king to raise the gate that they might see the play, else would the people cease to live or be. Then summoned Uht his counsellors and priests and asked of them what were the thing to do. And they gave answer that the Bhahdishih might enter if a covenant he made to quit the land before the madness came and swept the people from their duty's way. When heard the Bhahdishih the council's word he laughed and quickly made the covenant, whereon the gates were straightway opened wide.

Glad were the people when he entrance made, and crowded round to see his arts of joy, to be made glad by things he knew to do. And when the king beheld their joy was ripe he cried: Begone; but rose a mighty shout that told him not yet had they had enough. And never were the people satisfied until the madness came. So came it oft.

Then Uht sent forth his messengers of fire and stationed them upon the mighty gates and cautioned them upon the pain of death to let the Bhahdishih not enter in. Stern men they were, these messengers of fire, and men of mighty vows and valor loyal, and them the king knew well that he could trust as he had trusted them in deeds before. But when the Bhahdishih made his approach he cast his spell upon the men of fire, upon the warriors, until they slept, and went his way among the men of Bhor. And so the madness came again to Bhor and Uht was made to tremble for his life.

Slain were the messengers by Uht's command and others, stronger, mightier, set to watch, but ever wove the Bhahdishih his spell, and ever came the madness on the land. And all the counsellors that served the king could counsel naught and could no more advise, so darkness filled the land of Bhor, and grief. The Bhahdishih could not be kept without, and men ceased if the Bhahdishih were slain.

Then went the king unto the sorceress, Gaya, who dwelt upon the lonely isle that rose amid his kingdom's inland sea. Seldom he came upon that lonely isle or spoke with her, and when she did advise he only half believed the words she spoke. But now that counsellors of wisdom wide were silent, came the king to Gaya's shore. He spoke:

"Fair mother, often have the gods bestowed their wisdom in thy honored head. Let then that wisdom speak and save the land wherein the Bhahdishih spreads fast his ruin."

And Gaya answered him:

"Wherefore should I grant this, the greatest boon that thou couldst ask? Yea, I shall truly speak when thou thy son shall bring to me to wed. Is this too much?"

But Uht made answer sternly:

"Speak to me. I am thy king, and I command thee, speak."

And Gaya fell before him on her face, because she feared his frown, and said to him:

"One boon thou canst command. Name, then, that boon, but till it is fulfilled thy power can another not evoke, though thou art king."

And Uht considered how to name the boon, and said:

"Let forth thy wisdom now and say how shall the Bhahdishih be kept without the walls of Bhor. For mighty men have stood upon the gates but they have stayed him not."

And Gaya said:

"Go thou upon the gates."

Then said the king to her:

"What meanest thou to trifle thus? Full oft within the land I have commanded him to go his way when all the men of Bhor were round about, but never did my royal will avail."

But she replied:

"Go thou upon the gates."

Then went the king of Bhor upon the gates and sent his messengers of fire within and waited till the Bhahdishih should come. He waited through the watches of the night when no man stirred within the land of Bhor, and weary was when broke the dawn of day. Then came the Bhahdishih to weave his spell upon the watcher stationed on the gate. Hard struggled Uht against the weaving spell, until, with labor weakened, ceased the guest. Then said the king:

"Thou shalt not enter here."

And seeing that it was the king who spoke the Bhahdishih departed whence he came and entered not the king-kept gate of Bhor.

But when the evening shadows fell again and darkness crept upon the land of Bhor, again the Bhahdishih approached the gate, more terrible to see than at the dawn. But Uht it was who

stood upon the gate and struggled with the weaver of the spell, until the Bhahdishih had weary grown. Then said the king:
"Thou shalt not enter here."

And seeing that it was the king who spoke the Bhahdishih went on his way again.

And when another day began to dawn the Bhahdishih came forth before the gate and those that saw him trembled at his look, for mighty were the spells he brought with him. But still the king was watching on the gate, and though the weaver wove with all his might he could not weave the spell upon the king, and once again departed on his way.

Then in the land of Bhor the people came and told the king how darkness filled the land because the Bhahdishih with joyous arts had not been there to spread the light of mirth. They told how many men had ceased to be, they told how those that still remained were sad, and Uht, the King of Bhor, was sore perplexed and all the counsellors had naught to give.

So went the king again unto the isle where dwelt Gaya, the lonely sorceress, and having come he asked again a boon:

"Fair mother, what I heard has been fulfilled: the Bhahdishih has not been in the land, but many men have ceased to live or be. Let speak again the wisdom that thou hast, that I may know how he may enter in to save my people from the death that comes and yet not bring the madness on the land."

And once again Gaya asked to be paid, asked that the king give up his son to her. But he replied this was the boon he asked and could command because he was the king. Then said the sorceress:

"When next he comes, the Bhahdishih, let him to enter in, and when he enters let him be well chained."

The king departed with the witch's word and he commanded that that she had told. And when the Bhahdishih came forth again he entered freely, but the king of Bhor, seizing him roughly, made him fast with chains. And so the joy in Bhor came once again and men no more should cease to live or be. And when their joy was ripe the king spoke forth: enough; and with the chains that bound him fast the king's men led the Bhahdishih away.

But was the peace in Bhor still incomplete, for ever stronger must put on him lest he break the straining bond. And then grew the Bhahdishih and as he stronger grew new chains they there came a time, so strong he grew, that all the chains in Bhor could hold him not, then once again the madness filled the land and men destroyed what ages' toil had raised.

Then once again unto the lonely isle the king repaired and sought the sorceress, and told her that her words had been fulfilled, and these the words the king addressed to her:

"The boon that now I ask is wiser far than those that thou didst grant me hitherto, and all thy wisdom may not answer me. Long have I seen that with the Bhahdishih is much of good, for he brings life to men and joy and light and being to the land; and there is much of evil with him, too, else would the madness not come on the men. Speak then and say what way it shall be done that we may have the mighty good he brings and yet know not the evil of his stay. This boon, as King of Bhor, do I command."

The sorceress was silent very long, the while she sought the wisdom that he asked, and, having found it, answered him:

"My king, what thou dost ask that shalt thou know when thou shalt know what is the Bhahdishih; for this to me, to know him, is not given. Ask thou of him, and if he answer not, look thou upon his face, and thou shalt know."

Within the palace sat the king of Bhor and summoned there the awful Bhahdishih, and when he came dismissed his counsellors. When they were gone and silence fell, the king arose and questioned of the Bhahdishih:

"Who and what art thou, awful Bhahdishih, that bring both life and madness on the land, whom men regard as good and kings as ill? Speak truly, for it is the king who asks."

And proudly raised the Bhahdishih his head and proudly spoke:

"A myriad men have asked what thou dost ask me now, oh noble king, but never have I answer given them. He who will know me truly, what I am, must seek and find, else shall he never know."

Then Uht remembered what the witch had said, that if the Bhahdishih refused to tell then must he look upon the awful face. So Uht gazed full upon the awful face that men have seen with joy and kings with fear, and as he looked he trembled at the sight. And when the trembling passed he looked again and saw what none had ever seen before. He saw the face the Bhahdishih had shown to countless ages was no face at all, naught but a shadow painted there by time. Then spoke he, sternly,

"Show me forth thy face!"

"No," said the awful one, "if thou wouldst see what is not, hast thou first to seek it out."

Then Uht seized on the awful Bhahdishih and struggled with him, seeking hard his face. For many days within the palace walls they struggled, where there was no man to see. Then after many days the Bhahdishih was turned about by Uht, the King of Bhor, and when he turned him, Uht beheld his face. Behold! It was the father of the kings!

And it is said that in the Land of Bhor peace reigns and madness spreads no more abroad. Men know the Bhahdishih abides with them; the king beholds the father of the kings.

Then said the king to those who heard:
"It is well said. The father of the kings comes among men and is the Bhahdishih."

But the Ancient Tarveler whispered to me that no man, unless he be a king, shall behold the Bhahdishih his other face; and this too, have I, Lipo-va, the Scribe, set down.

THE IMPERSONALITY OF INTELLECT.

Intellect and intellection signify to the common ear consideration of abstract truth. The considerations of time and place, of you and me, of profit and hurt tyrannize over most men's minds. Intellect separates the fact considered, from *you,* from all local and personal reference, and discerns it as if it existed for its own sake. Heraclitus looked upon the affections as dense and colored mists. In the fog of good and evil affections it is hard for man to walk forward in a straight line. Intellect is void of affection and seems an object as it stands in the light of science, cool and disengaged. The intellect goes out of the individual, floats over its own personality, and regards it as a fact, and not as *I* and *mine*. He who is immersed in what concerns person or place cannot see the problem of existence. This the intellect always ponders. Nature shows all things formed and bound. The intellect pierces the form, overleaps the wall, detects intrinsic likeness between remote things and reduces all things into a few principles.

—Emerson, *"Intellect."*

A DREAM OF ATLANTIS—THE LAND OF MU.

By Alice Dixon Le Plongeon.

(Continued from page 301.)

BOOK SIXTH.

Part I.

Atlantean ships are speeding now
Across the seas, and every prow
A triton has to point the way;
Or beauteous mermaid doth display
Her charms, most cunningly inwrought
By artists who renown have sought.
Gay pennons floating to the breeze
Make known what states contribute these
Good ships, whose taut and gallant sails
Are filled with balmy westward gales.
Triremes in order follow too
Urged forward by their willing crew—
For on these vessels great and small
  Each man some glory hopes to win
  On sea or land, amid the din
Of strife,—to triumph or to fall.
The ships sailed thro' Heracles Gate,
Not far within the famous strait;
And soon the way was bridged, to land
Where foes awaited on the strand,—
Contestants long and sorely tried;
Who vainly had on justice cried;
As vainly too for freedom died.
The power oppressive ever gained;
The tyrant on their soil remained.
So wearied, lost to hope they grew,
Beholding how their dead bestrew
The field, and how to slavery base
Must be reduced a noble race,—

That peerless Athens, undismayed,
Without allies, at last arrayed
Herself;—the cause of right to save,
Their valor all the noblest gave.

Thro' ages yet to come this bold,
Heroic deed must still be told.
Defeat had plucked from out the heart
  Of cohorts many what of hope
They erst possessed; no further part
Would venture these; alone must cope
The Hellenes, by Athens led
Against aggressors staunch and dread.
Deserted by allies, at last
Great Athens all her valor cast
Upon the field and tossing wave,
To perish utterly or save
From captive doom a host o'erborne;
And other hosts from so forlorn
A fate preserve—heroic aim
That set each warrior's heart aflame.
The hated foe might countless be—
No man would falter, yield, or flee,
While led by Kaltoas, Athen's king,
Who triumph to the cause must bring.

Atlantis too her princes sped
Where blood in torrents must be shed—
  Renowned for valor these:—
Beyond all others famed were two,
Mestro and Evamon, who slew
  Untiring, to appease
Their greed insatiate for power,
For fame, and all that wealth can dower.

Atlantean shields and helmets shone
Where marshalled ranks went surging on
To meet the swift advancing foe
With lust of battle all aglow.
The fighters in the van defend
A numerous throng; on these depend
The chiefs to see their chariots placed

A DREAM OF ATLANTIS

Upon the land, and featly graced
With right equipment; and their steeds
Safe brought ashore, with other needs.

While now the fighters hotly raged,
Not yet might be the strife presaged,
Till cohorts trained their forces bring
In spear and axe, in sword and sling.
   Loud rang the air with sound
Of those who fought, and they who toiled,
That valiant foe might be despoiled
   And unto serfdom bound.
On every side were orders shrilled,
And eagerly the fighters thrilled
To martial strains of pipe and drum,
   Loud trumpets, cymbals, plectrums too,
   As louder yet the summons grew
To win, or unto death succumb;—
While ready squiers the horses yoked,
And horses bitted; these were stroked
   And soothed with kindly word,
For out upon the briny deep
The creatures, waking or asleep,
   Were by discomfort stirred.

Beholding now the regal car
Of Evamon, who leads in war,
His legions count divine his cause,
Himself a god, and make no pause
To swell his serried ranks and press
Where most the enemies aggress;
His aids, all eager to beseech
What part will he vouchsafe to each,
Are restive as the steeds they ride—
So lately from the swelling tide.
Prince Mestro too defiant stands,
And proudly voices his commands—
His golden helmet, high, white-plumed,
   His armor and his gleaming shield,
   The weapons he is now to wield,
The glory of the sun consumed.
Kak-Upacat invokes he now,
And, triumph on his regal brow,

Drives on to lead the van—
Where ready hands have met the fray
Of Athens' men who naught could stay,
  For these to glory ran.
"Kak-Upacat!" Atlanteans shout
Their war-god's name the ranks throughout;
The while Athenians, too, invoke
Their deities, and quick provoke
Fierce slaughter, counting not the foe
Advancing from the ocean's flow—,
For Kaltoas, Athens' king, leads on,
And Zeus loves this favored son.
Loud rings the clangour of the strife;
For now the sunlit air is rife
With arrows, steely pointed spears;
While flashing everywhere appears
The sword, the falchion, and the axe
That soon the feeble arm must tax.

With shouts of triumph, awful rise
The groans of they who agonize.
Then faster beats the sacatan
To stir the heart of every man;
The pipes increase their piercing shrill,
While trumpets blare and cymbals thrill.
Each hero feels the burning flush
Of war, and swears the foe to crush.

Upon the field, now back, now forth,
The legions press with swelling wrath;
Until the sun attains its height,
When Kaltoas seems in sorry plight.
To Athens appealing, he
Beholds her beaming victory;—
And hastening to his rescue now,
The light of triumph on each brow,
His bravest cohorts come to spoil
The legions from Atlantean soil.
On rushing in their fierce array,
To Kaltoas' side they force their way.
He, like a god, untouched, serene,

Leads on again, their ranks between,
  And from his chariot cries—
"On, on, my heroes! At them, slay!
Yield not a footstep of the way
  Till yonder princeling lies
To rot among those carrion thieves
Whose hateful sight our vision grieves."

The fiery horses tear away,
By ardor moved to join the fray
As thro' the battle onward speeds
Kaltoas where King Mestros leads.

'T is here stern Fate must work his will—
A glorious day for one fulfill,
And on the other send defeat
That shall forever be complete.
The God of war his fiat passed
Long ere the legions boldly massed
Their forces; and no valor swerves
What harsh decree his mandate serves.

For martial skill was Athens famed;
Its valor none had ever tamed;
So able every movement planned,
So nobly every cohort manned—
Whose chieftains quick the word would heed
By heralds brought on winged steed,—
That not a spirit of the air
To doubt the issue now might dare.

Around Kaltoas for the strife
Are closing guardians of his life
Their blood to shed with joy and pride,
If only they o'erbear, deride,
Lay low, and gibe, invading hosts
That bring destruction to these coasts.
Near them, unto their monarch press,
Amid the slaughter and the stress,
Heroic fighters, famed in war,
Their chargers ever near the car
Of Kaltoas who with fixed intent

On Mestro's death is wholly bent.
Algoras, Saispa, Tocalis,
Peneor and Pandon, find their bliss
In deeds of daring where the cry
Of battle rages to the sky;
Where like a flame the blood leaps up
To lap the victors' brimming cup;—
These value less the life they drain
Than chaff left empty of its grain:—
The blood of paltry foe or beast
Of sacrifice, but swells the feast
For Nature's maw. But one dear life
Unscathed must come from out the strife.
If perish they, it matters not;
What death they gave, that same they got—
If they his person safely guard
Till Victory grant him her award.

The valiant Mestro onward leads
To meet Kaltoas where he speeds;
And close upon his chariot wake
Dash those who him will not forsake—
Hamil, his darling boyhood friend,
And Mokul who his life will fend
With love unfailing to the end.
Here, too, within their war cars stand
A noble and heroic band—
Atlantean lords, named Lepolal,
The famed and favored general,
Holcan, Cocom, Hokol, Kambul,—
Their hearts with glorious triumph full,—
In chariots edge their king about,
And insolent defiance shout.

The warrior steeds of Kaltoas fly
While showers of missiles pass him by,
Till from his mighty bow sends he
The challenge Mestro longed to see.
On leap the coursers; o'er their heads
Death ever darts and life-blood sheds.

Kaltoas swiftly makes his way

A DREAM OF ATLANTIS

Where Mestro's taunts rise o'er the fray:
"Me seekest thou, O Athens' king —
Thy shame throughout the world shall ring!
Playgrounds for me thy battle-fields,
Where unto us the bravest yields.
By all the gods protected, I
Thyself and legions here defy."

Too brief for his inflated pride
The moment he might thus deride;
For now unchecked, the charges fierce
Of Kaltoas' mid the chariots pierce,
To fight the creatures of their kind
As tho' possessed by fury blind.

Excited by the swift attack
The horses rear; the wheels turn back;
While now, obedient to the reins,
The fighting steed itself restrains,
As side by side each royal car
Gleams with the panoply of war,
And, filled with blood-desiring rage,
Their lives these princes will engage.
Full armored stand the potentates,
And deeply one the other hates,
King Kaltoas silence grim will keep
As from the tongue of Mestro leap,
   E'en while his foes assail,
The taunting insults that but wrong
The mortal from whose lips they throng,
   When deeds, not words, prevail.

The kings are close, face unto face;
Between their chariots sides no space
Is lost, and Kaltoas' fighting steeds
Stand fast as their brave master needs.
Still shouting, Mestro lifts his spear
And thrusts to make it disappear.
But armored safely Kaltoas stands
And urges with his royal hands
A spear of orichalcum red—
Unerringly doth this imbed
The flesh of him who loudly vaunts

His valor, and Kaltoas taunts.

Then he, the king of Athens, grave
Retorts, "Poor mortal! fight and rave—
A dying foe may well indulge
His venomed hatred to divulge."
The only words were these he deigned
Till he his purpose had attained.

From Mestro's arm a crimson flow
His gilded trapping stains. Let go
He must the weighty shaft, and seize
A dagger that with more of ease
The combat he may quickly close,
Rejoiced at his opponent's throes.

This seeing, Kaltoas too forsakes
His spear, a dagger also takes.
Now fierce must rage the deadly strife
Till one or both shall yield dear life.
Around the chariots banded lords
Their valiant aid to each affords,
In shielding, fighting, holding back
Those partisans who would attack
What king they hoped to see laid low
Ere fatal issue theirs may know.
The air is cleaved by flashing steel,
Before whose blows the valiant reel,
And soon the soil is sodden mud
Empurpled with heroic blood.

The broad champaign with battle raged
For thirst of blood to be assuaged;
In furious combat chieftains pressed
Where mighty kings fought on to wrest
The life from out a noble frame
That death must rob of pride and fame.

Kaltoas, of Athena blessed,
No thrust had taken in his breast,
Nor any hurt received to stay
His action on this fateful day.

But Mestro, eager still to fight,
Himself beholds in woeful plight—
His knees are giving; on the floor
Of that brave chariot flows his gore;
No longer may his strength suffice
To consummate the sacrifice
Of Athens' king, who guarded by
His lords, unscathed can yet defy
The onslaught of Atlanteans brave
Who constant strive their king to save.
Beholding this, with failing strength
A fatal blow he'd deal at length;—
But Kaltoas thrusts his anelace
Close where the gorget hath its place.
The king from out Atlantis sent
Falls moribund, his forces spent.

Kaltoas to the golden car
In leaps and lauds the god of war;
His foe sees breathing yet; unclasps
The armour at the throat, and grasps
His battle-axe. One stroke cuts shear
The head from off the neck. A spear
He seizes; thrusts the head upon,
And gives it to the brave Pandon;—
"Tear down his oriflamme. His head
Set up aloft, to fill with dread
This host, while criers hasten to tell
That Athens every foe can quell."

Now fiery coursers, aliped,
Glad heralds waft where death is spread.
The victors hold the chariot prize—
But Kaltoas sternly on them cries,—
"Forbear! Let paltry gold await
The end. On victory rests the fate
Of generations yet unborn. Set guard
To keep your well-deserved reward.
Athena glorious points to where
Prince Evamon our arms will dare—
Away!" At once his horses leap
And thro' the carnage onward sweep.

Within that captured chariot lies
A headless form. No longer flies
The standard royal, golden bright—
That emblem of unconquered might
  To hosts that followed on.
But where that ensign first had flamed
A bleeding head, still helmet-framed,
  Now gleams beneath the sun.
The earth is heavy with the drain
Of heroes who a bloody rain
Have spent to save their leader stern
Who would from danger never turn.
Hamil, his boyhood friend had died.
His skull cleft open; at his side
Brave Mokul lay, his frame pierced thro'.
Here dead and dying thickly strew
The earth. But still survived Holcan
Who seeking comrades swiftly ran,
And cried out, "Vengeance! Rally here!
Let every brave Atlantean spear
Beset the cursed one who dared
Destroy a life so illy spared."

His call repeated travelled far,—
But, trifles turn the tide of war—
The heralds forth by Kaltoas sent
Not vainly had their forces spent.
Where loudest rang the battle din
A panic soon came sweeping in
When cried a voice, "The day is lost!"
From tongue to tongue the word was tost.
And now rolled out the deep chamade;
That pressing cohorts quickly stayed;
Some turned and fled to seek the shore,
While anger swelled into a roar.
Alarm was roused, and spreading fast,
It reached the heart of war at last.
"Our kings are slain!" cry one and all;—
And this must every heart appall.

The king of Athens like the wind
Pressed on, the Atlantean king to find.
Devoted champions, never loath

To fight, with ardor guarded both.
Evemon's piercing eye discerns
The car of Kaltoas, and he yearns
To face this regal foe. He cries,
As now the shaft from bowstring flies,
"Thy Zeus sends thee here to meet
A victor who shall set his feet
Upon thy neck." Kaltoas makes no boast,
But god-like cleaves the shouting host,
To press the car whose gleam might daze
The eyes that too long on it gaze.
To combat he'll at once provoke,
So cries: "Athena! I invoke
Thine aid to crush the hateful foe—
That freedom hosts again may know."

A demilance Evemon wields;
But matchless armour Kaltoas shields
From every thrust, while Evemon,
In prowess not to be outdone,
His savage onslaught blindly speeds
Unheeding that he freely bleeds.
The helmet towering o'er his face
A blow receives from Kaltoas' mace;
Mad rage is surging in his breast
As mastery he aspires to wrest
From his opponent, who betrays
No anger, tho' his hand ne'er stays.
Thus Evemon his life-blood poured
Erewhile when he defiance roared.
Loose-kneed he tottered where he stood,
And valorous death unto him wooed.
His limbs gave way and down he sunk;—
E'en so, his demilance had drunk
His foeman's blood if Saispa's lance
Caused not the dagger off to glance.

As hotly pressed the strife around,
Kaltoas quickly dealt a wound
That stretched the king inanimate;
And, still the legions to amate,
Bid Saispa raise aloft the head,
That all might know their leader dead.

On every side now raged the shock
Of battle, and the cruel mock
Of those who triumphed. On the plain
Made sodden by the gory rain,
In torture lengthened out expired
The valorous men who late aspired
To win a foremost place and lead
Their cohorts to triumphant deed,—
Imploring death the living cried,
And counted happy they who died
  Escaping harder fate:—
Thirst-tortured, nevermore to move;
Beyond the aid of pitying love,
  Their end must they await.
Here lies the valiant Epaphon
  So handsome and so strong!
Who in the games great honors won,
  Admired by all the throng;
Spurned now beneath the victor's heel,
Death's agony he yet must feel;
And on his closing ears will come
Harsh taunts, while weakness chains him, dumb:—
"Lie there! Foul birds shall pluck thine eyes
While for thy darling carcass cries
Some woman fond, on whom shall light
A fate to make thine own seem bright."

While Kaltoas with the king had fought,
His cohorts dreadful carnage wrought;
Till bodies spread the champaign o'er,
Pledged unto death, and victims tore
What spoils they might each one retain
If living they should yet remain.
Kaltoas swiftly drove away
To find the thickest of the fray.
A herald, speeded on the wings
Of joy, his welcome message brings:—
"Hail! Kaltoas,—puissant art thou!
Bright Victory wreathes thy noble brow.
The foe gives back and to the sea
In consternation wildly flee.
The sturdiest men alone will stay
To bide the issue of this day.

Outnumbered we no longer stand;
The heroes in thy wise command
  Will triumph soon attain"—
He said, and Kaltoas' heart rejoiced
While rapidly his will he voiced,
  The end to quickly gain.

The leaders of th' Atlantean hosts
Invading ever foreign coasts,
By Kaltoas and his chiefs were brought,
Thro' death with honor, unto naught.

Beholding Mestro's bleeding head,
  And hearing far the trumpet peal
  That more disaster must reveal,
Whole cohorts, urged by fear, had fled;
Abandoning the field to reach
The boats not far beyond the beach.

The valiant ones will yet await,
Unterrified at any fate;—
Tho' dead their kings, their leaders slain,
Atlantean heroes still would drain
The victors' cup e'er they return
To where in sacrifice must burn
Some trophies taken on the field;—
While anelace and bossy shield
Will serve in triumphs yet to come
Abroad, or in defence of home.
Some lords are here not yet laid low;
On these all aid will they bestow;—
Thus hasten they to take a stand
Where valor is by anger fanned.
And ever on the foughten field
Men raged like beasts and deathward reeled;
The joy insane of combat burned
Each heart; athirst for blood still yearned
The fighting mass that, pausing not,
All things save slaughter had forgot.

Kaltoas and his chiefs prevailed
Where hotly they the host assailed;

Till Athens valor overbore
The dauntless foe from foreign shore.
Mestro and Evemon were slain,
Eke valiant lords that swelled their train;
Which seeing, courage frenzied grew,
And, furious, their avengers slew:—
But all their might was spent in vain,
And many captives now were ta'en—
While ever back to find the strand
Fled they who would escape the land;—
So eager they the ships to reach,
O'erladen boats sank near the beach.
The seamen ready made their sails
And waited but the favoring gales.

A band of horsemen strong and bold
Survey the field and there behold
What triumphs crown Kaltoas' men.
A daring, valiant noble, then
Cries out, "Advance! Strike we a blow
That with us to the shades may go
Increasing numbers of the foe."

But not with such might these compete—
Before them glowered black defeat.
Yet forward swiftly on they came
  Their speed increasing still—
All shouting as they rode to aim,
  With fixed intent to kill
The leaders who, with lifted lance,
Awaited firmly this advance;
While trampling over prostrate forms
The reckless cohort onward swarms.

Their chieftain with defiant cry
Is wounded, and unhorsed must lie:—
  By Fate's unyielding frown
Outdone, defenceless now is he—
Too wounded from the worst to flee,
  With Death he lies him down.
There mowed like grain beneath the sithe
The heroes fall, in pain to writhe

A DREAM OF ATLANTIS

Till Yum-Cimil, fast drawing near,
Shall free them from a fate so drear.
Groans, shrieks, and curses on the air
Launch they who nevermore shall dare,—
Incarnadined all helpless lie
To welter in their gore and die.

Now shadows creep and darker grow
Upon the horrid scene below—
Night veils the mourning Earth in black,
While overhead the marshalled rack
Of storm-clouds hasting to the strife
Grow dark with thundrous anger rife;
The waves yet higher upward surge
As Tempest drives them with his scourge.
Retreating foremen fain would sleep
Upon the bosom of the deep;
But clouds in deafening war engage
While storm-lashed waters fiercely rage.
To be continued.

COURAGE OVERCOMES FEAR.

In regard to disagreeable and formidable things, prudence does not consist in evasion or in flight, but in courage. He who wishes to walk in the most peaceful parts of life with any serenity must screw himself up to resolution. Let him front the object of his worst apprehension, and his stoutness will commonly make his fear groundless. The Latin proverb says, "In battles the eye is first overcome." Entire self-possession may make a battle very little more dangerous to life than a match at foils or at football. Examples are cited by soldiers of men who have seen the cannon pointed and the fire given to it, and who have stepped aside from the path of the ball. The terrors of the storm are chiefly confined to the parlor and the cabin. The drover, the sailor, buffets it all day, and his health renews itself at as vigorous a pulse under the sleet as under the sun of June.
—EMERSON, *"Prudence."*

THE SEPHER HA-ZOHAR—THE BOOK OF LIGHT.

Containing the doctrines of Kabbalah, together with the discourses and teachings of its author, the great Kabbalist, Rabbi Simeon ben Jochai, and now for the first time wholly translated into English, with notes, references and expository remarks.

By Nurho de Manhar.

(*Continued from page* 315.)

THIS union and harmony between the finite and the infinite, God and man is the highest and deepest of mysteries, the mystery of all ages since the creation of the world. Happy are they in this world and the world to come who have attained unto a knowledge of it. Observe furthermore that the destroying angel known as "the end of all flesh" derives benefit and pleasure from acts of charity in this sense, that as such acts and deeds of charity and gratitude are a source of joy to the angels on high, so the material part of sacrifices symbolising the element of the impurity and imperfection of human nature becomes a source of strength and enjoyment to the inferior orders of spirits and this being the case, the Holy Spirit Israel's Watcher that neither slumbers nor sleeps, provides against their troubling her children and preventing their good deeds from becoming perfect and freed from impure thoughts.

At the rising of the moon in the early part of each month a goat is offered up as a supplementary sacrifice which the demon delighting in, cease or the time being from troubling Israel who is thus able to make its offerings in peace that bring them into closer relationship with their Lord and King. As a he-goat is what demons delight in, so is Israel the delight and choice of the Holy One as stated in scripture "for the Lord hath chosen Jacob unto himself and Israel for his peculiar treasure" (Ps. CXXXB. 4). Still further, "the end of all flesh" joys only in what is carnal and when he acquires power and influence over any one, it is over his animal or lower nature and not over his higher self. This is spiritual and celestial in origin, that is earthly in its production. So is it with the two elements or parts in a sacrifice; like goeth to like, the material part remaineth below, take spiritual part ascendeth on high. When any one lives the higher and diviner life, there is a continual sacrifice, that in a measure atones for the sins of humanity in general, whereas the life of an iniquitous man is of no benefit or advantage whatever to the world or it is blemished with sin and wrong doing and therefore it is written, "Whatsoever hath a blemish ye shall not offer, for it will not be acceptable" (Lev. XXII. 20). From what has been said we can understand and gather the true meaning of sacrifice and how the lives of good men subserve to the benefit and salvation of humanity.

The Occult Meaning of the Six Hundred Years of Noah's Life.

Referring again to the words "And Alhim said unto Noah, the end of all flesh is before me," Rabbi Simeon spake and said: "These words mean that the destroying angel presented himself before the Holy One, demanding power and authority to mark for destruction the race of the antediluvians. We further read, 'And behold! I will destroy them with the earth' (Gen. VI. 13). make thee an ark of gopher wood wherein entering thou mayst be preserved, and he may have no power over thee. And Noah did according to all that Alhim commanded him, "and in the six hundredth year of Noah's life, in the second month, the seventeenth day of the month, the same day were all the fountains of the great deep broken up and the windows of heaven were opened" (Gen. VII. 11). These words imply that only in that year of his earth life and incarnation, did Noah attain unto human perfection and by thus becoming a just man and perfect, was able to escape the doom impending over the wicked generation in which he lived, whose iniquity had then reached its climax. When Noah had attained unto this age, then the forbearance and long suffering of the Holy One ended and the destruction so long deferred overwhelmed the world and the race of the antediluvians was suddenly swept out of existence from off the face of the earth. Note the words, 'Behold I (ani) even I (hinneni) do bring a flood of waters upon the earth.' Wherefore the repetition of the personal pronoun, the one being the synonym of the other? It is because wherever in scripture Ani (I) is found it is used to designate God and having the same relation to Him as the soul has to the body. Thus it is written, 'I (ani) will make my covenant with thee' (Gen. xvii. 4), implying that God sometime or other will manifest himself and make himself known to mankind. Again, why is it written, 'Ath hammabbul mayin' (the deluge of waters), because thereby to show by the word 'ath' that in addition to the waters of the deluge, Alhim sent the angel of death to destroy the world and gave him authority to accomplish it by the element of water. We know also from tradition that the words 'I (ani) am the Lord' have the same meaning as, I am faithful in my promises of recompense to the righteous, as also in my denunciations of punishment on the wicked in the world to come, and all are made under the name of Ani. The additional words 'to destroy all flesh' also imply that the death angel is the real destroyer of the world and is alluded to as such in (Ex. xii. 23). 'And He will not suffer the destroyer to come into your houses to smite you.' That is to say, that the destroyer, who in the account of the deluge is designated 'the end of all flesh' shall have no power over you, nor authority to afflict and injure you. All this occult teaching in the secret doctrine respecting the deluge was imparted to me by Rabbi Issac."

Adam Sitting at the Gate of the Garden of Eden.

On another occasion Rabbi Simeon spake and said: "It is written, 'I said, I shall not see the Lord even the Lord in the land of the living; I shall behold man no more with the inhabitants of the world' (Ps. xxxviii. 11). How great the number of those who are ignorant and take no interest in the secret doctrine. They expend their strength and energy in the acquisition of worldly knowledge, oblivious altogether of that true wisdom which is both spiritual and divine. When a man departs out of earth life, he has to account for every act and deed committed in it and meets many with whom he has been acquainted and held intercourse in the world. Eventually he beholds Adam seated at the Garden of Eden rejoicing over those who have faithfully observed and kept the divine commandments. Surrounding him are the righteous who were wise and avoided walking in the way that leads down to Gehenna and found the path of light. Such are termed by scripture 'inhabitants of the world' hadel, not haded. The inhabitants of this latter are mouselike in their habits of heaping up riches and know not who shall enjoy them; but the just and upright are termed dwellers of hadel, which word signifies to shun and avoid, because they have learned to shun the way to death and found entrance into the Garden of Eden. Another interpretation is this: by 'the inhabitants of the world' (hadel) is signified those who through repentance, ceased to do evil and learned to do well, as did Adam who was afterwards appointed leader into Eden of all repentant souls, and thus termed inhabitants of hadel, and therefore is it written, 'that I may know what I lack (hadel)' (Ps. xxxix. 5). Note the words, 'I shall not see Jah.' 'Who then is able to see him?' the other part of the verse explains, 'Jah in the land of the living.' When souls encircled with an aura of light, the result of righteous living, ascend on high to the sphere especially prepared for those who have attained unto the higher life, they are then able to gaze into the Zohar, the luminous mirror, or in other words the beatific vision whose splendor and brightness are reflections from the highest heavenly sphere, since a soul clothed in any other raiment than this light would be unable to behold and endure its intense vibrations. For even as souls in their progress and development on earth life and clothed and girded with an aura, so in the world on high, they become encircled with one brighter and still more luminous, by which they are able to contemplate the transcendent light coming down out of the lightest of the heavenly spheres known as 'the land of the living.' It was this aura of the higher life encircling him that Moses was able to behold what he did, as it is written, 'And Moses went into the midst of the cloud (as it seemed to human vision) and ascended the mount' (Ex. xxiv. 15). That is, he became clothed with an aura of divine light, in order to gaze into the luminous mirror, or beatific vision, similar to that which the just or perfected human beings on their entrance into the higher heavenly spheres are clothed, of which the aura surrounding them during earth life is only a faint shadow and reflection. We now understand why the word Jah in the verse just cited is found repeated. 'I shall not see Jah in the land of the living,' were uttered by Hezekiah and mean that he feared and had no hope of ever experiencing the joy and delight of gazing upon the splendor of the light emanating from 'the land of the living,' through his dying childless, and therefoe he said also, 'I shall not see Adam sitting at the gate of the Garden of Eden on high.' But why should he be afraid of this? because Isaiah the prophet had said unto him, 'Thou shalt die, thou shalt not live,' that is, thou shalt not live in the world to come as thou shalt die childless; for whoever leaves and quits the world without offspring is not admitted into the garden of the celestial Eden and is therefore altogether precluded from contemplating the glory and splendor of its light. If therefore Hezekiah with all the inherited merits of his forefathers, besides being an upright and just person, feared lest by dying childless, he should fail to attain unto the beatific vision, or enter into 'the land of the living,' so ought he be alarmed who, lacking ancestral merit and virtues, transgresses divine laws. The aura surrounding the just and perfected in the world to come who have lived the higher and diviner life is known and designated by initiates of the secret doctrine as 'The Master's Robe.' Happy they who wear it, for it is on their account the Holy One has reserved and put by unnumbered joys in the world to come, as it is written, 'For from the beginning of the world, men have not heard nor perceived by the ears, neither have seen, Oh God beside thee, what thou hast prepared for him that putteth his trust in Thee.'" (Ps. lxiv. 4.)

REMARKS ON THE DESTROYING ANGEL AND THE ANTEDILUVIANS.

" 'Behold I even I will bring a flood of waters upon the earth,' " said Rabbi Jehuda. "These words have reference to the waters of strife (Meribah), when the children of Israel murmured against the Lord and caused his holiness to appear amongst them. But was this act of insubordination and murmuring against God the only occurrence in the history of the children of Israel, that scripture should thus characterize it? The fact is, it is recorded as the occasion Israel afforded to the executors of divine justice of overcoming and afflicting them. For there are waters sweet and bitter, waters clear and turbid, waters of peace and waters of strife, to which scripture alludes as waters of Meribah where the children of Israel strove with the Lord: that is, they attracted to themselves the impure, unclean spirit that defiled them (vayiqqadesh bam) (Num. xx. 13).

In objecting against this exposition, Rabbi Hezekiah said: "If your interpretation was correct, the word vayiqadshou (they were defiled) would have been used by scripture. The true meaning of the words is I think as follows: 'He whom the children of Israel should have worshipped and adored became degraded by them, if I may so express it. They became so obdurate and wilfully irrational both in mind and heart that the sense of the Divine presence with them became lost and extinguished, as doth the light of the moon at its fall. Therefore as the word vayiqadesh used by scripture should not be translated in its best sense of being sanctified; so the words, 'Behold I even I do bring a flood of waters,' should be understood as meaning, 'I will send unto them the impure and destroying angel by whom they have allowed themselves to become defiled.'"

Said Rabbi Jose: "Woe unto those who are unwilling to repent of their evil ways and deeds before the Holy One during their life on earth, for if, continuing unrepentant, at the close of it, they become cast into that outer darkness, where their torment ceaseth not and there shall be wailing and gnashing of teeth. Observe that by the open persistence of the antediluvians in their heinous and flagitious iniquity they were condemned and punished by the Holy One in a remarkable and open manner.

Said Rabbi Isaac: "Even when a man sins in secret, the Holy One is long suffering, and if he repents, has mercy upon and forgives him. On the contrary, if he continues in his evil and secret deeds, they become at last revealed and manifested and he is punished openly. Of this ordeal of the 'mey hammarim' (bitter waters) is an instance. It was so with the antediluvians, and how were they punished? They were exterminated from the face of the earth. The fountains of the great deep became opened and poured forth rain and mighty volumes of boiling water, so that their fleshless skeletons only remained to show they had once lived and had totally perished from off the face of the earth."

Said Rabbi Isaac: "The words 'and they were destroyed from the earth' (Gen. vii. 23), have the same meaning as 'let them be blotted out of the book of the living' (Ps. lxix. 28). Thus by the use of the word mahha (blotted out, destroyed off) in these two passages of scripture we are taught that the names of the wicked and evil doers are expunged out of the book of life —that they will never use again and appear in the day of judgment.

KABBALISTIC REMARKS ON THE COVENANT OR UNION OF THE HIGHER AND LOWER SELF.

Said Rabbi Eleazar: "It is written, 'But with thee will I establish my covenant' (Gen. vi. 18); as the continuity of the covenant or good law on earth is the same as in the higher spheres, we infer from these words that when men become just and upright in this world they contribute to the stability of the good law in both worlds.

Said Rabbi Simeon: "The words just cited have an occult meaning. The love of the male for the female is based upon jealous desire. Observe, when there is a just man in the world, or one whose higher and lower self have become harmonized and unified, the divine spirit or Schecuna is ever with him and abides in him, causing a feeling of affectionate attachment towards the Holy One to arise similar to that between the male and female. Therefore the words, 'I will establish my covenant with thee' may be rendered thus, 'Because of the union between thy higher and lower natures giving rise to a yet diviner life, I will abide with thee forever. I will never leave nor forsake thee. Come thou therefore into the ark into which no one unless he is just can enter.'"

Said Rabbi Eleazar: "As long as this covenant or union remains intact and undisturbed between himself and the Holy One, nothing can injure or afflict him. It was so with Noah who keeping the covenant was preserved along with his children, whilst the wickedness of the antediluvians caused them to perish from off the face of the earth."

Rabbi Jehuda whilst on a visit to Rabbi Simeon entered into a discussion with him as to the meaning of the words 'And Elijah repaired (vayerape) the altar of the Lord that was broken down' (1 Kings xviii. 30). "What," said he, "is the occult meaning of this word vayerape, which literally signifies to heal."

In answer to this Rabbi Simeon remarked: "Note that in the days of the prophet Elijah all Israel had forsaken the worship of the Holy One and transgressed against his covenant made with their forefathers, to such an extent that it had become altogether forgotten and sunk into oblivion. Seeing and recognizing this, Elijah brought it back to their remembrance and thus restored it and made known again to them the everlasting covenant, and therefore it is written, 'And Elijah took twelve stones according to the number of the tribes of the sons of Jacob;' implying by this that it was by the occult virtue of the number twelve that the altar of the Lord was erected as aforetime; and then we read further, 'Unto whom the word of the Lord came saying, "Israel shall be thy name."' Why is this name of Israel here mentioned? Truly because when Israel attaches itself and adheres to the good law, it is so called; but when they forsake it, they are termed the children of Israel, or sons of Jacob. This is therefore why the word vayerape is written, because Elijah causes the covenant to become a subject of faith with the children of Israel and thus healed the breach between them and the Holy One and restored love and affection between them. Observe further that Phinehas, filled with zeal, inflicted punishment on Zimri and thus helped to reestablish the covenant, and so it is written of him, 'Behold, I give unto him my covenant of peace' (Num. xxv. 12). Now it is certain that Phinehas had in no way violated the covenant and needed not this gift. The real meaning is that he prevented it from becoming regarded as obsolete, a thing of no avail and therefore not worth consideration. For so doing he secured the blessing of the 'Covenant of Peace' the occult signification of which is, the mysterious Word, the Mediator between the two worlds, the celestial and terrestrial, and so it is added, 'And he shall have it and his seed after him, even the covenant of an everlasting priesthood, because he was zealous for his God and made an atonement for the children of Israel.' " (Num. xxv. 13.)

Said Rabbi Simeon: "There is no greater transgression in the sight of the Holy One than the breaking of the covenant, as it is written, 'and I will bring a sword upon you that shall avenge the breaking of my covenant.' " (Lev. xxvi. 25.) Note that the sin of the antediluvians reached its climax by the practice of self pollution, so that the earth itself became corrupted and defiled thereby (va thishaheth) before God, and for this reason he said, 'I will destroy them with the earth (mashitham).' There are, however, some who affirm that the measure of their iniquity became full when ignoring all moral right and justice, and might with them becoming right they broke the laws of heaven and earth, of God and humanity, and reaped their karma, the executors of which never fail to avenge the wrongdoing of those who infringe the Good Law."

VARIOUS KABBALISTIC EXPOSITIONS OF BIBLICAL TEXTS.

Said Rabbi Simeon: "We read, 'And God said unto Noah, enter thou and all thy house into the ark.' Wherefore in the narrative of the deluge is the divine name of Alhim used throughout, except in this particular passage in which the sacred name I H V H is found. The explanation is this. It is not in accordance with the rules and custom of good society for a wife to receive a guest into her home without the consent and permission of her husband, so Noah though desirous to enter into the ark, it was first of all necessary that the husband of the ark, designated here by the Holy Name, representing divine goodness, should give Noah authority and permission to do so, and not before this did he enter the ark; and it is added, 'For thee have I seen righteous before me in this generation,' from which words we infer that no one should ever be received as a guest in a house whose character is blemished and has a stain upon it."

Said Rabbi Jehuda: "We find written in scripture, Ps. xxiv. 1, 'A psalm of David. The earth is the Lord's and the fulness thereof, the world and they dwell therein.' We know from tradition that wherever the name David occurs in the psalms, that it was composed by him himself, but whenever it precedes a psalm it was composed and written by the aid of the Holy Spirit's influence. The words, 'The earth is the Lord's and the fulness thereof' refer to the land of Israel which is called the Holy Land, whilst 'the fulness thereof' signifies the Schekina, as it is written 'for the glory of the Lord filled male the houses of God.' (1 Kings v. 11.) Why in this passage is the word mla (full) in place of mile (filled). Thereby is meant that the Schekina was as the light of the moon at its full. The Schekina is full of heavenly blessings as a treasure house is with jewels and gold so long as it remains and abides in the land of Israel which belongs unto the Lord. According to another exposition these words refer to heaven on high wherein the Lord delights to dwell, but 'the fulness (oumloah) thereof' are the souls of the righteous filled with the principle of justice, the divine attribute that sustains the universe. Should it however be said, 'Is the earth sustained only by a single pillar?' observe what is written. 'For He hath founded it upon the seas (yammim) and established it upon the floods or rivers (recharoth).' He here refers to the Holy One, of whom it is written, 'It is He that hath made us.' (Ps. c. 3). 'For He looketh to the ends of the earth and seeth under the whole heavens' (Job xxviii. 24). These words also designate the seven pillars or columns upon which the world stands and when these columns fill the earth then, as scripture states, the earth is said to be full; that is, when the number of the just increases, the earth becomes fertile and fruitful. When however they are outnumbered by the wicked then as it is written, 'The waters fail from the sea, and the flood decayeth and drieth up' (Job xiv. 11). 'The waters fail from the sea' signify the Holy land watered by rivers of life from on high, but the 'stream (naahr) decayeth and drieth up' refer to the column of justice and righteousness repaired in the Holy Land in order to enlighten it and have the same meaning as the words, 'The righteous perisheth and no man layeth it to heart.' " (Is. lvii. 1.)

(*To be continued.*)

SOUL THE LIGHT IN ALL THINGS.

If we consider what happens in conversation, in reveries, in remorse, in times of passion, in surprises, in the instructions of dreams, wherein often we see ourselves in masquerade,—the droll disguises only magnifying and enhancing a real element and forcing it on our distant notice,—we shall catch many hints that will broaden and lighten into knowledge of the secret of nature. All goes to show that the soul in man is not an organ, but animates and exercises all the organs; is not a function, like the power of memory, of calculation, of comparison, but uses these as hands and feet; is not a faculty, but a light; is not the intellect or the will, but the master of the intellect and the will; is the background of our being, in which they lie,—an immensity not possessed and that cannot be possessed. From within or from behind, a light shines through us upon things and makes us aware that we are nothing, but the light is all.

—EMERSON, "*The Over-Soul.*"

MOMENTS WITH FRIENDS.

"What are the essential differences between Theosophy and New Thought?"

Motives, methods and definiteness.

These differences are not based upon the talk and actions of so called theosophists nor of new thoughters, but upon the books of the theosophists and those of the new thought. Most members of present day theosophical societies make claims and act as unreasonably as most of the people of the New Thought. Each set of people shows the side of human nature which is working out at that particular time. The doctrines of Theosophy are: karma, the law of justice; reincarnation, the development of the mind and of the matter of the physical and other bodies by means of the mind's return from life to life in human bodies into this physical world; the sevenfold constitution of man, the principles and their interaction which enter into the makeup of man; the perfectibility of man, that all men are potentially gods and that it is in the power of every man to attain to the state of highest perfection and become consciously and intelligently one with God, the Universal Mind; brotherhood, that all men come from one and the same divine source and that all men are related and the same in essence though differing in degree of development, and that spiritually all have duties to and are related to each other as members of one family, and that it is the duty of each member of it to help and assist the others according to his powers and capacities.

The motives advocated or suggested in the books of theosophists and of new thoughters differ widely. The motives as urged by theosophical doctrines are: to comply with the requirements of Karma by fulfilling one's obligations, that is, duty, because it is demanded by the law of justice; or because by so doing, one will make good karma; or because it is right—in which case duty will be done without fear and without hope of reward. Immortality or perfection is looked forward to not because by its attainment one shall escape responsibilities and enjoy its fruits, but because by reaching it one is the better able to assist others in their overcoming of ignorance, sorrow and misery and attaining the same goal. The motives which prompt the new thoughter to action are first his own betterment, generally for physical benefits, and the enjoyment of that, and then to tell others that they too can have their desires along these lines satisfied.

The methods which Theosophy advises for the attainment of its objects are by doing one's duty wherever placed, by acting, unselfishly for the good of others, by controlling the desires through the intellect, by becoming illumined and by devoting a reasonable amount of one's time, money and work to the spreading of the doctrines. This is done, without money or charges of any kind. The methods of the New Thought are to promise physical benefits and mental satisfaction, and money is charged for courses in instruction in the thought and for practical application.

Another difference is that the doctrines of Theosophy are definite, as to principle and statement; whereas, in the New Thought societies vague claims are made, and a lack of definiteness in terms and philosophy is shown in the teachings. New Thought teachings speak mildly, if at all, of karma and reincarnation. Some of their writers speak of the seven principles or of some of them; they hold that man is divine in origin and fact, and believe that men are brothers. But there is a lack of definiteness in all these New Thought teachings which is a marked difference from the direct and insistent statements made in theosophical books.

The distinguishing features then are: that the motive which prompts the follower of Theosophy is unselfishness and service for the purpose of realizing the God within, whereas, the motive which prompts the new thoughter is to apply such information as he has for personal, material gain and advantage. The methods of work of one who follows Theosophy is to spread the doctrines without pay; whereas, the new thoughter says that the laborer is worthy of his hire and he charges money for benefits, or alleged benefits, conferred. The follower of Theosophy has definite objects and doctrines which are distinct in themselves, whereas the adherent of the New Thought is not particular as to doctrine, but has a hopeful and cheerful disposition and is confident that he will get all he desires. These are differences according to doctrine and books, but the so called theosophist is human and frail as well as the new thoughter; each acts according to his nature notwithstanding his particular convictions or beliefs.

Where Theosophy begins New Thought ends. Theosophy begins with one's duty in life, and aims to reach perfection in the physical world; and through that perfection, perfection in the spiritual world. New thought begins with a cheerful and confident belief in one's divinity, and seems to end with physical health, wealth, prosperity and happiness—sometimes and for the time being.

"What is the cause of cancer? Is there any known cure for it or will some method of treatment have to be discovered before its cure can be effected?"

There are immediate and remote causes of cancer. The immediate causes are those engendered in the present life. The remote causes originate in and come over from the action of the mind in previous human births. The immediate causes for the appearance of cancer are such as a bruise or continued irritation, which cause an obstruction to the blood circulation, tissue proliferation and which furnish soil favorable to the development of, what is believed to be a cancer germ, or they may be due to improper foods which the body is unable to assimilate or excrete and by reason of which the cancer germ develops, or that disease may be due to the restraining, suppressing and killing, but retaining in the body of the vital fluid during sexual practices. The killing, retaining and accumulation in the body of the life germs of the vital fluid is fertile soil which calls the cancer germ into existence; by continuing the practice the body abounds with cancerous growths. Again similar conditions may be furnished by the inability of the body to bring the vital germs to maturity, failing to do which the life germs die and decay and remain within the body which is unable to assimilate or excrete them.

The remote causes are brought over by the mind from its actions in previous incarnations in which the mind took part in excess and indulgence, but in which incarnation it did not reap the harvest which it then sowed, in the same way that those who are addicted to morbid and wrong sexual practices in the present life may not now reap, but are sowing, the causes for future harvest—unless they set up contrary causes by present thought and action. Unless cancer is physically transferred or transplanted, all cases of cancer are due to karmic causes; that is to say, they are caused by the action and interaction between the mind and desire in the field of one's physical body. This action between mind and desire must have taken place in the present life or in a preceding life. If it has taken place in the present life, it will be recognized as the immediate cause of the cancer when the attention is directed to it. If none of these or similar causes have been set up in the present life, in which cancer appears, then the disease is due to a remote cause which may be recognized. One may act against the law for a time, only, but he is checked in time. The cancer cell and its development may be destroyed, but the cancer germ is not physical and it cannot be destroyed by any physical means. The cancer germ is astral and is the form in which the cell grows and develops, although the cancer cell shows the form of the cancer germ. The cancer cell and germ can be treated and transformed by physical means.

There is a treatment for the cure of cancer, and cures have been effected. Cures have been made by the Salisbury treatment. This treatment has been known for over forty years, but comparatively few physicians have tried it. The Salisbury treatment of diseases has not found favor with the medical profession. A few who have tried it fairly, have had remarkable results in the treatment of most of the so called incurable diseases. The basis of the Salisbury treatment is the eating of well broiled lean beef from which all fat and fiber and connective tissue have been removed, and which eating is accompanied by the drinking of hot water not less than an hour and a half before and after meals. This treatment is too simple and inexpensive for most physicians. Nevertheless this treatment, when it is consciously applied, strikes at the roots, and effects cures of nearly every known disease. Well cooked lean beef, from which tissue and fat has been removed, and water furnish the simplest and most important material for the maintainance of healthy human animal bodies. The eating of lean beef and the drinking of pure water affects the physical body and its astral counterpart, the form body. Lean meat will not supply the material favorable to the growth and development of any germs which may bring disease to the body into which the lean meat is taken. When the supply of food is withheld from a disease and such food is taken in the body as cannot be used by the disease, but is wholesome to the body, the disease dies away. So when lean beef is taken into the body, it will not supply food favorable to the cancer or other disease germs, and, if other food is withheld, the unhealthy growths in the body gradually die and disappear by a process of starvation. This may take years and the body may appear emaciated and feel weak and physically exhausted. This condition is due to the sloughing off of the diseased portions of the body, but if the treatment is persisted in, the body will regain health. What takes place during the process is that the old diseased physical body is gradually being allowed to die off and is eliminated and in its place there is being grown and developed gradually, another physical body built up on the lean beef. The drinking of the boiled water taken hot an hour and a half before and after meals is as important as the eating of the meat, and the meat should not be eaten to cure disease without drinking hot water and at the times stated. The drinking of a quantity of hot water neutralizes the acids and injurious matter and passes them off from the body, and in that water this matter is passed off from the body. The meat is the food of the body; the water irrigates and cleanses the body. The lean beef builds healthy cells of the body, but the meat cannot touch or directly affect the invisible cancer germ. Hot water does this. Hot water affects and transforms the cancer germ and other germs in the body and adjusts these to the needs of the body. The meat builds up the physical body; the water supplies the needs of the astral body.

A body built up on this basis is clean and wholesome and is a good working instrument for the mind. By such a treatment not only is one's physical and astral body changed and made healthy, but the desires will also have been affected, curbed and trained. Only the Salisbury treatment of diseases deals directly with the physical body which is the field of the cancer cell and with the astral body which is the seat of the cancer germ. By the Salisbury treatment the mind also is trained, indirectly, because considerable determination and will must be exercised by the mind in order to hold the body and desires strictly to the treatment. Many fail in the treatment because they will not hold to it and because of mental discontent and rebellion which often appear in those who try it and which they do not overcome. If the rebellion is quelled and discontent replaced by a patient and confident attitude of mind, a cure will inevitably result. By training one's body according to reasonable methods, the mind is self-instructed by the operation and learns mastery not only of the body but also of its own disquietude and restlessness. When there is a harmonious relation between the body and the mind disease can find no home in that body. The cancer germ and cell will not cause disease unless the constitution of the body is unable to use them. There are many cancer germs and cells in nearly every human body. In fact myriads of germs swarm in the human body. Any of these will cause virulent diseases if the condition of the body is not such as will keep the germs in order and preserve a well organized body. Germs of diseases yet unknown teem in the body, but the body and the mind have not yet provided the conditions which will let these germs become known to the world as special diseases. They may be called into evidence at any time when the mind becomes aware of the possible disease, and the pathological conditions are provided by improper eating and living.

The cancer germ and cell belong to the period in the history and development of the human race when the human body was bi-sexual. At that period it would have been impossible to have the disease now called cancer because that was the normal cell used in the building up of bodies. Our present race has reached a point in its evolution which brings it to the same plane as that which the race passed in its involution, that is, the plane on which took place the involution or development of bi-sexual male-female bodies into the sexual male bodies and female bodies we now know.

The physical body is built up and maintained by a constant creation and destruction of germs. It is a war of the germs. The body is established according to a certain form of government. If it preserves its form of government it maintains order and health. If order is not preserved, opposing factions enter the government and cause disorder, if they do not cause revolution or death. The body cannot remain inactive or passive. The armies of germs which build up the body and other armies of germs which defend it against the attacks and invasion of opposing germs must be able to capture and assimilate the invaders. This is done when the body eats of wholesome food, drinks of pure water, breathes deeply of fresh air, and man entertains healthy thoughts and tries to think of influences and actions according to right motives.

A FRIEND.

OUR MAGAZINE SHELF

NOTICE.—Books, coming under the subjects to which this Magazine is devoted, will be received, and, as space permits, impartially reviewed irrespective of author or publisher.

The duty of the reviewer is to present to our readers a true and unbiased account of his charge. There is no deviation from this principle.—Ed.

THE LIFE AND THE DOCTRINES OF PHILIPPUS THEOPHRASTUS, Bombast of Hohenheim, known by the name of Paracelsus, extracted and translated from his rare and extensive works and from some unpublished manuscripts by Franz Hartmann, M. D. The Theosophical Publishing Company of New York, 1910. 367 pages, 8 vo. Price $2.50.

This is a new edition of one of the standard theosophical works, commonly known as Hartmann's "Paracelsus." It furnishes the student with first hand information concerning the chief teachings of the greatest of the mediaeval occultists as far as known to the world. Paracelsus dictated most of his works to disciples; few of his works were printed during his life time; many are still unprinted and remain manuscripts; many were by the disciples delivered to the printer after his death, but in such defective and confused condition that the study of these works is no easy matter; further, many spurious writings are attributed to the famous Paracelsus. Dr. Hartmann has found his way through all this. But the works are numerous, written partly in Latin and partly in mediaeval German, and the feature which is the greatest obstacle to the understanding is that they are written in the alchemical jargon, generally used by occultists, and pseudo-occultists as well, in those days. For instance, what in modern Theosophy is called the astral body is called by Paracelsus, evestrum, mumia, astral body, caballi, according to different aspects. Then such words as iliaster, firmament, beryllus, astrum, alcol, adech, magisterium, mysterium magnum, scaiolae, astrologer, alchemy, electrum, tinctura physicorum and sulphur, salt, mercury, to name but a few, are constantly used. Aside from all this, the terminology of Paracelsus is not exact; that is, he does not use one term for one thing only, nor one term with a defined meaning Therefore his terms, mystifying at best, overlap in their meaning. Hence while Paracelsus was an occultist of great attainments, many critics have voiced their opinion in substance as follows: "No one can take up a book of Theophrastus' without becoming convinced that the man was insane." That view is principally advanced by those who suffered and those who still smart under the rude attacks of Paracelsus, who was in the first instance a fighter of fighters. What he fought were shams, hypocrisy, arrogance, dishonesty, generally, and especially in the church and in medicine.

Others extol Paracelsus. The general student finds it impossible not only to form his own conclusions, but to get at the priceless treasures cunningly hid by the strange, wandering healer and philosopher in his dictated and unrevised works. Hartmann has changed this. He gives a fair biography of the peripatetic philosopher. Then he furnishes a dictionary explaining the characteristic terms used by Paracelsus and finally, he has translated and presents excerpts from the many different and inaccessible works of Paracelsus. These excerpts often contain Paracelsus' definitions of his strange terms and are placed in order according to subjects and are connected by fair commentaries.

So an opportunity is given us to become acquainted with Paracelsus and his writings which the author has examined and excerpts from which he has grouped under such headings as Cosmology, Anthropology, Pneumatology, Medicine, Alchemy and Astrology, by which terms something quite different is meant by Paracelsus than the modern externalist in science and art understands.

Through Dr. Hartmann's industry, understanding and sound philosophy, the treasures left by Paracelsus are made accessible to the general public. Readers of theosophical literature find a new field opened, in which however, the main theosophical doctrines find confirmation in an unexpected manner and are illustrated by new revelations. No one who reads this book of Dr. Hartmann's will lay it aside without thanks for the labor the translator and extractor has done for him; and a new light will shine on the reader's future path from the formerly obscure writings of Paracelsus. B. B. G.

FROM PASSION TO PEACE or The Pathway of the Pure, by James Allen, New York. Thomas Y. Crowell Co. 16 mo. 53 pages, $0.50.

Mr. James Allen is an English representative of the New Thought movement. He intends to show how in man's unhappy conditions in the spasms of passion, the bondage of vice or the fetters of slovenliness and indolence, the forces which bring on these conditions, may be transmuted so that peace is achieved. Peace is, to Mr. Allen, the consummation of man's destiny. There is much in the look that is worth reading and remembering, and which, if remembered, cannot but influence the conduct of life. The following are a few quotations: "The man who continually dwells upon the selfishness in others will not thus overcome his own selfishness." "The way from passion to peace is not in the outer world of people; it is in the inner world of thoughts; it does not consist in altering deeds of others; it consists in perfecting one's own deeds." p. 5. "If a man thinks: 'It is through others, or circumstances or heredity, that I am impure,' how can he hope to overcome his errors? Such a thought will check all holy aspirations and bind him to the slavery of passion." p. 11. Of him who is a lover of the pure life, the author says: "He rises early, and fortifies his mind with strong thoughts and strenuous endeavor. He knows that the mind is of such a nature that it cannot remain for a moment unoccupied, and that if it is not held and guided by high thoughts and pure aspirations, it will assuredly be enslaved and misguided by low thoughts and base desires." p. 14.

Temptation he holds to be a condition in which thought reverts from purity to passion. Some of the statements he makes on this subject would alone repay the reading of the booklet. He says that the stronghold of temptation is within a man, not without; that while man continues to run away from outward objects under the delusion that temptation subsists entirely in them, and he does not attack his impure imaginings, his temptations and falls will be many and grievous. By self-examination, the tempted will find that he is both the tempted and the tempter, and what appears as a temptation from the outside, is something which his lack of self-knowledge, and his own selfishness and desires, have formed and attracted. "Foolish men blame others for their lapses and sins, but let the truth-lover blame only himself. Let him acknowledge his complete responsibility for his own conduct, and not say, when he falls; this thing, or such and such circumstance, or that man, was to blame; for the most which others can do is to afford an opportunity for our own good or evil to manifest itself; they cannot *make* us good or evil." p. 22.

After temptation and enough grievous falls, comes the knowledge of the mental cause of temptation. That leads to transmutation of thought, thence to a deliverance from the bondage of error. Passion is to be transmuted into intellectual and moral forces, and thereby becomes a new power for accomplishments of high and unfailing purposes. He says that while men are involved in the passions of self, they load themselves with cares and trouble over many things; and more than all else, do they trouble over their own little burdened painstricken personality, being anxious for its fleeting pleasures, for its protection and preservation, and for its eternal safety and continuance, but that in the life that is wise and good all this is transcended and personal interests are replaced by universal purposes, whereby as an incident, all cares, troubles and anxieties, concerning the pleasure and fate of the personality, are dispelled like the feverish dreams of a night. p. 36.

The book is readable and inspiring. But, as in most New Thought publications, no great value is placed upon the terminology of characteristic terms, and, therefore, the terms are not distinct. As a rule, these writers do not value the meanings of words. Their books are written so as to present the matter dealt with in a soft, easy, indefinite light. Terms are not comprehensive and not exclusive. Definitions and analyses are not as evident as might be expected from those who assume to stand for the leadership in a movement for the development of the powers of the mind by thought.

Mr. Allen shares these faults to some degree. Passion is the basis, upon which his book is written. But he has little to say about the nature and origin of passion, and the relation it bears to other principals and forces in man. He holds passion to be the lowest level of human life. He says that "lust, hatred, covetousness, pride, vanity, revenge, envy, spite, retaliation, slander, back-biting, lying, theft, deceit, treachery, cruelty, suspicion and jealousy are the blind and brute forces which inhabit this world of passion. He fails to see that these different attributes are not passions, strictly speaking, all of them, though desire and passion are component parts. Some of them are vices and nearly all of them have an admixture of mental qualities, which is different from passion. He does not trouble himself to take up and analyze and consider the word "passion," although it is the foundation of his book. It is a word of some interest. Our words are an embodiment of pictures taken from the sensuous world. As we do not live in the mind world, we describe mental conditions and operations of the mind by pictures taken from the sense world; "understanding," "apprehension," "conceiving," "recollection," "perceiving," "swaying," "propensity," are so taken. "Emotion" is something which merely moves the mind, whereas "passion" is something which involves a suffering of the mind, either by an intense violent, inordinate, overpowering, feeling, or by a continuous or temporary affection.

Passion is something very different from the animal desire, and light ought to have been thrown properly on this subject; much uncertainty exists in the popular mind, as to the terms dealing with mental conditions, but the New Thought writers ought to define these terms. For only then, will an understanding of these terms, and after an understanding a mastery of the thoughts, which they embody, be had.

Mr. Allen's book, it may be said, is less burdened by these faults than many New Thought publications, and the spirit which pervades this book is one which will be appreciated by the reader and will help over some of its shortcomings. B. B. G.